THE WRITINGS OF WILL ROGERS

IV-4

SPONSORED BY

The Will Rogers Memorial Commission
and Oklahoma State University

THE WRITINGS OF WILL ROGERS

SERIES   I: *Books of Will Rogers*
            1 Ether and Me, or "Just Relax"
            2 There's Not a Bathing Suit in Russia & Other Bare Facts
            3 The Illiterate Digest
            4 The Cowboy Philosopher on The Peace Conference
            5 The Cowboy Philosopher on Prohibition
            6 Letters of a Self-Made Diplomat to His President

SERIES   II: *Convention Articles of Will Rogers* (in one volume)

SERIES III: *Daily Telegrams of Will Rogers*
            1 Coolidge Years 1926-1929
            2 Hoover Years 1929-1931
            3 Hoover Years 1931-1933
            4 Roosevelt Years 1933-1935

SERIES   IV: *Weekly Articles of Will Rogers*
            1 Harding/Coolidge Years 1922-1925
            2 Coolidge Years 1925-1927
            3 Coolidge Years 1927-1929
            4 Hoover Years 1929-1931
            5 Hoover Years 1931-1933
            6 Roosevelt Years 1933-1935

SERIES   V: *Magazine Articles of Will Rogers* (in two volumes)

SERIES   VI: *The Radio Broadcasts of Will Rogers* (in two volumes)

WILL ROGERS MEMORIAL COMMISSION

James C. Leake, *Chairman*
John Denbo
Harry Hoagland
Jarrell L. Jennings
Paul Johnson
David R. Milsten
Will Rogers, Jr.

Governor George Nigh, *ex-officio*

MEMORIAL STAFF

Reba Neighbors Collins, Director
Delmar Collins, Manager
Gregory Malak, Curator

SPECIAL CREDIT

The late Paula McSpadden Love
Curator, 1938-73

OSU ADVISORY COMMITTEE

George A. Gries, *Chairman*
W. David Baird
J. O. Grantham
Edward P. Pharr
Roscoe Rouse
William A. Sibley

President Lawrence L. Boger, *ex-officio*

EDITORIAL CONSULTANTS

Ray B. Browne, *Bowling Green State University*
LeRoy H. Fischer, *Oklahoma State University*
Wilbur R. Jacobs, *University of California, Santa Barbara*
Howard R. Lamar, *Yale University*
Russel B. Nye, *Michigan State University*

Will Rogers' Weekly Articles

STEVEN K. GRAGERT, *Editor*

Volume 4

THE HOOVER YEARS:
1929-1931

OKLAHOMA STATE UNIVERSITY PRESS
Stillwater, Oklahoma
1981

© 1981 Oklahoma State University Press

Printed in the United States of America
Library of Congress Catalog Card Number 79-57650
International Standard Book Number 0-914956-18-3

CONTENTS

INTRODUCTION   xiii

Weekly Articles 1929   1

Weekly Articles 1930   100

Weekly Articles 1931   220

NOTES   242

INDEX   266

Illustrations courtesy
Will Rogers Memorial
Claremore, Oklahoma

INTRODUCTION

Will Rogers was a multi-faceted individual who was as much at home on the vaudeville stage and the motion picture set as he was astride his favorite cow pony. He was a world traveler, a California rancher, an expert roper, an enthusiastic sportsman, and a dispenser of witticisms and wisdom. Although a person of enormous energy, Rogers spent countless hours at the keyboard of a well-worn portable typewriter, from whence came his popular daily "telegrams," his numerous magazine articles, advertising copy, his feature-length weekly newspaper columns, and assorted other writings. Through his literary work he became a spokesman for many Americans, offering insightful and humorous comments on politics, foreign affairs, public—and not-so-public—figures, business, lifestyles, and other topics.

Rogers' weekly newspaper columns comprise the fourth series of *The Writings of Will Rogers*. The *Weekly Articles: The Hoover Years, 1929-1931*, volume 4, continues the series of weekly columns through the first two years of the presidential administration of Herbert C. Hoover. Herein Rogers takes the reader through the early years of the Great Depression, touches on many of the crucial diplomatic crises of the times, allows a glimpse into the entertainment world during a critical era for that industry, and casts his ever-observant eye on a wide variety of contemporary events and individuals.

In the introduction to the first volume of this series, readers were provided with background information about the *Weekly Articles* and were informed on the editorial procedure on the annotations. No changes of a substantive nature have been made in this volume. We again have attempted to limit our editorial remarks and annotations. Only in instances where Rogers mentioned some individual, place, or event that necessitates explanation, have we supplied such information. As a source for the articles, we have used Rogers' original typed manuscripts where they have been available. In all other cases we have used copy from the McNaught Syndicate, which was Rogers' distributing agency, or have chosen from among the *Tulsa Daily World*, the *Los Angeles Examiner*, or other reliable newspapers that carried Rogers' columns.

A number of persons have played important roles in the production of this and earlier volumes of *The Writings of Will Rogers*. Foremost among them is Dr. James M. Smallwood, immediate past director and editor of the Will Rogers Project at Oklahoma State University. Dr. Smallwood contributed much to the organization of the present series and rendered valuable assistance in the research and writing of the annotations in Volume IV. His professionalism and concern for editorial exactness set the standards by which the staff of the project operated. On behalf of the staff, I thank him for his past untiring efforts and for his continuing interest in our work.

Other individuals have also contributed significantly to the work of the Will Rogers Project. Dr. Reba Neighbors Collins, director of the Will Rogers Memorial at Claremore, Oklahoma, has generously supplied manuscripts, photographs, and other material for inclusion in these volumes and has offered insightful advice for the annotations. Judy Buchholz of the Oklahoma State University Press has made significant contributions to the design, lay-out, and promotion of the books. The president of Oklahoma State University, Dr. Lawrence L. Boger, and his predecessor, Dr. Robert B. Kamm, have supported the project fully, as has Dr. George A. Gries, chairman of the Will Rogers Advisory Committee at Oklahoma State University, and Dr. Smith L. Holt, dean of the College of Arts and Sciences at the university. Dr. W. David Baird, chairman of the Department of History and a member of the advisory board, has encouraged the project staff and has provided many services that have enabled the project to function effectively. Ms. Jacque Lanier has rendered outstanding work in her capacity as secretary of the project.

Finally, special recognition is made for the continued support and assistance of the Will Rogers Memorial Commission and staff, the Oklahoma State University regents, administration, and advisory committee, the Edmon Low Library at Oklahoma State University, the Oklahoma State Historical Society, and the Oklahoma Legislature. Earlier in the project the Kerr-McGee Foundation, Phillips Petroleum Corporation, Mrs. T. S. Loffland, Mr. Sylvan Goldman, and the late Mr. and Mrs. Robert W. Love provided valuable assistance.

Steven K. Gragert,
Editor

WEEKLY ARTICLES
1929-1931

WEEKLY ARTICLES — 1929

325   HERE'S TO MEXICO

Well, all I know is just what I read in the papers. Of course as I write this about all we are reading in the papers are about Mexico. We got Hoover all set now for four years.[1] After that he will have to hustle for himself. There is an option clause in his contract, but we will look him over carefully before we exercise it.

But he is starting out pretty good. The night he was inaugurated why Mexico broke out. So this ain't going to be one of those "Let nature take its course" Administrations.

And Calvin is just settled down up there in Massachusetts.[2] He has wanted solitude and it looks like he will get it. Just think of having a breakfast in the morning and not having to feed some senator.

But the thing I want to take my text from today is "Mexico." Now it was just a little over a year ago that I was down there for weeks, and it looks like every fellow that I met and got well acquainted with down there is now mixed up in all the headlines on the day's news, some are on one side and some on the other.

Now take General Escobar.[3] He is the Leader that is operating in the North East. I have been his guest at his home in Mexico City. He is one of their most popular generals. He is the one that took me to the Bull Fight. He got a great kick out of it for every time the bull was anywhere near the horse I would bury my head down on my arms and look down at the floor. (We were sitting in the front row and there was a big concrete ballustrade where our elbows were resting on). Then he would tell me when to look up again.

Finally it got to be the laugh of everybody around there. My friend President Calles and his Party were kinder around the circle almost facing us and Calles got to kidding me about not looking up.[4]

They had pictures in the Mexico Papers the next day of "American Comedian enjoying Mexican Bull fight," and all you could see was the top of a hat buried on a couple of folded arms on the railing, and General Escobar laughing and pointing to me. I could stand part of it for there is some very clever things done in the ring. But when it come to the horses I sure couldent go that, and say by the way the most famous fighter in Spain now is a fellow that fights the Bull from his horse and don't get his horse hit at all. He has splendidly reigned horses, and he gives a great exhibition. I think he was to be in Mexico this winter. Now that is worth seeing cause that is real work.

But let's get back to personalities, when you read this you may be reading on the front page of the same paper, "Cross marks spot where Rebel Leader General Escobar stood when he faced the firing squad."

Now he is an awfully nice fellow, well educated, speaks English. Very fine personality. He told me the whole story of how he had captured the Leader of that Revolution. (For one was just being finished when I was there.)

That's the one where Serano, and Gomez were the Leaders and were shot.[5] Gomez was the last one. He had been hiding in the hills for weeks and Escobar was the government General that caught him. He captured him one night on a trail as he was coming down to the house to try and get something to eat. He had lived in the hills and was about half starved and weak. Escobar took him to his tent and had him shave and put on some of his clothes and clean up. Gomez couldent understand why he dident take him out and shoot him then, (as he naturally thought he would be shot on arrest).

He and Escobar had gone through Mexico Military School together (their West Point), and had both been Generals in the Army for years, but had never been particularly good friends, and Gomez couldent understand Escobar showing him this much courtesy.

From what I could gather from it Escobar wanted him to look well at the funeral.

He turned him over to another General who shot him the next morning.

Now it had been reported that Gomez dident die game, and just the day before Escobar told me this story, why Gomez' Mother and Sister come to Escobar's house and asked him to please tell them the real facts of his death.

You know that is one thing you got to hand to those Mexicans. They do know how to die. Course I guess they get a lot of practice out of it. But when they line 'em up against the wall, the most they ever ask for is a cigarette. There is none of these Alabis, and "Oh honest I dident do it" thing.

They got no excuse to offer, they lost, and they die like a man.

Well, he told these two ladies that the report was not so, that Gomez died like a real man, and he told me that they put their arms around him and cried and thanked him and seemed to be relieved as much to hear that as they would to have heard of his escape.

Now he is in the hills, and he will be the one to get lined up. Well

1929

I bet he don't flinch. And another General Almasans, he is the one that is hunting Escobar.[6] I got awfull well acquainted with him, in fact I had he and Escobar to dinner one night and they took me to a "Teater" after. He is a dandy fellow kidding and full of fun.

Then there is a General Limon, that was defending Juarez.[7] (That's the Town right across from El Paso.) He was the President's special Aide, on the two weeks trip that I was with President Calles and Ambassador Morrow all over the country.[8] He is a great little fellow. There was two of them brothers, Limon Grande, and Limoncito. I always called 'em big and little Lemon. He was a Polo player and when I got back to Mexico City he mounted me and I played several times with him.

It makes you sick to hear of these things happening down there. For they are no difference from us. They love peace just as much, they love life, and they want to be let alone. But these Leaders get overally ambitious, and think they are not getting a square deal from somebody, and there is just enough adventure in 'em to take the chance. But I think they are on the way to good government. These revolutions are getting more useless all the time. This one is not Popular. If it was it could win. I hope they get straightened out, for they are an awful nice people. Hospitality is their middle name. If I wasent acting a fool here in New York and have to stay I would be in Mexico in 24 hours. I would try to kid 'em out of fighting. So Viva Mexico.

326 A HISTORY OF MEXICO

Nothing has gained as much Publicity and is known as little about as this Mexican Revolution. Hoover hadent been sworn in over three-quarters of an hour till the desire to be President on the part of half of Mexico broke out.[1]

It just looks like his being inaugurated kinder put the same idea into 34 generals' heads in Mexico. So they started issueing ammunition to their men and said, "Come on Boys let's be inaugurated, how would you like to be personal bodyguard to the President of Mexico?"

Up here in our country every boy is taught by some old disappointed spinster that "Every one of you boys have the chance of becoming President, provided you were born in the right part of the country, and were not born of Democratic parents."

We are taught that from birth, and some of the most feebleminded ones take it seriously, and start to preparing, by reading what

Washington did, and what Lincoln did, and what Roosevelt did.[2] And as a matter of fact, no one of the whole thirty of them that we have had ever did what any one of the others did.

All of the prospective candidates study what to do, and who to do it to, and here comes Coolidge and does nothing and retires a hero, not only because he hadn't done anything but because he had done it better than anyone.[3]

Now in Mexico they have their fairy tales that are told to their children, the same as we do here. Where we are taught that every boy has a chance to be President, they are taught, "If my ammunition holds out, and I can get them before they get me, I not only can be President, but will."

Now we have come to look on a Mexican revolution the same as we have come to expect the farmers to cry for relief. We may not know just what day it will be, but we do know that it will come as soon as enough notes come due with the farmer, and in Mexico as soon as enough generals have had a dinner together, got full of mescal (Mexico's TNT) and decided on who would be President first out of the bunch.

Mexico used to have these things years and years ago, and then along come a fellow named Portfolio Diaz.[4] Now nobody has ever to this day discovered what's in a Portfolio. (Boston carried more of them for no reason than any city in the world.) But this old Portfolio down there it dident take long to see what he was loaded with. He just sit and waited till one of the generals got too full of "Teculia" (that's mescal before it's been diluted).

Well, old Portfolio would just play a little trick. He would see if this certain over-Patriotic General could stand up in front of a "Doble" wall while some other fellows playfully tried to bowl him over with a series of Mauser bullets. In that way he kept what has since become known as the Peace for about thirty years.

A Revolution under his administration just dident seem like it could get organized. The fellow wouldent any more than get an idea that he would like to be the God Father of one than the last words he would seem to remember would be spoken in his native tongue, "Ready, Aim, Fire!"

There was no disarmament of Conferences, no League of Nations, no World Court. Life in Mexico was just perpetual peace outside of just burying Generals. One day instead of the usual routine of "have you any Message you would like to leave to your folks," why he give a fellow a jail sentence instead.

That was his first mistake in thirty or forty years. He was getting old and his judgement was getting faulty. Instead of relieving this fellow of his over abundance of patriotism in the usual way why he put him in jail.

That was a fellow named Madero.[5] Now a jail will detain you for an indefinite period, but a firing squad will just practically ruin you. Now it's never been quite clear how Madero got out of there, neither has it ever been any clearer how Portfolio Diaz got on a Boat. You see he had broke his rule. The best way to keep a good man down is with Bulletts.

Well Madero hadent any more than got in till a Guy named Huerta come along, and Poncho Villa saw that the stage needed a new Character for Holbrook Blynn, so he charges into Columbus, New Mexico, one night and that gave us a chance to see Mexico first, before seeing France.[6]

So our troops went down and used that as a rehearsal for the main event overseas. Someway or other Madero and his Vice President Suarez were being transferred from the White House to the jail and come to an accidental death by murder.[7] Huerta was supposed to know nothing about it, and he was very much surprised on appointing himself President.

Well then when the whole of Mexico saw that all you had to do to be President was to shoot the one that was, why that brought on some pretty fancy marksmanship. Carranza started him a school of marksmanship.[8] Villa joined him. Villa would join anybody that had any ammunition.

Then Obregon comes into the picture.[9] Up to then he was an Amateur, but he entered in earnest now. Huerta saw that old man Diaz knew more than just how to rule a Country, he knew how to leave one when the leaving was good, so Huerta used the same Ocean for the same cause. He decided to get seasick instead of shot. Carranza moved into Chapultapec Castle, whiskers and all.

Another revolution bobbed up in the State of Sonora, whose principal product is Revolutions. Villa and Obregon were sent to either assist it, or hinder it, but at any rate not to let it stay dormant. They fell out with each other on the way and started one between themselves, had a battle, Obregon lost an arm and Villa lost the battle.

Then Zapata come along.[10] (That means shoes.) Well he walked into a personally conducted Revolution of his own. Then another Huerta, Adolpho.[11] (Not any relation to the other one.) He takes out a Revolutionary permit, and starts revoluting. About this time Carranza died what is a natural death in Mexico, he was shot, practically totally.

Weekly Articles

De La Huerta (he was only supposed to be Provisional President). That is president until he was shot, banished or thrown out. Obregon however comes in by an election, something unheard of up to then, that was a new way to get to be President. So everybody wanted to try that so another man from Sonora, Plutarco Calles, follows in Obregon (as a Mexican President can't succeed himself even if he is living he can't do it).[12]

Calles served and Obregon was to follow back in, (you can go back in if you stay out awhile) same idea that Coolidge has. But Obregon died a natural President's death. Then they appointed Portes Gil.[13] (Pronounced Heel.) Now Escobar getting tired of this back to the old way of electing Presidents by the Bulletts instead of the ballotts.[14] So it's just a question of whether he will be shot before he becomes President or after.

327 WOMEN 'PURIFY' POLITICS

Well all I know is just what I read in the papers, and what I run onto around the old Opera House here in New York. It's been so warm and nice that most of the people have been coming here from Florida to spend the winter. There hasent been five overcoats sold here all winter. Tammany Hall held the Comedy record all last week trying to nominate somebody to have his name on the stationary saying he was head. Course to an outsider we don't know what all the shooting is for, we don't know what it is. What is it he is head of, why and for what reason. There has been more people try to explain what Tammany Hall is and fewer succeeded than there has that have taken a shot at the Einsten Theory.[1] It's just a bunch banded together under a Constitution which says, "Get these Jobs and stay with 'em, and if the time ever does come when you have to give it up, give it up to another Tammany man."

Well the first time they had a meeting to elect a Leader why the Women come in and wanted to vote. Well they had never considered that, they had forgot about the Nineteenth Amendment on account of being so busy thinking about the Eighteenth. Well nobody knew what to do with these women. Then somebody thought of the idea of adjourning. When a meeting ain't running right why the thing to do is to adjourn, reorganize and meet some time when the ones that are against you don't know when you are going to meet.

1929

You know Women are getting into more things that are embarrassing to them men. You see the first idea of giving them the vote was just to use the vote. But the Women contrary like they are, they wasent satisfied with that. They started to take this equality thing serious. They begin to think they really was somebody. The women figured that "While we may not be as good as a Man, we are at least as good a Politician." So the Scamps commenced to want to get in on the loot. As soon as they found out a Political Job took no experience to hold, that it only took experience to get, why they commenced to making themselves rather embarrassing around the Political employment Bureau, and now every one of them call themselves as a Number 2 Company of Mabel W. Willerbrandt.[2] It was all right with the men when the women took the little Committee assignments where there was NO salary connected, but when they started to want to put their powdered nose into the feed trough, why that brought on complications. Now they are wondering, "Was the Women's vote worth what they are asking for it?"

It's not only that way with Tammany, but it's getting that way all over. Women that used to wouldent think of gossipping anywhere but over a back fence, now won't say a word about you till the meeting has been duly called to order. It's scattered Scandal around more. It's brought it more into the open. It's changed lots of things around. Families that used to dident know there was a Restaurant in town are looking over the Menu cards on days when the Ladies Auxiliary of the "Pork Barrell Political Society" is in session.

To us fellows that are not in Politics we are tickled to death, to see the Women folks dealing such misery to the Politicians. And in the long run it's good for humanity. Every job a Woman can grab off it just drives another Politician to either work or the poor house.

And you know this next Congress that meets now pretty soon. Did you just notice the amount of Crepe De Chine and Laungerie there was mixed up in it? Why pretty near every prominent man we ever had in Politics has got a Daughter entered in that Congress. Course that's another trouble with Politics, it breeds Politics. So that makes it pretty hard to stamp out. The only way to do it is at the source. We got to get Birth Control among Politicians. We have to do that in order that they don't bring more Politicians into the World. They may not purposely mean too, but it just can't be helped. Now you take some of these very Women that I am speaking of that are entered in this forthcoming Farm Relief Burlesque. Their Fathers worked hard and saved, and thought they had left them so well off that they would never have to resort to Politics. But here they are, you see that the breeding crops out, and that's why we are going to have to do something about it. You see there is no stopping these Women when they get started. Why I wouldent be a bit surprised that it won't be no time till some Woman will become so desperate Politically and just lose all prospectus of right and wrong and maby go from bad to worse and finally wind up in the Senate.

Now you know that no Father or Mother ever had any idea that the offspring would ever darken a Senate door. Course up to now there has been no need for anything resembling a Woman in actions in the Senate, especially an Old Woman, for there is more old Women in there already than there is in the old Lady's home. But they been in there on a pention for years, and they are awful nice old fellows, they don't do any particular harm to anyone. Course they don't do any great good. But they about break even and if they was out maby somebody worse would be in.

But this Nineteenth Amendment is worrying more people in the Country than the Eighteenth. It's not only caused millions of men to go hungry, (by their wives being away at a rally) but it is causing a lot of them to go Jobless, all because the whole thing was misunderstanding. The men give 'em the vote, and never meant for them to take it seriously. But being Women they took the wrong meaning and did.

328   PROHIBITION HAS ITS INNING

Well, all I know is just what I read in the papers, Politics, Innaugarations, Base Ball training, Cabinets being sworn, Indignation over Vanderbilt book in Reno, Mexican persuit race, and all those things are all as nothing in the press the last week or so compared to what has happened along the prohibition enforcement lines.[1] Sinking that Boat down in the Gulf of Mexico come pretty near being another sinking of Tea in the Boston Harbor.[2] You know we had a World Series with England over that little incident, and when we sunk this one it looked like the Dollar a year men would be out again.

The whole argument was, "How far out away from land was the boat when they first took after it?" The old time law said three miles was the limit that a Country owned from its shore, then when Prohibition come in we wanted to take in more territory. We was enforcing it so good out as far as three miles that we had a Treaty made with

1929

England. For it has always been considered that England practically owns the Ocean. So naturally in dealing with anything that comes up regarding water, (especially if it is salt water) why we have to confer with England. Not on account of her importance as a Nation, for perhaps they are no more important than France, or Germany, but it's their Navy that makes the difference. It's like a rich man in a Town, he may not really be as important, or know as much as dozens of others, but it's his dough that makes the difference.

You give Equador England's Navy and right away Equador's ambassador would be seated next to the President at official functions, and England would go to the foot where Equador is now. A country is known by its strength, and a Man by his Check Book. So we met England and made a treaty with them that would give us about 12 miles to enforce in. In other words we were just enforcing so good that we figured in order to keep the boys from just laying off all the time why we would give them nine more miles. Well we took care of that so well that we met England again and asked for some more of their Ocean, so we drew up a Treaty that give us something like this, "It's our Ocean out as far as a Boat can go in one hour's travel." It dident state how the boat was to travel. It dident say whether it was as far as a sailing boat could go in an hour with no wind, or whether it was as far as the same boat could go if it had 25 Wright Whirlwind Engines in it. It was just to be an hour's travel. Now evidently this "I am Alone" this one they sunk could travel pretty far in an hour, for it went so fast that it took our Coast Guard Cutters the biggest part of a week to catch up with it and sink it. Well they shot at him for days before they could sink the boat. If they had taken all the bullets they shot at it, and put them on the boat it would have sunk immediately from the weight.

Well, we was just getting over the excitement of all that in the papers when away out in Aurora somewhere they shot a woman, beat up her husband and then their little boy shot one of the officers. Well that caused more arguments than the boat sinking. I don't know which side you are on in that argument. But you got to admire the kid. He come through when his parents were in danger. Whether your parents are good or bad, that's not your business, but stick with 'em when they are in trouble.

Well then to cap it all and make 100% prohibition week why a bunch of Congressmen landed in New York from Panama Canal where they had been at Government expense to see if it really did connect the two Oceans, or was it just propaganda. Well they got back here to New York and they only searched one of their baggage and found four quarts. He had forgot to claim Government privalege. (That's a gag where if you leave the Country, you can come back with anything you want and they can't search your baggage.) The other 14 had claimed it and they got home with theirs. All but Congressman La Guardia, an Italian American (and a good one).[3] He admitted that he had had started from down there with a few steins of Grog, but had drank it up before arrival at quarantine, purposely. Now he will be ostracised in Congress for honesty.

Then all this was no more than happening than this fellow Wesley Jones that put in the Woolworth bill 5 and 10, five years in jail and 10 thousand fine, he up and says that he has never seen any drinking either among Congressman, or TOO MUCH drinking even among Senators.[4] Some young lady interviewed him in Washington and what the man hadent seen is almost remarkable.

On the same day our great author, and Dramatist, Booth Tarkington had admitted that he was blind and had been for some time.[5] Well to Mr. Tarkington's statement and to read Wesley Jones, (author of the Jones Bill) you would have thought that it was Jones that was blind, and had been for the course of his natural life, and you would think Tarkington was the one that could see.

And by the way wasent that wonderful what he said about the blind, (I mean Tarkington, not Jones.) He said it was so wonderful to be blind and not have to look at a lot of things that he dident want to see, wasent that great? What an encouragement to the blind! What a real love for his fellowman!

Well Jones is all right too. We wants to give this fellowman free room and meals for five years, and all he has to pay for it is ten thousand bucks. That's two thousand a year. Well that's about as cheap as you can live outside. Course what I have always thought was that Jones could have improved on his bill by making it Ten and Five. You see if you get ten years in jail and only have to pay five thousand why you get your rent and board five thousand cheaper. It's a great world though, watch her go by.

329 THESE EXPLORERS ARE SO SHY, THEY SHUN TOURISTS

Well, all I know is just what I read in the papers, or what I can pick up as I try to keep an ear to the ground. Had an awful interesting evening a week or so ago.

1929

Mr. Putman the Publisher had a Dinner party.¹ It was given I think to this man Wilkins, that's just been prowling around down near the South Pole.² Around the table was just about everybody that we had ever seen in the Sunday supplement with a coonskin Coat on (not for fraternity purposes). There was men there that had eaten more meals with Esquimos than Mr. Stearns has with Mr. Coolidge.³ This Guy Putman he kinder messes around on the fringe of the Artic himself. I reckon he is about the only Book binder that knows the difference between a snowshoe and a La Crosse racket. There was Guys there that had flew over the North Pole, walked over it, jumped over it, and here was this Wilkins announcing that night, (at this very dinner) the fact that he was going to "Dive under it." He was going down in a Submarine and see what the pole was really anchored to underneath.

Sitting right by me was a mild, rather meek voiced individual, that I kinder wondered how he got in this bread line, he didn't look like he had ever been any further away from 14th Street and Fourth Ave. than a Tammany Leader, and here he had spent more years in the Arctic than any man living. He had spent nine winters and 13 summers with a floating Iceberg for a putting green. It was this fellow Stefansson.⁴ He is the one we have been reading about for years.

Then right across was Martin Johnston and his wife (the best looking woman that ever had her picture taken with a foot on a dead Lion).⁵ Here they had been years in Africa, and the South Seas among the Cannibals. A Cannibal is a good deal like a Democrat they are forced to live off each other. Come to find out this Johnston and his wife both come from right up above where I was raised.

One had come from Independence, Kansas, and she had come from another little hay barn right near, Coffeyville. It used to be our Post office from our old home down in the Nation. It was forty miles away, but then we didn't get much mail anyhow. In fact I have known some of us to make the whole trip and never get an oil circular. That just shows you, us down in the old Indian Territory, (now called **IMPEACHERINO**.)

We always did know those Kansas people was queer. Imagine two fine young people going and spending their life trying to make a Rhineosoris look pleasant in the Camera! Amelia Earhardt, the Girl that flew the Atlantic Ocean to escape Boston Society, well she was there, a very charming young lady, one of the few Aviatrixes whose excapades have been with a Plane and not with unappreciative husbands!⁶ Mrs. Kermit Roosevelt, a might pleasant little Mother was there by us.⁷ I wondered how she got in with all this "Safari." Then I

11

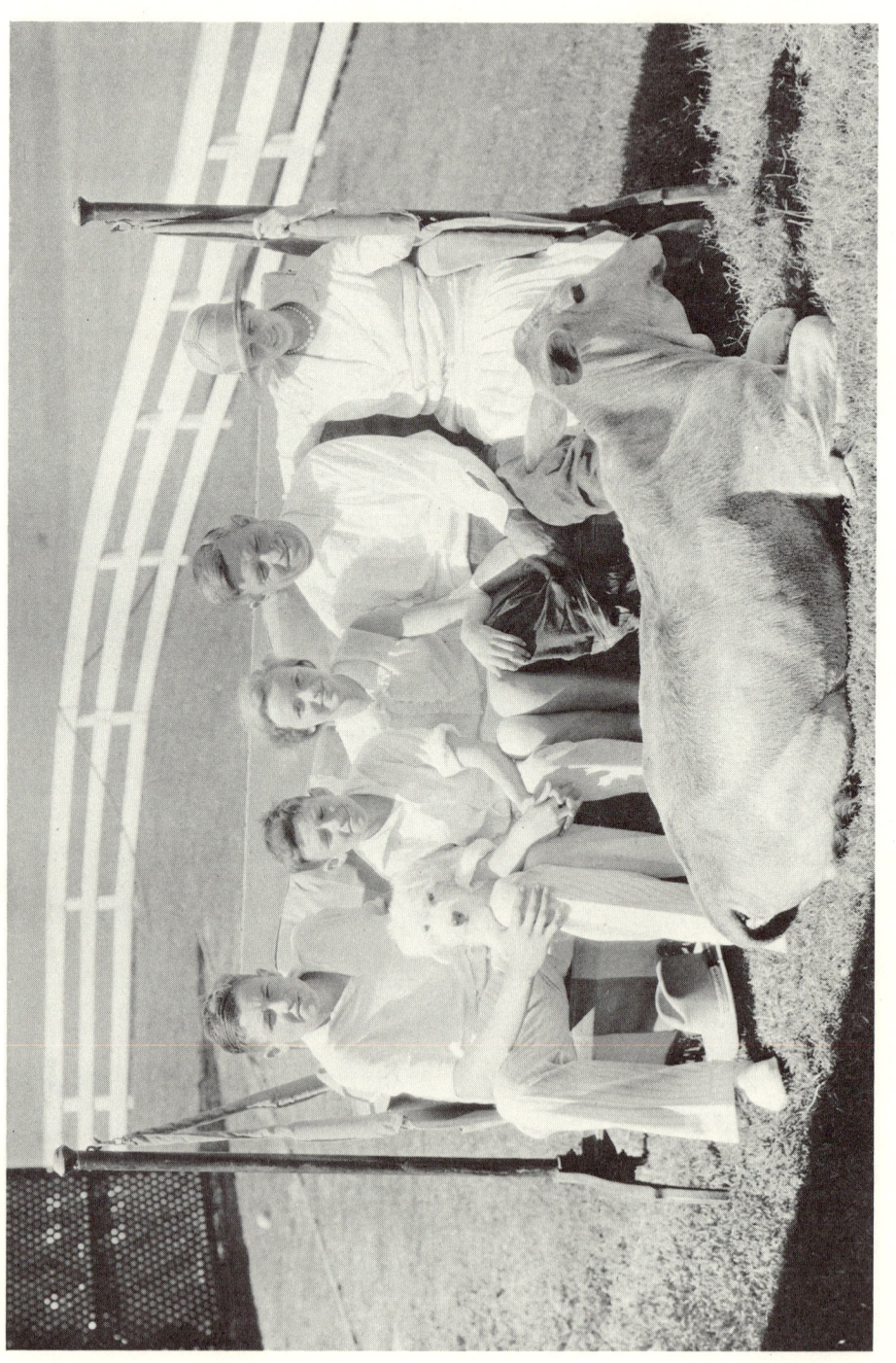

Will Rogers and his family at their ranch near Santa Monica, California. Left to right: Bill, Jr. (holding the family's Sealyham, Jock), Jimmy, Mary, Will, and Betty. The Rogers' pet calf, Sarah, came from the King Ranch in Texas.

happened to remember being out to their home the Sunday before her Husband and his Brother Ted started for some outlandish place called Tibet, to shoot some specimens of queer things for a Chicago Museum.[8] You would think if Chicago wanted to see some queer things that was shot they would just go to the Morgue.

It begin to look like Mrs. Rogers and I were about the only ones who had never said, "I smoked your Cigarette and really found it took all the danger out of my entire trip."[9] The furtherest I had ever been from a Cook's guide was just hollering distance. I had visited some strange places in the world, but it was always so full of Tourists by the time I got to it that the Tourists were stranger than the place.

Then I happened to spy Jesse Lasky (the big Close-up and Long shot Guy of the Movies) and I thought well he has never been out of sight of a head Waiter, and here I happened to remember a trip he took floating down the Colorado River away down into the wilds of Mexico.[10] They floated down and dident have energy enough to row back, so they just kept on going. It was a mighty interesting group.

This Stefansson fellow told me he was in the Arctic for five and a half years, and that they didn't know the war was on till it was a year old and didn't get home till away after it was over. Think of coming out and asking, "Well, what's the news, anything happened since I been away?" "Oh no, the boys had a little argument, and there was some pretty cross words between a few of the countries, but nothing much come of it, outside of a little war."

Then Wilkins and him got to talking about this submarine Gag. Wilkins said he would come up every day for air. If the Ice was over them, they would bore through it with an auger, or with some kind of Chemicals. Chances are the chemical he would use would be some bootleg liquor. That would melt the ice and leave a sear on the Pole. He figured he could go across in 21 days from Spitzbergen to Siberia, or Seattle or one of those northwest towns.

Stefansson suggested they should go the other way on account of the current (those Guys know everything). But Wilkins said it would be too hard to get his Submarine around there to start, have to take it through the canal. The Pole has been flown over three times with a Plane, and twice with a Dirigible. So just being no. 6 don't get you anywhere. Peary made it with a pack of flea hounds, Cook found it twenty miles north of Duluth.[11]

What a scenic trip this will be, 21 days under the water! That will be just like wanting to see something on a train and a bunch of Box Cars in your way. I want him to lay out some place there at the pole, for I want to hold the next Democratic Convention there. Course that won't attract much attention to it. Wall Street wants to take up a collection and send the Federal Reserve bank members up there. They couldn't dissrupt the Icebergs with any statement. But they were all a mighty nice pleasant bunch of people, and I am awful glad I went over. Course on account of having to work in the Theatre I didn't get there for the dinner, and didn't get anything to eat, so that's why I could remember what everybody said and did.

330 PLOTTING AGAINST HEFLIN

Well all I know is just what I read in the papers. Texas Guinan has been so busy hugging and kissing everybody over her aquittal that the old Town just can't seem to get organized again.[1] She said she had no idea that drinks were served in her Night Club, and twelve jurymen agreed with her.

President Coolidge surprised us all again by joining the Board of Directors of a big life Insurance Company. I had always said you would never see him hooking up with any big Company, that it might be brought out against him in 32. But it seems like he is not to do much for this one. He only gets $50.00 when the Board meets, which is about once or twice a month, unless he calls it oftener. He certainly will not give much for that wage.

So it's really kinder hard to tell just what he is supposed to do. He was supposed to take Mr. Herrick's place on the board.[2] Well Mr. Herrick was Ambassador to France, so if he takes his place he evidently won't be supposed to do much. I wish he had taken some real job where there was something to do and it would look like he was really doing something. Course if you can get into enough of these Companies at fifty bucks a gathering why it wouldent be bad employment. You know these big Companies are having a hard time trying to get names on their list of Directors that look BIG. It's kinder like trying to find somebody to give a dinner to. There just ain't many that look important enough to be fed free. Funny thing, on the same day that Mr. Coolidge signed up with the Insurance Co., why some fellow committed suicide because he couldent get rid of an insurance Agent.

Poor old Tom Heflin, he no more than gained quite a bit of sympathy with the statement that he issued about his Son, "I wish people would not exploit my Son's weakness but try and help him, and I will be ready to meet him when he comes with open arms."[3] Now that was lovely and very fatherly. But he come right back and

1929

spoils it all with, "It was the Son of a Roman Catholic that give my Boy the drink, and then insisted that he take another." Tom even insinuated that the Liquor was made by the Benedictines. It just seems that Romans won't lay off Tom. The Christians in the early days wasent chased around by the Mountain Lions any more than Tom is persecuted by 'em today.

Course if this Roman Catholic did give his Son a drink, it don't seem to signify much only that they must be an awful liberal race of people. And if the effects of that round of drinks lasted till they got back to New York, it looks like an awful good add for the brand turned out by the Benedictines.

But he is all right Tom is, and I bet the Boy is all right, and Tom will sure go to bat for a friend. When it looked like they was going to make the Curtis Family eat at the second Table Tom come to the front for 'em. He forgot for the moment that Charley was a Republican, and he broke Democratic precedent by complimenting him.[4] Tom figured that it was really the Vatican that was trying to make Charley eat in the kitchen, and he wasent going to stand by and see 'em get away with it. If they hadent given Charley the rating that he deserved, Tom was going to put a Bill in Congress to make 'em all eat at an Automat, and the one with the most Nickles would be the Head Man. But they got it all fixed and they had a big Dinner last week at the Chilean Embassy and everybody got their Chili Con Carne according to the latest Emily Post standard.[5]

But poor old Washington, that's all they got to think about. When you pay your tax there it really is nothing but a gossipping license. Nobody has anything to do but just sit and Gab and Gab, and have dinners. That's why so many of them stay there after their term of office expires, they just havent got through talking about everybody yet.

Secretary Stimpson got out of that thing pretty slick.[6] He left it to the Ambassadors from all the other Countries. That's about the only thing they had ever been called on to decide since they been there, so they was glad to get something that made it look like they were doing something. He must be quite a fixer this Stimpson fellow. He got out of Nicaragua alive, lived through a Taft Cabinet, arrived in America two days ahead of a Phillipine Deligation looking for freedom.[7] He seems to be quite a fellow.

Well we had some more argument started here lately. The Leviathan left here after being sold to private parties and they decided they would peddle a little Liquor on the way over to kinder help keep the Wolf from the Gangplank. It seems they are allowed to have seven hundred Bottles of Medicinal Joy Juice in case some of the

15

Weekly Articles

passengers dident drink water. Well then the howl commenced coming in, and now the poor fellow that bought the Boat may have to switch it and put it under the Nicaragua flag instead of ours. They are not supposed to sell till they get twelve miles out. You have to bring enough of your own to last that long.

When this gets to you Congress will be in session again helping the farmers, so if you have a farm don't sell it for there is no telling what a farm will be worth when we find the amount of relief they are to get. Why they may have the Federal Reserve give as much to the Farmer as they do to the Stock Market. That would make farms be worth more than General Motors.

Now that Marion Talley the opera Singer is turned agriculturist things look bright even without Congress.[8] I can see Marion winning all the Hog calling Contests around among her mortgaged neighbors.

331   PAUL REVERE HAD A RUNAWAY

Well all I know is just what little I read in the papers. Benn up among the Yankees in New England for a couple of weeks. They are mighty fine old folks, and they take a joke on themselvs great too. I was kidding 'em about not making Coolidge a present of a home when he returned to the old State from serving as President. I really always felt like they ought to got Mr. Coolidge a nice home. They laughed hartily at my little quips on it, but no one started a collection. But they are mighty loyal, well read and a dandy audience.

I was here last week during the celebration of "Patriots Day," that's a thing they just have up here. It has something to do with the time when the English overestimated their fighting qualities and they started a Revolution. Well that's the time Paul Revere unhitched an old Buggy Horse, jumped on him bareback and announced, "This is Paul Revere broadcasting from Bunker Hill Station, shut off your sets and grab a musket. The British are coming and if they don't stop to get tea they are liable to be here any minute. This programme is being brought to you through the courtesy of George Washington, a Virginia Planter. A farmer that needs no relief. But just wants to clean the British out, and figures we can run it ourselvs and cut out the overhead. Wake up Pilgrims, and shake a leg, and when you see a Red Coat coming don't shoot till you see if they got white eyes. Any of you Birds know the road to Concord. Loan me a pair of spurs or I never will get anywhere. Good night Patriots, remember this is station B. H. (Bunker Hill) broadcasting Goo-oo-d Ni-g-h-t."

16

1929

Now I just want to show you how much smarter these New Englanders are than all the rest of us. We thought Paul was the only Western Union Messenger Boy that night, we had never heard of another one. (Not in Oklahoma History there ain't.) Well there was another fellow, that worked a different territory that same night, his name was Dawes, and he had a Horse too.[1] I don't know where he went, I think he went down to Newport to see if he could interest any of the Millionaires in Local Government control. Now how many of you that knew that there was a Dawes that made the race? Course it attracted no more attention than a Vice President, but he did it. He had a long Corn Cob pipe and here was his appeal against Taxation without Representation, "Wake up there you Plymouth Rocks, and stop laying and go to crowing. Hell and Maria what do you think this is, a United States Senate? Get up and do something for your country. If you havent got a Country get a Gun and make you one. Come on, after fighting the Indians all these years, fighting the British will a fiesta. Hell and Maria, you think I am lopping through this Country in the middle of the night for nothing? If we can get the British out of here maby we can get the Senate Rules changed. Who's got a pipe full of good smoking tobacco? I want you all to clean these British out back here, I don't want to have to go out to my home in Chicago and bring them back here. They would kill all the British, and all the minute men too. How's that road to Lexington now, have they still got those detours? Remember as I told you when I first gallopped up to the bar here and got off, the British are coming. If that's of any particular interest to you. No thanks, had enough, got to be getting on. Goodnight everybody."

Well now last week here in Boston on Patriots day April 19th, they went through this whole thing. It was a big Holiday up here. Well you might know it was a big Holiday when the Braves won two games. They had all the patriotic Societies out, and had a wonderful parade, and they reproduced Paul's and Charley's ride.[2] Well Dawes he got lost, there was a traffic light against him so he started off another way, and the crowds along the way never did get a peek at him any more. He was supposed to have an escort. But none of them had ever made the route before, they were picked more for historical than geographical knowledge. Paul did a little better, he made the trip but his old barrelled headed Army Horse run away, and just delighted on running into where there was the most people located. This old Jug head had never heard bands playing and people hollering before. Some cops finally caught his horse, but Paul hadent had any time to yell the British are coming. He finally changed horses with an escort, and I think finally reached Concord in a Ford. So I guess if the war had been held this time, we would have lost it, so I doubt very much if our present generation is an improvement over the old Forefathers.

It's quite a leap from anything historical to Congress. But did you see where already there has been over 1,000 Bills introduced in there? Now it was supposed to just be for Farm relief, but they got 'em in there for everything from Birth Control to Mass Production. Congressman Louie Ludlow from Ind., he used to be head of the press club in Washington and is a fine newspaper man.[3] Well Louie's contribution to farm relief is to do away with "Slugs" in beating vending machines. He figures if we can just prevent lead nickles, that it will pay every mortage in Indiana. Representative Fish of New York introduces a Bill to stop war.[4] That's an original idea. Another Representative wants a bill to stabilize money. It can't ever change, no matter whether the Country is rich or poor, the money is the same. Bills to build over 300 bridges are in there. Those old Babies in there want something to get back into Congress over. Nothing beats a bunch of bridges as a National graft. Some Guy from Minnesota wants to make the home a "Nuisance" if liquor is found in there, and Linthicum of Maryland wants to make the Star Spangled Banner the National Anthem.[5] And then they ask, "Will, where do you get your jokes from?"

332   PEACE ON EARTH —
       AND WAR IN BROCKTON!

All I know is just what I read in the papers. Now let's see what has taken place since I communed with you last week. Tom Heflin lost his encounter with the "Heirachy."[1] Tom wanted the Senate to go on record that it condemned the action of the Town of Brocton Mass for not paying strick attention to one of his adresses. Well he could have come nearer getting the Senate to go on record that they sympathised with Brocton. For Lord the Town of Brocton only had to listen to one, while the Senate never gets over 'em. Well anyhow this longwinded drawn-out thing afforded the one best line and laugh that has been pulled in there for this session. Senator Gillette of Mass told Tom, "The State of Mass. regrets it.[2] The Town of Brocton regrets it. The Mayor regrets it, the Police regret it, and the Man that threw the bottle, and MISSED you, regrets it."

Well farm Relief would get a little help in between. Grundy would try to get some higher tarriff on anything Manufactured in

1929

Pennsylvania.³ But Tom would bob up the next day during lull and say, "You've got to make this Country safe for United States Senators to speak in."

Well we finished our Theatrical engagement up in Boston and are moving over to Philadelphia for a couple of weeks, then one week in Detroit and one more in Pittsburg and then on the old Plane and out "Where Men are beginning to be heard." We had some laughs in the Theatre in Boston last week. One night Babe Ruth was in and I introduced him and his new Bride, and then sitting near him was Charles Francis Adams, Our new and very distinguished Secretary of the Navy, a real blue blood.⁴ The only living American that has had two American Presidents that he descended from, John Adams, and John Quincy Adams. Then I introduced them to each other and Babe got up and went over and shook hands with Adams. It was a big laugh and applause, then I told the audience you wouldent think after having the two men as great as these, One a Descendent of two Presidents and the other the greatest Sports favorite that we ever produced, you wouldent think we possibly could have a BIGGER man here tonight than either one of them, in fact, BIGGER than both of them put together. Well I just want to introduce you to the Giant of the Ringling show, and sure enough there he was.⁵ The Circus was to have opened there the next day. He was sitting in the back of a Box and no one had noticed him. It was one of the biggest laughs I ever heard in a Theatre. These Adams'es, and Lodges, and Lowells, they are just about the whole thing in the way of Tradition up there.

Well I see where we have offered some plan at a Dissarmament Conference over in Geneva and everybody is all excited about it. So I suppose we will be kidded into entering into another sinking. We are just about to live down the humiliation of that last one in 22. I told the Secretary of our Navy right from the stage, that I wished we had the biggest Navy in the World, the biggest Army, and by all means the biggest Aeroplane force, but have it understood with the taxpayers that they are ONLY TO BE USED ON THE HOME GROUNDS. Now how in the world will you tell me is there a better way to prevent war than that. Be ready for it and stay at home. When they know they can't lick you they certainly are not coming away over here to try it. He applauded it, and I believe he thought it was all right. In fact it looks like the League of Nations could just about prevent war by deciding "Who starts a war?" Well just have the League pass the following resolution, "We consider the first Nation that sets military foot on the other is the starter of the war." Now you put that on 'em, and they won't be in such a hurry to grab up a lot of men and start prancing into Belgium, or somewhere. Then they can be as sore at each other as they want but they will know that the first one that invades the other is the starter of the war, and they will be leary of that, and as long as each one will be waiting for the other to start it, why neither one will want to carry the ultimate blame, so the first thing you know they will calmed down and meet on the line and have a drink. Personally I can't think of anything that would encourage a war more than for a couple of Nations to know that they had Equal Navies. If you know your Navy is equal to the other fellows, you will always figure that your men are superior to theirs, so you are ready to go to any time with him. There is enough sportsmanship in every Country to want if they knew they had an equal break to take a try at the other. So this old thing of regulating Navies so they are equal is the Houie.

Did you ever notice how much more peaceful it is all-around when our Marines are at home instead of prowling around? Why if we keep at home awhile why we are liable to get out of the habit of wanting to send 'em away off every time we heard that some little Nation was about to pull off a local Amateur Revolution. I believe this fellow Hoover has been around the World so much that he won't think it's any novelty to have them away off in all those places.

Say here is one that Coolidge pulled when someone was telling him about Mr. Hoover moving the six White House saddle Horses away, and sending them back over to the Army Post. You know it had been reported how much this move of Hoover's would save, the feed and care of the Horses, and when the fellow got through Coolidge said, "Guess they will quit eating when they get to the Army Post." So as a matter of fact it dident save anything, and also the Mayflower going out of Commission, the Government has to pay all those men just the same, they are all Navy men.[6] They just as well be on the Mayflower as the "Robert E. Lee." We kinder thought Calvin might come down and see our little show while in Boston, But I guess the prices scared him out.

333 WILL TURNS LITERARY

Well all I know is just what I read in the papers, and I kinder went out of my way while I was up in the City of Culture week before last and I decided to improve myself literarily. So I says I got to do some real highbrow reading. I am sorter like Al Smith, I never was much on this Book reading, for it takes 'em so long to describe the color of the eyes of all the Characters.[1] Then I like my sunsets from

1929

eyesight and not from adjectives. Congress has got more fiction in it in a day than Writers can think of in a year.

Old Henry the eight might have been a Bear according to the Book of the month Club.[2] He broke loose from the Holy Church at Rome and went at it with nothing to back him but an Axe and a series of Wives. But listen, that's five hundred years ago. Why old Henry with all his portfolio full of marriage certificates never saw the day he ever broke off relations with Rome any cleaner than Tom Heflin has right here in our own generation.[3] Tom may lack the sex appeal that Henry had but he can go him two to one on denouncing qualities. He has got no Cardinal Wolsey to advise him.[4] But the old Alabama Kleagle has handed him over some circumstantial evidence that has kept him on his feet more hours than Farm Relief has occupied. But being up in Boston why your mind naturally turns to "Higher things." The week I was there they had just barred the "American Tragedy" from being sold over the Bar, And the Committee was then reading Pilgrims Progress, to see if there wasent some underlying meaning in it.

So I said well up here what Book can I get that I won't be breaking any City ordinance, and at the same time will improve my mind, and I started looking through the adds and I saw a Girl sitting straddle of an old Gin case with her toes wrapped around the lower spokes of a steering wheel and her hands assisting her toes to guide the ship. Her hair was blowing in the breeze, and she had on one of those hats you wear with a slicker. But there was no strap under her chin, so I don't know what held it till the photographer could get the Picture. The adds all said it was a true story of a Girl that went to Sea when she was eleven months old, and was finally Shanghied ashore at the age of seventeen. The adds had some samples of the cussing in it, and I wanted to see how Sea cussing compared with New York stage cussing during the past season, which really reached its heighth in high grade profanity. I guess there was more good straight away cussing this year than ever before. But most of it had been confined to scenes on land.

Well I go literary and say never mind all this Fiction, I want some facts, and all the things I had read about this book said here is the real McCoy. Here is a Gal that was Born in the Crows Nest, Weaned on a Porpoise, Cut her teeth on an Anchor, Learned about sex from the Statue of Liberty, Could spit in a Shark's eye, and him under water. Her bottom was Whale hide, but her Heart was Gold. She could swim the Channell with a litter of Cats on her back, and never dampen a Kitty. The Northern Lights was nothing but a lightning Bug, and the Southern Cross was religious propganda. The

21

Equator was an extension of the Dixie Highway. A storm at sea was music to her ears, and a Typhoon was a Buggy ride. A Shipwreck wasent even a punctured tire. She combed her hair with a live Shark's tooth, and wore a couple of Octapuses for Garters.

She was just a female She Serpent that had vaulted up on deck and was ready to take out a stack in anything that come along from scuttling a Ship to poisening the ocean.

The Book had a time table on its folder and it told just when profanity, and Sharks' insides, and murders, and loads of Guano, would be run onto each 15 minutes as you read the Book.[5]

Well I was going along on schedule, a little leary right from the jump as to how a Mother could part with a seven month old Baby Girl, But not knowing sea people much I thought well maby they part with their young young. When she would pull an extra scary one it might arouse your doubt, why she would drown you in Latitude and longitude, so fast you would overlook whether the thing could happen or not. Well anyhow I got through it, and I was a saying to myself that's a pretty good tale even for a Able Bodied Male Seaman to go through. I was just a complimenting myself on what a great mental improvement it is to read Books, and that I must read more of these REAL life experiences. And the next morning a paper screams a headline across the page that they had just discovered the Boat out in Frisco tied up and rottening at the docks there, the one where she said sunk off Australia and she swam with the cats. They found the log of the boat, that's sort of a history of it. Her Father had been Captain but he seems like he always had a weakness for a family of Females at sea. Her Mother and sisters had traveled on the boat more than she had, for they was older. Seems like it used to ferry parties of Girl Scouts from Frisco to Honolulu, and Sydney.

Why from what the log said it was men that would get lonesome on there for the companionship of other men. This old "Stitches" why they find out now that he was an old Dame, a kind of "Hostess." She was the Texas Guinan of the Pacific.[6] They are figureing out now where most of Joan's Deep Seaing was on the Ferry from an Apartment in Jersey City over to her Publishers. And that profanity was all gathered from two trips to the "Front Page."[7]

So it's been an awful blow to me. Here I start in on my literery carreer and have my hopes shattered right on the first jump. How am I to know anything if I am not able to rely on the Publishers? How do I know that Shakespeare had a beard and wore knee breeches? I can only go by the pictures on the front of his books. Now wasent that funny that I should have my ideals shattered right on the first book I read? So me back to the Congressional Record where they ain't

1929

supposed to be doing nothing but lying when they say it. I am going to look mighty throughly into Coolidge's life before I start reading it.

334   'PHILLY' COPIES TULSA

Well all I know is just what I read in the Papers. There's been an awful lot of printing in 'em lately but not much news. Personally I been over in old Philadelphia for a couple of weeks, and you would be surprised at the life the old Girl is showing. They are organizing and trying to raise $1,300,000 dollars to advertise Philadelphia, to make it known outside of sonambulastic circles. It's always been known as one of the first places of where our Capitol was located, and it's been fairly well established that Washington slept here in not only one but various beds.

The old Liberty Bell is here. It's cracked but it's here. Washington crossed the Delaware (with everybody rowing but him) somewhere near here (wherever the Delaware is). I don't remember whether he crossed it to get to, or away from Phila. In fact I think the Constitution in its original form, (without amendments) was cooked up and signed here. In fact there has just been so much old History took place here that the place is practically saturated with our early scandal.

But what these boys is taking up this Million for is not to buy more Histories and distribute 'em among the night Clubs. It's to try and *live down* this History. They don't want it known that Washington slept here, what they want it known is that everybody here is not doing just what Washington did, sleeping here. They want it known there is more alarm clocks here than sleeping powders. They are not appealing to the poor straggler with "Nowhere to rest his weary head," they are after the Tourist and the prospective business man that rest is the last thing he wants. In fact they are doing just what Tulsa, and Claremore, and Los Angeles did twenty years ago. They want to show you that the great Pennsylvania Railroad goes through here, but that it stops. They know that we know from our great learning at Kemper Military Academy that Benjamin Franklin started the first tabloid newspaper here and called it the Saturday Evening Post, and originated the idea of making the Story be continued over among the pages with the adds on 'em.

A story run it till it went by all the adds and then it was "Concluded in an early issue." Franklin grabbed off all of William Penn's advertising, and that kept him going till Wanamaker come

Weekly Articles

along and opened up the first glorified Drug Store (a place where you sell everything).¹

William Penn through this press sheet of Franklyn's, become so well known that I was named after him. Course it was kinder second handed. I was named for the smartest Cherokee Chief we ever had. He had been named for William Penn, and he give me that and his too, William Penn Adair.² So there is really some dignity about my name when I really cut loose and want to use it all.

William Penn got pretty well linked up in early Philadelphia Real Estate and tradition. He was just about the Boise Penrose of his day.³ Franklyn in this little American Mercury of his got to giving so much favorable publicity to George Washington and his dappled gray Horse. In fact it was in the Saturday Evening Post where the Cherry Tree Story first broke. It was originated by Lincoln just to show you could "Fool all of the people enough of the time to get away with it." Well Washington made Franklyn Ambassador to France in return for this favorable publicity.

Franklyn made the best Ambassador since Alexander Hamilton, who wasent really an Ambassador but was the man that originated the "Put and take" system into our National Treasury. The Taxpayers put it in and the Politicians take it out. Hamilton was going good till he run into Aaron Burr, who wouldent pay his income tax, and that turned into a feud that had never before been equalled only by Andy Mellon and Jim Couzins.⁴ Burr and Hamilton had to use guns as the United States Senate had not been invented then as a means of attack. When Franklin went to Paris that left nobody to run the Saturday Evening Post, as Brisbane was working with Webster on a book called, "Don't sell America short."⁵ Well Hearst had not thought about selling it at all.⁶ He said, "I will keep it and some day I will worry Horace Greely and Munsey to death."⁷

So Franklyn heard of a fellow out in what was called Chicago, (for want of more ammunition.) This fellow was named George Horace Lorimer.⁸ The George was for Washington the Horace for Greely and the Lorimer was a combined family contribution. He was then working for Armour.⁹ Those were the days when we eat meat and not lettuce sandwiches. Armour was doing fine in those days, there was no tarriff to help him or no Federal Reserve to handicap him. Big Bill Thompson was in good favor with the Court of St James.¹⁰ Sam Insull was in his infancy and the whole City of Chicago was happy.¹¹ Lorimer come east with a double page colored add from Wrigley, and Sam Blythe.¹² Sam Blythe had managed Dolly Madison's campaign and knew as much about Politics as Alice Longworth.¹³ He lived a long and useful life and died when he quit drinking while listening to a Keynote speech at the Houston Democratic Convention.

But it's these modern things that Phila wants known. They don't want to drag up that old historical stuff of what the Susque-Centennial lost in 1926, what they charged the Government for Hog Island just to stable our silk shirts on away back in the war is not the things they want known. They want to coax some boats up the River. Their advertisements call it a Port of Call for European Liners, and they want to call some of them loud enough to get up here. It's only a hundred miles down to the Ocean. But what's a hundred miles to an add Writer?

There is very few Democrats here. That, if I was them, would be my main focus of attention. It's the only State that only has ONE Senator. That should be a sales argument. It's got all kinds of Baseball, Both the Athletics and the Phillies. It's the only Town too tough for a Marine. Smedley Butler left here and joined the Bandits in China.[14] But it's a great old Town, in a great old State, the Cradle of Political Corruption.

335   QUIET ON THE POTOMAC

Well all I know is just what I read in the papers, and in addition you have to do a little outside observing or you won't know much. I was in Philadelphia for a couple of weeks and I went so far as to decide to spend Sunday there. I stood it till about two o'clock in the afternoon when I discovered that I was the only one there, so I called up the Airport and asked Bob Hewitt, a splendid Pilot, if he had anything that would get me out of this isolation.[1] He says where do you want to go? I says, Well let's go to Washington. He says, "Well there is not much doing in Washington on Sunday either." I told him I knew that outwardly Washington was pretty dead on Sunday, but inside the homes there was many a "Conference" and "Huddle" and deep plans against the taxpayer.

So it was a beautiful afternoon and we flew down to Washington in about an hour and a quarter, landed at Bohling field. Just missed quite a sight as there was 18 big Martin Bombers had gone out of there on their way to Dayton Ohio for a big war maneuvers they held there. Met an old Marine Pilot there, that said, "I got it in for you. When we was fighting down in Nicaragua you wrote a piece about us going out and shelling the Nicaraguans from our Planes, and they was fighting us back by throwing sticks and rocks. Say listen Comedian, I wish you had been in one of those Planes some time. We have come in with more Machine gun bullets through our wings and fuselage than you ever told jokes about Coolidge. Don't you think those Guys dident have modern guns, and listen there was no place to land either."

Well I guess the Boy was about right at that. Course we dident like the idea of us fighting them with Planes and them have to defend themselves with nothing but what we thought was bean shooters. But it was the system that sent them there that most of us was hollering and not the Boys who really had to do the fighting. You know you can be killed just as dead in an unjustified war, as you can in one protecting your own home. We lost lots of fine men down there, for what? To make Nicaragua elections as pure as Chicago's? We are always going out to catch some native Bandit like Villa, or Sandino, and if we caught him we wouldent have anything to do with him.[2] After a Senate Investigation he would wind up in vaudeville. You can't go back in those native mountains and Jungles and catch one lone man.

Somebody killed Arnold Rothstein in a big hotel in the heart of New York and we can't even catch him, so what's the use sicking the Marines on somebody away off in those bush League Countries, where if we lose ONE Marine we are loser more than if we had caught old Sardino and even sentenced him to our Senate.[3]

So I am glad for once in our lives we got our Marines back home. I know they are laying off waiting for some war somewhere. There is one in Alfagistan, or Alfalfa, or some joint away over near Turkey. But we got nobody in Washington that knows where it is, so the Marines will have to stay till Hoover tells the war Department where this place is.

Well before I forget it, you must fly over Washington. It's beautiful. Flew right down over where the old "Mayflower" used to dock, in the days when we had a real Sailor in the White House, a man that knew how to take his recreation in a gentlemany way, with the old Cap and white "Panties" on, not with a pair of rubber boots, and can full of worms.[4] Went up to the Willard Hotel and staked me out a room, picked up quite a bit of local scandal from the clerks, who know more about what's going on down there than anyone. Went out to "Friendship" to see the McCleans.[5] They got a thirteen year old Boy, "Jock" named after their race horse, and say he beats grown men Tennis Players.[6] But the hit of the outfit is the little Girl, Emily, about six.[7] She must have 15 dogs, no two anywhere near alike, all sizes, all colors all breeds. There is just sixty legs equally distributed among fifteen dogs, all following this kid. Went to Mrs. Longworth's and made my jokes string out till after Dinner had been served.⁸ Her and I tried to get some news out of Nick as to just what relief would be delt out to the Farmers.⁹ He just kinder smiled. He had been there a good many years, and he had never seen the farmers go away with anything yet. But he hoped they would this time. He seemed sorry that the Tarriff had been dragged in as he said that was just like argueing religion, no people of opposite beliefs ever agreed. Somebody asked him how long he thought this special term would last and he said, "See the Chaplin, he is in more direct communication with God than I am."

Nick was against the Die-Benture, and said it would Die in his hall of Horrors.¹⁰ Saw the two branches of fun and amusement operate the next day. Some Guy in Nick's fun factory was trying to make the "Star Spangled Banner" the National Anthem. I couldent see where the Farmers would get much nourishment out of that. So I went over to the Senate, The Mack Sennett end of our Legislative Body.¹¹ Brookhardt of Iowa was supposed to denounce Fess of Ohio.¹² Well as everybody knew there was plenty of subject material for him to work on, why the place was packed.

Well in the meantime, Mr. Hoover had got 'em to the White House and fed 'em the day before, and you feed a Senator and he is just like an old stuffed house cat, he is no good for practical denouncing. You got to keep 'em hungry to make 'em work good. In the meantime Alice and Mrs. Gans happened to come up on the same Elevator and into the Senate Gallery and sit down togeather.¹³ Well Farm Relief, National Anthem relief, Smoot and his Sugar relief, it all vanished.¹⁴ If Mabel Willerbrandt had been caught going into Texas Guinans with Bishop Cannon it wouldent have caused any more of a commotion.¹⁵ What a Senator does is of no interest in Washington for he will do the same thing over again tomorrow. But what Alice does at anytime is news to the World. If Tom Heflin had been caught at Mass it couldent have been more front pagy.¹⁶ So I happened to hit the old Aquarium on a day when the fish wasent doing much but the Visitors saved a bad show.

336   WILL HAS READ ANOTHER BOOK!

Well all I know is just what I read in books. You remember a few weeks ago I was telling you about starting in to improve myself with some book learning and I started in on that Girl's book "The Cradle of the Deep."¹ She was the Girl that would just walk up and slap a

Shark in the face if he started pulling any wisecracks at her. Well buying that Book got me into a Book Store. Well I had no idea there was as many books as there must be. Half the world that don't know what the other half is doing well they are writing books. Busy men that you would think would have something important to do, have got some book that they have written.

Well I had heard in a round about way that Henry the 8th was a having a revival year, and as I was headed for Hollywood for a couple of years I says to myself I will read about old Henry, and see where all these Movie gang got their idea.[2] I knew a little about him for years ago in Ziegfeld Follies we had a Shakespeare revival.[3] (All the sketches were about things he had written about.) And Sam Hardy the fellow that is so good out in talking Pictures, he was Henry 8th, and we had six beautiful girls as his wives.[4] Marion Davis I remember was one of them and she had one line to speak, "And a hell of a King was he."[5] And I always did say I am going to read about this old Bird, if Congress and Heflin, and Reed Smoot and his sugar tarriff will give me time.[6]

There was a fellow named Hackett, they said he had spent practically a lifetime, (course everybody has their own idea of what a lifetime in England is) just working on material for this book.[7] Well I don't know how long he spent. But he sure come out with something. Talk about suppressing books. I would think they would extinguish this one in England. Not because the book is bad, but this old Henry, Why if the English nobility have gone down in a direct line, and if King Edward and George, and The Prince of Wales are all direct descendants of that old reprobate, I would rise up and say, Folks you got me wrong, I am not of that strain at all, He was no forefather of mine.[8]

Why if somebody told all those things about one of my ancestors, I would take it up with the Al Capone gang and I wouldent care how much it cost me to extinguish him I do it.[9]

This old Henry was just an old fat big-footed chuchled-headed Baby. He had an older brother named Arthur.[10] Oldest brothers got everything in those days, a younger Brother was just a Democrat, he had to take what was left. This Arthur wasent well and he dident know much even when he felt good. England wasent much of a country. It stood just about like the Red Sox in the American League. They wanted to marry this Prince Arthur off to somebody with a pedigree. They looked in the Stud book and found there had been a filly colt sired in Spain a few years ahead of Arthur, but that whos mating might add to the prestige of a fast slipping Organization, so they got ahold of Queen Isabella of Spain.[11] She was about the Mabel

1929

Willerbrandt of that administration.[12] There was a King along with her, I think it was Ferdinand.[13] But they kept him sitting on the bench season after season. This Isabella is the one that a Dago from Italy come up and got her to back the first non-stop flight of the Atlantic. He went in for safety, he wanted a three-motored job, he wouldent take a chance on one ship going dead on him, so he made her fix him up with three. He missed the whole of the American Continent, but found San Domingo. The next man to find it five hundred years later was Charley Dawes and a Commission of financial experts.[14] For Dawes discovery he was made Ambassador to the tea parlor of St. James.

Well this Isabella not only had jewels to pawn to back these cross-country tours, but she had children to distribute around where they would bring in the most revenue. She had landed one in France as a king's wife, and one in Rome, (whoever had it that day). When Nations in those days had nothing else to do they would take Rome, then sit and pray for somebody to come and take it off their hands.

Well they had a Daughter Catherine, so about the best they could do with her was an offer from England.[15] That was kinder like slumming for it dident mean much to Spain who was the General Motors in those days. But they sent her over and married her to Arthur, who I think was about fourteen years old. They wanted to get him settled down before he had a chance to start running around too much. Well Arthur was disgusted with the whole proceedings, and to get even with all of them, he just died.

Well that brought this old round fat-headed boy into the proceedings. For a second Son in England only has one chance in the world, and that's for the older one to die. So that was Henry's first good break early in life. He not only inherited the direct line to the King but he took over all Prince Arthur's estate, including a wife. In order for Henry not to marry a widow, why they dug up a Guy named Woolsey.[16] He was a Lobbyist to Rome and the Pope, and anything like old Marriage ceremonies, or dates or deeds, why he could arrange and change them to fit the times, so he thought of the bright idea of saying that Prince Arthur and Catherine were never married, that it was two other fellows. So Henry took her over. I think he was about twelve. He had to start in marrying early for he had a lot of marrying to do. About all you could say for him was that he was big. If he had lived in these days he would have been a wrestler, or a Doorman outside some New York Hotel.

Catherine couldent speak English and he couldent speak Spanish so there was no chance of an argument.

His Father whoever it was, I forget his number, (you know they

Weekly Articles

have numbers on these Kings like they do on race horses) well I forgot whether it was a George the 7th, or Edward the 11th. Well anyhow he died, and left young King Henry a disease in one leg and Cardinal Woolsey, that's the only two things he willed him. Well Catherine seemed to have been all right as a wife for a Prince of Wales. But for a King, well she just wasent the type. No male heir had been born, and of course everybody was to blame but Henry. To have a Girl baby in those days was not only a total loss but practically a social disaster. It wasent that Boys were anymore comfort to you, but if there was no heir to follow up the graft might slip out of your Families hands and into some other. It was the days of high ideals and square dealing.

Well lookout now the story is getting hot. Ann Boeyln was a local Vamp, and don't fail to follow up and read how Ann took Henry.[17] She made all the fat go to his head, so don't fail to read the greatest love, graft, corruption, murders, wars, and be-headings galore. Remember History in minature, you don't have to read. Let me do your learning for you. Remember 15 minutes every Sunday with Professor Rogers, and you will be able to be the life of the Party at any Rotary, Kiawanis, Or Lions luncheon. Remember next week, Anne, two more Katherines, and a Jane.

337 KING HENRY'S WIVES

All I know is just what I read in history. Last Sunday our lesson was Henry 8th, the John Barrymore, Jack Gilbert, Mussolini, Heflin, and John Roach Stratton all rolled into one.[1] I told you about his first wife, Catherine of Arragon.[2] Arragon translated from our old College days latin means, "Somewhere in Spain." Well Henry just "lost his taste for Catherine." He was trying to raise him a bunch of Boy Babies and Catherine's inclination ran more to the effeminate.

Now we get Anne Boelyn.[3] Ann was the Greta Garbo, Peggy Joyce, type.[4] Catherine was a devout Catholic, and didnt believe in a divorce. But Ann could regulate her religion and her morals to fit the situation. She just said, "If this big fat round headed Bird is going to start in on a series of promiscious weddings, why I better get in early, while he is really only an Amateur."

But wait a minute, before we get to Ann, we got to stop and do something for Mary Boelyn, Ann's sister four years older.[5] Mary had a husband named Carey.[6] But what's husband between friends? Henry give him a job, it says, in the Court where he could see his own

1929

wife and Henry. I don't know what job Mary had at the court, but it was nothing trivial for her and Henry raise a baby Boy, Carey was still around there. But Henry was the "Head Man."

Now Ann comes in. Ann was nineteen, "Hen" was 35. Catherine his wife was 41. Now who of the two will win? You said it.

Ann had already been stuck on a young Noble named, Percy.[7] But he was kinder of the drugstore type. This Cardinal Woolsey who was really the William Borah of that administration, He was the one that King Henry kept promising that he would see that he would be made Pope at the next vacancy.[8] Well Woolsey had the backing of Hen but he lacked the vote of some 55 Cardinals. If it hadent been for that little oversight he might have been elected. Henry was for him on the platform of "Divorce relief." Clement the Pope couldent see any reason why Henry should have a spare wife when he already had one, but if Henry could make Woolsey Pope he could have have given him a bill of sale to go out and marry who and what he wanted.[9] Why there is practically no telling who all Henry would have married.

No woman would have been safe from becoming Queen of England. Woolsey would go to Rome when a Pope would die with what Henry thought would be enough votes, But some other King from France or Spain would send an entry with more "Doubloons" and before poor old Woolsey could cummunicate with Henry to make another Campaign donation, why the new Pope would be elected. Radio, or even a good Bicycle would have been a godsend to Woolsey in those trying hours. But it just looked like Woolsey was a Democrat in a Republican administration. So when Henry the 8th saw that Rome was going to veto his divorce bills, why Henry and Woolsey started a religion of their own.

It wasent exactly a free love religion, But they would listen to reason in case some "Gentleman" run onto a younger Lady friend. Had Rome given Henry a divorce there would have been no Church of England, For Henry wasent particular about what religion it was, all he wanted was, "Bigger and better Divorces." So this Anne Boelyn really should be their Patron Saint. She not only started a row, but a Religion.

Henry kinder suggested to Ann that there really dident have to be any marriage ceremony, But this Anne had seen where her sister Mary had finished when there had been no wedding bells. So she just kindly informed the old King that there would be a session with the Justice of the Peace before he started any of his funny business.

This Anne lived in 1529 just four hundred years ago, but Boy she knew her Onions. She not only knew her Onions but her King. Henry started a couple of wars thinking maby that would attract some attention to him and his Country and make it look so important that Rome would have to listen to reason. That's when he issued that famous historic statement, "My Kingdom, My Kingdom for a divorce." Anne stood pat, and the Catholic church lost England, which was of such little importance to them that it was about like Hoover losing Rhode Island. Martin Luther over in Germany was kinder kicking for a minority religion at this time, and I guess that's really about where Henry got his idea from.[10] Luther dident want to get married again, he just wanted to get free.

Well when he got his own Court and made his own laws, why of course he said that Catherine was not married to him. He had it annulled on the grounds that he had never seen Anne Boelyn when he married Catherine. Mistaken identity. So he grabs off Anne, and leaves Catherine and his daughter Mary, marries Anne and in five months she has a baby and it's a Girl so he starts looking around again.[11] This baby was Elizabeth, that we are later to hear so much of.[12] What happened to Anne? The Ax. What had she done? Nothing. But Henry had run onto Jane Seymour, and in the meantime Catherine had died of a broken heart, so his batting average was met two, defeated two.[13]

Here is what Anne Boelyn said, "I heard say the Executioneer is very good, and I have a little neck." That night Henry give a big party, he had found a better way than to divorce 'em. He married Jane who dident have much to recommend her outside of just being of the female gender. Well they hadent any more than got home from the church till they had a baby, and it was a boy, and she died at once, which was fortunate for her, for he was already in communication with Germany to import a new wife from over there. Her name was Anne of Cleves.[14] His Ministers had picked her from a Holbein Portrait, so they brought her over and I will say one thing for old Henry, he had no conscience but he did have judgement.[15] He went to the docks to meet Anne from Germany, and got one flash at her, and chopped off Cromwell's head for being such a bad Judge of beauty.[16] But it looked like it would strengthen the Kingdom with Europe if he married her, so he shut his eyes and went at it. She had been what the Japanese call a Picture bride, all they see is the picture. But Holbein was a painter, not a camera. If Cameras had been in use it would have saved Henry that marriage. One snap shot with a No. 2 Brownie of her, would have kept her right at home. She had a lot of breeding but no class. She was a Princess 31 years old; she made up in virtue what she lacked in charm. Well Henry had never been very high on virtue. What he wanted was beauty, and how!! The only

English word she could say was "Ja, Ja." And Henry dident know what that was. Neither do I.

Cromwell said, "Yes, me Lord, but she hath a Queenly manner." "Hen" wisecracking back, "Well she don't need it to protect her." She missed beheading, by his divorcing her and sending her home.

Now we get Katheryn Howard, a cousin of Anne Boelyn's.[17] She went to the block with these kind words, "I die Queen of England, But I would rather die the wife of a Culpepper," (I wonder if he was any relation to the Virginia Culpeppers who owned a Court House).[18] Well that dident make Henry feel any too good, to know that he wasent in as good favor as Culpepper, so he just hunted up Culpepper and off with his bean. Oh what a cheerful little ancestor our folks that come over on the Mayflower had in this Gentleman Henry.

Well he was death on Katherines. He gets another one, only they all spell their name different. This last one is Katherine Parr.[19] She was a motherly kind of a soul and they do say, (and all hoped it was true) that she poisoned him, anyhow she beat him to the Ax. She had been married twice before, and you got to learn something in that time, course Henry had her Six to three, but her and that English Grog bumped him off before he could get her. She buried him and then married the man of her choice which was No. 4 for her. And then we say "What's our Country coming too, we are getting worse and worse."

Well it looks to me the only safe man in those days was the Ax man. So I just want to meet some Colonial Dame now that likes to claim she can trace her ancestors back to the Tudors. But don't miss Henry the 8th by Hackett.[20] They say it's the best written book of this Generation. It's the best one I ever read next to the Illiterate Digest, and my new one coming out called, "Ether and me."

338 SATISFYING THE SHRINERS

Well all I know is just what I read in the papers. The best thing that was out of the papers in years was the Lindbergh Wedding.[1]

The old Boy certainly hung one on 'em. Talk about embarrassing moments, I can think of none that must have equalled all those Camera men and Reporters that were standing out at the Morrow's front gate and Lindy and Ann drove out waved at 'em and drove on off. The gang dident even stop shooting craps long enough to notice 'em.

They just figured "Off for another ride." Then three hours later have some one come out and announce to you, "They have married, boys, and that was their departure on their honeymoon that you just witnessed a short time ago. Too bad you was too busy to follow them."

The Guys started eating their cameras, reporters were wondering where their next jobs were coming from. Well, they hounded 'em into it. The press wouldn't give the family a minute's peace since the engagement was announced.

Now, instead of having pages and pages of pictures of the bridal couple as they walk to the altar, why all they can do is dig up old ones showing him on his arrival in France, or flying the air mail to St. Louis. Tunney has the right idea, get on an island in the middle of the Mediterranean, even if you have to be pestered with Bernard Shaw.[2] But at least there is no tabloids after you.

Now what else we had? We was pestered for a week out here in California with the Shriners. That's a funny trait of Human Nature, especially American nature. You wouldent think a bunch of what is ordinarily considered a fairly smart type of men, would leave their comfortable homes, families, business, and right in the midst of a summer, gang together on hot trains, loaded in like sheep, and for four and five days cross the continent, just to get to wear badges and march in the heat.

Everywhere they move it's a shove. Gang up in hot hotel lobbies. Do everything that is against all the laws of ease and comfort that we are supposed to be such a martyr, too. But they just eat it up, men that when there is no convention on have pretty fair intelligence and dignity. But just let a band start playing and give one a Fezz, and a badge and he is practically useless for the rest of the season.

But they do have a lot of fun, and it's really a good thing for 'em, for if it wasn't for fool things like that, they would all get too serious and business like. They are a great bunch, about the best I guess of the noisy organizations. There is some live bunches among them. It always struck everyone odd that Philadelphia should always furnish about the livest and most up-to-date Shrine bunch of all, LuLu Temple to the Shrine is just about what Chaplin is to the Movies.[3] My own Shrine, Akdar of Tulsa, Oklahoma, a branch of the Claremore Lodge, they was just about as live a bunch as any. And by the way Claremore would be an ideal town for them to meet in another year or so. We are getting a fine Hotel there where they can rub badges against each other. We are building the only Indian Hospital in the United States right there in Claremore. Well these Shriners act like Indians when they are on a convention, so we will take 'em right out there and sober 'em up.

1929

We made some pretty good real estates sales to 'em while here that week. We guarantee a Screen star with every lot. We turned on the "Unusual Weather" for 'em. Mabel Willebrandt layed off 'em, while here.[4] The City Council got all the Rackiteers together and said, "Now Boys, go easy, keep the prices without reason. Make it up in amount sold. Remember two quarts at a fair price will make you as much as one Quart at an exorbitant figure. And of course you know it costs you no more to produce two than one, and the authorities will see that the overhead is kept within reason. Cost you no more for protection for a thousand quarts than one, so what we want to do is to send 'em away satisfied."

So I will say this, that everything went off fine. There was no kick on prices. Course there was a little hollering on quality. But the cheap price enables the purchaser to procure enough quantity, that he soon dident notice the quality. So all in all everything was handled mighty nice, and they finally got 'em all carried to the station out of town. Course nobody got on the right train, but as long as we got 'em out of town why our responsibility ended.

It don't make much difference where one is anyhow. A Seattle Guy might just as well wake up in Jacksonville as at home; his summer is spoiled anyhow. But they are all dragging back home now and will start resting to get ready for their next vacation.

Well we better get some Comedy in this Article, so let's get to Congress quick. Hoover put one over on 'em, when it commenced to get hot in Washington a couple of weeks ago, why they thought well we will just adjourn and go home for the summer and come back when it's cool and take this up. Hoover says, "Who is going to adjourn to whose home till it's cool?"

He just told 'em you stay right here and either give these Farmers relief, or something that looks like relief to them. But you are not going to meet here and just do a lot of argueing and then just because it's hot go home. So now he has 'em there he is going to make 'em stick till they do something.

The Die-benture thing looks like it's about washed up.[5] The Gans vs. Longworth case is about over.[6] The tariff bill, settling that is just like argueing over "who won the war."

Mr. Hoover sneaks out every Saturday and catches enough fish to last through the week. Mrs. Hoover went up to Radcliffe College and pinch hit for the President and made a splendid speech, that's about the first time we have had that, and she is liable to be in great demand.[7] All invitations now will read, "Either you or your wife will be acceptable." But Lord I guess to fill all the invitations that he gets he would have to have as many wives as a Movie Star.

35

Weekly Articles

And speaking of the Movies, they are going full blast out here, all "Noisies." Everybody that can't sing has a double that can, and everybody that can't talk is going right on and proving it. You meet an actor or girl and in the old days where they would have just nodded and passed by, now they stop and start chattering like a parrott. Weather, politics, Babe Ruth, anything just to practice talking, and they are so busy ennunciating that they pay no attention to what they are saying.[8] Everything is "Annunciation." I was on the stage 23 years and never heard the word or knew what it was.

339   WALES SETTLES DOWN

Well all I know is what I read in the papers. What do you know about the Prince of Wales getting married?[1] Looks like the Kid is going to settle down. You remember a couple of lessons back I was telling you about old Henry the 8th doing all his rough and tumble marrying, Well you know these Titled Birds seem to have one tradition that they are pretty jealous of, and that is that it is bred into them to try and cop off a Princess if possible.[2] Course some times the Boys go out among the plebians and take a spouse to wife, but they just practically ruin themselvs with the rest of their family.

We had a lot of Gals over here that went practically haywire when the Prince was over here, and they would practically cut off a leg to even get to dance with him, and if he had been out strictly for money I expect he could have picked up more over here than anywhere else in the world. So it does go to their credit that they don't always go out for a monetary consideration. It's just as I tell you, it's this "Grab off a Princess" idea that is so deeply rooted in them, that they are always out for that first. Now take two or more Princesses, and let one of them possess a little more of the World's goods than the other. I am not saying that that would make any difference in his choice, but she would be the one that he would pick. Course that may be accidental but it always happens, so there is a chance that it is premeditated.

Here is the way the whole thing is done. King George and Queen Mary have one of the Privy council bring in a Directory of all the living royal Families, that are really operating now.[3] When Russia and Germany dropped out that almost ruined the Directory; they had to tear out about 20 pages. I don't care how royal your blood is, and how far your breeding goes back, if you are not at the present time employed in the business of ruling, why there is no more thought of marrying into your family than we have if all the members of a family happen to be at the time incarcerated in a jail.

Now there is just thousands of Russians that are eligible and their breeding is as about as it ever was, but as far as matrimony with some reigning family they are just what you might call null and void. England is especially handicapped in this present crisis, as they have always used Germany as a mating ground. In fact the English family have just learned to speak what little English they do in the last couple of generations. They was all kin, and they just kept their marriages in the family, a little thing like being a cousin, or an Aunt, dident stop them in the least. Well you see all that available talent is now out of the question. The late big war not only showed that civilization don't pay, but it just eliminated over 70 percent of crop of available wives and Husbands that a self respecting Prince had to pick from.

Well now we have them eliminated, let's get back to the ones left. The King and Queen take the list and go over it carefully. You would think they was looking for a telephone number. Instead of taking the numbers alphabetically, they start down in Italy; that's about as far south as you can safely pick up a wife and not take a chance on her being a little "Off color." You get any further south than that and you are liable to find that the hair grows out, turns around and grows back in again.

Now they take Italy. They have an awfully nice breed of Princesses. Their Mother was a Monte-negroian, and their Father an Italian. But they can't consider them, Why? On account of a Gentleman named Mussolini.[4] They never know when he is liable to get peeved at them and declare the whole shebang a Republic. Well that would do away with any standing that the Royal family had. Now suppose the Prince was bethrothed to an Italian Princess, and Mussolini went on a rampage. Well, see, she would lose her Amateur standing, and become just a professional commoner. Well that would mean that he would have the right to annul the engagement, or even if they was already married, it would give him the right to be divorced, for he could prove that she obtained him by false pretenses. So that lets Italy out, and he lost a fine girl just really on account of Mussolini.

Now that brings us to Spain. They have two fine Girls there. But there again we have Primo Revira, the Amateur Dictator.[5] He is a kind of second company of Mussolini. Kinging there is not what you would call a steady job. So it's too unstable to monkey with. You couldent possibly take a chance on being linked with a Republic. Portugal is out, for they would have three Revolutions between the

Weekly Articles

time of the engagement and the marriage. France, Nothing there worth while. Belgium, I havent looked over the chart but I don't think there is anything available there.

Holland, They and the English don't mix so much. When an Englishman is having his tea he don't want to be interrupted by a clattering of wooden shoes clattering through the house. So that dident leave him anything but the Scandinavian Countries. There is three of them, Sweden, Norway, and Denmark. Well there was "Something queer in Denmark" so he dident go there, Norway sounded too cold, so that leaves Sweden, and a beautiful lovely Girl 19 years old, Who perhaps is in love with some nice young man of her own age and country, but the old heads must keep up the "Prestige" of this marrying business, and find somebody that will do Royalty the most good.[6] It's just like Queen Isabella told all her children, when she was doleing them out to Henry the 8th and King Charles, "It's not a Princess place to love, it's a Princess' place to breed."[7] She sent 'em out to marry for their Country.

A Thoroughbred race horse breeding establishment is more in line with royal marriages than anything I know of. Only they are careful to never inbreed. But as far as the Love that's a lot of Hooey. They think it brings Nations closer to each other to have the heads marry to each other. Well it dident do so much for Germany and England. But anyhow let's get him married off and let the Girls all over the world get their minds on somebody else. It's wonderful I reckon to be a Prince or a Princess, But they pay for it.

340 THAT WHITE HOUSE TEA

Well all I know is just what I read in the papers. Let's just run over a few of the high spots that have jammed up the press in the last few weeks. A week or so ago there was quite an attempt to try and make something out of the fact that the colored Congressman's wife got so far in the White House that she got three saucers of tea before anybody knew it.[1]

Now wait a minute, let's get this straight. If there is one thing that this Country has been especially happy in it's been the fact that we have been continually blessed with some fine charming Women in the White House. Some of the men might have been able to stand a little overhauling. But I tell you, there has never been a chirp of regret out of anyone about the Female occupants. It's all right to say the Coolidges, the Hardings, the Wilsons, and all those dident do it.[2]

1929

But the opportunity was not put up to them. There was no colored Congressman in their time. Dixie hadent reached Chicago.

Now Mrs. Hoover knows what she is doing. If it was a custom for the first Lady of the White House to entertain all the Congressman's wives, then when a colored one come along there was nothing else to do. When he was elected and ready to be seated there was no one in a position to say they wouldent sit with him in Congress. No it was a custom and nothing was thought of it. So that's just about the way that Mrs. Hoover looked at it. Neither party refuses their votes, and you got to give 'em a little consideration.

So that blew over pretty quick and we were in the throes of some other scandal. Some Bird made arrangements with the French Government to Stowaway and prevent their plane from making France. Suppose Lyndberg had taken somebody along for Publicity to write the Story of the trip.[3] Pretending to hide on an Aeroplane trip strikes me as having about the same value as to jump on some friend's back and ride them when they were in a foot race. That's about the amount of aid you would be to them.

Well then that had no more than quieted down till some Professor (I guess it was Harvard, we always look to them for the freak things) he made the Boys a talk about not aiming too low. Said instead of marrying the Stenographer aim for the Boss's daughter. Now wait a minute. Have you seen ALL the Boss's daughters? You look 'em over and it will take quite a sacrifice to give up the Stenographer and take The Daughter.

Course when he advised the Boys to be as "Snooty" as possible and do anything they could to advance themselvs, why that raised a yell that went round the World. Well there was no use howling about it. It was nothing but "An Old English Custom." Englishmen have been working that system for years. They always aim above 'em. What really hurt was that the old Professor really had about the dope on it. He dident have to tell 'em to do that, they are doing it already. Higher education is doing more to teach it to them than all the professors that would tell them to do it.

Course everybody broke into print and said it shouldent be that way. But there was so much truth in the old Professor's advice that it had 'em winging to answer it. What's the use kidding ourselvs? What makes 'em high hat any quicker than education? They got to be high hat to keep up with the rest of their gang, and maby it's better that they are. It's pretty tough on us but we just can't have the children do like we do. We are always drilling into them, "When I was a Boy we dident do that." But we forget that we are not doing those same old things today. We changed with the times, so we can't blame the children for just joining the times, without even having to change. We are always telling 'em what we used to not do. We dident do it because we dident think of it. We did everything we could think of. We drove a horse and Buggy but we don't drive one now. So we just got to sit and watch 'em go, and I tell you they got to go some to keep up with us. If anyone of us had a child that we thought was as bad as we know we are we would have cause to start to worry.

Well now I got Youth all set, and old age on the run, let's see what our Government has been doing. Well it was the funniest thing. It commenced to get hot in Washington and they wanted to go home and they started to "passing." Say, they would pass anything. They would have cancelled the debt if it had come up when the thermometer was hot enough.

Now they go home for two months, and that will give 'em enough time to think up some devilment. They dident get the tarriff fixed; they are leaving that. They go home and wait for offers, see which side will do the best by them.

Mr. Dawes opened his Campaign in England before the boat had docked and it looks like him and that Labor Government will hit it off pretty well.[4] They havent got a laboring man in England that can do more work than Charley. We havent sent anybody to France yet. That's a good idea, about the best way to get along with them is to stay away from them.

Prince of Wales marriage is declared off, which means I suppose that it will happen, that's generally about the type of stategy that they always use.[5] That's called Diplomacy, doing just what you said you wouldent.

Owen D. Young, (AND A DEMOCRAT) is back, after a fine record in Europe.[6] J. P. Morgan was with him over there.[7] But kinder in the capacity of a Vice Pres. See where Mr. Coolidge is going to write for some Magazine.

That's just about all there has been lately in the papers. Unless you want Murders, and those of course you got to order. Whatever kind of murder you want why just write to your favorite tabloid and they will, if you get ten signers, have the murder for you.

341   PUT CAL TO WORK

Well all I know is just what I read in the papers, and the Magazines. You know if you want to get what Mr. Coolidge says, you got to get it in the Magazines. When he was just President you could read what he said in the newspapers for three cents. But since he is the Late Ex President why it's 35 cents. Not only Mr. Coolidge but all of our big men are breaking out in small thick periodicals.

I just last night read two very nice human stories, one in the American Magazine and the other in the Cosmopolitan, both of which Mr. Coolidge had written. One was on his life up around Plymouth notch Vermont. He told of his early school days, he said when he was three years old he knew his letters, and started to school at five and at twelve he knew as much as the Teacher, in fact he said he knew as much as any teachers up there. The way he kinder explained it he just was on the verge of being a Child Prodigy.

At twelve they sent him away to school at Ludlow. I was up through there and visited Plymouth and Ludlow and all those historic places, and Ludlow is just about two hills and a valley away, but in those days it constituted going some place. He paid a mighty fine tribute to the upbringing of the Country Boy, said if he had to be brought up again that he would just go ahead and be brought up in the same place. Course he knows how it's done now and the next time wouldent be so hard.

I never was President, I never was even a Senator. But so would I choose to be brought up where I was brought up. But I bet you there is a lot of things I did that you bet I would know better than to do them again. If I was going to be brought up again, the first thing I would specialize in would be boxing, then the next time I would just go through life getting even with a few that kinder hung it on me then.

He said it was winter and the snow was on the ground when he left for school and he went in a sleigh. Him and a Calf. The calf was going to market and him to Washington, (only then he dident know it). His whole story was a mighty human document. You know that's one thing about Mr. Coolidge he has never been spoiled.

Then in the other Article he dwelled on his life in the White House. He could tell you the exact number of dinners that they entertained and the exact number they went out too. In fact he could tell you what they was supposed to eat at each place. Told about feeding the Senators and Congressmen at breakfasts at the White House. He laid particular stress on the fact that he fed some Democratic ones. He seemed to bring that out to show his liberality. Fed 'em even when he knew he would get no favors from them. Paid a lovely compliment to Mrs. Coolidge which was richly deserved.

You know it's kinder nice to have our Presidents and big men get right down human and tell us what they are thinking about. But they should never be allowed to have all this time to do all this reminiscing. I tell you with all our boasted generosity we are an ungrateful Nation: we don't do a thing for our retired Presidents. I don't mean declare a pension for them. It's not generally money they need, (though very few have a competent income to keep them in comparitive luxury for the rest of their lives). But it's employment; it's work they need. They should be paid a handsome sum but know that they were delivering something for it.

Who knows more of the workings of our Government than the man that has run it for four or eight years? Who knows more of our Foreign relations? Cabinet men know of their Departments, but the President knows of all Departments. There should be some position created where we could benefit from the knowledge and advice of a man that we have had in training all these years. It should be something where he would be a Member, we will say, of our Foreign Relation Committee. Now they are disscussing something that he is bound to know more about than any of them. For he has had access to knowledge that never reaches them. He could explain to them why it might be advisable to take a certain course, and give them reasons that before that might never occur to them.

He would have no vote so he couldent possibly be a balance of power. Not only Foreign Relations but various of our very important Committees — Agriculture, Federal Reserve — even if he should be of the opposite Political faith of his successor, (which don't happen often). His duties should not conflict in any way with the President's policys. He simply expresses an opinion, an opinion backed by knowledge.

Then he would feel like he was a real benefit to his Country. It would keep him active, and would bring us back a thousand fold what we paid him. Make his salary at least fifty thousand a year. That's about what you can get for managing a little chain of Drug Stores, or a small Oil Company. Then it would also give him a chance while in office to give more and better service to us. For his thoughts would not be continually on what he was going to do for a living when he had to get out. He would know what he was going to do.

Now you have often heard about pensioning them, but that's no good, (course it beats what we got now) but this scheme of mine is to keep him working for us.

I will take it up with Congress and if anything comes of it, I will expect my commission from Mr. Coolidge and also Mr. Taft, for the Bill will be made retroactive.[1] It's such a good Bill it will go through along with Farm Relief.

342 DISCREDITING LINDY

1929

Well all I know is just what I read in the papers. Lindy was just out among us a few days ago and opened up his line to the East, I predict that to be a great success in the near future.[1] It's just a nice easy jaunt from New York, two nights on the train, two days flying, no tremendous long hops that can't be made, but just a fine sure trip, they allow themselves two or three hours for delays and then can make their schedule each jump. I came out over the line when I came west six weeks ago and I think it's the ideal trip. The only thing, it's awful slow getting on those trains at night, it looks like losing a lot of time crawling along on them. But by doing that you have no night flying, and it helps to take off six or seven hundred miles.

And speaking of Lindy, some of the writings of our eastern newspaper men have been trickling into my view and it brought to light a kind of a concerted idea to try and cut the boy from up around the heart of his country and re-deposit him down along its footpaths. I had no idea they took it so serious when he so completely made a sucker out of them during his late honeymoon. I was out here in the west and didn't get the undercurrent of rumblings that they were letting out, and trying to insinuate that he "hadn't done right by our press," that they had made him and that he was ungrateful.

Now we will just stop and take up that bit of propaganda right now. Lindbergh was made by just two things. The Lord and a Wright Whirlwind Motor. Newspapers couldn't have flew him from one side of a razor blade to another. They reported the fact that he arrived there. Sure they did, but don't you think the French would have found it out sooner or later, and eventually have got the news back over here to us, even if it had to gone by word of mouth? I think that sooner or later after hearing of it that we would have suspected that it was considerable of a feat without even seeing a headline of it. Somebody would have no doubt given us the facts of the trip by book, and it might possibly have been announced over the radio, for those fellows are awful scarce of things to talk about sometimes.

Our Savior performed some pretty handy feats in the early days and his exploits have been handed down through the ages and made him our greatest hero, all accomplished without the aid of a newspaper. No weekly camera man recorded his daily adventures, he had to receive his publicity by word of mouth. Still he become quite famous even during his lifetime.

I am making no comparison, I am only showing what has been done. For after all the greatest publicity and interest in the world is to be told about something, not to have read about it. So I am going to argue with anybody who says that they made Lindbergh. In fact the less printed about people sometimes make folks more anxious and more interested in them, so when he drove out through the gate, with his bride of only a few minutes by his side, and waved the boys "a merry how de do" why I don't think he owed 'em a thing. Any man that flown the ocean alone, and returned to his people even though they be Zulus, and couldn't read, they would have been awful apt to consider him quite a boy. Being a good navigator, did him more good than all the editorials ever printed.

But when we turn the tables, what did he do for the newspapers? We get a different story. He gave 'em the next most publicity to the war, if he had been paid for his stuff at just a fair author's rate he would have been the highest salaried man in the world, what would some millionaire newspaper owner have given him if it had been possible to have, bought and controlled the entire rights of everything that was to printed about him and photographers? They ought to change the Lord's Prayer to read, "Now I lay me down to sleep, I pray the Lord Lindberg to keep. If he should die before he wakes, I pray the Lord his picture to take." He has paid their rent for two years.

No, you writers when you try to pull that boy down you are just trying to fill up the Grand Canyon with old chewing gum, it's all right to try and be different and not string with the mob, but before you start doing it announce that that's what you are doing it for, it's not a case of ordinary hero worship. It's that the boy licks you at every turn. He won more friends by the way he conducted his engagement and his honeymoon than he did by his flight.

The flight only showed daring, ability, and of course good fortune, but his last adventure, showed shrewdness, modesty, and 100 percent common sense. When her family had to ask the police for protection against the press, that just about threw the last doubting vote over to the Lindbergh column in favor of "give a lover a chance."

He has never made a wrong move yet, everything he has done has reflected glory on his country, he has been a gentleman under some pretty trying times. And we must never forget the one great thing of his flight, (whether he was sent over as a stowaway under auspices of the *Oolagah Banner,* or whether the trip was a blindfold cigarette test) he turned America's mind to aviation, just at a time when we was on the verge of going back to covered wagon days instead of the air.

After all, there is a mighty little line between do and don't, a small margin between success and failure. His exploit just give us that

1929

little push that sent us over into the aviation line, instead of decided that "it wasn't practical."

No, let's don't tear him down, at least while he is living and conducting himself in the manner he is. Wait a few years and then show that he didn't cross himself at all but used a double.

It's all right now in these late years to show that George Washington would have fought on the British side if they had given him a commission and if Grant hadn't got drunk he wouldn't have won the war. But don't denounce Lindy because he didn't marry the press instead of Miss Morrow.

343 STAYING UP IN THE AIR

Well all I know is just what I read in the papers, Or what I see as I prowl around. You know there has been quite an epidemic here lately all over our Country of trying to break the endurance record for sustained flight in the air, by re-fueling while still up there. Of course the Army fliers really started the thing out in California when they were up for five or six days. Then two old Boys from down in Amon Carterville near Dallas broke the Army's record.[1] That was a great flight and they received and deserved a lot of credit. Well that record held till Cleveland Ohio could get a Plane and then two fellows from there went out and broke the Fort Worth Boys record. Well they hadent even come down in Cleveland till a couple of old Country boys from out at Culver City California went up and stayed till it looked like they was going to have to shoot 'em to get 'em to come down.

Now that is the flight I want to tell you about. The reason I want to tell you about it is that I was over there when it was made. Now in the first place "Where is Culver City?" Culver City is a mighty thriving little City right in the edge of Los Angeles. It was founded by Harry Culver, a young hustling fellow, and he is now the head of the whole United States Real Estate Board, and incidentally one of the greatest boosters for Aviation we have.[2] He has his own plane and Pilot and flies all over the United States and he hasent tipped a Pullman Porter in years. And it seems a kind of a happy coincidence that he is the founder of the Town where this record flight was made.

You all, all over the world hear about Hollywood, and hear of it as the home of all the films, when as a matter of fact there are more pictures made in Culver City than in all Hollywood. This Culver landed some of the biggest Studios there years ago and they have grown bigger ever since. It's one of the few towns that have not been

Weekly Articles

swallowed up by Los Angeles. It and Beverly Hills. You see Los Angeles got all these adjoining towns in because they had a fine water system and water in what is normally a desert Country is just about the whole thing, so they held this water over these other towns' heads and they had to come in to get some water. In other words they started the boys in bigger taxes. But old Culver City, and Beverley Hills dug themselves up some water and stuck it out. But let's get down to the flight.

I was working at a Studio not so far over from there, and we never paid much attention to these two fellows. We read that they were up in the air for one of these tests, but that dident mean anything. Every town that could get together two planes would send one up for a test and keep the other to reload it. Well some of them stayed up till dark and some got through the night, but we kept on gradually reading about how these two Birds from right under our nose at Culver City was still up. Well I got to driving over to see what was holding 'em up and to see if they had a Stowaway on there.

But I think we are about cured of the stowaway craze, that last one just about killed it for all stowaways.

I happened to be on the field the afternoon they broke the record; then they had to fly one more hour to make it official. It was about one thirty in the afternoon when the refueling Plane went aloft to give them more gas, and let me tell you something about the credit for one of these things. Don't overlook the men that take up the gas. You know there is some mighty ticklish things about this continually re-fueling in the air. The way these fellows worked it, Paul Whittier, a mighty fine young Pilot, son of a very wealthy family out here who were the founders of Beverley Hills, piloted the Gas Wagon, or as they call it the Nurse ship.[3]

It was an old "Curtis Pigeon" with an old Liberty motor. Then Slade Hulbert was what they called the contact man.[4] He had a hole in the bottom of the ship and had to lay down on his stomach in there and let the hose out through the bottom, first with a rope that the man in the other ship would grab. He was standing up through a hole that had been cut in the top of a closed job. He would reach out and get the rope, now here is where the great danger come in was to keep that rope or that hose from getting caught in the propeller of the lower ship. If at any time during all those contacts it had ever touched the propeller it would have been all off. They would generally have to fly out over the ocean to do the refueling as the air was more smooth out there.

One day they couldent get the old Nurse ship off the ground, and the boys above, Pilots Mendell and Rhinehardt were just about out of gas when another ship went up with no hose attachment, but just a rope and a five gallon can of Gas in a canvas sack and just lowered that over to the boys who grabbed it and saved the trip.[5] Another time they got lost in the fog and the Nurse ship went up and they hunted each other for a long time over the top of the fog, which was twenty five hundred feet thick, they got together back down under it just as they were on their last gallon.

The boys got terrible seasick up there the first two or three days. They were sent up all kinds of stuff for it. Then as time went along they got stronger and more cheerful every day, and they always kept their sense of humor with them (they sent down some awful funny notes, mostly kidding about the old Mack Truck, as they called their ship they were re-fueling from). It was so hot up there they dident wear their clothes, just run the ship in their underwear, with all the windows open. They fixed up a sort of a blown up bed that they could take it time about sleeping on. You know when you just think of fellows staying up there and one lone engine going and carrying all that weight all that many days it sure does give you a great confidence in the Motors that we are using in Planes nowadays.

You know Young McAdoo, W. G.'s oldest Boy and his Partner, a Mr. McManus, were really responsible for this remarkable flight.[6] There is a whole lot more to this than just saying I will go up and break a record. It takes a lot of cooperation and work and much planning ahead. But it all helps aviation tremendously, and it was a real kick to stand on that field and see them at the very moments that they were breaking the record, the longest that any humans had ever stayed up. In fact, I guess that took in birds and fowls too.

344   DON'T ARGUE WITH CHINA

Well all I know is just what I read in the papers. Things been going on pretty good the last few weeks. I knew things would pick up as soon as Congress quit. Mr. Hoover has stuck around Washington and it's away in the middle of the summer it looks like the Summer Resorts will have to look for some other add than him. The Black Hills, or the White ones are out of luck as far as the weeklies are concerned this summer. He kinder goes out there in the edge of Maryland, and Virginia some place and catches a few old cat fish ever Saturday. But outside of that he has been right on the job all the time.

His Farm board met a couple of weeks ago, and a funny thing

happened. The day they met the price of wheat went up. But as soon as they saw the board wasent going to do anything, why it went back down again. They just met and kinder got organized, and we really don't know what they will try to do. They have got I believe it's five hundred million dollars. It's to kinder help stabalize prices, or do something, anyhow the Boys are not working exactly what you would call empty handed. There will be some money put in circulation. But it will be passing by the Farmer so fast and often that he will think it's on a Merry Go Round.

Then Mr. Hoover's Prohibition Commission is all organized and on the look out to see if this drinking has been exaggerated or is it a habit. The Head Man of that, Mr. Wickersham I believe it is, he issued a Statement to all the Governors who were assembled and asked the States to try and help.[1] New York and a lot of the others got their annual laugh. They won't join in any enforcement at all. Well about all that that Commission has done is just to make that appeal. It sounds like it was awful reasonable, but it won't get anywhere.

There are just little things that have been happening around home here, of course if you want to get out in the World and start making observations, why there is really something doing. China and Russia, while they don't speak the same language, have in some way hired an Interpreter and informed each other that a war would not be uncalled for. So they been drawing up the contracts. Nobody don't know what it's all about so you might say it is a typical war. Wars always start by somebody wanting somebody else to apologize for something, maby for something which the other dident even do. Then they Alabi it with calling it a war of honor. Maby neither one of them havent really got any more honor than a Rabbitt. But the old Propaganda gets to working, and the big men let it be known that the country has been insulted, and that they must arise and make the other nation take back water.

The same old Bull is going on in the opponent's camp, both sides trying to manufacture a national hate, that don't even exist. Now what's Russia care or got to do with China. Both of them are the biggest Nations in area in the World. There is nothing either one has that the other wants. But they must have a war. Other Nations have become famous through wars so Russia feels like that is just about what they need to make the front page.

It's supposed to be something about a Railroad in China that China owns, but they don't run it like Russia wants it run. Course, Japan she is watching to see where she can dip in to the best advantage, and we are watching Japan, and the first thing you know we will all be lining up and forming little alliances, and the same old combinations will getting togeather again. Diplomacy will start operating, and that's the match that starts all the wars. Now how could anybody come to be having an argument with China? She is the most peaceful Nation on earth outside of Switzerland. China goes her own way, minds her own business, and would like to live off to herself if these other Nations including us would let her. But, no, everybody must horn into China. China never in her life had any private business. China's business is everybody's business.

Saw a picture in the Movies the other night of Ramsey McDonald the new British Premier.[2] He was introducing his Cabinet. He has a lot of humor and a fine personality. Just think of those old Britishers, with all their pomp and tradition, having to be rule by labor. They grin and bear it fine for they are fine Sportsmen but you know it must be pretty galling to those old Titled ones. I would like to be over there now and get all the real dope from Lady Astor, she is the brightest Political mind I ever run into.[3]

They been having an awful time over in France about paying us the debt. But this fellow Briand and Poincaire seem to have finally won.[4] They told the Chamber of Deputies, "One time Germany was at our very doorstep, and we asked the United States to help us and they did. Now should missfortune ever again threaten us, let's don't have them say, 'No once was enough for us; we helped you once and you dident seem to appreciate it, so never again.' " Well that convinced the Boys that even a war debt has some grounds of equity. You see France wanted to wait and see how this Young Plan worked, (and by the way I want to remind you again that his fellow Owen D. Young that drew it up is still a Democrat) I just dident want to let it be forgotten.[5] These Republicans grab off everything, and when us Democrats get ahold of something good why we want the credit.

So get this straight. Young is a Democrat, but don't make the mistake of running him for President, we want to have him well known for a long time yet.

Well that's just about all the big news that's happened in the last few weeks. Aimee has been away from us here in California.[6] She went back to try and civilize Detroit, but give up. Young Senator La Follette is here.[7] I had a visit with him the other day. He has a lot of the old Gentleman in him, and seems to be a mighty sincere boy.[8]

345 SOME SENATORS ARE REAL NICE

Well all I know is just what I read in the papers, and what I run into hither and yon. You know I like to make little jokes and kid about the Senators. They are a kind of a never ending source of amusement, amazement, and Discouragement. But the Rascals, when you meet 'em face to face and know 'em, they are mighty nice fellows. It must be something in the office that makes 'em so honery sometimes. When you see what they do officially you want to shoot 'em, but when one looks at you and grins so innocently, why you kinder want to kiss him.

We got a young fellow in there that you have all heard a lot about, and maby lots of you never met him personally, although you would like to. Well that's the way I was, I had always admired his Father, for he was a real fearless Fighter, with a world of ability. I expect he was admired more by his enemies than any man we ever had in public life. For they knew that he was on the level. Now it's a funny thing about off-springs in the human race.

It's not like its animal neighbor. A race horse is almost sure to breed another race horse. He may not be as fast as the old Father Horse. But he will show a lot of speed nevertheless, and Dogs follow along in the make of their ancestors. You take a couple of pretty well bred Airdales and you can rest assured you are not going to get a Pot Hound. But with the Human race you may just as well throw your register book in the creek, for what the mating brings forth no human mind can even guess, much less be certain of. You are just liable to have some fine old stock bring forth a family of human Mutts as to produce an amateur Lincoln.

That's one of the main places where the Human race differs from the purely and totally animal. In nearly every other respect, the human race is just about on a par with its animal brothers. Given the same conditions they will both do about the same thing. In intelligence they run about even; in self preservation, they are 50-50. The animal will kill to improve it's food supply just about as quick as the human. The animal is about as untrustworthy as its 100% Human brother. So if it wasent for the breeding why there would be no reason to distinguish one from the other. We would just be classed as another breed of Cats, or Bears, or some other Species. But on account of us being so uncertain as to what we will produce why we are known as the Humans.

Human comes from the old Spanish word "Huber." Huber's used to be a Museum on 14th Street, New York. And they had everything in there, and from there they gradually got to calling people, Humans. It's just a name and has practically no significience at all.

Ancestors don't mean a thing in our tribe. It's as unreliable as a political promise. Able bodied Newfoundlanders produce Scotch ter-

1929

riers in the breed Human. A western range Mare is liable to produce a Man of War in our strata of existence.¹ You just don't know what will happen. You just have to raise 'em up till they are 22 or 23 and then start guessing. They no more take after their Father and Mother than a Congressman will take after a good example.

Mind you, I am not in the least criticising all this, for it's like everything else; it's for the best. If this Country did take after it's Fathers, God help it. It's because most of them are an improvement over their Fathers is why we have such low taxes, good Radio announcers, and Farm relief.

But every once in awhile we get ahold of a great Father who begets a great Son, and this offspring I am referring to is of that very type. He looks mighty like he was going to pick up the old man's pack and carry on with it. I had met him before, that is casually. It was in a crowd and I dident want anybody to know that I knew a Senator. But the other day he come up to my place with his Brother in Law, and a friend of mine, Mr. Middleton the Playwright, and I had the pleasure of knowing and chatting for two or three hours with Young Senator Bob La Follette, of I think it's Wisconsin, or Minnesota, (I always get those two mixed up).² But wherever it is, it's where Glenn Frank has charge of an experimental Laboratory, and instead of using Guinea Pigs, they used Football Players.³

Well Sir, this young fellow and I took up the Government business, just where it should be taken up, which is at the source, and I wish Coolidge and Hoover could have heard us. They would have learned something to their advantage. This Boy has got a lot of the old Father in him. He knows there is a lot "Hooey" in Washington and they know that he knows it. I heard him make the best speech that was made at the Republican Convention in Kansas City. I don't know what he was doing there, he would have fit in just as well at Houston.

He has a lot of ideas that on account of their merit won't get anywhere, and he is smart enough to know they won't probably be adopted for twenty years. But he must get a certain kick out of suggesting them first. He is just the most pleasant congenial, square thinking, plain talking fellow you ever met. He don't feel that he has any great work to carry on, Has no cause. He was born and bred in Politics and knows you must give lest you won't receive. He takes it serious but not solemn.

It's just a pleasure to meet and spend the hours with him. He don't think the Country is going to H——. But he sees no reason why we shouldent.

My wife as usual summed him up in one remark, "That fellow would have made good in a legitimate business."

THAT RUSSIAN-CHINESE WAR MAY FALL THROUGH

This Russia China War has had us all worked up here for the last few weeks. But it looks like they just can't work up much enthusiasm. In the first place it's too far away from civilization. (Wherever civilization is.) You can't sell any war bonds to people when they can't get over and see how their war is getting on. None of our other big Nations have enough concessions and interests in there to make them want to protect them.

Japan who would perhaps prosper more from a war of that description, they don't hardly know what to do about it. They have been fighting China for generations, and naturally feel that they have the exclusive privilege. They have whipped China so much that they have just gone by default. And they have already got about all of China that is any good. And they also hold a decision over Russia. So Japan is what you might call the "Smelling" of the Far East.[1]

But in this case they don't know who they want to win. The one that wins will be much stronger, and might some day give them opposition. And unless they both whipped each other why Japan don't know who she would really be pulling for.

China has been awful nice to us, they have let us use their home grounds to send our Marines when we didn't have any other war on for them at the time. They have let us mingle in every private war they have had. Why there has been times that if it hadn't been for China allowing us to go in and shoot at them, why we wouldn't have had a soul in the World to shoot at. We have made 'em keep what we call the "Open Door." That meant that they wasn't allowed to charge too much tariff on our stuff coming in, or they wasn't to keep us out of any family feuds they might have. In fact we was taken in as one of the family.

They are the most self sustaining Country in the World, and would like to live and exist all off to themselves. But of course countries like us and England and Germany and France, we can see right away that that wouldn't really be the thing for them to do, so we have to go in and help them out. Some times we have to shoot 'em, they are so hard headed and won't see it our way. So we all manage their affairs so well that they don't have anything to do with their own customs.

There is five hundred million of them, that was at the last Census, which was taken on Confuscious' 10th birthday. Next to poor people they breed faster than any other race. Lots of them can't talk to each other, which is no great handicap, for they probably wouldn't

1929

have anything to say of interest. In that way they are civilized. They figure that there is enough Chinamen alive today that if they come to Los Angeles, and each bought a lot, that it would almost take up the amount that is sub-divided now. We send many Missionaries there. They go through Chicago on their way out. Missionaries teach 'em not only how to serve the Lord but run a Ford Car. Then the American Agent sells 'em one. You take religion backed up by Commerce and it's awful hard for a Heathen to overcome.

They are getting more civilized though all the time. They are not only learning how to use opium from us, but they are learning how to sell it to us. We control the Automobile Industry of the entire world, which kills off more people in one year than the whole Opium Industry in ten. But they are ambitious, and are doing their best to catch us.

There has been an awful lot of internal dissension in China. There has been a gang up in the North in Manchuria, that have kinder compared to our Democrats down south. They have been trying to get in and see what the shooting was all about. They are headed by some fellow called Chang.[2] He is kinder the Al Smith of the Prairies.[3]

England has been awful nice to them and helped 'em run their business even more than we have, if that is possible. There is one town called Shanghi that the Chinese were running it so un-English that the English had to go right in and go to the trouble of taking over the whole thing, and now a Chinaman has to come in on a Passport. English Gunboats are so far up the Chinese Rivers that it takes Chinese Guides to bring 'em back down. If a Chinese Gunboat ever got in Radio hearing from Liverpool it would bring on International complications. When a problem comes up in China and the Chinese are in doubt as to what to do, why England tells 'em.

Yet through all this they have lived and existed and raised more children than an Englishman or an American could even count. They have taught more love and instilled more respect in their families for each other, than we even have for the law. Now Russia kinder wants to jump on 'em, for they figure a war would just about give them enough advertising that it would get them recognized. China hasn't done anything to 'em. That's what makes Russia sore at them is because they have given 'em no reasons to fight.

A war either makes or breaks a Nation, so you always got a fifty-fifty break. But I think since Russia got so hostile, that they have kinder counted China. Then too they have figured that it's a long way to go for the eggs. That Trans-siberian railway looks all right on a map, but you try to ferry an Army across it, and it's like getting across Fifth Avenue. But it wasn't so much that as it was that the other Nations just didn't hardly see their way clear what they would get out of it, so the war had no outside boosting. You know you can't get a war in a minute. It takes years of hard boosting and planning and scheming, and a lot more arrangements than you would at first think. Did you ever read Lord Grey's books, and all the other Diplomats ones too?[4] Why there was a time there before the World war that it looked like it would fall through. So China and Russia will fight, don't forget that, but not till the Nations that are not in it decide that they should.

347 THOUGHTS ON FLYING

Well, all I know is just what I read in the papers. Now lets just see what has been flitting across these truthful organs front pages in the last few weeks. Course Aviation got a great boost when the German Zep come zooming in and on by. I would have sure liked to have been on that old Sister. Not as a Stowaway. I don't know why those birds get my "Nanny" so but they sure do. Let me see a Stowaway and I sure see red.

It's been a mighty eventful last few days in that nobody has broken the refueling record. That seventeen-day thing was just on the verge of being discouraging to Aviators that wanted to stay away from home only a few days.

They opened up a line from out here on the west Coast to Mexico City and Central America. They just got 'em going pretty near everywhere now. I see where Capt. Eddie Rickenbacker, our great Ace (and by the way, one Hero who really never received anything like his proportionate share of Hero worship. I want to drop you all a line about that very thing some time and discuss it with you. He has never let a yelp out and has conducted himself in fine, high-class manner all these years since then), says that the demand for air travel in this country in the next few years will far exceed the amount of available planes.[1]

Here is twelve different and well equipped landing fields right here in Los Angeles, every one almost with a line running out to some place. It's got by the boosting stage, it's in with the necessities now.

It sure has been hot all over the country. Course these papers out here never refer to our heat. It's always the amount of heat prostration in the east and middle west that make the front headlines, but just between you and I it's been so hot out here that the headlines of other heat waves have melted on the page while you was reading it.

I been working on one of those talking pictures, but it's been on one of the new soundproof stages and it's all air cooled, and we have had it pretty soft, we was fine till we started home in the evening.

But I guess it's been pretty general all over the country. I don't see how President Hoover has stood it staying practically right in Washington all summer. Course he went over in Virginia on what we learn from England to call the "week end." But even when you are in Virginia you haven't helped out the District of Columbia much. He has been doing a little amateur Dam building on his camp up there.

He has been trying to fix one to make a swimming pool, but he hasent been able to get one to hold water long enough to get yourself wet in it yet. He has been away from construction work so long since he got mixed up in politics that he just can't get any real constructive personal work done. But he goes out and catches a few old cat fish every Saturday and feeds the renegade Senators that drop in over Sunday to escape going to services in Washington and to talk over the tariff.

Reed Smoot brings out some foreign and some domestic sugar every week end and shows him the inferiority of the foreign brand, claims Phillipine and Cuban sugar are what's causing all the discontent in this Country.[2] He lays all the late jail breaks on the lack of tarriff on sugar.

By the way some guy several weeks ago shipped some apricots back east and had them labeled that they were raised on Mr. Hoover's private ranch, and they sold like gold Nuggets. Mr. Hoover heard of it and sent 'em word that he was no more responsible for them, or where they come from, than Dr. Mayo was responsible for that 18 day diet that they tried to lay onto him.[3] That whole thing was got up by the Grapefruit Growers Association and has taken off less pounds and ruined more stomachs than anything outside of Carbolic acid.

Somebody ought to figure out a reducing process where you don't have to go through any hardships in the way of denying yourself anything but just slice off a chunk someplace. They take off an arm or a leg with no danger whatever, so in this plan they could remove it from spots where a diet can't generally reach it. They whittled down Peaches Browning's underpinnings by some outside process, and while I haven't been fortunate enough to feast my eyes on them, they say you can't hardly see where any has been taken off.[4]

If I was one of these big Surgeons that's what I would specialize in. My calling cards would read something like this, "Drs. Moore and White, removers of protruding hips, remakers of body lines, distorted calves removed while you wait.⁵ Legs brought back with the bounds of garters. Why reduce and have it come off the wrong place? We level all bumps and you can eat a box of chocolates while we are doing it."

I know just lots of Women that if they could get certain outer sections removed, as long as the Madula Oblong Gota was not disturbed, would fall for it in a minute. Besides look at the conversation it would give them after the thing was over.

But that has nothing to do with what-ever I was talking about. I just happened to think of it and want to see it adopted, so we can start feeding Women again.

348 WHAT'S HAPPENED TO THE CAMERA MEN?

Well all I know is just what I read in the papers. With Congress out of session most of the time, the Comedy is mighty slack around this time of year. Hoover has really been the direct cause of a lot of these slack times. Where is the Photographers that they don't give us some idea of how he is making out with the Finney Tribe? How do we know he has caught any fish? Monday morning comes and goes in our papers and we just as well not have a President. Where is the usual week end story of what the week end loot was?

Why, the Black Hills of Old Virginia might as well be the home of some defeated Democratic President as far as the publicity they are getting. I am kinder glad now he dident accept my offer to go to Oklahoma and take over the old Rogers Igloo for the mosquieto season. Where is the stories of the old Guides? Why for all we know he might be down there and not fishing at all. Well if that's the case he could be impeached. He led the people to belive that he was a Fisherman before election. Now he hides himself away every Friday and even Dave Reed can't locate him.¹

Why Reed Smoot had some defective sugar that he had received from foreign parts that he was gloating over and wanting to show Mr. Hoover.² But do you think you could locate him? Talk about Lindberg being ungrateful and not marrying the Camera men instead of his wife?³ Why what's the matter with Mr. Hoover being unmindful of his duty to his Tabloids? Do you realize we haven't seen that man with a Perch in his hand since March the fourth. Why he is just liable to be out there vetoeing Bills or doing some other unnessasary thing, and not fishing at all. I think it must be the State of Virginia.

They are ashamed to have the outside world see the type of fish that they have. And they don't want the World to know that they haven't got anything but an old Cat Fish.

Why you remember how nice Mr. Coolidge was about all this. Why he even took a pet Coon out to help us out on our stories of "Presidential Life in the Wilds." And here Mr. Hoover don't take nobody but Mark Sullivan.[4] Why there is no story in Mark like there is in a Pet Coon, that climbs a tree backwards and won't come down for the weeklies. Mark is an awful nice man, a fine newspaper man, and an excellent fellow. But for news for us fellows that are supposed to keep you all posted, why Mark can't touch a Pet Coon, even a Coon that ain't a pet.

But the summer is a drawing to a close, and the old Camera men are oiling up their tripods, and while he might go to Virginia to escape the Lenz, They will get him this fall if ever sticks his head out of his office while dodging a Chamber of Commerce deligation with an invitation to open some new Police Station. They may not land you Mr. Hoover in the middle of the creek with the long rubber boots on, But when you step outside with the old Prince Albert the boys will be pressing the bulb.

All we have ever read is a week or so ago Colonel Lindberg was out with him and drove him back to the White House in less time than he had ever been driven there before. But not a picture of them did we see, so where is your evidence? And it also said that the Colonel had won the Horse Shoe pitching contest out there wherever it is. Nobody don't even know where it is. Some say it's Maryland, and some say it's West Virginia. But anyhow wherever it was, Lindy heaved the old Mule Slippers for some tree point landings around the little peg. Now where was our staff Photographers? We want when we go into our favorite Movie Emporium see the Col. take off with a hand full of Horse Regals and start flipping 'em for safe landings.

Course they are going to gather Congress in there again right away and in fact it may be done by now. So that the old humor will start percolating pretty pronto from now on. They are gathering in to argue over the Tarriff. George Washington argued over it with Thomas Jefferson. Columbus had a session with the Cherokees near where Claremore Oklahoma is now located. In fact, the tarriff is to the Politicians what Jonah and the Whale is to the Stand Pat religionists and the Futurists in religion. It's just one of those things that will be going on when Jackie Coogan the third is Senior Senator from the great State of Los Angeles.[5] Tarriff don't hit any two men the same. It's like the weather. What suits you don't feel so good to me.

You want everything you buy to come in Tarriff free, you want

Weekly Articles

everything you sell to be protected by having a tarriff on any of that same stuff coming in. Now unfortunately everybody in the Country is not in exactly the same business. Reed Smoot comes from Utah. They raise Sugar beets. So the Sugar Beet Boys have retained Reed at the usual Senator's Salary to go back east and represent them in any controversy that comes up in regard to sugar. He don't care what happens to Peanuts, his mind is on sugar. So each one is sent there to dig something out of the National Treasury, or the people in general to take back to the folks at home.

You are a Politician just in proportion to the loot you have pilfered while there for the old home State. If you can come in with a Couple of Boulder Dams, a few Government Hospitals and Jails, and an appropration to build a road somewhere where nobody lives or wants to, why if you do all those things you will be putting yourself in line with becoming a Statesman. But that's all as it should be I reckon. It's there the money is, and they won't pay off the National debt with it, that's the last thing that was ever suggested. So as long as we are going to spend it anyhow why there is no reason why the old home town or Home State don't grab off what we think is more than our Pro Rata.

So that's what all this Tarriff is about. It's about Who is going to get something that the other fellow won't. Grundy, the Santa Claus of the Republican Campaign, is working out what little we are to have left after Pennsylvania gets all it can carry.[6] Lobbyists are reaping a harvest. There never was a time when a good Lobbyist was in such demand. A Lobbyist is a person that is supposed to help a Politician to make up his mind, not only help him but pay him.

349   WASTE-BASKET POLITICAL SCORES

Well all I know is just what I read in the Papers, and what I have to personally get out and accidentally come in contact with. Last night I kinder went out of my territory in the way of Intellectual relaxation and got from the newspaper to the Magazine herd. I saw a Magazine on the stands with Mrs Coolidge and Myself as having contributed to its output, so I just feel mighty proud that I am in the same one as our much beloved Ex first Lady of our land.[1]

So I make an original outlay I think of twenty-five cents, and go home and start in. Not to read mine. For when I write 'em I am through with 'em. I am not being paid reading wages. You can always see too many things you wish you hadent said, and not enough that you ought to.

1929

But I certainly was pleased with the one that Mrs Coolidge had. It was very plain and chatty and homelike. She told about having some rats in her Hotel at Washington where they lived when he was Vice President. I know this can't by any means be construed as an add, so I will name the Hotel, as it is where I always stop too. It's the Willard. And rats go with each room but they don't charge you extra. Well do you know Mrs Coolidge told the nicest cutest little Rat episode you ever read. It was like one of Rex Beaches animal stories of the North, but it was just about mice, and two rats.[2] The two rats were the father and mother, (apparently) of the mice. Just home talent animals.

She tells how she made friends with 'em, how she fed 'em, how they played around the room, and got in the waste Paper Basket and she would turn it over with them in there, and they would get back in again. The Coolidges stayed at the Hotel a short while after they were made President and the Rats were perhaps some Lobbyists that were trying to get in the basket to see what Bills the President had vetoed. Then she tells about the Senators' wives coming there to the Hotel to her "At Homes" or receptions. But she don't dwell much on that. The Rats get two pages and the Senators' wives two paragraphs. Just shows you which made the more lasting impression.

Now when a woman can make friends with a Rat she is not only humane, but very unusual. She dident grab her skirts and jump on the transom, she just went out and made friends with those little Rodents. She had been mixed up in the turmoil of politics long enough to know that with your husband continually running for office it's best to stand in with everything and anything, as you can never tell when they will grow to manhood and have a vote. She says they come back to the Hotel there away long afterwards and she looked for the rats but they were gone. Probably had a job lobbying for the Power Trust.

But you never saw a rat made so human as she pictures him in this article. She tells another thing that I sure did like to hear her say and that was the kindly and generous reference to Mrs Tom Marshall, who was the Vice President's wife that preceeded her.[3] That was one thing that first made a hit with me with Mr Coolidge. The first time I ever saw and talked with him I was taken in there by Nick Longworth, (also married) and it was the night of the Gridiron Dinner that I had come down to gab at.[4] Well, Mr Marshall was one of the announced Speakers. I had never heard him, and was looking forward with much pleasure to the treat, for he had a great fund of humor, and something come up about him at our chat with Mr

Weekly Articles

Coolidge and he said, "Mr Marshall won't be there. I just got a wire from him. He and his wife was to have been our guests here at the White House, but he is ill."

Then we talked a lot of him and how everyone looked on him as a mere Humorist when in reality he was a great Statesman and would have made a fine President, and should have been President at one time when Mr Wilson was incapaicated. In fact it was his extreme modesty and loyalty to the President that was all that kept him from being, as they all wanted to have the affairs turned over to the Vice President. Well Mr Coolidge liked him, (and he was a Democrat, and Darn good one too). His affection and appreciation for him made a real hit with me, and a year afterwards and Mr Marshall had passed away, I saw and chatted with the President again and he remembered our talk of Mr Marshall, and remarked on the misfortune of the passing of our mutual friend. Well Mrs Coolidge does them proud again.

But here is the main and the meat of the whole Article outside of the rats, and that is the inside story of the "I don't choose to run." We had heard that Mr Coolidge had not consulted Mrs Coolidge and that he made the statement to the Press unbeknowns to her, and that when it was repeated to her she was very much upset, as naturally one would be. Well here is a little inside story about it. When it was known that she did not know it before, why the folks in charge of Republican Skullduggery got their heads together and said, "Here we better not let this get out. It would lose us all the Women vote in the Country if they knew he had done a thing like that without consulting his wife."

So the whole thing was kept quiet till around now. For while he said he dident choose, he could have been induced to change his mind, and they dident want a thing like this to come out in case he did. While it's mighty nice and sweet of Mrs Coolidge to say that she dident want to know any of his business and had to read the papers to find out what he was doing. It just don't seem any too clubby with him to do such things.

When a man don't discuss things with his wife why it don't hardly hit the other weaker (Ha-Ha) sex any too well. If he didn't talk about his plans why it evidently didn't leave much else to talk about. Anyhow I know they kept it mighty quiet, the leaders did after Senator Capper told it, until after it was a certainty that he wouldn't run.[5]

350   DIPLOMACY AND TARIFF

Well all I know is just what I read in the funny papers. Things have been mighty quiet along the Political front here lately. Mrs Poindexter kinder went into a huddle against Peru, but it was kinder short.[1] The Sharge de affairs of that Country wouldent argue. He just up and packs his dress suit and went home. It seems she had brought some native Peruvian up here with her, and when he got here and found the price of "Mescal," why he wanted more money, so he went to the Peruvian Embassy and they told him he should have more money and that he could work there for them till something showed up that was in keeping with his talents, so that's that.

Mr Hoover took a lot of week end guests out, and instead of fishing as they thought they would get to, why he put 'em all to carrying rocks to build a dam, so now he is having trouble getting week enders.

This fellow Phillip Snowden over in the labor Government grabbed all glory of the conference to distribute the dough that Germany is to pay.[2] I don't know how much money he is going to get out of it but he certainly grabbed the front page and went south with it. You know I met him when I was over there. I first met his wife at Lady Astor's (and by the way she is a very brilliant woman, and has been a great aid to him so they say).[3] Then I met him. His party was out of power then and he wasent very particular. I dident pay any more attention to it than to meeting a Democrat. But now I can recall him that he is back in again. Well you know England has been the Daddy of the Diplomat, the one with the smooth manners. But still be going after what he wants but always the Gentleman. You know that's one thing about an Englishman, he can insult you, but he can do it so slick and polite that he will have you guessing till away after he leaves you just whether he was friend or foe. Well when this new Chancellor of the Excheaquer (that's perfect English for Secretary of the Treasury) well when this Snowden Lad got to the conference where they were splitting up the Jack, why instead of coining a few polite phrases, he just up and said even before he had said Ladies and Gentlemen, he just said in what really was not their English, "Boys, I am here for some more dough. In the divvy, I feel that the British Empire was handed the Hooey, and I am here to see that amends are made in a financial way. I don't want to be rough. I want to be a Gentleman as long as possible, BUT under the auspices of the Prince of Wales and the King's Royal Navy I am here for collecting purposes. Now it don't make any difference to me who pays it, but just let it be here, Get Me?"

61

Well nothing like that had ever been heard since Heflin defied the entire Vatican.[4] Here was an Englishman asking for something without diplomacy, in fact he wasent asking for it, he was just telling them who's doorstep to leave it on, and he left mighty explicit directions, so they wouldent get the wrong step.

Well the other Nations went right in secret and meditative conference, and up to the time of going to press they are still passing the hat. They dident quite have the total amount but had borrowed some lead pipe and were reporting progress. I read the whole thing over and it looks like they got a mighty just claim. England wasent getting as much as Charley Dawes had given them.[5] So for awhile it looked like there might be another war over the spoils of the last one. But anyhow this labor government has spoken right out, and they got the "Gentlemen" with 'em in England too.

It's hard to unite both classes over there. For a Gentleman in England is a man that disagrees with whatever the laboring Party wants. But now they all agree, for this means money, and where there is money involved, (coming in) you can generally interest what is humorously called the "better classes."

Well our arguments are starting now. This Tarriff, it's what started Politics. It's what started Partys. It split Washington and Jefferson, what will it do with Borah and Pat Harrison?[6] Mr Hoover pulled a bad one when he ever let them kid him into promising to monkey with that thing. It was before election and he was trying to please everybody. All he had to promise to do was to get some sort of legislation to assist the Farmer. He dident have to have a grab bag for Grundy and his Pennsylvania Manafacturers.[7] If there is one deed in Mr Hoover life he would like to live over and have another crack at, it's this same opening up that Tarriff debate. For twenty men can enter a room as friends and someone can bring up the Tarriff and you will find nineteen bodies on the floor with only one living that escaped.

There is only one answer to it. "I want everything protected that I make, or raise, and I want everything to come in free that I have to buy." So as no two raise, make, eat and wear exactly the same things, there is no two that would ever agree 100 percent.

Been having quite some little minature wars over in Turkey somewhere. It's sort of a religious war. They are pretty bad, these big wars over Commerce. They kill more people. But one over religion is really the most bitter. Turks have been pretty quiet for some time now. They generally have quite a few wars booked, I never saw a year when they were so slack. So I guess this is in the nature of a rehersal for something they got coming up later. I want to get over there some time to see this Kemal Pasha, he must be a Baer.[8] He made the Women change clothes, and anytime you can tell a whole Nation of women to slip on or take off, You are a MAN.

351 ELIHU ROOT KNOWS HIS ADVERBS!

Well all I know is just what I read in the papers. It seems like old times to have the World's Court bob up again in our midst. Just when you think a thing has about died out, why the first thing you know up it comes and it kinder sounds new, you havent heard it in so long. Mr Elihu Root, a very learned Lawyer, in fact second only to Mr Hughes as our most distinguished Statesman, is over there working on it.[1] He has devised some plan by which we can get into it in a painless manner with none of the old objections.

You see since it come up before we have had time to study our neighbors on the other side of the World and they have shown us that given the breaks that they will be good and behave themselvs. They all want us in, not for any monetary consideration as most of our objectors seem to think. But it's just like the fellow who comes to you and wants to use your name in some very profitable enterprize. "We don't want a cent of your money. We don't want anything you have. But we just want the privalege of your being with us, we like you, we don't obligate you to anything. But we just want to use your name as sponsoring our enterprise."

Well that all come up years ago. And the Senate after discussing Prohibition, The Klan, Religious freedom, Mississippi relief, Nicaragua and Coolidge's third term, they accepted the World Court but with such reservations that you would have thought it was a Pullman window, there was so many resevations being made. Cause when that Senate gets through resevating, Resevating is practically null and void.

These Resevations said in toto, "We the United States of Borah, and Reed Smoot, assisted by Grundy, do hereby and hereon agree to join this Court, BUT with the following clauses and How.[2] We are to furnish eleven of the twelve Jurymen on each case. The Prosecuting Attorney and the Lawyer for the defense are to be either Elks or Kiawanis. We reserve the right to appoint the Judge, if we can't appoint him, we reserve the right to name the Nation that does appoint him. If any decision goes against us, we reserve the right to name the judgement that shall be visited on the said Judge, Jury and court attendants, including the Sob squad. We want the right to all radio privaleges, and reserve the privalege of appointing our own announcer. On account of high Republican tarriff we want to charge an Ad valorium duty on all witnesses that may or may not be intending to testify against us. We feel as a Nation that having saved the World for Wall Street and the Republican Party and Aimee McPherson we think it is no more than proper, (in fact we don't think it as much as proper) to demand these few little amendments, (and speaking of amendments that reminds us of a story. The eighteenth Amendment, that's the story)."[3]

Well never mind let bygones be bygones. Mabel Jimmy Walker Willerbrandt wrote some awful amusing Articles and there is no doubt they will be published serially.[4] Each day she said what was wrong with Prohibition and they run 365 days, (including February which has but 28 when Leap Year comes and gives it 29).

"Its a funny Lane if it don't either turn or stop," so we just kept right on making resevations. Whether anybody agreed to any of them was beside the point, we was out to make a record in demands. We demanded so much that Rockefeller, Ford and Joe Toplitsky even couldent fullfill them, much less England, France and Montenegro.[5] (That Monte Negro was appointed by Congressman De Priest of Chicago.)[6] De Priest says, "If Monte Negro don't make good in West Point, gets kidney feet and can't stand the march for the Movie weeklies, I will appoint a bigger and blacker Monte Negro. I picked the blackest one. But if he ain't black enough, we will cross 'em with Polangus and breed 'em blacker, and if you got a White Political Leader in your district throw him out, and put in a black one, if you can't find any blacker one than a White Political Leader why call for a change of venue." These are the words of Oscar De Priest who says he has got more publicity than any man in Congress with the exception of Tom Heflin and Peggy Joice.[7]

We also demand in our resevations that Bobby Jones is not to meet, pass through, or even read of, anyone conected with Omaha, even if they are Brandies something else, so help me Calamity Jame.[8] But as long as Gus Nations works for Prohibition, and his brother for the Griesedick Brewery, just so long will he be in argument with Mabel.[9] But Mr Elihu Root has worked out a more injeanous scheme, and he has concocted a scheme of getting by all these various resevations, and here is how he did it.

"There shall be individual negotiations between the United States and the Council of the League in cases where the U.S. has any opposition to the proposal to ask for advisory opinions." Now you can see yourself how clear that is. Why after an amendment like that even a child couldent help but join. It's all so lucid that it's funny no one

1929

thought of that before. Just that little paragraph that I quoted above was all that it took to put us in Europe again. So now the thing comes back to the Senate all straightened out and they can during the discussion of it bring up Mr Hoover's summer Camp, Boulder Dam, Federal Reserve Percentage system, The Mediterranian Fly, local flys, Reed Smoot Sugar Baby Bill, and so we will finally get into the Court room, all for why? Simply because Mr Root happened to think of this, "Individual negotiations in case there is any opposition to the proposal to ask for advisory opinions."

352   PUBLIC LANDS TO LET

Well, all I know is just what I read in the papers. Well, let's see what took place since we communed last week. One of the biggest things is the attempt of President Hoover to give all the lands belonging to the United States back to the Individual States.

But he recommends that the Federal Government hold all the Oil and Mineral rights. Well that's just like offering a hungry man a meal and reserving the rights to issue him no food. You give him a plate and knife and fork, and you put him in a position to eat in case something shows up.

Course originally in our Country the Government owned all the land there was outside the original 13 colonies, and England owned that. Then Washington had a war and took it away from them and annexed most of it personally himself.

What he dident get a Democrat named Jefferson got. He was the most far-sighted Democrat in either his or any other time, and they named the Democratic Party after him. There is no reason with the start they had that the Democrats couldent just as well have been the Party of Prominence as the Republicans. The Democrats had the first start, and they could just as well have taken the part of Capital. But they took Jefferson's high ideals. That is, he was for the poor but was himself of the rich.

So the Democrats wanted a wonderful talking argument, where they could get up on the stump (they had stumps in those days; that was before stumppullers were invented), and it sounded great to announce, "I and the party I represent am for the poor man (cheers), and we believe in every man having an equal opportunity, and if elected I will personally see that he gets it." (Cheers even more louder, if that was possible.) Now he would really finish with a big round of applause. But he never could get enough votes to keep him in free postage stamps. But that's one peculiar thing about a Democrat, he would rather have applause than salary. He would rather be told that he is right, even if he knows the Guy is a liar, than he would to know he is wrong, but belongs to the Republican Party.

But all this has nothing to do with the Public land. Nobody knows why Mr. Hoover got it in for the states and wanted to sick the land on them. If the Federal Government can't keep it up, what could some poor state like Nevada do with it? Why, the U.S. Government owns 75 per cent of all the land in Nevada. Utah is next. You wouldn't think it, but Brigham Young and Mr. Joseph Smith only took over 53 per cent of the land in Utah, leaving the government (if my Rays green back arithmatic is correct) 47 per cent.[1] The government owns 27 per cent of Wyoming, including the biggest party of Charley Irwin.[2] Now these are all poor States. (That is, poor in financial standing, BUT RICH IN TRADITION.)

Now if you are going to force this extra percentage of land on them you are just going to make them that much poorer. Any time Reed Smoot and Senator Kendrick can't make sugar and cattle pay, why what chance has some poor state with no Senator on the Tariff Commission got?[3] There is nothing that can break a man quicker than land, unless it's running a Grocery Store or dealing in secondhand cars.

About all you can do with this public land is make a park out of it, and you have to make roads into it if it's a park, and that costs you more than you can make out of the Soda Pop and Hot Dogs that the Tourists will buy on their way through it.

I tell you a Tourist is one of the worst, if not the worst investment there is. He knocks everything and buys nothing. He don't know where he is going only that he wants to get away from his own home. He is sore at his wife and family that are in the car and he takes it out on your part of the Country. A tourist contributes nothing but empty tin cans and profanity to the upbuilding of your State.

Now the Government wasent able (with all its Republican Tarriff) to build roads through these Public lands, so what can a State do? Even if there was no graft in the Highway Commission I doubt if you could do it.

So we just better announce to Mr. Hoover that while we as public tax Dodgers if possible, appreciate what he is trying to do for us, we just can't accept. That he will have to take these deserts and mountain sides back and put them under the Secretary of the Treasury as he is the only man I can off hand think of that has enough money to maintain them.

Mr. Hoover's argument was that he wanted to give the States

individually a little more leeway in conducting their public affairs. But he had no more than done that then the Anti-Prohibitionists hopped on him and said, "Well, if you want the States to run their own business why don't you let them run their own Prohibition business?"

Well, that brings on more argument. So it just looks like a President better lay off of things like that. I guess little Calvin had the right idea. He didn't let on he knew who owned these lands, as long as he could fish on them why that was all he knew about them. It only shows that no matter what a President does he is wrong according to some people, so I couldn't even say YES or NO if I was him; I would just stall along and if asked I would remark, "I don't choose to answer." But take it all in all it's a tough life, this thing of being President and trying to please everybody. (Well not exactly everybody but enough to re-elect.)

353 STORY OF A MISSPENT BOYHOOD

Well all I know is just what I read in the papers. Course football is getting all the play now and it beehooves us old Alumni's to get out with the cash and do our bit for old (I forgot the name).

I don't mean spend the money now. I mean get ready to spend it for later on when you see whether they need ends, or backs, or tackles. But get out now and go all over the country and see all the Prep school games you can and when a promising head arises why get on the job. Every time a good tackle is made go to the boy and explain to him the advantages of a free education under a splendid coach at old "Bohunk College."

I was just a thinking what I would have to do if I was to start out to help out my old schools. "Drungoul" was a little one-room log cabin four miles east of Chelsea, Indian Territory, (where I am right now writing this article).[1] It was all Indian kids went there and I being part cherokee (had enough white in me to make my honesty questionable).

Now that school is not now in existance. Why? Why because the old Alumni let the football material fall down.

There must have been about thirty of us in that room that had rode horseback and walked miles to get there, and by the way it was a Co-Ed Institution. About half of 'em was Coo Coo Eds. We graduated when we could print our full name and unumerate to the teacher, or Principle, or Faculty, (Well whenever we could name to

Weekly Articles

her) the nationality of the last Democratic President.

But as I say the school went out of business. We wasent able to get games with was profitable. It seems that other schools grabbed off all the other good dates, and got the breaks in the newspapers. We couldent seem to ever be accused of proffessionalism. I could see the finish even as far back as when I was there along in 1887. I could tell then that the old Grads wasent getting us the material that we should have to complete for the big gate receipts. We could tell it there in the school.

Why I can remember when the Coach couldent get enough out of us 15 Boys out to make a team. We got to running Horse races instead. Why there was just lots of days I dident go out for Skull practice at all. I had a little chestnut mare that was beating everything that any of them could ride to school and I was losing interest in what we was really there for. I was kinder forgetting that we was there to put the old school on a Paying basis by seeing how many times we could get through that Goal with that old pigskin.

I got to thinking well Horseracing is the big game, that's where the money is, that's what the crowds pay to see. But as years went along it showed that I was a Lad of mighty poor foresight. Little did I dream that it was football that was to be the real McCoy. Course we had no way of hardly telling it then, for we was paid practically nothing at all. In fact we had what I would call a Real Simon Pure Amateur Team. Course we got our side line, (Schooling) free. The Cherokee Nation, (we then had our own Government, and the name Oklahoma was as foreign to us as a Tooth Paste). Well the Cherokee Nation paid the Teacher, and I guess Rockefeller paid the Football Coach.[2]

But anyhow there was mighty few of us what was there under any kind of a guarantee. Course I will admit one of the Alumni got me to go there. He had spent three weeks there and couldent get along with the Teacher and he wanted to do what he could for the old School so he procured me. I looked like a promising End. I could run pretty fast. In fact my nickname was and is to this day among some of the old timers "Rabbit." I could never figure out if that referred to my speed or my heart. But I, like a fool, dident make him put up anything, or guarantee me any privileges while at school.

Mind you, you wouldent believe it, but we dident even have a Stadium. Think of that in this day and time! Thousands and Thousands of acres surrounded us with not a thing on it but Cows and not a concrete seat for a spectator to sit on. Well you see as I look back on it now, a school like that dident have any license to exist. It had to perish. It just staid with books, such as Ray's Arithmatic, and

McGuffy 1st, 2nd, (and two pupils in the 3rd) Readers.[3] We had even a Geography around there but we just used it for the pictures of the cattle grazing in the Argentine and the wolves attacking the sleighs in Rusia. Well you see they just couldent see what was the future in Colleges. They just wore out the old books instead of wearing out some footballs. We was a printing our ABC's when we ought to have been marking down "Tackles Back" and "Lateral Passes." We had Indian Boys that could knock a Squirrel out of a Tree with a rock. But do you think the Regents knew enough to get a Pop Warner and teach 'em how to hide a Ball under their Jerseys?[4] No. They just had the old fashioned idea that the place must be made self-sustaining by learning alone, and you see where their ignorance got them. Now the weeds is higher than the School house was, and that's what is happening in a few places in this country. We got those same "Drumgoul" ideas. Course not many but a few. They won't switch and get to the new ideas that it's open field running that gets your old College somewhere and not a pack of spectacled Orators, or a mess of Civil Engineers. It's better to turn out one good Coach then Ten College Presidents. His name will be in the papers every day and it will always be referred to where he come from. But with the College Presidents, why as far as publicity is concerned they just as well might have matriculated in Hong Kong. So don't let your school be another Drumgoul.

354 WILL BUMS AROUND

Well all I know is just what I run into as I prowl around. I was a sitting around home after finishing an "Audible" and as it was to appear with a sort Ballyhoo opening why I figured I better kinder take to the woods till the effects kinder blew over.[1] I wanted 'em to kinder fumigate around before I appeared in person back home. Well then the thought come where will I go. Now just offhand that is more of a problem than you would think. Here you are with some time on your hands, have to get out of town. But nowhere in particular to go. In fact you could go wherever you wanted, so where?

Well naturally my first thoughts was back to see the old Home folks back in Oklahoma. My Wife had just returned from a visit there with my folks and over into Arkansaw with hers. But I had not been there for, well since I was on my way from the Republican Convention in Kansas City to the other one in Houston last summer. The children were all getting started in school, which of course was her

Will Rogers relaxing while reading Homer Croy's They Had to See Paris. *Rogers starred in the 1929 motion picture based on the best selling novel.*

Rogers and Fifi D'orsay in a scene from the film They Had to See Paris *(Fox Film Corporation, 1929), based on the novel by Homer Croy.*

job anyhow and not mine getting them off, so I announced that Father for perhaps the first time in his life was just out for some travel, sun and amusement.

Just think, going somewhere. Dident have to go at any certain time, dident have to make some Town to lecture the people out of anything on any certain night, dident have to make a Show at eight oclock in New York. I just dident have to do nothing. Well of course my mind turned to Planes. Well the Western Air Express gets you further from Los Angeles in one day than any other, so I called 'em up and told 'em to reserve me a seat the following morning. (Oh I tell you I work fast when I decide to step out.) They told me we left for Kansas City at five oclock in the morning. Well that's pretty early to be woke up and shoved on an Aeroplane and it still dark, but I made it. And the Plane was full 10 or twelve people. There was some Boys and Girls on there that were going back to their homes who had made a ten thousand mile trip as the Guests of the Western Air Express Co. on their Planes. They had won a Song Title Contest, in their respective Citys all over the Country. I had always wondered what kind of people it was that answered Puzzles and entered all Newspaper contests. It was a kind of a mania that I couldent hardly see what would drive 'em to it. But do you know they was an awful normal bunch. Old ones, young ones, School Boys and men with good jobs. All had answered some add and sent in a Title for a song. You would have been surprised what a rational crowd it was, Awfully normal. One Girl in the bunch who tried to make love and DID to all the rest.

We had a fine trip, the Pilot in flying over where the accident was tried to point it out but was not able to find it.[2] It was in a very bad territory and with a storm and a fog on, why you could see that it was an accident that could be accounted for in no way only by the elements. It was just one of those unfortunate things that had to happen like some are killed by Earthquakes and lightning. But it don't mean that we are going to abolish either one of those.

I got off in Wichita at eight o'clock that same evening. Just think across the whole width of California, Arizona, New Mexico, Texas and most of Kansas, and a corner of Oklahoma, all in one day. Staid there all night, then on a regular, organized line, on a regular daily schedule from there down to Tulsa, Oklahoma, and by the way saw more Planes and more Aerial activity there than at any field I have ever visited. Was met by my Sister and driven to her home in Chelsea.[3]

Well for the next few days I did nothing but just visit around with all my folks and old Cronies, made no dates, just get in the car and go see 'em. The family couldent get over the idea that there was

Weekly Articles

not some place I had to rush to make a Lecture date every night.

I received a wire from my Wife from California saying the picture had opened and I could come home, that's all the wire said. So you see we got two Comedians in the family. Left Tulsa in a fast single motored Lockhead Viga, with Oklahoma's favorite Pilot Robert Cantwell, stopped at Fort Reno a beautiful old Fort that I had always wanted to see.[4] They were having a big Polo tournament there, among the best Army teams and the best Civilian ones in the middle west. They are doing a great work there. It's the Government Remount station and they are keeping up the breeding and caliber of our Army Horses and also of the whole country.

Next was an old Friend's ranch away out in western Texas, where if it hadent been for Planes, I would never have been able to spare the time to make the trip. Then I degenerated down to the speed of a car. Another old Cowpuncher Cronie loaded me in his car, (as this Plane that had brought me out had gone back to Tulsa) and he and I drove from Amarillo Texas to Cimmaron New Mexico. We was half of one night, up at five oclock and most of the day. Could have made it in a Plane in three hours. But did enjoy looking at all the ranches. Cattle was never fatter, and grass was never better.

The old Staked Plains that we used to think wouldent raise a thing but grass has farms all over it. But there is still some tremendous ranches, for lots of them have blocked up and bought outright big tracts of land. There is several of a Quarter and half million acres each. My friend had a big Horse ranch away up in the mountains and we rode and looked at horses and lots of wild game for two days. All this time I was just going where I wanted too, and doing what I wanted too. Had nowhere to go, or no particular time to get there. Finally I says I better go home, cause I got to make another one. So into Raton New Mex by car, then by train down to Albequrque where I would catch one of the transcontinental air lines into Los Angeles. Left Albequrque at eleven oclock in the morning, landed at Los Angeles at four thirty. So I finished ten days of just Bumming. Course it was high class "Bumming" but it was bumming never the less.

355   THE CHANGING MOVIES

Well, all I know is just what I read in the papers. I got home a week ago from prowling around in the various states visiting relatives and old friends and what had been going on in Hollywood during my absence. My picture had opened amid no casualties and I had been

1929

practically forgiven for it; wasent bad enough to shoot or good enough to cheer. Went over to the studio and our general manager showed me the new "grandeur" screen.

That is you can't take one old bed sheet and tack it up on the wall and throw some movies on it. This is a great big thing as broad as a Gettysburg painting that covers the whole of the opening of the theatre. It's about two and a half times the width of the old screen. It has to be taken with a different camera and it has to be projected with a different projecting machine and the width of the film is just about twice what the other was.

They say it will speed up the movies as it will take in so much territory that it will do away with the old idea of continually cutting to a "close-up." That when a scene is being played and there is a bunch of people that you will have to get over your "emotions" all at once and in the same picture, that they won't cut to each of you in a close-up.

I sho will be glad of that for I sho do hate those close-ups. When those old wrinkles commence coming and the old mane is turning snowy, why we don't want either cameras or people to commence to crowd us.

This broad screen thing looks like almost as big an innovation as the new talkies were. You just get twice as much to look at as you used to. Then the color thing is coming along fine, where they are going to get our natural complexion right in the camera, without artificial coloring after the film is taken.

Oh we are just getting so many new things that you almost have to go every night to get 'em. A theater no more than gets in one type of apparatus than it has to start installing another one. They have more workmen in the theaters now than they have audiences. Everybody that can speak above a whisper is out here to have their voice invoiced.

The old town is just a-humming. Broadway, New York, has moved out — spats and dogs. This talking picture craze has got more actors out of New York than "Abie's Irish Rose" did.[1] They come thinking the screen actor can't talk. Say, the screen actor can talk, but nobody ever listened to him before.

He has been speaking words in these things for years, but nobody heard him but the crew. You know, after all, talk is not exactly a new industry among any Americans. Talk was the best thing we did. And when a chance come along to record it for prosperity (posterity means people two weeks later), why, we just snapped at the chance.

I was over to the studio today and who do I run onto but little Ann Pennington.[2] I hadent seen her in years since we used to work

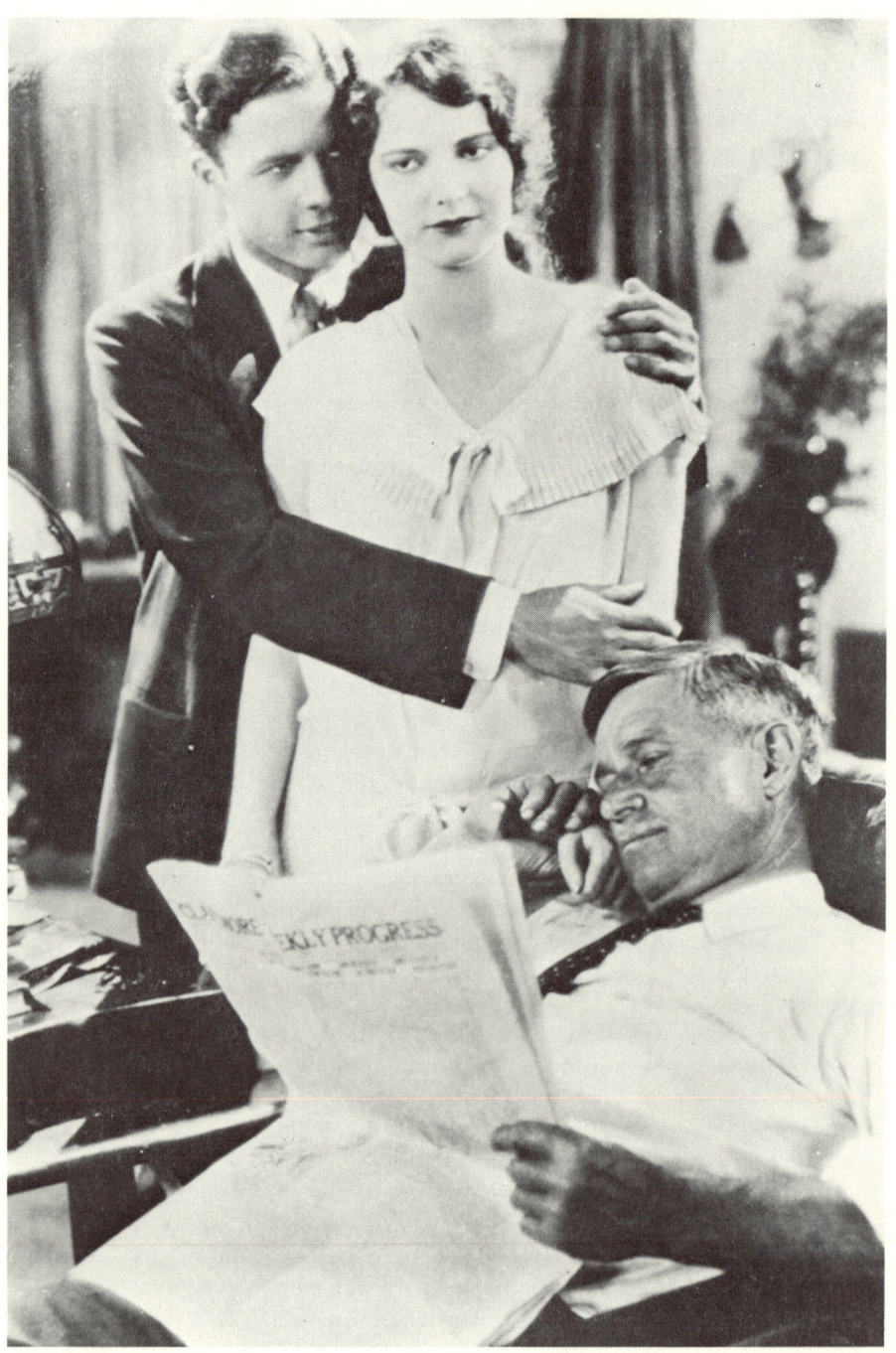

Will Rogers as "Pike Peters" in Rogers' first film with sound, They Had to See Paris *(Fox Film Corporation, 1929).*

1929

together in the "Follies." She has collected more money off her knees than most people have off their heads. My wife always said that Ann was the only woman that had a child's leg. So you see it's not only me in the family that's high on Ann's underpinning.

Not only actors but writers are all out here. Ben Ames Williams, that you all have read after in the Saturday Evening Post so much, is here.³ He wrote the finest story it was ever my privilege to work in. That was one called "Jubilo," where I played a tramp.

It was the only story ever made out here where there was no scenario made. We just shot the scenes from the various paragraphs in the story in the Saturday Evening Post. When we took a scene we just marked it off and went on the next.

I think, and he verified it, that it was the only story ever made that was absolutely filmed as it was written. Here is the big novelty to it: We dident change his main title either! They will film the Lord's Supper and when it is made figure that that is not a good release title and not catchy enough, so it will be released under the heading, "A Red Hot Meal" or "The Gastronomical Orgy."

I passed a theater down by the ranch the other night and we wanted to go in and had intended to, but what stared us in the face but something like "Fast Company" or some such idiotic title and we just drove on. A few days later the children got to talking about a good and funny picture they had seen, a baseball picture. I got to asking them about it. It was the one by Ring Lardner, the "Elmer, the Great" play, based on his famous stories of the rookie in baseball.⁴

Andy Tombs and I had done a sketch in the "Follies" of '22 that Ring wrote that was the nucleus of this play.⁵ Well, here this thing called "Fast Company" and featuring some girl was nothing but "Elmer The Great." Now I know that title they had drove out more people than it ever brought in.

So no matter what famous book you have read and want to see in the pictures, why you better start going into every theater you come to. Don't look up at the title, for "Pationate Pal" may be just what you was looking for as "Romeo and Juliet" or "She Stoops to Conquer" may reach your corner labeled "Baby You Are a Wow." Sometimes you just think there ain't enough crazy titles to go round and that when they end, that will be the finish of pictures.

But really the whole business is flourishing and weddings were never more at a premium. Divorces permeate the air. High-powered roadsters are skitting here and yon. Beach houses are closed and the sand is covering up the old bottles. There will be little to recognize the old place in a few weeks. It and Wall Street are two businesses you can't explain.

Weekly Articles

356   WILL EXPLAINS 'GRUNDY'

Well all I know is just what I read in the papers. It sure was fine the way America responded to somebody that had some vague connection with labor. It was really an inspiration to our Politicians to see the way Ramsey worked even while here.[1] He made a mighty fine impression, and his evidently charming daughter was a tremendous hit over here. Just when we were on the verge of having our Women reach for "Henry Clay" instead of a dish rag, why this Girl comes along and announced that she dident smoke, chew, dip, Powder or rouge, and she "dident take care of her Father." Well that knocked American society right back on its flasks, and had the old Dem-me monde breaking their Lornogettes trying to pick flaws in her complexion. If England have got any more like her, and I imagine they have, why we could use 'em over here. Not that we haven't got a lot of that type. But we got a lot that would be that type if they were sure that they could get anywhere by being that way. For the painted Dolls and the Ga-Ga Girls have kinder grabbed off all the paying boys here lately. But we got many an old fashioned one that will be in at the payoff.

Course here is one thing you got to keep in mind on all this disarmament thing. Mr. McDonald is for it, Mr. Hoover is for it. But it takes years to get ships sunk, or even plans scrapped. Now there is one thing about England's Government where they are more Democratic than ours. When a Guy don't suit there is no waiting five years to oust him. The minute the majority are at outs with the reigning Premier, why they can call for a new election and he is out, maby before he had time to learn where the ice box is at 10 Downing Street.

Then, even over here you know what three years will bring in the way of a change of opinion. Well what I am getting at by the time all these marvelous plans are about to be in effect why neither of these men might be in power. Most of this is their ideas. But who knows what the next men's ideas are that might follow them in these two high offices? You know it is not just everybody in the World, (and that may include quite a few smart people) that think the best way to never have any more wars is not to have any Navy.

It's going to be an awful good tax saving thing, the same as economy in any other line of business would be good tax saving. But they are conscientious men, and let us hope that they are followed by men of the same high type. You can't get nothing without trying, and if no effort is made toward peace why we can't expect any.

Well now what else has rolled over the old Press since last we communed? Why nothing but the Tarriff.

1929

Our old friend Grundy.² (And by the way I get more communications wanting to know who this Grundy is that I am always boosting to the skies.) Well Mr. Grundy is kinder the Federal Reserve of the Standpat Republican Party. When the boys need a little more nourishment in the way of some financial fodder for the forthcoming election, why Mr. Grundy is the Lad that OK's the shipment out to the needy Senator, and his benefations have been known to reach as far down as a mere Representative in Congress.

"Yes, I know, but where does Grundy get all this?" Children, What was the first thing you learned about Politics at school? It was that Politics was business wasent it? That is that it was advertised under the heading of idealism, but that it was carried out under the heading of business, and the bigger the business the bigger the politician.

Now the great State of Pennsylvania houses many manafacturing concerns, don't it? It's a rich State. Well everybody in Pennsylvania that makes anything have joined in a Giant Society. That is, everybody but the Farmer. He is not a member. He is just a campaign slogan.

He is just the fellow that they are "Going to help" every four years. He would join a Society, but he don't make enough to get in. But everybody that makes things, I don't mean that makes things you need, I mean the ones that makes things that you buy. Well they got a Society and they got to have a President. Well, right there is where Mr. Grundy comes in. He not only comes in, but those Republicans have the door open if he even looks like he is going to pass within a block.

I knew you was going to ask, "What is Grundy doing in Washington?" That is where his offices are.

"What's his offices doing in Washington when he is President of the Manafactures Association of Pennsylvania? Why ain't they in Pennsylvania?"

Say, Grundy has more offices in Washington than Hoover. Hoover only tells the Senate what they should do. Grundy tells 'em what they will do.

"Well, what's the answer? What's it all about?"'

It's all about the tarriff. Grundy has a list of everything made in Pennsylvania. (That is all that are paid up.) He sends that list to the Senate, and then the tarriff is changed.

"What do you mean it's changed?"
Why, it's raised.
"Why is it raised?"
Because Grundy sent the list.

"Can't they raise anything that's not on Grundy's list?"
They can but they never have.
"Well why don't Grundy run for the Senate?"
Would you get out of the driver's seat to go down and pull with the other horses?
"But I see by the papers here lately that they are to investigate Guys like Grundy."
There is no Guys like Grundy, he is in a class by himself.
"Well they are going to investigate 'em anyway."
Yes investigate them, but not Grundy.
"Well who will they investigate then?"
Why Guys that Grundy puts on his list for 'em to investigate.
"Well this Grundy must be quite a fellow then."
Quite a fellow. There in only one man stronger.
"Who is that?"
Mussolini.

357 ALL THIS FUNNY POLITICS

Well all I know is just what I read in the reading papers. Ramsey left us and everybody predicted that there wouldent be any war at least till after the next disarmament Conference.[1] He made a mighty fine human speech over the radio before he left and it made him lots of more friends if that was possible.

Then come the World Series and that knocked the tarriff, the Investigations, Shearer and Aimee's argument with a Precher right off the front page while the series was on.[2] Even Mr Hoover got all warmed up and bothered over it and went clear to Philadelphia to see the last game. If he had just let 'em know they would have brought one of the games to Washington. He had been the first person to make a special trip to Philadelphia since the time those two people took in the Susqui-Centenial there. They put him on a fine game and plenty of excitement. Connie Mack arranged it so his boys wouldent make any home runs till along about the last inning.[3] He even had 'em wait til one man was out. Then he told the Boys, "Go ahead and get back to normal." So they all started hitting. Chicago played a fine set of games and if they could have played indoors where the sun dident shine they would have perhaps won. But Connie Mack had it arranged so they would start the game at a time when the sun was right in the center fielder's eyes at that particular time of day, and he made all his Boys knock them to Hack.[4] If they had knocked 'em to anybody else they would have got caught. But Hack lost them in the sun, and it really was not his fault at all. But it was a fine series and The National League really come back into its own. They dident win but they got one game that is more than they have done in the last two previous series. Hoover going there was a big boost for the whole game. He took his whole Cabinet with him, so in case the tarriff come up and they had to vote on it why he would have them there with him. None of them were busy so there was no time lost by them going away. Lots of them had never been off the train in Philadelphia before and a good time was had by all.

The Senate wanted to go but they wasent invited gratis, so they started an investigation instead to see what was the matter with a Man like Connie Mack that he stopped the World series so quick and not grab off that dough.

But after it was all over and I read about the Cubs coming home I don't know when I ever felt so sorry for anyone in my life. You know when all is said and done I doubt if any club ever had so many lucky breaks come their way at the very right moment as the Athletics did. And there really wasent that much difference in the two teams.

But let's see what the Government is doing, Baseball only operates in the summer but Senatorial Investigations go on all the time. The one about finding out who is a Lobbyist and who is a Bootlegger in Washington has started now and that will be the best one of the bunch. There is no law against Lobbying any more than there is against a man going out and trying to get votes for the Senators when they are running for office. It is simply a case of trying to convince someone that this or that is the best thing under the circumstances. But Washington is going to investigate them and see how they make this living. For it looks like a terrible easy graft, and during the investigations will be brought out perhaps the finer points of Lobbying. Then of course Shearer will be led out again. They dropped that while Mr McDonald was here so Shearer could go to some of the dinners. But they will put on a second edition of that investigation now, and you will hear some good ones from him when he starts in questioning those Senators. There will be no chance to get any legislation through Congress as all the Senators are on investigation Committees and they will never have a Quorum.

Mr Hoover went out and made a fine address at the Ford Factory for Mr Edison.[5] That's about the first running around he has done. He even brought his fishing right near home.

That was a great affair they had for Mr Edison. He had no idea when he invented that all day Lantern that it would lead to so much Glory and confusion. He just invented it because he needed it to work

Weekly Articles

by. It was appropraite that Mr Ford should give him that great celebration for it was through Mr Edison's electricity that Mr Ford was able to get those things started without breaking an arm.[6] Then they have always been great friends. They go out camping and fishing together. They lost one of their old Cronies, Mr Burroughs, the Naturalist.[7] He went along to show 'em where to camp and tell them what the names of the trees were, and all the Birds. Then Mr Firestone would be along and he would show 'em what tires to put on.[8] Mr Harding used to go with 'em. They never could get Mr Coolidge out with 'em. He kinder watched his company. He was afraid to be seen with so much wealth, it might lead to a bad impression by the voters. They might think he was listening to a Lobby.

But it was a wonderful thing for us to have lived in this age and have seen in person this great man Edison. For he will get bigger and bigger as the years go by and our Grandchildren won't believe it when we say "Why yes your old Granddad saw him right on the street, passed right by him. Think of that Lad, saw him with my own eyes."

358   THAT DEARBORN PARTY

Well all I know is just what I read in the papers or what I see as I prowl from hither to yon. Well the first of last week I had the finest and most remembered day I ever had in my life. It was what the advertising man would call a Red Letter day. I had received by Air Mail a lovely engraved invitation from Mr Henry Ford and his Son Edsel to be present at Dearborn at the celebration of Mr Edison's.[1] So grab the old Plane and reserve passage and away I went.

Got there on Monday morning the day of the big doings. Was first taken to the hotel and then the Guests were sent to Dearbon. Mr Hoover come in by train from Washington and he and his party was transferred to an old time wood burner Engine train on the Port Huron railroad. It was the same one Mr Edison used to work on. He was what was called a News Butch, that is he sold everything, papers candy and all that.

Well he even as a young boy was of an inventive mind. He use to keep his junk in the baggage car, and along with it a lot of chemicals and tools that he would experiment with. Well one of the first things he invented was setting a train on fire from the baggage car while it was in motion. It had never been done before, and they dident leave him on the job long enough to ever repeat the experiment. The experiment worked and he left.

1929

Well Sir do you know this man Ford has reproduced that whole thing, the train, the little depot where he was fired. They put on everything but the fire and would have done that if Mr Edison had just had some matches. Mr. Hoover and Party were on the train. Mr Edison was in his old role of Candy butch. He went through the cars crying his wares. The President took a peach, charged it to the Republican Pennsylvania tarriff Commission. Charley Schwab bought a joke book from him, for which all audiences will be grateful.² Then when they got off at the depot there was a whole town of that early period reproduced.

There was dozens of Cabs with horses hitched to 'em, and they hauled everyone all around from one place to another. It was drizzling a little light rain all day. But no one noticed that.

The President and Mrs. Hoover had to be down in the City of Detroit, as they were to be paraded through the streets of the city, and they insisted on it being in an open car. Mrs Hoover was smiling through the rain dripping off an unpowdered nose. They risked Phneumonia but they saved Michigan to the Republican Party. It made a big hit with everybody, them going through with the program as they did regardless of the weather.

Mr Edison of course was taken back to Mr Ford's home to rest for the night festivities. Then the riff raff of Guests were left pretty well to themselves to just wander from one place to another in this old remade village. In this class was prowling around in the rain and all having lunch in an old time Inn, was such undesirables as Young John D. Rockefeller, the President of every railroad from the Cotton Belt down, Mr Otto Kahn, who retails Art at so much a Box at the Metropolitan Opera.³ He was the only one with Spats on. Judge Lindsey was advocating to a bunch of Automobile Manufacturers, Chrysler, Irskine, Fishers, and Briggs.⁴

They had an old Store with it all stocked up with the very things that they used to have in 'em, cracker boxes, Cheese for the local rats, rolls of Calico, boxes of old brogan boots.

I saw an old fellow looking it all over mighty minutley and I went up and got in conversation with him, and who do you think it was? It was Julius Rosenwald, the great Philantrophist and head of Sears Roebuck, the man who sells more stuff in a year than any man living.⁵ Here he was looking over this old store, and maby you think he wasent getting a kick out of it. We bummed around a good deal together there the rest of the day. I was trying to see if I couldent nick him for an appropriation for "Starving Actors whose voice dident register well." He was interested in my charity, but finally decided that they should be radio announcers.

Weekly Articles

But it was just a joy to see just hundreds of the men that we read about all the time in every big activity going on, well here they were just bumming around, everything they looked at it must have brought back old memories, for after all pretty near all of our big men are country or small town boys. There was the old school house where Henry Ford had gone to school, with the original benches, an old mill, an old church. In bringing the old Labratory of Mr Edison's from Milo Park, New Jersey, he had even brought a dozen or more car loads of Jersey clay. This old red sticky stuff, and had it around the front of the labratory and Mr Edison noticed it too. It was I think one of the greatest thoughts and the most perfectly carried out things ever attempted in America. All these great Financiers and men of big affairs just felt like kids at a County fair.

It was marvelous, and the dinner that night in an exact reproduction of the old Liberty Hall in Philadelphia. There was real splendor and old time magnificience. I heard all of them say that it was the greatest banquet in every respect that was ever held. And the old Gentleman made a fine little talk, the longest perhaps in his entire career. I was sitting near his son and he told me that his Father had been worried about it for weeks and had even practiced it, but could never quite get through it. He did that night, but he was overcome with emotion at the end, which made it all the more wonderful. Mr Ford was persuaded on to rise, but he wouldent speak, but he certainly got a rousing hand. The only sad note of the day was that one of Edsel Ford's children was very sick with diptheria that day and he or his charming wife was not present at all.

But it was a proud day for Henry Ford, and it was a great treat to everybody else. Just think we all got something worth while to hand down to our grandchildren. It will be like men living today who saw Lincoln. "Say you kids asking about that wonderful man, Edison? Why I lived when he did. I have seen him pass by with my own eyes! Say you little Brats, your old Granddad lived when there was Real men."

359   BEATING WALL STREET

Well all I know is just what I read in the Papers. Awful lot of news percolating here and there. This Stock Market thing has spoiled more appetites lately than bad cooking. Some fellow named Roger Babson a month or two ago predicted that lightning was going to

1929

strike the margins, and because it dident do it the day his warning come out, why they all give Roger the laugh and said "This Country is too big and prosperous to have any let up in prices."[1] Well it looked like Roger had pulled a bone and he had to stand for a lot of kidding. But as the old saying, "He who laughs along toward the finish, generally carries more real merriment in his tones." So as things have turned out why it looks like the whole market has just tried to help Roger Babson make a sucker out of his detractors.

Now that Stock Market is all a puzzle to me. I never did mess with it. One time in New York last year when everybody was just raking in money with a shovel, so they all told me, well Eddie Cantor the Actor of Jewish contraction, I had known and been a friend of Eddie's for many years and I was hearing that Eddie was piling up a fortune that Rockefeller couldent vault over.[2] So I hold out some dough on Mrs. Rogers out of the weekly stipend and I go over to the New Amsterdam Theatre one night and call on Eddie.

When I was admitted I felt like a Racketeer that had finally gained admission to J. P. Morgan's sanctum.[3] Eddie thought I had come to persuade him to play a benefit for some improvedent christians, (as I had often done with him in the past). But when I quietly whispered to him that I wanted him to make a few dollars without telling jokes for them, (or what went for jokes) I told him about the amount that I had been able by judicious scheming to nick from Mrs. Rogers. Knowing her he wouldent believe that I had been so shrewd, and immediately he said "you don't need me, just keep this thing up and grab it off from her. What does it matter whether you make it from Wall Street or her?"

But I told him I wanted to get in on this skinning of Wall Street. Everybody was doing it and I wanted to be in at the killing. I dident have anything particular against Wall Street, but knowing the geographical and physical attributes of the Street, I knew that it was crooked. (You can stand at the head of it, and you can only see to the bend. It just won't let you see all of it at once as short as it is). I just said to myself I would like to be with the bunch that has the credit of straightening this Alley out.

Well Eddie had just that day made fifty thousand according to closing odds on the last commodity. I says show me the fifty. He then explained to me that he hadent the money, that that's what he could have made if he had sold. But he hadent sold, as tomorrow he should make at least another fifty, or even if he only made 49 why it would help pay for burnt cork. Then he explained the stock market to me in a mighty sensible way, he told me who had told him this, but anyhow it had repeated well, so I will repeat it to you.

Weekly Articles

The Stock market is just like a sieve, (one of those pans with holes in it). Everything and everybody is put into it, and it is shaken, and through the holes go all the small stuff. Then they load it up again and maby hold it still for awhile and then they start shaking again and through the little investors go. They pick themselves up, turn bootlegger or do something to get some more money, and then they crawl back in the hopper and away they go again.

Well that made a mighty pretty Scenario. But I said, that's only the Boobs that go through the hole. I am going to grab a root and hang on with the big boys. He dident much want to take my money, knowing how hard I had worked for it, both from the Theatre Manager and Mrs. Rogers.

But I went on telling him I was 49 years and had never in my life made a single dollar without having to chew some gum to get it. So he says, "Well I will buy you some of my bank stock. It's selling mighty high and with this little dab you got here you won't get much of it, but it's bound to go up, for banks make it whether the market goes up or down. Even if it stand still they are getting their interest while it's making up its mind what to do."

So he said I will get you some of this. You don't need to pay me for it, just let it go. Put it away and forget about it. Then some day when you want you can send me a check for it.

Well I shook hands and told him that I had always known and said that he was the greatest Comedian on the stage but now I knew that he was best financier we had in our profession. Well I went back to my own dressing room at my Theatre and I never was as funny in my life as I was that night. I had Wall Street by the tail and a down hill run.

I stayed up the next night till the papers come out to see what OUR Bank had closed at, and after reading it stayed up the rest of the night wondering if Eddie could possibly be wrong. Well one little drop brought on another, till one day I received a letter from Eddie's Broker saying my check would come in mighty handy and for me please remit undernamed amount.

Well in the meantime I had used most of the money celebrating the fact that I had bought the stock. In fact I had really spent most of it in advertising Eddie and his humatarian qualities. Each night I begin to get unfunnier and unfunnier. This strain of being "In the Market" was telling on me. Eddie could laugh at a loss and still remain Komical. But when there was minus sign before my lone stock, I just was not unctious. I dident want to tell Eddie. But finally I sent for his personal Aide De Camp and told him that on the morrow when the market opened, among those desiring to dispose, I would be among those present. I got out with a very moderate loss. Next day it went up big. But the whole thing is no place for a weak hearted Comedian, and from now on when Eddie wants to help me, he can just give me some of his old jokes.

360 POLITICAL RODEOS

Well all I know is just what I read in the Advertisements. Been a lot of Scandal in the last few weeks including elections all over the Country. New York's of course attracted quite a little attention, but was no surprise to anyone when Walker won by half a million.[1] One big fight was in Virginia. The Civil War was the issue there and the Confederates won, Bishop Cannon turned his pulpit into a rostrum and wound up with the minority.[2]

Kentucky threw out a mess of Republicans that had accidentally got in during the boom days. Another Dinner Scandal in Washington. When Mr Hoover was pouring tea for Mr. and Mrs. Dawes why it seems that the invitation of Senator Hiram Johnston was misplaced, perhaps purposely, and instead of Hi getting into the White House why he had to eat with some Democrats in the Capitol Restaurant.[3] Well that brought up a big scene out here in California. Our Papers played it up very big. For they are both home town boys, both members of the same club, (Republican).

These Lads seem to have had different views for some time past. When they come west looking for a President why naturally Mr Johnston couldent see why they had to pass his house on the search. He was in Washington and wouldent have to move his things far, and it looked like a good move all around. But the Republicans always claimed that while Hiram was carrying a Republican labor card, he was at heart for the open shop, and they claimed that everything they started he would not only disapprove of, but he would even go so far as to lend his support to the Democrats. Well that's one thing the Republicans won't forgive. They can excuse you being against them, for in their heart they know that you are right, but when you go and throw that support to the Democrats, that's the last straw.

So along comes Mr Hoover and naturally he had some ideas of what he would like to have done in the way of Civic good for the entire Commonwealth. But every time he would suggest something why Hiram was there with the veto. Mr Hoover would suggest fishing in Virginia, and Mr Johnston would suggest that he fish in California. Mr Hoover suggested relief for the Farmer, Mr Johnston suggested Relief was what put the Farmer where he is now.

Then the Tarriff come up and for awhile they dident know how to disagree on it for neither knew how the other stood on it. But it finally worked out satjsfactory to each of them, they disagreed. I can understand this invitation being lost in the mail.

Now that brings us down to Senator Brookhardt who a week or so ago related the ingredients of a wild party he attended.[4] He said Liquor just flowed like Oratory in the Senate. Said he sat next to Otto Kahn which sounded to me like a boast.[5] For it was certainly a social concession on Otto's part. He told the names of the Senators that were there, but couldent remember what they drank. When you can't remember what people drink, you must be drinking some of it yourself. For that's what it does is destroy your memory.

He said Mr Kahn asked him about some Railway legislation and told him that it wouldent work. And he told him he knew that, that's why they passed it. Well anyhow the other Senators could have choked him for telling all this, for it just made it that much harder for them to get into another Dining room.

Senators' lives are getting tough enough as it is without losing out on any invitations that might crop up.

Look at Senator Bingham; they said he had disgraced the dignity of the Senate, and everybody couldent understand what he could possibly have done, so he was reprimanded.[6] The Democrats wanted to have him thrown out, and his place taken by a dignified Democrat. But they couldent get him to resign. It's awful hard to get a Senator to quit. In fact, Mr Bingham wouldent even appoligise to 'em. I always like this fellow Bingham. He is strong for aviation. And I like Hiram, he has done some mighty worthy things, and anyhow it takes years in this country to tell whether anybodys is right or wrong. It's kinder of a case of just how far ahead you can see.

The fellow that can only see a week ahead is always the popular fellow, for he looking with the crowd. But the one that can see years ahead. He has a telescope but he can't make anybody believe he has it.

But anyhow its been a great fall in legislative matters. Nothing has been accomplished, making it a typical session. But there has been a lot of laughs, plenty of what looked like excitement at the time. But which in the general results dident amount to anything.

They had Grundy up for awhile and he gave them the lecture of their lives on, "Protection."[7] They was going to try and prove he was a Lobbyist. Well he not only admitted it, but seemed proud of it. Well that dident leave them a thing to do, but just look amazed. Said he had been a Lobbyist for fifty years and never lost a Lob. He raises a million dollars every Presidential year for the good of the Party, and is down there to collect dividends.

Don't want a thing but protection for everything that is made in Pennsylvania. Said the only thing that Idaho, Arkansaw, and Montana raised was Senators and they made too much noise. He said every State should make a noise according to what it manafactured, and that as Pennsylvania manafactured more things, it was his night to howl and he was there to Howl. The Senators couldent think of any answer to that so they adjourned the investigation. And they cuss the day they ever called Grundy.

361   WALL STREET HAS A HEADACHE THAT'S CATCHING

Well all I know is just what I read in the morning Papers. The evening ones don't have much unless they grab off a late murder that dident make the early editions, or a delayed divorce. So it's with the old Ham and — that we get our early scandal. This Stock Market thing has kinder had the front page groggy here lately. They thought we had the thing just about as low as they could possibly get it but here lately it's been getting still worse.

Course all that's great for the rich, for they just sit around and wait till somebody goes broke and then buy in. But the old Margin Boy has got a mustard plaster on him all over. He can't take any good stocks of his to protect the weak ones, for there is no good ones, the good ones are the ones that are going down. England says our Market is all cockeyed and that it will eventually get so stabalized that if a thing pays around five percent it will be worth right around 100, and that if it pays ten percent it will be worth 200. That is everything will be based on just a fair percentage of what it earns. Our Folks been buying without even having any idea what they were earning. We been buying just alphabetically, the nearer A you could get the more it seemed to be worth.

If the President of the concern was a good after dinner Speaker and made a good appearance, why his stock would go up to two or three hundred. Nothing determined the worth of the stock but the fact that it was going up, and it hadent reached a thousand yet and there was no reason why it shouldent keep going till it did.

Oh it was a great game while it lasted. All you had to do was to buy and wait till the next morning and just pick up the paper and see how much you made, in print. But all that has changed, and I think it will be good for everything else. For after all everybody just can't live on gambling. Somebody has to do some work.

So I hope Oklahoma farm lands come back. They been about the cheapest thing there is, and our little neck of the Country has been mighty bad hit, but maby we are in for a change. This session of Congress was rounded up to try and do something for the Farmer but they went into a private fight of their own, and nobody has got a thing out of them. The Republicans hatched 'em up a high Tarriff bill and all they thought they had to do was to pass it, which looked like about the easiest thing there was too it, and of course they knew the Democrats would be against them. But they dident pay any attention to a little opposition like that.

But all at once they got to looking around and there was the renegade Republicans cavorting with the Democrats. It was the first time they had ever knew enough to go in together and beat the Republicans. Well the fact of the matter was that they dident figure victory was worth that much. They wanted to win but they just dident want to stoop so low to conquer. But they buried their pride and now when the Bill comes up why they will knock it right in the head. You see this session of Congress was called primarily to help the Farmer, and then when they all got to Washington why they learned from the Manafacturing State Senators that Industry was in a terrible shape, and that would they mind giving it a helping hand as they went along.

Well that looked reasonable. They dident go to the trouble of looking at Industry's earnings, they just took the Senator's word for it. Then they got to making up the schedule of the raises, and when they got it all done, why it was the old Farmer that they had forgotten, and they had raised the price of the things that he had to buy so high, that even if he had raised anything he could never have had enough to buy anything. Grundy got in among the Boys and handed 'em a list of raises that a Poker player couldent have stood.[1] You see where the whole mistake was, was in Mr. Hoover ever allowing them to drag in every known article under the face of the sun. It was originally just to be a Farm relife session. And that's where he should have stood his ground and held 'em to that alone. Course nobody hates it I imagine worse than he does. For he sure is sick and tired of them by now, and then to make it worse they are to go from this session right on into the next one, without even giving him or the public a vacation.

This Lobby investigation has kinder helped to liven up things. They have found out that there is some Lobbyists there and now all they got to find out is "What to do with 'em." They will be finding

1929

out there is some Policemen in Washington the next thing, or that there is some crooked streets that nobody knows where they go only around circles. But they have had a lot of fun investigating them.

A Senator is never as happy as when he is asking somebody a question without the party being able to ask him one back. But I guess these Lobby Guys had got to going pretty strong and if this will kinder scare 'em out why the whole thing will have done some good. Grundy bragged on being one and said he was a good one and glad of it.

Been reading some mighty nice things that Miss McDonald said about us on her return home.[2] Well we are doing the same over here about her. I don't know when anyone has visited that come in for any more whole hearted praise.

Thanksgiving is right on us and we got to do some thinking over just what we got to give thanks for. Course we are glad to be living. But we got to have a better excuse for it than that. I guess we will all just give thanks we had it in land instead of Wall Street, even if we can't sell the land and have to pay taxes on it, we can at least walk out on it. Still I got some you can't unless you have divine power. But take it all around it looks like a pretty good thanksgiving.

362 WHOOPING IT UP FOR WALL STREET

Well all I know is just what I read in the papers. And I just haven't had much time to read the papers lately on account as you know, that I have been trying my best to help Mr. Hoover and Wall Street "Restore Confidence." You take confidence, it's one of the hardest things in the World to get restored once it gets out of bounds.

I have helped restore a lot of things in my time, such as cattle back to the home range. Herded Folly Girls toward the stage door near show time. Helped to revive interest in National Political Conventions. Even assisted the Democrats in every forlorn pilgrimage, and a host of other worthy charities. But I tell you this "Restoring Confidence" is the toughest drive I ever assisted in. When I took up the work two or three weeks ago, confidence was at a mighty low ebb, that is so all the Papers and speakers was saying.

Wall Street had gone into one tail spin after another. You would pick up a paper in the morning and read the stock report and you wouldent think there was that many "Minus" signs in the world. Well the effect of it was just like going to Monte Carlo, and hearing that everybody was betting on the Black, and the red had been coming up continually for two days. That would just simply demoralize southern France and the whole Riviera. Well that's what this Market was doing here. It was just taking all the joy out of gambling. If it kept on like that it would discourage Gambling, and that of course would be bad for the country. (That's what they said.)

Course there was a lot of us dumb ones that couldent understand it. We said, "Well if somebody lost money there, why somebody else must have made it. You can't just lose money to nobody, unless you drop it somewhere and nobody ever finds it." Then they said a good deal of the money was "Lost on paper." That is it was figures but it wasent real money. Well I had done that, I could remember every contract I would get for a season's work on the stage or screen, my wife and I would sit down and figure out what all we would have by the end of that season. Well at the end of the season we had the figures but we couldent find the money. So Wall Street Men had nothing on us. In fact, I don't think it had anything on anybody, for we all can take a piece of paper and if you give us enough pencil we can figure ourselves out a pretty neat little fortune in no time, so when I heard that most of the money had been lost on "paper profits," why I felt right at home with them.

But then everybody said it would have a demoralizing effect on the country for so many to have their paper profits all rubbed out at once. That it would have the effect of making people more careful with their money, and thereby make it bad for speculation. That if people dident trade in stocks why Wall Street couldent exist.

So I says what can we do for 'em so they will keep on existing? "Why restore confidence." And that's what I been doing for weeks, writing and talking. Course I haven't been buying anything myself. I wanted to give all the other folks a chance to have confidence first. There is none of the greedy Pig about me. This confidence was for sale and I wanted them to have the very first chance of buying it.

Course I never could understand what the price of the stock had to do with keeping the company working and turning out their product. For instance if "Consolidated Corn Salve" stock had all been sold, and the Company had that money it had brought in and was operating on that, what difference did it make to them if the stock was selling at a thousand bucks, or if people was using the stock to kindle their fire with? Their business was still to keep after those corns. In other words they should be watching corns instead of the market. If the shares had sold for 564 one day and $1.80 the next, what had happened during the night to the afflicted toes of the country? Well I couldent get that.

Course they explained it off someway. Said, "Trading was good for the country, and kept things a-circulating." So I finally went over to their side. I really did it for vanity, for I could see all the big men over there, and I felt flattered when I saw that I was one to join in this great work of getting people back to contributing to Wall Street agin. Course there is a lot of them that is going to take me time to get back. They not only lost confidence but they lost money, some of them all of their money. So we will have to wait till they get some money in some other business, perhaps in some business in which they really have no confidence. Then they will be able to get back into the market not only with new confidence but new money. That's going to take time in some cases.

But I am telling them that the Country as a whole is "Sound," and that all those who's heads are solid are bound to get back into the market again. I tell 'em that this Country is bigger than Wall Street, and if they don't believe it, I show 'em the map.

Mr. Hoover called all the Railroad men in and they decided to do all they could to keep people from riding on Busses. Then he had all Bankers there, and they announced what their annual Jip would be for coming year. They agreed to be more careful in their loans, and see that the borrower dident buy a farm with it, as Agriculture was so uncertain. Try and get them to invest in some business where he could read the paper in the morning and see what he had. But it's a great work, and I am just crazy about it. Viva confidence.

363 DOWN IN THE BOTTOM OF THE SEA

Well all I know is just what I read in the Movie weeklies, or what I happen to run into as I prowl hither and thither. Was you ever down below sea level? Well I am like you, I thought the only way you could get down there was to go to Australia or some place on the under side of the ocean, or to go down below the level of the ocean in a submarine. But here a week or so ago, I spent two or three days prowling around down below sea level, riding in cars eating and sleeping in nice beautiful homes and all the time the ocean could have come right in and covered us up.

It's in California. Everything is in California, all the great sights of nature, and along with all these wonders we have out here is the World's greatest collection of freak humans on earth. We maintain more freak religions and cults than all the rest of the world combined. Just start anything out here and if it's cuckoo enough you will get followers. But its not of the alleged humans I am talking to you about now, it's of the freaks of nature. It's down in what's called the Imperial valley. Some old Preacher years ago named it. It was up to then called the Colorado desert. But he could see no reason why it shouldent be called the Imperial Valley. Well it was about like all desert valleys except you had to climb up hill to be able to see the Ocean. If there had been an ocean there. There is a good big lake down there and it's all salt, for years ago the ocean used to be in there. But the real estate men and the Chamber of Commerce passed a resolution and either it or them had to get out. Well the Lord saw that while he might be able to handle nature, He couldent do anything with California Real estate men. It was a new form of pestilence that he had never encountered before. So he just washed his hands of the whole thing, picked up his ocean and took it down into Mexico, where they appreciated God's original handiwork, and the Preachers were not selling Real Estate. Well that just left 'em the place where an ocean had been.

Did you ever look at a place where an ocean has just been? I doubt if you ever did. For very few communities do things on that big a scale like they do out here in California. It takes real enterprise to move an ocean. They left a little of it there, to show that they were not as big a liars as the rest of country generally suppose them to be. This Salton sea is evidence. The Salton Sea is something like the Dead sea only·this one is not mentioned in the Bible, (except in the California revised de luxe edition).

The Dead sea got a lot of publicity in those days on account of its odd name. Everybody wanted to see it, and wondered what it died of, and how long would it stay dead. It's the sea that the then Kaiser Wilhelm went down on, on one of his big new Battleships and of course it couldent get up to the dock.[1] So instead of going ashore in a small boat or lighter, he just stepped out on the ocean, and started to walk ashore. He had heard that this feat had been performed years ago by another great man, (if any of you haven't read the original book, there is no use of my continuing with this narrative). Well it seems that the Kaiser had kinder overestimated his aquatic feats, and after they had fished him out, to show that while he had perhaps suffered humiliation, and perhaps contracted pheunomonia, he still retained his egotism, for he immediately remarked, "I don't believe the other fellow did it either." That was on the Dead sea, but as time goes along and as California historians get going good our Grandchildren will perhaps be taught that both events took place just eight miles west of Calapatria, Imperial Valley, California, in Ed Vail's horse pasture.[2]

This town of Calapatria was named by taking a part of two

famous historical names. The Cal, comes from Calvin Coolidge—first name of Calvin, and the Patria, comes from the last part of Cleo-Patria, a woman of doubtful reputation, who I am sorry to see Mr Coolidge get mixed up with.

The next town they establish down there will be called "Hershe." It's not a Chocolate, it will be a town. The Her, will of course come from Herbert, (Mr Hoover's given name), and the She, will be from Sheba's, one of the best advertised Queens. Her, and She, Hershe, after Herbert and her Majesty. But you want to go down there, where there used to be whales swimming around scratching their stomach on the bottom, why now there is Real Estate offices, Cafetaria's, and Department store Druggists.

And Fertile, say you ain't seen nothing yet. They can raise anything. It's another Rogers County Oklahoma as far as productivity is concerned. That County and the valley of the E-U-F-R-P-H-A. I can't spell it, I will just make it the Nile, that's easy to spell and maby just as fertile as that hard one. Cotton is one of the big things, half the linen goods we buy is made from Imperial valley cotton. And their Grapefruit is every day squirting on wealthier and more immoral families all over our land. Of course it gets hot there in the summer. But only for those who are able to get out. For those who can't afford to leave "why its really not bad at all. It's hot but there is no humidity, so we really don't mind it at all, and won't till we get enough to get out." But when the Chamber of Commerces in these other Towns have seen what can be done with the bottom of an Ocean, why I can see 'em moving them all over the country. But you got to hand it to California for starting it. But if you have never been below sea level you just ought to go down and see what all they have, luncheon clubs, and mortgages, and everything even below sea level.

364 HAIL TO ROCKNE

Well all I know is just what I read in the papers. We ought to start going right along now from the Comedy standpoint, for Congress is back in its regular stride. This is the real session, the last one was one that was called to just reherse for this one, so this is the Big Show.

Mr. Hoover delivered his message to 'em about ten days ago, he is supposed to tell 'em the shape the Country is in. Well as Countrys go nowadays, we wasent so bad off. Course we wasent so well off either. But we was better than most of 'em. We are in the first division as far as "Condition" is.

He dident deliver the message himself, he sent it. You know some of our late Presidents delivered them themselvs. They wouldent trust the Senate or Congress to read 'em right. He picked a kind of an oppurtune time to deliver it. Football had just passed out in a blaze of raccoon coats and empty Gin bottles, and that left the papers nothing in the world to do but pick an all-American team, so all Mr. Hoover had to do was to sandwitch his message in between the team Coolidge picked and the one Texas Guinan picked.[1]

Football had a great year. Course the market failure cut into it at the finish. But most of the big operators had their game tickets bought before the crash, and of course while they dident get to go themselvs their Brokers had taken them as margins, and they closed 'em out and give the poor victims credit.

Notre Dame come through like the real forward passing Institution that it is.

They can talk about all your Dean Lowells, and your Elliotts, and Littles, your Glenn Franks, but I tell you Knute Rockne's name will live when the following generation can't tell you whether Nicholas Murray Butler was an Educator or a Politician.[2]

Knute just went out there on those Prairies and said to the graduating class, "Now you are going out in the World, with no aim and no purpose. Well I want to tell you that from now on you got an aim and a purpose. Henceforth and hereon you are to desecrate your lives to a cause. There is going to be no more monkey business from now on. You have a reason for living. If you are from Notre Dame, show it to me. Not now, but in the future. Every time you hear of a Football game, no matter how small, High School, Grammer school, or Kindergarten, go to it. Get in some way, no matter what the hardship. Get in there and watch 'em, and if you see a six months old baby grab a Milk Bottle and heave it across the room for a forward pass, watch that Baby. If as a growing child, its Father or Mother starts for it to punish it, and the Child shows any ability at all in dodging and keeping out of reach, through cut backs, and delayed runs, why cultivate the aquaintance of these parents and start showing them the advantages of the training table at South Bend, Ind. Tell of the wonderful advantages of travel. Show 'em where you recite your mathematics in the Stadium in New York on Saturday and the following one you do some Physics in the Rose Bowl at Pasadena. Show 'em that there is no education like it. The minute that child can write its name get it on an agreement to some day receive its forward passes from under the shade of the Studebaker factory, and make a run toward Oliver Chill Plows. That's the spirit of old South Bend.

1929

Go Ye into the Highways and Byways and deliver back to your old Alma Mater a man that can stand on his own two yard line, receive a pass intended for some Protestant, Grab that Pass, tuck it to your consecrated bosom and show those Athiest's your heels! That's what I want you to go out in the world and do. When you have done that then you can say, I am a Notre Dame man. Get out of here you Graduates, and don't you dare hang up your sheep skins in your homes till you have delivered to old Man Rockne a man that can Run, Punt, Kick, Pass, and Receive. When he has led his own State in all these then send him to your uncle Knute, and even then don't hang up your Diplomas till I have sent you an O.K. on him. I don't want College cheers, and good wishes sent in by this Alumni. I want open field runners, hard tacklers, and ten second men with mole skins on. They are to be had. If you don't get 'em somebody else will. Where was you when Cagle was booting 'em for some high school?[3] Where did the Army come in to grab him off? When we could have shown more of the world in one session than he will see in the Army if he travels as Pershing's aid.[4] How did you let him get away? West Point never saw the day it could show a prospect the advantages that old South Bend can. Where did this Abie Booth get by you?[5] Don't let the name Abie scare you. We will take any Nationality, the odder the better. We got to have some queer breeds to keep the Irish mad enough to play. Bring him in. Whether he is a Schecko, Slovakian, or an Esquimo, or Siamese Twins, just so he can get that old Pigskin down that field. He don't even have to be a Catholic. He can be Grand Kleagle of the Klan at his home Wickiup so long as he can make first down. So go send me back a Real Football Player, and then you can truly say, I AM A REAL SON of OLD NOTRE DAME."

And that's the spirit. They are all doing it, only he inspires more confidence and does it better than any other college. So viva Rockne, long may you live.

365   THE NEW PROSPERITY

Well all I know is just what I read in the papers. Football had no more than dropped out till Congress took up playing to a packed gallery.

Mr. Hoover has just about finished with his Conferences. He run out of men to confer with, that is men that had anything. He wanted men that he could get in there and make 'em sign the pledge that they would go back home and spend something, that is if they ever intended to spend anything "To Spend It Now." And it looks like it is having mighty beneficial results. It's really astonishing the amount of things that are going to be done in the way of improvements and public works. Never did things look brighter for the working man, but none of us want to work.

If Mr. Hoover could have persuaded these big men to divide up, why I believe it would have been a better idea. But if we got to work for the money we are just as bad off if there was no prosperity.

Henry Ford raised everybody's salary and tried to shame some of the others into doing the same, but some of these old Babies are pretty hard to shame. They offered to help prosperity but they dident want to hardly go to that means to do it.

But anyhow I believe it's going to be a good year. It just shows how two men can get at the same results by directly opposite methods. Here was Mr. Coolidge that never delivered a message that he dident always add a postscript, "Save your money, don't spend, be economical." And here comes Mr. Hoover with "What's the big idea of having money in the Bank? Get it out, blow it in, let's get some action around here, the more you spend the more it gives everybody else to spend thereby creating an active market for everything." And he may be right, and so was Mr. Coolidge right. You see it was only through Mr. Coolidge having them save some, that they was able to spend some during this time. So that makes a splendid arrangement, have everybody save during one administration, and spend during the next.

So it looks like Wall Street might have done everybody a favor after all. Course some of them got pretty hard hit. But they would have only spent it in going to Europe anyhow, so this will keep 'em at home and let 'em see California and Florida, and Oklahoma.

You know Politicians, when Mr. Hoover got to calling in all the business men of the Country to ask them something about the country instead of calling in Politicians, why that was such a radical move that it had never been heard of before. The idea that a President would call in Henry Ford, Owen D. Young, and John D. Jr., instead of calling Senator Jasbo, and Congressman Whiffletree had never been done before.[1] It was all new, and looked mighty radical. But this fellow Hoover is a kind of a queer Duck that way. He can take a bunch of business men and talk to 'em a little while and before he gets through they are eating out of his hand, and purring and rubbing all around his legs.

Now of course the Politician feels hurt that he wasent called in, for while he couldent have given the country any practical relief, he could have passed a bill in Congress, "Demanding Prosperity."

Then Mr. Mellon comes in with a mighty welcome suggestion.² He says we can cut the taxes $160,000,000. Course that many millions is not much when you are used to dealing in billions, but it's a good trade argument. We deal in Billions in expenditure, and millions in curtailment. But Andy is a mighty fine business man and he will do what he can for us.

Mr. Vare of Pennsylvania wanted to get his regular elected seat in the Senate a couple of weeks ago but he only got to stay in there in his seat till the roll was called on his case.³ They said he was a splendid man, but too free hearted for that organization. That spending money that much money on his election was not against the law, but set a bad precedent, and that as each of them was coming up for re-election in the near future, they dident feel that they wanted to squander that much money for their seat. As they had been in and knew what it was worth, and he hadent. That naturally he might overestimate the value of it. But he is going back to Philadelphia and at the next election he will be returned with no expenditure at all. In fact the people of Pennsylvania will no doubt make up a purse and present it to him, so then it will be amusing to see what happens.

Then to cap the climax Mr. Grundy was appointed in his place.⁴ Well taking out Vare and sending in Grundy is the same as being sorry for a Bull Fighter and taking the bull out, and replacing it with a Mountain Lion. But it's going to be a great year and we will have plenty of prosperity, and plenty of excitement. Course it may not reach everybody, the Prosperity. But the excitement will, so we will all get a 50 per cent break anyway, so what more can we ask?

366 GOLF IS GOOD—WHEN THERE'S DOUGH IN IT!

Well all know is just what I read in the papers.

We have had a lot of Golf Players out here in California with us lately, they are just playing a regular circuit of Tournaments. Why it's like show business in vaudeville. All the good ones are out here. By that I mean the Professionals, men who make a living at it, and a mighty good living too. They are about as fine a lot of fellows as you ever met, and fine bunch of sportsmen.

You know it's a kind of a funny business at that. You see these fellows don't get anything at these Tournaments unless they win it. The prizes generally run to about the first ten. Well sometimes there is sixty or eighty that start, so you can see somebody has got to have some other visable means of support than his "Putter." They pay their railroad fare and all their living expenses and if they can't find that Gopher Hole in less knocks than the other sixty why, it's just too bad.

I saw 'em all playing in the $10,000 Professional Championship, where the winner got I think $3500. Now Golf is no joke when it gets into jack like that, I have done my fair share of kidding about it, but when there is $3500 bucks strung along on the green and you have to project a little Gutapercha missle into the empty end of a sardine can twenty feet away to get your clutches onto any part of that dough, I want to tell you neighbors the humor of the game immdiately vanishes into cold prespiration.

Most of us that think it's a kind of a Nursemaid's knee game. If you laid thirty five hundred in front of us and informed us casually that all we had to do to get it to eat on, was to spank that little marble over a hill to a spot that we couldent even see, why say, with that much collateral at stake, we couldent take a whisk broom and get down on our hands and knees and even brush it off the tee. I would be nervous carrying a ball in a sack to deposit somewhere, if I knew everyone else had one going for the same hole. It's not like a lot of games where you loaf along till you get down near the finish and then turn on some speed.

You are shooting for your marmalade on every shot, on every hole, on every day, the thing lasts. There is no three strikes here. There is no yap hollering, "Never mind old Boy you got the big one left." Every move is the big one. When one is sliced out into the forest reserve nothing goes with it but your week's board bill, and fare to the next Niblick Rodeo. There is not only a story, but a meal hanging on every putt. You just get the worry of one hole out of your system and onto your handkerchief, then all you have to do is walk up to a nearby executioneer's stand, and look from there down across a beautiful valley (That is it's beautiful if you are only a spectator) and by exact geometrical survey just 543 yards and ⅞th inches is located another of these cunning little resepticles in the ground with a mouth no bigger than a Higlander's heart, and to give aid and comfort to you in distress there is a well painted sign staring you in the face with the information that if you are any kind of a Golfer whatever that four swipes at this little cascaret is all that "Should" be required. That any you take over that, you are simply deducting from your own Bank account.

Then there is a pardner, or accomplice, who plays along with you. You are not sent out for company but to annoy each other, if it wasent for watching what he was doing you could do pretty good.

Sometimes it's (what I think) is called a match play that is all you have to beat is the Guy with you. But generally it's medal play, (I think that's it) then all you have to beat is eighty professionals (that you know in your own heart are better than you) and Bobby Jones, and Par, and O. B. Keelers Typewriter.[1]

That's all you have to do to start eating regular. I want to tell you Lads it's no place for a nervous person. I got the Jimmys just looking at them, and I had nothing at stake but a Two dollar admission ticket. I knew William Fox would feed me that night whether the Guy made the putt or not, but you would have thought that I was to dine with the guy putting.[2]

Then there is wives. Yes Sir these fellows actually have wives, and they are following around. What must those poor creatures go through. They all look young. I guess there never was an old woman Golfer's wife, either the strain or starvation get 'em along before middle life. I would think one tough season of tournament would wear out about three wives on a fellow. Think of the prospects of a new dress hanging on every approach. If he goes in the bunker she goes back to last years "Cerise." Just think of having to see your husband's every mistake. Other wives know of them, but they don't see 'em happen. Not only you seeing what a fool he has made of himself by missing a ten inch putt, "But it was right before everybody. What must they think?" Then when you get through the game, the strain is not over, you have to wait till the last Guy comes in at sundown to find out what happened to you. Oh, It's a game, don't kid yourself about that. I don't mean this Junk these old fat Birds go out and call Golf, I mean it's a game when you have to do it right, or you don't eat. Anything to be done right has got to be done by people that make their living at it, like football, look what it has done since it's for the old ham and eggs.

But these Golfers are a cheerful lot, win or lose, wives and all. They laugh it off, take the husband home, dress him up and send him back for another beating on the morrow. But don't kid yourself Comrades that there is nothing to this game. Put $3500 smackers down and tell us we had one putt to win it. I think I would be so nervous I would pick up the caddy and swing him at it.

WEEKLY ARTICLES — 1930

367   ARE WE TOO SMART TO BE HAPPY?

Well all I know is just what I read in the Papers. Well let's see what we got to "Blather about" this weekend. I know you all had a fine Xmas and New Years. Those that dident have it will have it on "Roshashona and Yomkipper." But a funny thing is that our good Jewish Citizens are getting so they get as big a kick out of our Xmas as we do. It's just about a real Universal celebration.

Take it all around everything passed off pretty good. Xmas is getting kinder like one of our old time western dances. They wait till the dancing is all over and then they sorter sweep out to see how many was left laying around. We are killing off some mighty good citizens with our Xmas cheer and it has been discussed quite openly as to whether the whole thing was worth the tallow or not. Since Santa Clause has been pretty thoroughly disscredited by even our Babe's in Arms, and on account of Xmas cost to everybody, there has come up in this country quite a wide movement to just let the yuletide go by default. Of course in the old days when the Democrats were at their Zenith, and the old Reindeers and the jingling Bells were considered official, why then there was cause for all this. But now when they dress up some poor old fellow as Santa, why the kids get one peep at him, and say, "Oh look at the old Geeser trying to fool the old folks."

That's the trouble with the whole things. Kids are getting too wise. Why I was a big old chuckle-headed Nestor maby ten years old before I really even suspicioned that our old friend of the long whiskers wasent delivering into my stocking every Xmas morning the sack of candy, horn, and cap pistol. But nowadays you start asking a Baby, "What he wants Santa to bring him," and he will bounce his empty nursing bottle off your bean.

In other words we just ain't fooling nobody, and are buying a lot of stuff and giving it to folks that don't understand why you was so half-witted as to get that particular object. It was the last thing on earth they would want. In fact we ourselvs have gotten so wise that even when we are buying it for them we know it won't suit, but the etiquette of Xmas tells us that we must get them something. Of course the whole thing started in a fine spirit. It was to give happiness

1930

to the young, and another holiday to the old, so it was relished by practically everybody. It was a great day, the presents were inexpensive and received with much joy and gratification, and it was a pleasure to see the innocent little souls as they rushed down to the big room with the fireplace on Xmas morning in their bare feet, and generally the back end of their little sleepers unbuttoned and a dragging. They remembered right where they had hung their stocking, and they dived into it with great glee and anticipation. No matter why they dug out, it was great. It was just what they wanted him to bring for they had confidence in him. The merest little toy was a boon to their young lives, and what a kick it was to the parents to have them rush back up to the bedroom and show you "what Santa brought."

Then the mother would finally venture down and look into her big-top stocking to see what the sly old father had deposited during the night. Maby it was just more cotton stockings. Maby it was a new "sofa." Maby it was a new Axe for wood splitting. Maby a hot water bottle. But whatever it was it was the most acceptable thing in the world. It was just what she wanted "her man" to get her. Ah! Them was the days lads! When you could satisfy 'em with a squirrell Muff, and a box of five cent Cigars practically cinched your friendship with a Male friend for the coming year. Then they talk about Civilization. Say there ain't no civilization where there ain't no satisfaction, and that's what's the trouble now, nobody is satisfied.

In the old days where a nice crayon Picture would be just the thing as a present, why now an unborn Lamb would be unacceptable. They would wonder why you dident send Mink. And a wife, why she will sneeze at a Buick! If she don't find a new Cord auto in her short sock why you will be the cheapest husband she ever had. The whole prospectus of the thing has changed. We not only don't believe in Santa Clause, we don't believe in anything, and the Kids say they don't care anything about a "Train that will run if you wind it up." They want an Aeroplane that will Fly, and NOT wound up either.

You start talking about sending them a ten-cent horn that will blow and they want a Saxaphone that will annoy, and as for a Cap Pistol and a dozen boxes of caps, why say, he wants a machine gun. He has read about Chicago. A football? "Is it regulation?" If it's not, you are wasting your time giving it. They know better than you do. If it's a Girl Baby and you are sending some pink Sachet Powder you are all wet again. The "She" infant will rise up and demand an overnight bag, some Nose Paint, and a lip stick, and when they get it they will examine the brand.

So you just wonder sometimes if the ones who want to abolish

Xmas are not about half right. Everybody faces it with, "Oh my goodness, Xmas is coming, and how I dread it!" Then you decide "The whole thing is the bunk I will just send cards." Then about three days before Xmas you commence to get a few little boxes and remembrences from alleged friends, and you say, "I can't do this. I have to return something." Then out you go at the last minute to round up some tokens for friends who in your heart you curse for sending you anything. So the whole thing is an uproar from about Thanksgiving on.

In fact that's what they have Thanksgiving for, it's your last day of peace for that year. I sometimes think some bright merchants are not really taking advantage of their opportunities. Suppose along about a day or so after Xmas, the merchant went to each house and said, "Now this is confidential, but what did you get for Xmas that you don't want and what do you want in cash for it?" They buy it for ten cents on the dollar, they hold it over a sell at some simp the next Xmas, and you are ten percent ahead. But anyhow it's worth thinking about, this doing away with it. It would be all right if we could again believe in Santa Clause. But our smartness has defeated our own happiness.

368   WHAT'LL WE SINK NOW?

Well all I know is just what I read in the papers. Now just what has been adjitating the Natives in the public prints here lately? Course they got Xmas and New Years off their minds and are just now getting through exchanging all the presents, and so we can settle down to the serious side of life.

It's only a few days now till the opening of the big Dissarmament Conference in London. I wanted to get over there and see what the boys were doing. But it looks like these people that I am working for are actually going to demand some of my time here in Beverley Hills making faces and odd sounds for the benefit of posterity.

Can you imagine just when I wanted to get to London and see what my old friends Mr. Dawes, Mr. Morrow, Joe Robinson, Dave Reed and Admiral Hilary Jones was doing, why these Fox people got the nerve to tell me I have to go to work![1] Just for a little I would tell them something. (A little salary.)

Course I don't need to tell you that I don't think the Boys are going to do much over there. Mind you I think it's a fine thing, and it may be a step in the right direction. But the road is so long that step

1930

don't make much showing. You know they say that all the education, all the learning we have is just from reading and studying what was done in the past. Everything after all according to the learned, is what has the past taught us. Mind you that's what all the educated people say. But I am kinder personally like Henry Ford. History don't mean much to me. Never mind what some other old Geeser did in 324 B. C. It's what are you going to do in 1930. And to my mind the less you read about him the better. For no condition that existed during his time is around today. Now mind you that's only the ignorant view. We must string the educated for they are the ones that taught us what little us ignorant ones know.

So the educated say that everything is based on what has happened, in other words there is a historical precedent to everything. Now here is where we will lick 'em on their own argument in regard to the success of this conference. If there had never been a Dissarmament Conference in the past why we would look to this one with great anticipation. We would figure that they was going to really dissarm. But since 1922 in Washington at one when I had the good fortune to be, (Not as a Deligate) Secretary Hughes was pinch hitting for me there, and then there was another in 1926 at Geneva.[2] I went over on the Leviathan with our Deligation. Mr. Hugh Gibson, (who was then not an Ambassador as he is now but only Minister to Switzerland) and a very very competent man, he will be on this one too, then Admiral Jones, Admiral Andy Long, Mr. Alexander, all a fine bunch of men.[3]

Well I went down to Geneva too, to see what they would do. Well outside of paying board they dident do anything. We had sunk and sunk at the Washington Conference, till we dident have anything else left above water line, so naturally at the Geneva one as we had nothing to sink, there was no sinking. So it flopped.

It was like going to a Prohibition New Years party, there was just nothing to keep the thing going that was all. Then the next year they had another. But it did nothing. Now this is just another one. Of course mind you they will decide on some little thing such as the limiting of Battleships, (which are washed up anyhow) and they may do something about Cruisers. But there will be nothing done about Instruments of war.

If some fellow gets up and says, "What do you say about prohibiting the entire use of Chemical gasses during the next war?" Say they will throw that guy in the Thames River.

Suppose some Deligate says, "Aeroplanes are an unfair method of warfare, for they can drop things on defenseless people, what do you say we abolish them?" Well I will tell you what they would say, they would say, send that Deligate home to have his head examined.

Now you see what I mean by us profiting by what has taken place in history is that we have held all these Dissarmament Conferences and nothing has been done, so if we base the future on the past why nothing will be done. It just is not in the cards. Naturally every Nation wants to protect themselvs according to their own needs. They don't want war. Neither do they want to be left entirely defenseless, so you can't blame 'em. England and America may make a big too-doo about cutting down till it's a parity in Battleships and Cruisers. But that won't mean a thing. If you and I are evenly matched, that don't mean that we won't fight. It really means that we are more liable to fight, for each will naturally think they have the edge on the other.

But the whole thing may lead to something. It sets people thinking in the right direction. But as far as doing anything to prevent war, why it's not liable to do that. There has been war since the beginning of time, and we are no smarter than the people that have gone before us, so there is awful apt to be some more war. So let's sink something with 'em, but don't sink anything that we are liable to need.

369   TARIFF, HOOTCH AND ROYALTY

Well all I know is just what I read in the papers.

We got some pretty big things been happening in the last week or so. Our Deligation to the Conference of Peace Propaganda landed O.K. and have rehearsed and are ready to open Tuesday. We sent over a mighty fine cast. It opens with great expectations, and I do hope something good comes from it. But I kinder look for the Boys to come sneaking back here one by one exausted with really nothing done, unless we decide to do the sinking.

Prohibition has been the small table talk here lately. People are getting so they get pretty excited in Boston and New York when there is a run-in between the Coast Guard and Gentlemen of our fastest growing industry. You shoot a Bootlegger now and they take it up in Congress.

You shoot the Town's leading Citizen in an attempted Holdup and even the local papers won't make much of a to-do over it. That shooting up along the New England Coast, I don't know what they thought the Coast Guard Boys should have done when the boat wouldent halt. Just let 'em go and lay it to unruliness I guess. The Commission that Mr. Hoover has out now "to see if there is any drinking going on, and if so why?" why it's turning in its report now. Well when that comes in the Senate will break out again. The same old argument will start again. How much time in the way of salary do you suppose has been wasted in Congress just on argueing on Prohibition? And you just as well argue on the tarriff. Nothing is ever going to be done about either one.

Well we are going through the siege now of looking at the pictures of the Italian wedding.[1] Say she is a pretty stern-faced young Lady ain't she? Boy I would hate to beat her to a parking space. She looks like she took that Queen stuff serious.

Did you know that her Mother was Montenegroian? No it's not as bad as it sounds. She came from a country called Monte-Negro. I looked all this up when I was over in Italy prowling around writing about them. Her father was the king there and he had a pack of daughters, and either he or someone was a mighty fine matchmaker, for he married every one of them off to somebody who would be King some day. He had 'em scattered all around those little "Balking" Nations. It got so you couldent hardly meet a Queen over there that wasent the daughter of the King of Monte-Negro. Course this one to Italy really landed what would be called the Piece-De-Resistance of the bunch of them. Course lots of these others dident stay Queens long, but that wasent their Father's fault, he couldent be responsible for knowing that there was going to be a war and send pretty near all the Kings back to the bench. He was the King of a pretty poor little Country, and one time somebody asked him "what was the principal product of his Country?" He said, "Raising Queens."

They were all very pretty and very domesticated. You know there is a great deal of missunderstanding in regard to the standing of the Royal Family of Italy, on account of the great publicity and prominence of Mussolini. It is most generally supposed that the King there is nothing. Well nothing could be further from the fact. That's one of the smart things that Mussolini has done is to always show great reverence and respect for the King and his family and their position, and say if you think the King there is not popular with the people you are away off, he is very popular, and don't think Mussolini don't know that, and he always gives the King preference (unless he is really going to do something important.)[2] But no, really he does get on great with him.

They claim at any big public function in most parts of Italy that the King will get a much bigger public reception than the "Duce."[3] He is a very small fellow, and he has always been very self-conscious about it. He only likes to attend functions where it's on a hill, and he can be on the upper side. He did some very nice things during the war, and all the Soldiers like him very much. He really went right up to where they were at the front and helped to minister to their wants and ills. And the Queen did wonderful work then.

There dident seem to be any of the "Hooey" and Applesauce, about that Royal family that surrounds all those others. Course they had a lot of it, but they are modest, plus, in comparison to all the others. That old thing of doing away with the Kings, it will never be done there if the people themselves have anything to do with it, at least not while he is alive.

You know this Mussolini is a wise Bird. He knows that, and he knows that they don't do any harm, and like the one in England, and all of them, they fill a certain social place, that the men who run the Country havent time or wouldent monkey with.

Those people over there like it and we eat it up over here. We are the biggest Yaps in the World to fall for stuff like that. Buckingham Palace has the Iron railings all wore off with the noses of Americans trying to peep through the cracks of the bars.

I really think the King of Spain has more to do with the affairs of his country than any of them.[4] They have a Dictator, but the King put him in, and he can throw him out. But this little fellow in Italy is very popular, no more so than King George is in England, but much more so than people think, who have the impression that Mussolini is the only one in Italy that ever got a hand. So happy life to the young folks, they are no better or no worse than the rest of us. They got their troubles cut out. This Kinging is a tough job I imagine. And just think where would we be with our weeklies. You know Mr. Hoover don't come out and be shot with everybody like Mr. Coolidge used to, so a Royal wedding now and then is mighty welcome.

370 A QUICK HOP TO LONDON

Well all I know is just what I read in the papers, and what I see as I prowl hither and thither, and Boy I did some prowling right lately before setting sail for our former Proprietors' land. Just before I jumped over here to England, I was all set out in California to go to New York on some business, and was to take the plane the next day. Well the Company called me up about dinner time and said that the weather was none to good and they wasent sure about a Plane getting away the next morning, so I decided that I would catch the train that night, (the Chief) that left at nine oclock. So my wife hustled me around there and we called up the aviation and told them if they did

1930

leave in the morning to wire me and I would drop off the train and they could pick me up along the line.

Well away I come and the next day as we was poking along I kept waiting for a message to get off, but finally one come saying the plane couldent go so that meant I had to stay on the train for the trip for it was snowing and a terrible storm all over the country.

It's the first whole trip I have made on the train in a long time. But I enjoyed it. We had a lot of folks aboard that I knew, among them Tom Mix.[1] He was going down to Florida to confer with his boss Mr. John Ringling, as Tom was a big success in the Circus last year and he is to go out with the same show again this year, the "Sells Floto" show.[2] You know Mr. Ringling bought it and all the other shows. Did you know that he owns all the Circuse's there is now, every one of them. All but the 101 Wild West, that's still Zack Miller's.[3] And by the way did you know that John Ringling is ONE of the richest men in America? Well he is. He has property everywhere. You know he had a great chance to tell where the country was growing and where it wasent. Talk about a weather report, that circus could tell you about to a "two bit piece" just the amount of money that was in every community and then he had these year after year records and having plenty of money he knew where to buy, and he did and today there's not a growing town or State that he don't own something in.

You can't fool that Baby; he knows how good your town is. The Circus business is about the smallest thing he is in, and he owns it all. The Dr. Gianini, one of those famous Italian brothers that made such a record with the "Bank of Italy," all of us in California owe them.[4] Dr. runs the New York end of all their business and I had borrowed from him even before we hit California. Well Dr. and his wife was on the train. You see it's kinder like a party. You are on there three days. I visited with Dr. but paid nothing on account. He said to me, "Will, what do you do with your money? It's about time you was paying your debt." He finances all these Movie people that make productions. You know it's one of the most wonderful tributes to the opportunities of our Country that a couple of Italians could start with a little working man's saving chest in a little shack in San Francisco and in just a few years have the third largest banking Institute in the World. Their Father wasent Morgan, or a Rockefeller.[5]

Then Earl C. Anthony that runs our finest Radio Station out there where we get all our amusement from was on the trip.[6] So it passed mighty fast. Well I landed in New York on the Century and made a date to see Winifred Sheehan, the head man in the Fox Organization at two o'clock.[7] We talked over a story that I am to do for my next picture and found that it would take a little while to prepare it so that there was nothing I could be doing for the next couple of weeks. So I said, Winnie I believe I will jump over to London to this "Dissagreement Conference" and as our Deligation had already sailed we called up the Steamship line and here the Bramen, the newest and finest boat, was sailing that very night. This was three oclock, and I had no Passports, Visa's or anything.

So we hustled around and grabbed off an Emergency passport, then I had to go get my picture taken to put on the "Suponea," so I rushed to one of those Passport Photo places, got the "Wanted in Oklahoma," then I had to make the British Embassy Offices to get the thing Visayed for their Country or I couldent land. Then to get some Boat accomodations, then it's knocking right on six oclock, for this is all away down in the wrong end of New York.

Well I had clothes. I dident want a dress or Tuxedo, but I did want an old dark blue serge that I could get in the dining room on the boat with, so I found a little place open, not exactly second-hand, but they had been there so long they tasted like it. Then some black shoes, and a black tie, and I was ready to fool the head Steward. I was just thinking some people plan for years to go to Europe and wonder what they will get to wear, and all that Hooey. But Boy, I had to do it all in just fifteen minutes. Course I looked like fifteen minutes, but I made it. The whole thing was originally my Wife's idea anyhow. She had been saying all the time that I should go to this Conference. I had been to the Washington one and the Geneva one, and she insisted that I needed some new gags, and told me when I left if I had the chance to run over and see what it was all about, for my Public.

So I hope some good comes from it. I am just landing here and mailing you this back and I can't tell yet what will happen. But even if they don't dissarm, it's been a great trip, and next week I will tell you about London.

Oh, by the way, the little suit fell apart the first night out.

371 PRESIDENTS MESSAGE AND ROMAN PROGRESS

Well all I know is just what I read in the papers. About ten days ago our President delivered his first message to Congress. You know that's one of the things that his contract calls for. One of the few stipulated duties of the President, and that is that every once in awhile he delivers a message to Congress to tell them the "Condition

1930

of the Country." This message as I say is to Congress, the rest of the country know the condition of the country, for they live in it and are a part of it. But the Senators and Congressmen being in Washington all the time have no idea what is going on in America. So the President has to tell 'em. The country must have been in pretty bad shape for it took 12,000 words for Mr. Hoover to tell how bad it was. You see when a thing is in fine shape, it don't need much explaining, you can then just write, "Country. O. K." Now we will just take up various ailments and see what he says about this land of "A dollar down and a dollar a week."

In the first paragraph he says, "In complying with the Constitution that I from time to time give to Congress information on the State of the Union, I wish to emphasize that during the last year it has grown in strength, advanced in comfort, and gained in knowledge." Well that don't look so bad for us, we have "gained in strength," in plainer words we have got stouter. That proves that our reducing has been a failure, if a Country can get stouter while they are on a diet, what could we gain if we wasent. This observation of the President's will be of no knowledge to lots of middle aged women of the country. They have realized their strength, ever since they all procured a bath room scales.

Now the next paragraph, "Advanced in comfort." Now why have we advanced in comfort? Maby it's because we have gained in strength, or have we got more comfortable in spite of our fat, but at any rate we are "fat and comfortable." Now in both of those I think his observations are absolutely correct. I never saw a President more right than he is there. We are "fat and comfortable." Now I wish he had gone into it a little further there and kinder discussed the fact as to just how good is it for a country to be fat and comfortable. A pig being fattened for slaughter is fat and comfortable, but that's just about all he is. He ain't worth much to get out and do some rustling around for himself. So I wonder if the President dident just about sum up the condition of this country in those two observations. Wasent it Rome that was in that very shape one time? I never did read much about Roman history outside of the life of Mussolini, by Zurfatti.[1] But I have gathered from Hollywood Photographic annoyances that Rome gained her exalted position in the manly art of self defense at a time when they were anything but "fat and comfortable" but were as a matter of fact, "skinny" and "ill at ease." In other words little pangs of hunger drove them to deeds far beyond their natural capacities. They went out and cleaned up on the rest of the world not for glory but for "callories." Just look at pictures of them in that great bales of tin armor. They wasent comfortable by

Will Rogers as "Sir Boss" in the motion picture A Connecticut Yankee (Fox Film Corporation, 1931). In the upper scene Rogers appears with William Farnum who played "King Arthur." In the lower view, Sir Boss rebuffs the amorous moves of "Queen Morgan Le Fay," played here by Myrna Loy.

any means. (I know I wore one of those things in a picture once.) That's what made 'em fight was to get out of that thing. And Caesar wouldent unlock the thing and let 'em out till they had practically whipped the world. Caesar was kinder the "Head Man" down there then. He was the Grundy of his day.[2] He knew that Senators were a useless lot and that especially the ones from the backward states, should talk "darn small." Brutus was a Senator from Cicily kinder the Alabama of the Roman Empire, and the other Senators wanted to have Caesar investigated. You see Caesar had really no official capacity. He maintains a suit of offices in Rome and every time there was a Convention or an election he would bob up. There was two political fations in Rome then, the Republicans and the Christians. Caesar was of course a Republican and contributed generously to their campaign funds, and would kindly furnish Christians for the Sunday afternoon affairs in the arenas. In that ingenious way they kept the Christians the minority party. But the Christians said, "If we can't rule we will investigate. But Brutus being a learned man, far beyond the knowledge of other Senators, was the first person to have no confidence in investigations. He knew they were good for recreational purposes, and for a pastime till the next session was called, but not as a means of arriving at anything. So instead of investigating Caesar, he just procured a Bowie knife and just stabbed the gentleman, practically ruining him. It was a rather crude way of arriving at the facts, but you must remember Brutues was an honorable man, he was a Democrat. That called for a trial, to see if was a penal offense to stab a Senator. The Jury was to decide whether he was to get a medal or be reprimanded. It was the first trial at Cameras and Aielaniests took part. Nero the Paul Whiteman of his day, was called in to judge while he was rosining his bow.[3] Mark Anthony was the first District attorney to have ambitions of becoming Governor. When he started speaking they couldent tell if he was for Caesar or against him, for it was the first time that satire had ever been used publically. When he kept saying, "Brutues was an honorable man," why Brutues was taking it on the level, and he had to repeat it over twenty times to drive home his brand of humor. The Roman Senate at that time was a kinder modern House of Lords, and after Anthony for the 19th time said, "Brutues was an honorable man" why they got to looking at each other and saying, "This guy is either kidding us or Brutues" and they got to paying closer attention and they found it was both of them.

Anthony made a wonderful speech. But it practically ruined all Senates to follow, for they have figured that all legislation must be based on oratory, make up in jestures what you lack in ideas. So all these intervening years Senators have tried to emulate Anthony, and the only thing they have ever approached him in is, endurance. Anthony had one quality that the boys following have never been able to grasp. Anthony dident take himself seriously. That how he got Brutues off with a tune by Caesar, and a small bail. But all this is just to show you that Rome's turning point was just at that time. She had reached her heights through the American Magazine plan of hard work, perseverance, and taking advantage of her opportunities. Now she was "fat and Comfortable." She started putting in baths. Up to then when a Nation got any dirt on 'em, they wore it off. But the Romans commenced to getting High Hat. They had bath tubs. With this effiminatecy started their downfall, they had up to then walked everywhere, or rode horseback. But an ingenious fellow named Chariot, first name Henry, got to getting out a contraption to ride in, a thing where you dident have to walk. You looked like you was walking but you wasent. You was in fact riding. Well that just upset the whole lives habits and customs of a Nation. "Ride in a conveyance and take a bath." Rome was sitting pretty. Then somebody decided with these conveyances they must have some roads. Up to then they had had nothing but trails, for they dident need anything else to walk on. Then they appointed a Highway Commission.

That's where the first graft enters into history. The Highway Com wanted to build from Rome to Naples. As Naples was where a great many of the boys spent their week ends. They called it the Apian way for the same reason we call one the Lincoln highway. Lincoln was never on it and neither was Apian. Then there was a fellow on the highway com who lived away over at Venice, so he built it by his place, thereby starting a custom which has been faithfully handed down. A smart state nowadays will appoint all their highway men from one place. Then one road will do all of 'em. So the lad's commenced burning up the boulevards, more people crushed under wheels than met their death in fair competition with the lions. But what mattered the death, wasent progress on the rampage, "We are bathing and moving, what else do you want?"

With the riding come the flesh. Where they used to walk and keep theirselvs in shape to meet and defeat any enemy on a moment's notice now they were taking on beef. But they was happy, they was riding and bathing. To solve the industrial situation, why they decided to sell on credit, making the Chariot within the reach of all. Up to then Romans had never been in debt, but now they were really becoming to amount to something. They could afford to look down on the Greeks, and the meades and the Persians, and the Pharisees, for those backward people dident not only not have a Bath, or a Chariot, but they dident even know enough to owe something, they were a backward lot. So the Romans just kept riding, bathing, for they were selling Tubs on credit. Well that was great. They framed themselvs up a stock market, where they could sell something they dident have. They started selling shares in Vesuvious limited. Well these other Nations got to watching 'em, and as their waistbands expanded, their endurance lessened. Instead of standing on guard to see if any enemy approached they was week ending on the yacht in the bay of Napoli.

372 TONNAGE COSTS RISE

Well, all I know is just what I read in the papers, but as I havent seen a paper to read for over a week, and then for the three weeks previous so that I dident get ahold of any that had any American news in them.

So I don't know what has happened with you all here on the home grounds. All I can hear that has happened is Prohibition. Congress is still argueing over it. So I guess I haven't missed much by being away, for I have heard everything there was to say for either side in the first six months it was in existence.

So that leaves us nothing but London and the Conference, and that trip home. Now you have often heard people say, "The Captain said it was the worst trip he had ever experienced." Now I know it's terrible to pull that.

But honest, that's just what he said. He said that there was especially one day that it was not only a storm but a hurricane. Well old Claremore just keeled over and dident show up for days. We was on the French Lines crack boat the "Ille De France," and it's a great one in rough weather.

Of course we wasent making much time, but it did stand the weather great. It pitched a lot, of course, but it dident do any of that side rolling that is so popular with most boats. We come in right along side of the "Aquatania" that left a day and a half ahead of us.

I was awful anxious to get the papers to see what had been done at the Conference since I had been on the boat. Of course we had a little paper on board that gives us a few lines of each event that comes over the wireless. We couldent tell if they were doing anything or not, so when I landed I grabbed the papers to see what had been done, and do you know we hadent missed a thing.

There was something in there about Japan and America conferring on the tonnage of Submarines. Well when the conference started, everyone had been led to believe that they would be abolished all together.

Now they are discussing the amount of tonnage and it is far in excess of what either country has, so it will take a lot of money to build up to the amount that the Country dissarms down to.

They are talking about giving Japan equality with us on Submarines. Well, that's one of the coming war weapons; why, that will mean just what I told you one time. That a one-eyed man can tell you who will win the Conference, it will be Japan.

Our ratio in Battleships are: England 5: America 5 and Japan 3, 5-5-3. Now they are talking of giving Japan 5-5-5 on Submarines. Why, the more submarines? Because Japan wants them, that's why. Mind you, with all joking and kidding aside, it's going to be a pretty tough thing to really do anything worthwhile over there.

You are bucking human nature. It's simply an economic Conference and not by any means a Dissarmament Conference.

Nobody is going to dissarm in the least. You know the men that every Nation that is gathered there are not the "Idealists" that think, "Oh we can't have war; it's too terrible, we must not have war." Well that's wonderfull, but these men know history too well. They know each other too well, they know that is not only a possibility but a probably.

They know they can't go back home and tell their people that they have left them unprotected. England was raised on her Navy. Her Navy is what has made her great. Every British Kid 8 years old knows that. Do you think they are going to let a bunch of their statesmen just sit around a table and agree to let somebody else be ABSOLUTELY as big as they are? You know these things are not being done.

Something that you have held for life and you know it's been your weapon that has made you, you just don't give up that without a struggle, you don't just hand it over.

It sounds great, this parity, but you are not going to get it. In the first place, it would take us years to build up to them and it's a cinch they are not going to sink till they arrive at our level.

Then there is France and Italy, they were given equality at Washington. Why? Because France was down and out at that time, 1922. They couldn't demand more. Now they are a different France than in 22.

They are the "Cockyest" ones at the Conference. They want to be given a much higher rating. They feel, (and rightly so) that they are one of the world's powers, and they are not going to be humiliated by being called any less.

They have a tremendous submarine building programme. It's their only weapon against England's already great fleet. And you can bet they won't give up a pound of that.

1930

Italy will demand the same rating with France, and she won't get it. Now what will the Italian Deligation do? Will Mussolini bring them home if they don't get it?

You know those birds over there have a pretty tough time of it. It's all right to joke about them not doing anything. But when you have fought each other as much as they have this old trusting each other to never have another war is a lot of beautiful stuff, but not just exactly what you would want to bet all your whole mode of defense on.

One thing we can rest assured, we have some fine men there, we got a great Deligation. They are not thinking the World is going to kiss each other from now to eternity. They want Peace, but they want a Gun to help get it with.

You must always remember that their is more National pride in this Conference to divide up than there is Ships. Nations are not there so much to protect their Little Gunboats as they are their National Prestige.

And always remember they are not there to stop wars, they are there just to put some kind of a stop if they can of this Nation and France of making them build too many.

373   AROUND ASTOR FARM

Well, all I know is just what I read in the papers, and what I see in the old Country. Of all the places I visited on this last trip to England the one that really was the most impressive was the country place of Lord and Lady Astor.[1]

I had been lots of times at their London residence. But this one, out about an hour from London, was the real McCoy. It's got one of those long records that take you back and maby was where old Henry the 8th. did a big percentage of his marrying. I expect Caesar was registered there.

It's right up on a hill overlooking the winding Thames River. I don't know the acreage but the chances are that old Cromwell filed on the original 160 acres, and then had all his hired help homestead on adjoining 160's, and then when they had proved up on them, why "Crommy" conveniently sent them off to some little Nicaraguan uprising.[2] But before going he had them make their cross on some parchment, saying that in case of their not returning the holdings of the said Cross'ee were entirely at the disposal of party of the first

115

part, which was Cromwell. So the Astors practically hold all the country lying east of the Thames.

The house is a modest bungalow of not over seventy-five or a hundred rooms. It's laid out a good deal like Westminster Abbey, only without the Towers. It's rambling, but still kept within the bounds of good taste. There is a landing field in each wing, where you can take off and make the dining room by lunch. The ceilings are high enough that they give you plenty of altitude for taking off and landing. The first room you enter is kind of a cosy corner. It's about ten acres cut off from the rest of the subdivision. But now they have made it a lovely homely place.

It was a lovely Sunday afternoon, the sun shining bright, a kind of a historic day for that time of the year near London. The door tender told me that Lady Astor was out in the tennis court and she had left word for me to come out, and sure enough she was out there. She was going it great guns. You know she has more energy, can get more things done in one day, and have more of them to do than any creature either male or female that I ever saw. Well, she quit the tennis racket, and when I started in blowing about what a place it was, she said, "Come on, I will show you around." We were then out in front of the main house, and I was gapping at it, and then she told me:

"Right where you are standing is where my old colored woman, that I brought with me from Virginia when I was married, she got one look at the place and said to me; "Miss Nancy is here where we all goin to live?" "Why yes, Cynthia, here is our home." "My Lord, Miss Nancy you all done outmarried yourself." Well what a kick she got out of repeating that old favorite of hers.

Then we started in to see this wonderful place. We walked for about three-quarters of an hour then she saw a little old car there and she said "Come on we will ride." I asked her can you run this thing. Well then we commenced seeing the place right, a golf course, steeplechase course, flowers, beautiful colored Pheasants running about, stables where he breeds his great Thoroughbreds, and then we walked down a beautiful walk. There was a fine big monument with names on it. It was all the men killed in the war that worked on the Estate. Then on down on the side of a beautiful wooded bluff or hillside, and there was a kind of a lovely sunken garden effect, about 100 feet long, and maby forty wide, in oblong shape, with a marvelous statue of an angel faced woman with arms outstretched, and she standing at the back and over this garden effect, facing a wide strip of clearing through the trees away down below so you could see out across the river.

1930

What was in this spot? You wouldent guess in a million years. Well during the great war they had given up their place for a great Hospital, they had used a part of the house and built in addition great temporary buildings, and in this was the graves of boys who had died on their place, that lived in almost every country both England and all overseas. The stones were laid flat over the graves, all of one shape and kind, with their names and home; several of our boys, Canadians, Australians. There must have been as many as fifty in all and she could stand at any grave and tell you about each boy. She knew them all personally. She had held the hands of many as they passed out.

She would move from grave to grave and tell you the characteristics of each. How she had promised one a wrist watch if he would live till she could go to London and buy it, and he did, and he had it on smiling as he passed on. How she could go into a ward and say, "Now you boys either got to die or get well, we are not going to have you sick here all the time."

She is the greatest jollier in the world. If I was sick and dident even know her I know of no one I would rather have come to see me. There she stood with tears in her eyes as she spoke of each boy as though he had been her own, and related stories of them.

This woman that can get up in the House of Commons and stand the "Ragging" and "chaffing" of the roughest old politician, an American born woman, and first to sit in the great Parliamentary Halls of England, the center of every drawing room crowd, the Famous Lady Astor, but here she was, just a plain mother, all the fight, all the alertness of mind, all the Social graces, all the wit and sparkle gone, there almost under the shade of her great house lay buried these lads, she had tried to help and learned to love. She was just walking among "Her Boys."

She had had a great artist do the statue, it was symbolic of the Mother looking across these graves to the west, as they had "Gone West." The spot had been consecrated for those of its religions that asks for that. One woman knew of her son being buried there and she wanted to move him. Lady Astor paid her way and had her come from Canada and when she saw the spot she said, "I wouldent move him for the world, no spot could be more beautiful than this." How many will turn their beautiful Estates into a burial ground?

And when I hear some political or social opponent ever say aught of her, I won't even go the trouble of telling them of her wonderful heart. I will just smile satisfyingly to myself and rake up that vision of that woman walking among "Her Boys" with tears in her eyes yet telling jokes of each one. So let no woman, mother of a son, ever say evil against her.

Then we come back to the House and that's when I demanded the Port Wine instead of tea, and got it.

374   ME AND THE KING AT THE HOUSE OF LORDS

Well all I know is just what I read in the papers, or what I see as I prowl around. Of all the things on the English trip I have been asked more about was the big opening of the Conference where the King was present.[1] Well that was about all there was and has been to the Conference so far. The opening was so big and impressive that they havent been able to follow it up. It's like an act on the stage coming out and doing their very best trick first, then they have nothing to do afterwards. But in all seriousness I feel sooner or later (mostly later) they will be able to accomplish something over there. Nothing so big or radical as some had hoped, but they will do something.

Well this opening was in one of the rooms called the Lords Room in the House of Parliament. It's not the one where they meet, it's I suppose a lounge room. In fact I don't know what it's used for ordinarily, it's not so very big, just a big old long bare room with some great paintings all around the walls, and a funny thing right behind the speakers was a scene the Battle on the seas where Lord Nelson, their greatest Naval Hero, was in a hand to hand battle with his enemy on the deck of the ship.[2] Then facing all the speakers was another Naval battle scene where the English Navy had sunk somebody else. You would have thought their sense of humor would have made them change these things and get them out of there while this great effort to Abolish ships was on. It would be just like the Anti Saloon League holding their convention in a speakeasy.

I had heard of London fogs, and most of my trips over there heretofore had been in the summer and I had never seen a really great fog in action. But Broth! I want to tell you that on the very morning of this great opening ceremony, it was pitch dark. Cabs were poking along, people feeling their way about. The king coming from Buckingham Palace had policemen walking in front of his Auto with lights. Crowds of people had gathered along the route he was to take to see him but they couldent even see the street he was to come along, much less his car.

And that's how our poor Charley Dawes got late.[3] Here we had

1930

sent him over to England five months ahead so that he would be on time, and the poor fellow missed the King's speech and half the others. Guess he dident have any Policemen to guide him. Everybody of an official nature had on the usual morning dress, cutaway coat, stripe trousers and black shoes, and high top hat. All but the American Newspaper men, lots of us still had on our Pajamas. News Hounds from other countries they had all these costumes, some of them looked better than their Deligations. But these old Political News sleuths from Washington, they had been on too many trips and Conventions, this was just another gathering with them. Course the King was kinder new to 'em. But outside of that and the fog there was no novelty.

I sure was lucky. My seat in the Press section was the row just in front of where the wives of the Deligates sit, and right behind me sat Mrs Morrow, Mrs Robinson, Mrs Reed, Mrs Dawes, Mrs Gibson, Mrs Adams and Mrs Stimpson.[4] We could talk and visit without being rude, for we would do it during the time that the Interpreter was translating from English to French, or Visa Versa. You see every speech had to be translated. Not into Japanese. I don't know how they were supposed to know what it was all about. They dident come there to hear speeches anyway; they come to get more ships, and you watch 'em get 'em, too.

A thing that struck me rather odd was that there was no prayer, or benediction, or blessing, or a single thing to start it off. You would have thought that they would have made some plea for divine guidance. But they seemed to have enough confidence in themselves that they dident need any help from the Lord. However I think by now they wish they had asked him to give them some small assistance.

Now the King comes in. Prime Minister McDonald and one of his Cabinet walk on either side.[5] He looks fine. This is really his first public appearance since his severe illness, and the English people felt a little nervous that he might show the effect of it. But he dident at all. He walked in with a steady gait. He has a very infectious smile, and he bowed to the left and right very generously as he walked down the aisleway. He was escorted to the Throne Chair. All this time everybody was standing. Then McDonald announced who it was, and he started in. He read his speech, as all of them did, but a man from Australia, he had learned his. The king has practically no English accent at all. He speaks perfect English. He was by far the easiest understood of any speaker there. We all stood all during his speech. Happily it wasent long. The minute he had finished he was escorted out, and all remained standing. He dident even wait until it had been interpreted into French.

Weekly Articles

Then is when he sent four men carrying a long table back, and they carried the Throne Chair out. Of course that struck us Americans as funny. You would have thought they had enough Throne Chairs that they wouldent have to carry one around with him. Or knowing that Curio hunting mania of us folks over here, he knew that parts of that Chair would be in Arkansaw, and the throne part in Pennsylvania. Of course the Republican Senator would have taken care of that. But the King sent back for it after he had gone out, and we all stood while they carried it out, they put it on this table, and carried it like it was a stretcher. The king then went back to his Country Estate Sandingham, or something like that. He had only come up for this.

The Prince of Wales was of course down in Africa.[6] Then the other Speakers, then the long Interpreters, and that when I would get all the scandal from the Women. Mrs Morrow was telling me all about Anne and Charles, that's what she calls 'em, Anne and Charles.[7] She told me about the wedding, and how they fooled the newspaper men who were standing out at the front gate all the time. The family dident take so heartily to her flying. But after she got so enthuastic about it, and they figured that on account of the teacher she had why it was OK. Mrs Morrow of course then dident know about this Glider stuff they have been pulling. That sitting up there on a little dab of canvass and some boards with no engine, and no power, that wouldent look so encouraging to me. I want all the engines I can get, and I want 'em all going at full speed before I crawl into anything. I must write you next week about what Ambassador Dawes had to say about these American girls who their folks practically go as far as committing murder to get them presented to the Queen every year. You wouldent believe that such scheming and conniving existed. Remember next week, "Meet the Queen."

375   "MEET THE QUEEN," A GREAT AMERICAN INDUSTRY

Well, all I know is just what I read in the papers, or see when I am looking. You know I told you I was going to tell you about one of our American Industrys that you perhaps never knew existed, and that is "Trying to get to be presented at the Court of St James." The reason I happened to know anything about it, was not from actual experience, as you couldent hardly class me as a Debutante, but one day out at Luncheon with the Ambassador, Mr Charley Dawes, he got to telling about what he was up against with this mania.[1] You see it's getting along about the season for it now, it's "Meeting season."

I think its some time in the spring, that they have these "Presentations." Well fond mothers and doting Aunts don't wait till then. They go over sometimes a year ahead, and start laying their schemes. Each Nation is allowed so many, I don't know what determines the amount. I imagine it was an old custom that started away back when they was trying to drum up trade to come to their Country. It was perhaps the first Tourist bait. In those days there was no Prince of Wales to attract attention, so they decided to let a bunch of Girls meet the Queen.[2]

Our big interest in it of course started when we got to be a Democracy. There is no race of people of people that likes to see royalty like a Democracy. I imagine that the American Revolution wasent hardly over before a bunch of our "better class Citizens" started in trying till finally they had to limit it, and now we are limited to 40. The other Nations I guess have about a like Representation. Personally I think the thing was promoted for the Dressmakers, and Photographers, because all they do is dress up, and then after it's over have their picture taken in the Presentation dress.

Well here is something you maby dident know the Queen won't meet at one of these a divorced Woman.[3] She has got to have gotten rid of her husband by criminal and not legal means. Well when they cut out these Divorcees that just about cut our supply down to zero. Made some of them almost sorry they got a divorce. Our government tried to get 'em to kind of ease up on that strict rule, and cut it down to just bar ones who had been divorced MORE than once. Well this big elimination give the young Girls a chance. They had never had a chance to get divorced, but they had a chance to meet the Queen, so the competition gets hotter and hotter every year.

They found that no matter if you was presented in 1856 that when ever you married again or died, or shot somebody, that the papers would always remember that "Lizzie Presistent was once presented to Queen Helen of Troy." It has become a great trade mark. A girl comes back home and lives on that "Presentation" like a Channel swimmer. The folks at home want to meet the girls that took the bow in front of a Queen.

Now how do they get there. Ah' thats the story. Mr Dawes said that statistics showed that all Ambassadors died young, and that was the reason "Trying to pick 40 out of 120,000,000." He says that over 93 and 1/3 percent of the business that is transacted at the American Embassy in London, is trying to do something about these Debs that are trying to get their pictures in the home town papers, via the Queen.

The old ambitious Mothers use every ruse know to scheming science. They have letters from their Post Masters, their Congressmen, their Senators, Young Voters League, and do everything that they can to blackjack the Ambassador into thinking that if "Our Mollie" is not one of the favored that they will see that he is recalled from London and sent to Peru. They take Houses in London, and start their Campaigns early. They use dinners as bribes, would use money if they could. Find out some one back home that they know that knows the Ambassador and get them to start work on him. I suppose there has been more money spent on getting and trying to get presented than there has on Armament, which they are trying to abolish now on account of its expense. Mr Dawes said it just had him about cuckoo, and what he wanted to do was to turn the thing over to the Senate of the United States, they have a try at everything and he wants to give them a crack at this. Let each State select a girl, and the seven States that lost out would get in next year, and seven others lose out. Well there is two Senators from each State and can you hear the arguments in there as to why each of their Candidates should not be the ONE. But at least that would give us a new argument in the Senate and that's something that we havent had since Prohibition and the Tarriff was invented. Dawes claims that if an Ambassador could get rid of that thing that it would practically eliminate the cause of an Ambassador being there, and they could come home and we could live in peace forever. I think they ought to sell the privaleges, let the English do it. That's the way they do with the Titles over there; they auction them off. Why if England would raise the limit from 40 to 40,000 they could sell every one at a big price and soon pay their debt. But I am like Dawes. I want to see the Senate get ahold of it. In the meantime try and meet the Queen, everybody is doing it.

376 COOLIDGE TALKS BUT LITTLE

Well, all I know is just what I read in the Cigarette adds. Calvin and Grace were in our midst for quite a spell and went back last week.[1] I really believe he had a great time. He seemed in a mighty cheerful mood. He dident have anything to say, but he kinder smiled when he refused to say it. I really believe it kinder reminded him of old times, the crowds trying to get a glimpse of him and all anxious to hear even a word from him.

The weekly men were shooting at him as of old. I was at a little quiet dinner party where he and Mrs. Coolidge were. I told him all my little jokes on the Disarmament Conference (well not all of them), for there was so many that it would take a week. He knows about the difficulties of one of those things. He sent a bunch over in '26 and another in '27 to Geneva and he remembers all they sunk was their expenses. He thinks that Mr. Hoover made a a mighty fine selection in our Deligation. I was bragging on Joe Robinson and he said, "He was a very able man."[2]

Mrs. Coolidge wanted particularly to hear about Mrs. Dawes.[3] She likes Mrs. Dawes very much so she told me, and she is a sweet little old lady, just the opposite in manner from Charley.[4]

I was fortunate enough to be placed at dinner next to Mrs. Coolidge and she is a dandy. And you know a funny thing she would tell a story and imitate his twang, or New England voice and could she do it? Say, I make a living imitating Mr. Coolidge, but she has me beat and she did it right there before him. I dident think she would have the nerve.

We talked about the Stearns, their old friends up in Boston, and I told them I had met Mr. Stearns and liked him very much and told her the story that I used on the stage about her packing up to leave the White House and after I had finished it, she told me now I will tell you the story as it really happened.[5]

Mr. Coolidge and I were coming home from Church one morning and he asked me when we moved back to Northampton what I was going to do with all my clothes? I said, well I guess I will have to put them in the closet. He said, "You better put them in the bed room and we will sleep in the closet."

She was telling about them both writing for the Magazines, and I asked her if they diden't ever get mixed up on what they were writing and both perhaps refer to the same thing, and she told us, "One day Mr. Coolidge happened to pick up a page of my manuscript and said, 'I used that, you better leave it out.' " She said, however that enough things happened there that both had plenty to write about.

She had that day been over to the Studios watching them make the Movies and she was all enthused about it and she pulled a good one, as they had been photographed with all the different stars and in every conceivable "Set" or place, she said, "I think we are the only ones I saw working all day. Nobody else was taking any pictures."

As they went to the Studio and as they got out of the car, she said she started to take her little Movie Camera and Mary Pickford told her to leave it.[6] She couldent understand that and neither could I. She said,

Weekly Articles

"I suppose they thought I would take something that I ought not to show." But anyhow Mary gave commands to our Ex-First Lady of the Land.

I flew through El Paso the morning after they had passed through and the Reporters had asked him how he liked West Texas, and what he thought of its advancement. He replied, "It looks just like it did 21 years ago when I was here." That dident go so well with the Texicans.

He had wired ahead to a friend to get them "a room at the Biltmore Hotel. Nothing elaborate, and please meet us at the train and show us up there." Naturally the Hotel gave him the whole end of it. But wasen't that just like him and having the friend meet them at the Station and show them up there? Why that's like Lindbergh having letters of recommendation to the French.[7] Why, Lord, half the Town met them at the Station.

You know it's remarkable the hold that little fellow has on the people. They sure do believe in him. They know that he didn't do anything when in there. But he does nothing just at the time when the people want nothing done. You never caught him messing with any Tarriff he knew that was loaded with ill will and chances, no matter which way you raised it you hit somebody. They would never have got an extra session of Congress out of him. He knew that was Dynamite to any President. It's bad enought to let 'em meet when the law says they have to meet, much less gathering them in at other times.

Of course, ·Mr. Hoover was forced into it, but he shouldent have listened to Borah and that Gang before election.[8] He had it won if he had promised nothing. That's one thing, nobody ever heard Mr. Coolidge promise anything. He is perhaps the greatest Politician of our generation. He has forgot more politics than those birds back there know.

He knows a lot of human Psychology too. He would go to work right now for some big Company, but he is afraid it would be held against him in the future, that is that he had been connected with "Big Business." You see there is very few businesses that don't have business with the Government and he is afraid that it would be said that they hired him to help get something about their Income tax fixed, or something of that sort. So he is just laying off, AND YOU WATCH HIM. You are going to hear a lot more of him. I have already invited him to be my Guest at my ranch when he is Ex-President the NEXT time.

377   RED MEN GOT BIG LAUGH

Well all I know is just what I read in the papers or what I see as I go about the Country watching Calvin open Dams, or close 'em up

1930

rather.[1] You see he wasent going to go over into Arizona and do that at all. I think he kinder felt like it might be construed as a political move, for future reference.

So the Committee got the bright idea of wiring President Hoover and getting him to ask Mr. Coolidge. Well Mr. Hoover did and as he did he wired the Arizona Committee back that he had wired Mr. Coolidge asking him to go.

Well of course that put it up to Mr. Coolidge, and if he hadn't gone the Committee would have known that he really was disobeying the wishes of the President. It was pretty slick on Mr. Hoover's part in doing this, and anyhow after Mr. Coolidge got there I think he was glad he went.

It really was a wonderful sight away out in the Mountains and desert, and here was this huge affair that they not only had to spend millions on, but had to spend a tremendous sum to get the roads in there, to get in on, and bring all the thousands of tons of stuff to be used.

The Indians made it look mighty picturesque. One of the tribes, the Pima's is supposed to get some of the water for they are supposed to own the reservation just below the Dam. I am going over there pretty soon when the thing gets going good and see just exactly how much land the Indians really own that is watered by this.

It's as I told you before the Apache Indians owned the land the Dam is built on. But to be above a dam is very little comfort to you in the way of getting some water out of it. You got to be down hill from it. Living above a dam is just kinder like being a Democrat, you are living and voting, but you are not deriving any of the Benefits.

You know as you saw all those Indians you couldent help but think of the old days. Here was the old warlike Apaches that fought to hold all they had, and most of them wound up in jail, but there was a Washington that fought for his tribe against invaders and wound up with a flock of Statues and a title of Father of his Country. And yet I expect if the truth were known the old Apache Chiefs went through more and fought harder for their Country than George did. But George won, that's the whole answer to history, it's not what did you do, but what did you get away with at the finish.

That's why your dissarmament won't get anywhere much, it's just because all those Nations know that they are important in World affairs just in proportion to their Military strength. Is there any reason in the world why Japan should be the power she is and China with its millions and resources, that go to the four corners of the earth. But that's just the trouble, China has STOOD for so much from other Nations that they are not classed as one of the big shots.

Why because they concentrated on peace and not war. So Japan is at London now, and China can't even make a Rotary Convention.

Spain discovered half the world, her ships were on every sea, but she let her Navy run down and wound up in the class Z League. Look at Holland, great Country big as England, and they have Colonies, but do you ever hear of them when they talk of what the big powers want? No, you would think they were Rhode Island. Why? No Navy, and some of the rest of them the same. We don't rate their culture, we don't rate their achievements, their Art, their Literature, their Integrity, their population, their size, in fact nothing but How big is their Navy?

Why Brazil is bigger than all England, France, Italy and Japan, and has more National resources than all them combined. Yet she couldent get to a Chamber of Commerce membership rally. Same old answer. No Navy. They all know that.

So you can see why there won't be any tall sinking done by any of these Babies that are up there on top now. It would be a marvelous thing if all of them could see that there was to be no more war and go ahead and do away with their arms of defense. But unfortunately they have all studied history and they know that these ideas we are talking about now are not new, they have all been gone over before, and they just can't hardly bring themselves to believe that this is going to happen.

So it's as I said at first we were out there on Indian land dedicating a Dam to get water for white people to come out and use and gradually take more Indian land away. There is going to be nothing different. It started with Lief Erricson in 996, then skipped over Columbus in 1492, for he couldent find this Country in four trips. Then come the Spanish settlers, then the Mayflower was the last straw.

They dident have any Ex-President at the dedicating at their taking land from the Indians but they got it just the same, and they have kept right on doing it up to last week. So you see history repeats itself, the same as it has in wars.

It would be wonderful if people would quit fighting, it would be wonderful if people would leave the Indians alone and let 'em do what they wanted too. But what a chance? I don't blame Arizona, mind you. You can't blame anybody. It's just the way we are bred, that's all. If we see anything we want we take it. The more so-called civilized we get the more we kill and take. But I bet many an old Indian got many a quiet laugh out of the speeches of "good fellowship" there that day, that were meant to be serious.

MERGERS OPERATE WORLD

I had to do a little yapping over the "Rodeo" the other night and as the hook-up was principally over the Middle West States, and having been there recently, I knew that one of the principal things that was agitating the Natives was the "Chain Stores." I know in my own State of Oklahoma that it has caused quite a furror.

Well after the Broadcasting I got a lot of letters and Telegrams, lots of them from people that did not hear it, but wanted to know what it was.

Well they asked me to send it to them, so I just figure the best way to do would be to just use it. There wasent much to it, just a lot of junk, but it might interest you. It really, however, is quite a problem I can't and dident try to solve it. That's what the Politicians are for. I only bring these subjects up and let them fix 'em.

Anyhow here it is. I am working here for the Standard Oil of Indiana. In fact sooner or later we will all be working for 'em, or for somebody else. For the day of the Guy working for himself is past. We are living in an age of "Mergers" and "Combines." When your business is not doing good you combine with something and sell more stock.

The poor little fellow, he can't combine with anything but the Sherrif in case he is going broke, which he generally is. But "Big Business" merges with another that's not going good and both do "nothing together." But it's one of the mental weaknesses of the American people that if two things go together they think it must be great. They don't know how it will be financially, but they know that the stock will go up, and that's all they think about, never mind the dividends.

We used to think that it was only things of the same nature that could combine, but now it's liable to be the Pennsylvania Railroad and Mennens Borated Talcum Powder.

Blue Jay Corn Plasters are just as liable to go into a financial huddle with Whirlwind Motors as it is to join pedal extremities with Allens footease.

General Motors not only took over Chevrolet, but Frigid Air Ice boxes. Now what's a Buick car got to do with keeping the smell of onions out of the butter? What's a Caddilac got to do with keeping your milk cool? I don't know but Wall Street does. It knows that the stock went up. General Electric can take over a Tooth Paste, and Wall Street will turn a cartwheel in enjoyment.

Montgomery Ward has put in everything else. I look for 'em to put in Post Offices in every town in opposition to the ones the

Weekly Articles

Government runs. Then where is your little fellow going to be who has struggled along all these years trying to build up his Post Office? Here to fore he has only been troubled by the fact that the Democrats were liable to come in and dispossess him. But now the Chain Stores are liable to put him out of business quicker than the Democrats.

They can put out their stamps and Post cards by the millions, and they can even lose money on stamps in some little town where people mail out a lot of Stories to the Movies and then get 'em back again and then mail 'em out again to somebody else.

It just looks like the way of the Little Post Officeholder is over, and the little anything is over, little Newspaper man, Little Grocer, Butcher, everything. Why Sears Roebuck have opened up a store on every section line crossing. You can't possibly live over six miles out of their clutches. They will sell you a Mowing Machine, Standard Oil stock, U. S. bonds, a Farm, Town lots, Ice Cream soda, a house all put together like blocks.

If you want meat you don't go to the Butcher. The Chain will sell it to you and throw in a Radio set and mattress. Independent Druggists just as well pack up their unpaid charge accounts and their Asparin Tablets and Lettuce sandwiches and quit and join the Navy. For the chain will slice ham thinner than they ever could. They buy their Coca Cola in Oil Tankers.

They can serve your wife a case of Gin, and you a Ford Tractor and deliver it over the counter with your Apple Pie. If you die Piggly Wiggly or owner of my sole name, will buy you cheaper than your local Mortician can monkey with the body. They even got the poor old Bootlegger on the run, they can sell Oklahoma City people Jamaica Ginger cheaper than the Bootlegger can square the Authorities.

And the Minister's business is not safe. Julius Rosenwald, an old friend of mine, wanted me to go in some of their Stores and do a little fancy preaching for 'em.[1] They figured the people would buy something before they got out if it was nothing but an Old Testament. They figure that they can deliver you your salvation cheaper than you can get it elsewhere, and a better grade. Big Business has already corralled the big preachers. So in a year or so we will all be working for "Edsel and Henry, Incorporated," "U. S. Steel and Lip Rouge, Limited," or "Chicago and DuPont Powder Consolidated."[2]

We will either be doing that or else, "Or else what?" Or else not eating regular.

I don't know what's going to be done about it. One time the Government split up the Standard Oil into 31 parts, and in two years each one of the 31 was bigger than the original. So it looked like they just thrived on being split up. There is not much you can do about it unless you could change human nature. Americans are the greatest people in the world to blow and want to talk and go to big things. They will go to the biggest Hotel, regardless of service, the biggest Theater, regardless of performance, the biggest funeral, regardless of whether they knew the corpse, and the biggest store to get anything, whether it's the best or not, and naturally, as the Chain Stores are bigger than most of the others, there is where they hike to. They want to be seen where there is the most people.

Course I hope the Politicans can fix it, for my sympathy is naturally with the little fellow that has struggled along all these years and give the best he could for the money. He must have given pretty good value, for none of them got rich, so that showed he didn't cheat anybody. I don't know what to do about it. We are not only raising too much wheat, we are raising too many people. There ain't enough jobs to go round, and there ain't enough business to go round.

379 AL GRABS FRONT PAGE

Well, all I know is just what I read in the papers. Now just what has been agitating the natives? The fine humanitarin Ramsy McDonald visited this Country and received tremendous publicity, Mr. Coolidge closed up a dam and Indians come for miles.[1] But when Scar Face Al Capone was smuggled through half the jails in Pennsylvania to avoid the crowds on his release, that really comes under the heading of front page "Copy."[2]

Then anywhere you go some Bird will get up and tell "How our Civilization is advancing, and how primative it all was a few years back." Honest there is times when it looks like we havent got over two ideas above a flea. Just give anything enough publicity, and we would pay admission to see folks Guillotined.

I happened to be playing last spring in a theater in Philadelphia when this estimiable gentleman Capone was arrested there, that is he arranged for his arrest. An opposition Gang was just two Machine Gun lengths behind him and he was looking for a refuge, so he just had himself arrested, and put where the Industry couldent get at him. He had looked all the jails over and decided that the Pennsylvania ones were the hardest to break into. He told the Policemen that he was carrying a gun, and for them to arrest him on that charge.

Can you imagine arresting a man in America for carrying a gun nowadays? Why in Chicago there is Pistol pockets put in your

Pajamas. There is thousands there that are faultlessly dressed in artillery that havent got underwear on. He has a wonderful place at Miami Beach, Florida. He and Jess Andrews and Caryl Fisher all have arranged a Community Estate and interests there together, and they have great times romping together.[3] We made an offer to get him to come to Beverly Hills, but Jess and Caryl knowing what an asset he was made him a better offer.

Capone just run the poor old Dissarmament Conference ragged. We havent heard of them in years. They drew on us for $150,000 more the other day. We better put them on a Commission basis. They get so much for what they agree to sink. Poor Ramsey McDonald. It takes all his time finding out if he is still at the head of his Government. Every time a problem comes up and is voted on in the House of Commons why if the side he is on loses, why that means that he has been defeated, and should resign, that the people have lost confidence in him, and losing confidence in a Public Official over there means something. It means he is not with you long. Imagine what would have happened to our Senate if such a procedure had been in effect over here.

Course McDonald is still strong over there, and they are afraid to put him out as he would run at the next election and come back stronger than ever. They come home, they can't just leave and do absolutely nothing. But it just wasent in the cards to get anything done. For the very problems that have stumped 'em there, they knew existed before they went and what I never could understand is why they dident find out before the thing was called if it would be possible to do these certain things.

Well, let's see what else we got. Oh Yes, the Literary Digest, it has got us in the throes of another heated Campaign. We are straw voting around. Straw voting is about the lowest form of voting there is. It don't decide much, but it works 'em up while it lasts, but these old Literary Digest boys have got it down pretty fine, and the side that loses might try to kid it off as a joke, but at heart they will take it mighty serious.

Course whoever wins, it won't mean anything, only another argument, and it will just get the Digest in good practice for another vote in 1932 on the same subject. I don't know who they are mailing the ballots too. I havent SEEN ANY, OR ANYONE that has, but I saw a picture of one in the Digest, so whatever happens I won't be able to get mixed up in it.

380 THE TARIFF IS PASSED

1930

Well all I know is just what I read in the daily prints. Well sir what do you think happened? You couldent guess in a million years. The United States Senate passed the Tariff Bill. Everlasting life, and perpetual motion are the only other two things now that we have to look forward to, and after this, we can really look forward to them with more hope.

Of course Tariff has been to a Politician about what a bone is to a Dog, and fixed Jury is to a Los Angeles Culprit. It's not only his bread and butter, but it's his desert and toothpick. Any President with Political knowledge always fights shy of the Tariff coming up during his Administration. They tried their best to drag Roosevelt into it, and he just took a well worn elm Club and wrapped it over any friend or foe's head who suggested that his Administration get tangled up with that yellow fever.[1] That's where he got the reputation of the "Man with the Big Stick." It was for hammering on Guys who wanted some Tariff gravy.

Coolidge was another they tried to land. Say that little red-headed Yankee dident cut his political teeth on a District of Columbia License Plate. He knew the tariff was Jamica Ginger, and would paralyze anybody that libated on it. So when Mr. Hoover come along, the old Political Boy's mouth just watered. They said here is some new money in the game. Here is a fellow that learned his Politics feeding the Armenians.

Well they dident even let Mr. Hoover get elected till they started working on him. They got ahold of him during the heat of the Campaign, and got him to promise that if elected he would revise the Tarriff. Now if he had only known it he dident have to do this. Nobody was pressing him for Tarriff action but the Politicians themselves. Of course they made him think that it meant his election, but my goodness he was so far out in front that he couldent have been beaten with a Tammany Hall voting maching at every booth. He was in the bag the hour he was nominated. But he was foolishly made to announce, "If elected I will hold a Special Session of Congress, and revise the Tarriff to help the Farmer."

Now there is another thing, that extra session of Congress. That's just about as much misery to a President as the Tarriff. Why call 'em in Extra session, why call 'em in regular session? Here he was borrowing all this trouble for no reason at all.

The present Tarriff Bill originated in January 29, just exactly 14 months ago. It passed the House of Representatives on the last of May, last year, or less than four months from the day it went in there.

131

The House then kissed it goodbye and sent it to the Senate. That was last June, now its pretty near next June.

Well they wore out that special session with it, and finally Mr. Hoover had to let 'em go home to think up some new rates and come back in time for the regular session. They took up the debate right where they had left off and never missed a word. That's nine months those Birds have argued and debated over that Bill, and there is not one man in five hundred that you meet that know or care what in the world it's all about.

The best prosperity the country had ever had was under the Bill that this one replaces. But it must be changed. Factories wasent closing. Manufacturing was paying a fine dividend. But Uncle Joe says, "My boys are kinder kicking on some little competition that is creeping in.[2] It's not much, but we better nip it while it's young, and they have been mighty liberal with you Lads here during your various Campaigns, so we better give 'em some returns on their contributions."

Well "Uncle Joe" took it to heart so much, that he just swallowed his pride and went into the Senate himself, says "Here I will show you Boys how to make a Bill." He found out early that Reed Smoot was born, weaned, brought up, and turned loose just with one sole purpose in view, that was to get a higher Tarriff on Sugar.[3] The day there is a Bill passed to make it unlawful and punishable by death to extract the juice from the Utah Beet, that day will Reed be made a Mormon Prophet, and buried by the side of Brigham Young.[4]

Well Uncle Joe says to himself, "I am going to do for every Article Manufactured in Pennsylvania what Reed does for Sugar." So he says, "Reed I'll help you on sugar if you will help me on 1645 other Nick Nacks that are made up my way." Now you would think that would be an unfair trade wouldent you? But not with Smoot. You get him his sugar, and you can bring in your articles by the million and he will O.K. your raise on 'em.

Of course there was no vote trading done during all this time. Who said there was anyhow? Well he ought to be ashamed of himself for slandering a fine bunch of men, if he said it. Seven Democrats traded themselves out of their Party. Bourssard of Louisiana stuck with his sugar too.[5] Doc Copeland of N.Y. left the policies of Jefferson to string with the Doctrine of the best Treasurer the United States had before Andy Mellon.[6] Key Pittman of Nevada, Lord knows what they manufacture up his way outside of Divorces.[7] I guess the Sugar Beets has got over the line from Utah or else Smoot did him a favor in his early career.

Sam Bratton of New Mex., where the sheep vote, joined the

1930

Republicans to get a higher rate on Navajo Blankets made in Brooklyn.[8] Kendrick, a Cowman, Sheridan, from Wyoming, joined the sheepherders.[9] Trammell of Florida stayed in the Republican column, to offset Fletcher of Jacksonville who evidently Uncle Joe couldent come to terms with.[10] The final vote was 53 to 31. Fourteen months of steady Oratory to change something that was already going good.

381   COUNTING NOW IN STYLE

Well all I know is just what I read in the papers. When a man comes around to our House nowadays or you get a letter you don't know if it's a Census Taker, a Literary Digest Poll Vote or a Bootlegger.

This is the year of the census. We take a tally. That's what we used to call it when I was on a ranch and we counted cattle. In other words we run 'em by us and see how many we got. Well, Uncle Sam takes a tally every ten years, and it's a good thing, not that it means much to anybody to know how many other people there are. But it's an Old Spanish Custom, and it does give work to the ones that count and that's what we got to do this year is to do something that will give everybody something to do.

California is sure excited over this census. Most places just take it as a matter of fact, but not out here. These Babies take it as a business. They have instructed every one of us on just what assumed names to give to the different Census takers, and when we have registered under every name we can think of then not to forget to use our right one. That's how far they are going out here. They are all excited over the fact that the more votes we show we have the more Congressmen we will be allowed in the next Congress.

Well of all the silly arguments. Who wants more Congressmen? But they seem to think the more we have the more loot we will get from the National Treasury in the way of appropriations. Then the more we can advertise what we have out here the better they think it will make us. I don't know about that. There ain't much quality in numbers. But there is not an Editorial out here that don't tell us how valuable it is to register all we can.

The Literary Digest poll is causing a lot of talk. It's staying wet a little longer than I thought. That might be on account of the most of the drys can't write. But I think when the old back country gets going good they will throw the thing the other way.

It's given the Preachers something new to talk about anyway.

Weekly Articles

They are getting out now and working like it was a regular election. I just heard a Couple of them over the Radio tonight.

Well, it's a funny thing that a so-called busy Nation can take so much time to argue all this over something that can't be changed now, no matter what happened. This is no election time, and all this talk will be for nothing. But we are that way. We can get more excited over something that can't be done anything about. The Bootlegger is with us and like the Sunday Automobile accidents it just looks like both will be with us from some time.

The old Conference over in London is being slipped Oxygen between gasps. I don't want to brag but when I went there and heard the King make his opening and then I come home, why I think I didn't miss a thing. Here is all these poor newspaper men over there all this time. There was four hundred visiting correspondents there, just waiting day after day to find out something, and all this misunderstanding could have easily been found out at home before they left, for none of them have changed. We wanted Parity and we were never going to get it. Italy wanted equality with France and they were never going to get it. So these were things that should have been threshed out before anyone ever left. That is seen if it would be possible to fix such things.

I have always claimed that any International Conference does more harm than good, for they engender more hate than good will. It's hatreds formed at Conferences that causes the next war. If I don't meet you and have any business dealings with you, I think you are perhaps O.K., but the minute I meet you day after day and both of us are trying to do the best we can towards our own, why that just shows up our shortcomings, and we go home knowing the other fellow's weaknesses.

I tell you when you commence to talking war you are on a pretty ticklish subject, and that's all that disarmament is. It's just talk about wars.

You can't discuss Battleships without discussing what they are to each other in battle. Why the London Conference, I was there and heard them for two weeks, and when they had each discussed Publicly their needs why there wasent a Navy afloat that would have been adequate for them. Everybody got up and got to talking about the amount of Coast line they had. Why you had no idea that there was anywhere that there was so much ocean front. Here out here I had been putting what little money I had in Ocean Frontage, for the sole reason that there was only so much of it and no more, and that they wasent making any more, then when I hear Nation after Nation arise and announce the amount of coast line they had, it sure was discouraging to me.

I tell you this old thing of telling another nation how to defend itself is bad dope. Every man protects himself according to his own needs and his best methods. But we did have a mighty fine bunch of men over there and we can always rest assured that they did all they could.

Say old Wall Street is picking up again. The Boys must have saved up and started to contributing again. They always did say that the heart of the American people was sound, in fact it was sounder than most of the stocks that the sound heart bought. I will always believe that Mr. Hoover pulled that Gang through a pretty tough place.

Anybody that wouldent have come to their help like he did might have left them in worse shape than they would have wished to admit. That rallying all those business men around him, while it looked kinder funny at that time, I believe it had a fine effect. Just to see those men's pictures in the papers make us feel like we have something. So I still believe that Herbert will come through in fine shape, and I won nothing but two beach lots.

382   DISSERTATION ON LEGS

Well all I know is just what I read in the papers. You know one of the most welcome things that has hit us in many a moon is the return of the long dresses. It had to come but it was a long time doing it. You see according to law, fashions must change every year, sometimes every month, and in order to change dresses styles, you have to either go up or down, the crossways change don't count, or show much. So if you can only change one way or the other and you have been going one way for years why it stands to reason that the worm must turn sometimes, even if it's a silk worm. Well skirts had just gone so high there wasent anything to 'em, and the material people put up a howl. Men had just about lost interest in 'em, or below 'em.

It was just legs, legs, legs. The whole country had gone legs. Every imaginable shape, size, contour, was on free exhibition. Legs were one parade. Well you can get tired of anything if it's dished up to you morning noon and night. We will watch an Elephant parading quicker than we will anything, and I doubt if even they could hold our attention if we couldent turn without having an eye full of elephant legs all the time.

They first showed us their calves. Well that looked fairly promising, and we seemed enough shocked to add spice to our views. But

Weekly Articles

when they just practically overnight yanked another foot off their apparel and we woke up one morning with thousand of knees staring us in the face, why there is where I will always think they overstepped and took in too much territory. A knee is pliable but not what you would call gorgeous. There is 120 million people in this Country with knees, that adds up 240 million knees, substracting the He knees, and figureing on a fifty percent male calf crop, that leaves 120 million She knees.

Now almost every part of the human anatomy has gained fame in some way or another. We speak of beautiful arms, necks, heads, feet, Body hands, nose, eyes and ears, but do you know out of 120 million knees we have never heard a word about a one of them only two belonging to little Anne Pennington.[1] Now aint that strange? Of all the knees in the world there has only been one pair that rose to the distinction of ever being spoken of.

You read of some Girl imported from Europe to join Ziegy's Follies and it tells of her legs, but there is never anything outstanding about her knees.[2] The reason is they have a practical and not landscape value, in other words there had to be a joint somewhere for locomotion purposes and in order to get the joint in they had to break the line of the limb on the way down, that meant leaving some bumps there that it was practically impossible to get rid of. You see an ugly leg is just as apt to have a fair looking knee as a good looking leg is, that is if there was such a thing as a good-looking knee.

Now I was just telling you just now about Anne's knee's. I know Anne's knees pretty well. I was in the show with them for years. We both had our little meal tickets. I had my chewing Gum and my rope and Anne had her knees. If I appeared without my rope there would have been a row, and if Anne had appeared without hers there would have been a Riot. When she wanted to disguise herself and not be recognised in public she used to cover up her knees and no one ever knew her. Hers kinder blended into the leg, they dident protrude.

Most people's knees are practically knots, but little Anne's were symetrical. I used to do a dance with her in the Follies and I could black up some nights, or send in a double, and let him do it for me, and I would never be missed. For when Annes knee's were on the stage why your audience never looked up. But when the feminine world, or the dress designers who perhaps did it, thought "Why if Anne can startle the world with hers, why we will show 'em some knees."

And Brother they did, some knees and How, and why? It was just old bumpy knees to the right of us, exposed joints to the left of us, volleyed and rattled.

1930

Well to be honest with you the idea just dident get over. Women made a mistake, like everybody else makes the same mistake when they are allowed to much kneeway. They always spoil a good thing by going to far, and that's what they did when they showed us their knees. We would have thought much more of 'em, both morally and artistically if they had just kept 'em covered. So they had to do something, nobody was looking at 'em any more, and they was tired of looking at themselves. So they had to do something radical so some genius conceived the idea of not only covering the knee up but the whole thing again, and you would be surprised how much better they look. You see short dresses was made for certain figures, but fashion decrees that everybody be fashionable, so that means there is going to be folks try and keep up with fashions that while they might be financially able, are physically unfit, their purse is good but their build is bad. Now with long skirts that will all be remedied. Every girl gets an even break till she hits the beach. So long skirts mean democracy, there is no privalge classes. Society is not rated on its curves as it has been. You got to get by with your head now instead of underpinning.

Defects are hid now and not made exhibits. The big-legged Girl and the skinny-legged one are coming back. That's going to cut out a lot of this fool reducing too. That was what was the matter with the prosperity of this country, people wasent eating and buying enough. Course they can hide their legs for a few years now, and we grow up a new generation that never saw them why that will mean that they can take another whirl at the old exposure stuff. But We hope it don't come during our generation, for we have seen enough legs and knees to tide us over the balance of our existence. You watch the marriages pick up now. Concealment will beat exposure anytime.

383   WHY MR. COOLIDGE DODGES THE SENATE

Well all I know is just what I read in the Magazines, and about all I read in the Magazines is what Mr Coolidge puts in there. In one out a couple of weeks ago that just happened to fall into my hands because it had some nice dress advertisements in there that my Wife had bought it too look at, why among all these Tooth Paste, Linolium, "Stay sleep" matresses, "Pick me up Tonic" memory courses, Face massage cream, and Corn Plaster adds, why here was an Article by Mr Coolidge advising Ex Presidents not to run for the United States Senate. In the meantime Mr Taft had passed away and

Weekly Articles

that left practically no one left to take this warning outside of Mr Coolidge himself.[1]

But the way he put it it sounded mighty sound. He says if he was in the Senate that "it would not be agreeable to many of my Colleagues." Now he is right about that. There is some of them in there that might object cause you take a Body of men, and no matter how exclusive you try and keep it or how high you make the fees to get in, there is bound to creep in an undesirable element.

Well the Senate is no different. There is a pack of Democrats that have got in there, and been kinder lodged so long that it is going to take time to root 'em out. Now naturally they would kinder object to Mr Coolidge coming in there. They are just narrow minded enough to prefer some Massachusetts Democrat to the scholarly presence of an Ex President.

Then another thing that might have had its effect on Mr Coolidge's inclination to not desire to crave to run, was the fact that in his very District some lowly Democrat beat the ears off a Republican for the office of Congressman, and that was in Massachusetts where up to then Democrats had been confined mostly to Zoo's. Then too Mr Coolidge seemed to anticipate some little embarrasment to some of his fellow members of the Republican side of the Senate.

You see there is another ailment cropped up in the last few years. We had no more than eradicated yellow fever and small pox than "Insurgentry" broke out in our midst. Well it has quite a sprinkling of victims, and like all ailments it has naturally reached the Senate. Well Lepers kinder naturally flock together, so these observation cases in this Insurgentry ward kinder drifted in with the old Democratic Lumbago bunch, (they had weak backs from carrying their troubles). So these two naturally pooled their troubles, and you would be surprised the amount they had accumilated. Now what Mr Coolidge meant is if he went in there, he would naturally be called upon to be nice to them, and it would be embarrassing.

Then he knew also of a third group, that was recognized members of his own Doctrine, but members who who had failed to make the breakfast table when he was presiding over the pancakes in the good old days of the feed trough. They havent forgot that he kinder high hatted some of them, and if he come in there with nothing but just a membership card why he would not even get the loan of the privalege of the floor from them.

Then another thing he knew is that when you went in there, you had to start at the bottom, that is if you was not Grundy, course he was an exception.[2] He put all these in there so naturally when he come in, he got the best in the House.

1930

But Mr Coolidge had no list of Campaign contributions that he could show that he could swing, so about the best Committee he could hope to get on was the "Ways and Means Committee to find out what to do with excess empty bottles found in cloak room." Or perhaps be put on the funeral Committee that would be called on to visit the home with the body of a Brother member. You see he knows all these things and so that's why he said he would not be interested.

Now get this what he says, "Yet I do not mean to underestimate the Senate. IN ITS CONCEPTION, IT'S A GREAT LEGISLATIVE BODY." Get that, in its Conception! He don't say in its execution, it's great. He only says the idea of it is great. You know that fellow has always got his tongue in his cheek, he was kidding those Birds and bet they swallowed this just as it sounded. He is wise to those Babies, and he is too wise to get mixed up with 'em, he knows that they are laying for him if he ever pokes his nose in there, and he is not going to give them the chance.

Then in just the next paragraph he punches right in the jaw with this, "I passed to a higher rank twelve years ago when I was elected Governor of Massachusetts. To take a back track now would be to give up a position that I believe is important to the Country."

You see he kinder wants to keep his Social standing. He has got this home now in Northampton, and he wants to kinder put on some dinners, and he don't want it said in the morning paper, "Another Senator gives a dinner." He wants the name mentioned. Ex Presidents are awful scarce, but you can't hardly shake a bush without an Ex Senator running out, afraid that you are looking for him for an investigation.

He just won't let the Senate rest even in peace. Down on the same page he has this paragraph, "While I do not *altogeather* share the prevailing lack of esteem in which the Senate is held now." You see he practically tells them that they are "Jamaica Ginger" to the rest of the Country, and that he don't ALTOGEATHER hold this opinoin. In other words he says, You birds are terrible, but personally I don't believe that you are as bad as they say you are, in fact I don't think you could be that bad and live, so he don't Altogeather share the Country's unanimous opinion.

So you see if he ever went in there they would just resurrect this one article, and when he wanted something in the way of a new Post Office building why these other Boys would drag out this Article and say, "Oh you did knock us did you? Well try and get something out of our old Pork Barrell and see where you get."

So he is mighty wise in not going in there. He watched 'em work

Weekly Articles

for 8 years, two as Vice President where he had nothing to do but watch 'em, and six where he had to run the Country in spite of them, so asking a man to enter a Den of Lions after he has scars on his body from them, well it just ain't in the cards. What a wise little fellow he is!

384   PRAIRIE AND OIL NEWS

Well, all I know is just what I read in the papers or what I see as I prowl from hither to thither. Got to tell you about going back home week before last.

You know at Ponca City, Okla., they were unveiling a wonderful big Bronze Statue of "The Pioneer Woman." The Sculptor Baker made it and did a mighty fine job.[1]

It was picked from 12 models by 12 of the World's leading Artists. They sent the models all over the Country and exhibited them and let the folks vote on it and this one got by far the most. It's a beautiful figure standing 30 or 40 feet high, of a fairly young Mother leading her young son by the hand, and she has determination and grit written in her every feature. She has an old Sun Bonnet and long skirts, she is truly a Pioneer. I think she is a Democrat for she has a kind of dumb Democratic faith in what she is going to do.

The poor thing just don't know that the Republicans have taken over everything and we can only peep through the fence and see what they are doing.

This Oil man, George Marland, paid the whole cost of the thing, which must have run into lots of money, and he put on and entertained every body on the day of the unveiling.[2]

Well, it was the old home state and I knew there would be a lot of old timers there, so I rushed around and got a couple of days off from my Picture that I am making and grabbed a Plane out of here early in the morning, and was there for dinner that night, stayed all night and the next day, and left early the following day and was back here in Beverly Hills that evening at 4:30.

You know it's just uncanny where you can get to in one of those things, distance just don't mean a thing. You just get up in the morning and anywhere you think of you want to be, why you are there that same day. Ponca City is a beautiful Prairie City. It's fortunate in having some oil men there that have made lots of money, but spent it there, they dident have social Long Island ambitions.

Well, the old Timers sure did gather in there. They had a fine

Will Rogers making a nation-wide radio broadcast at the dedication of "The Pioneer Woman" memorial in Ponca City, Oklahoma, on April 22, 1930.

Weekly Articles

parade at 10 o'clock in the morning, old Prairie Schooners and outfits that looked like they had made the "run" in there in the early days. Cutest float was a bunch of little kids 3 or 4 years old, dancing and it was labelled, "Pioneer Dancers."

Saw old man Colonel Zach Mulhall that I hadent seen in some time.[3] I hit New York with a show in 1905 and showed in Madison Square Garden. He was a great old fellow and a good Showman, also there was another old time friend, Pawnee Bill, you all remember seeing his shows for years.[4] He is a prosperous Banker and Ranchman and don't ever get a day older.

Jimmy Rider, an old hand that ranched right side of me in those days, and forgot more about roping than I will ever know, well Jimmy brought his "Remuda" over, had a Ford full of the finest Kids you ever saw, one wild one named Bill Rogers.[5]

Zach Miller, the sole surviving one of the three Miller brothers, that own the famous 101 Ranch and show, Zach left the show in Wichita and come down, and after the ceremonies were over we went down to the big Ranch and what a place it is.[6]

My oldest boy, Bill, was out there spending his little Spring vacation away from Beverly Hills High School.[7] He was over around Chelsea and Oo-la-gah, and Claremore. Well he and my only Sister, Mrs. Tom McSpadden from Chelsea, they drove over and Bill and I flew home together.[8] He had flown, or flew (which is it anyway?) out a week ahead of me.

Mr. Hoover was mighty nice and opened the ceremonies from Washington over a National hook up, then come our own Oklahoman Secretary of war, Pat Hurley, he was sick and couldent come out, or he sure would have been there.[9] Pat's doing a mighty nice job of waring back there and if anything shows up during his administration he is liable to make a name for himself. Pat will act as secretary and soldier too, if we can match anything.

We got a Governor out there that I had never met before and I got to meet him before he was impeached, that's an accomplishment.[10] Well sir, this one is sticking and it looks like we are going to finally have something permanent. All these others we have had couldent send their laundry out and be sure they would be there when it come back.

There must have been fifty thousand people at this and what made it look colorful was the big amount of Indians, of all tribes, Poncas, Otoes, Osages and Cherokees. You see it was our tribe of Cherokee's that sold the original old Cherokee Strip that all this mess is living on.

I think the Government, only give us about a dollar an acre for it. We had it for hunting grounds, but we never knew enough to hunt oil on it. I can remember as a kid the payment we had, when the Government paid out the money to the Cherokees for it. There was something over three million dollars as there was that many acres and we got about $320 apiece, I think it was.

The Cherokees are supposed to be the highest civilized Tribe there is and yet that's all we ever got in all our lifetime and sold a fortune in oil and wonderful agricultural land to get that little 320 apiece. Yet there was the Osages lived right by us and they get that much before breakfast every morning, and they are supposed to be uncivilized.

So it really shows you it kinder pays not to know too much. I would trade my so called superior knowledge right now for an Osage headright. If you had their payments you wouldent need to know anything only where the payment was going to be held. But as a matter of fact the Osages got some mighty smart men among them.

But it was a great gathering and a beautiful thought in the erecting of that Statue. Why even Eve, one of our original ancestors never had a Statue built to her, till Robert Quillian of Greenville, South Carolina, did it in his front yard, out side of there in the little Town he lives in.[11] He took me out to see it.

You all know him, he is the fellow that writes these wonderful little short sayings that make up in thought what long ones lack in sense. He is a wonder and it took a Humorist to see that Eve wasent getting anywhere and if you ever go down there, go and see her.

385 BREAKS ABOUT EVEN

Well, all I know is just what I read in the papers. Our Deligates getting back home on one of our boats a couple of weeks ago was big news, for when they went over it was thought they would sink so much that they would have to borrow a boat to come home on.

Well they come dragging in, they dident bring much back in the way of a Treaty, but enough to save their skin. They layed it on to France and Italy that Japan dident get any further. In other words they used France and Italy as an alabi for them not agreeing better.

But take it all in all I guess the Boys did as good as could be expected. I know when I was over there listening to them for two and a half weeks I dident think they would ever get back home with their Pajamas.

Now comes the big fight in the Senate over what they brought back. Anything that has to pass by that Senate is just like a Rat having to pass a Cat Convention, it's sure to be pounced on, and the more meritorious the scheme is the less chance it has of passing. But there should be no serious opposition to any fair scheme they brought back.

They won't sink much, and it won't hurt us much. This dissarmament is very dear to Mr. Hoover's heart, and the Senate ought to at least let him have his way once. They have objected to everything else. I look for 'em to pass a resolution denouncing his brand of Fishing tackle.

Course the Eclipse come and went away and the Scientists had a Picnic. They got more pleasure out of some fool thing the sun or moon does than you or I would get out of a new wedding. They got pictures of it.

Why an Iowa Tourist that caught Mary and Doug out in the yard and got a snapshot of it wasent any prouder than those Boys when they found they had shot the Sun while it was hiding behind maby Venus or Neptune.[1] It wasent as dark as it was at that Eclipse five or six years ago. That was a dandy. We are not putting on as good Eclipses as we did under the Coolidge administration. Hoover is falling down on our Eclipses. What we want is bigger and darker eclipses.

Say, and you talk about these learned scientists that know all about when these are going to happen, will, let me tell you one, did you know that the Hopi Indians out in Arizona that put on that snake dance every year, know about as much about the Moon and Stars and what's going to happen as these College Birds do? Those Indians don't let it be known just when the dance will be held till they have figured out various happenings of the elements.

You see, this dance is in the nature of a prayer for rain, and what I mean they get it. They are doing some praying that is backed up by some previous knowledge. They don't just grab a snake in their mouth and jump around and ask the Lord to drown them out just because they are asking it. These old Indians study the heavens for weeks ahead, and they know about the time that rain is maybe leaving Honolulu and headed this way, well, then they say we will dance on the 6th of next month.

Well, I was up there year before last, and before they could unwrap these rattlesnakes from around their necks and ears and tongues, why, the old rain had started in. Those old Indians don't just take snap judgment on having their prayers answered. They know what's going to happen, and then lay their prayers accordingly. Then, we call 'em uncivilized.

1930

The trouble with our praying is, we just do it as a means of last resort. We just pray for anything, whether we got any dope on it or not. But these Indians. Say, the Rain come down so thick and the roads was so bad and slippery that the Indians had no more than stopped praying for the rain to come than the Whites started praying for it to stop, so their Fords wouldent slip over into the Grand Canyon.

Well, it's just as I told you, we had no previous data on what could be expected of the duration of this particular rain, so we lost our prayer entirely. Now, how do those Indians, with no instruments, no cameras, no observatories, no Fraternity Pins, not even a College Pennant, now, how do they go about getting their advance information? But they know so many things we don't, that it's got so it's no novelty to try and find out why they know it.

You know I believe the Lord split knowledge up among his subjects about equal after all. The so-called ignorant is happy. You think he is happy because he don't know any better. Maybe he is happy because he knows enough to be happy. Well, the smart one knows he knows a lot, and that makes him unhappy because he can't impart it to all his friends. Discontent comes in proportion to knowledge.

The more you know the more you realize you don't know, so you see after all the Lord evened it up, dident he? He evens up everything in the long run. Rockefeller has got a Billion Dollars and can't eat cornbeef and cabbage.[2] Hoover has surveyed the entire Universe and fed the World, yet he can't catch a Sail Fish. Andy Mellon takes up our collection, and cares for our donations, yet he can't control the votes in Philadelphia.[3]

Henry Ford can jolt the Gizzards out of humanity but he spends his time trying to master the old-fashioned quadrille. Coolidge was President of these great United States but he spends his time writing fiction for the Magazines.

Aimee McPherson has the whole of Los Angeles worshipping at her shrine, but over in Jarusalem they won't let her ask the blessing without she joins the Moslems.[4] And the rest of us we have our little blessings in one way or the other. Here I am scratching around trying to tell enough jokes to pay my taxes and interest on what I owe every Bank out here. But I can dance a quadrille better than Henry, can eat anything, have no ambition to catch a fish, and just crazy enough to be happy. So when we all figure up, the breaks are about even.

AMOS AND ANDY

Well all I know is just what I read in the papers.

"What did you read in the papers, Andy?"[1]

"Well Amos I jes been setting here thinkifying, I jest wanted to come out and help you run the Fresh Air Taxicab, but there has been so much regoations going on here in the office that I jes couldent get away."

"What kind a distortions been going on here in the office, Andy, outside of Madam Queens perpesual telephoneing?"

"Well, the's been a lot of news in the papers, Amos. It wouldent do much good to know what was in there, for you wouldent know anyhow."

"Well dident I brought you the papers that the people left in the taxicab, if it hadent been for me and my regenerosity you wouldent a knowed what was in the papers."

"Yes, Amos, you did brought in the papers, and the next time I want you to bring in some that was on the seat and not on the floor, and, too, I wants you to carry customers who leave some of the good papers there, and quit hauling these folks that jes reads the Tableaux Papers."

"What you mean those little papers thats got all the pictures of all the murders in 'em? Why, Andy, I thought that's the kind you wanted; you don't have to do no reading to puruse one of 'em."

"Yes, dats jes it, Amos, it makes me look like I can't read, when somebody comes into the office here on reportant business and dey sees me wif one of dem little old police gazetts turned white, why it drops me in dem folks respiration. What I wants you to bring in is some of de big papers with less snap shots and more reditorials. I am a man, Amos, whats got to keep reformed on whats going on, now take you, you don't have to know nothing, dats you has lived this long without it proves dat you don't, but with me running de business like I is, why I got to be able to reverse with anyone who comes in, and on any subject that they might want to reconsider."

"Yes, but Andy, you don't have to talk on nothing but, 'No I can't pay it today, but if you will come around tomorrow Amos will maybe have made something and den I can make you a small reposit on de undebtness.' Dats all you ever called on to say, Andy, to any of 'em that ever comes in, even de Sheriff you jes told him the same, so whats de good of all de reading?"

"Now, listen here, Amos, is you my friend, or is you aint? You got me all wrong. We's got a business here and I is de President, and you is de personelly?"

1930

"What's you mean I is de personelly?"

"I means you is de crew. I is de Captain and whatever de Captain ain't you is."

"What what's dat got to do with you setting here reading de papers all de day, with your big flat feet on de desk, and me out taking a chance with my life dodging these other roposition lines, where de drivers are for using me fur a green light and running right through me."

"Yes, but Amos ain't you riding all de time? Why jes think de folks whats in de cab are paying to get jes what you are getting for nothing."

"Yes, but dey ain't getting what I is getting when I is out on de street standing in de rain and sno', waiting for somebody to come ride wif me."

"Yes, but ain't it de 'Fresh Air Taxi Cab,' don't we advertise it as sich and ain't you there partaking in the fresh air all de time while de Customers they only partake in the air during de time they are part and passels of you Cab. So again you is getting something for nothing, while I is here in dis old stuffy office readin and skeemin how to let you have these blessings."

"Well why don't you distake of some of some of these blessings some time? You ain't been in dat cab in so long you couldent find de clutch, I wants you to know its hard setting and waiting for something to show up."

"Yes but dident I see by de papers dat Mr. Hoover is bringing us posterity and we all goin' to be doin' better before we knows it?"

"Well, mayby we's doing better now and don't know it, what's he keeping it from us fur?"

"Well de paper say dat Mr. Hoover has jes talked with Mr. Mellon and Mr. Ford and Mr. Rockefeller and Mr. Capone and dat means dat de good times is right round de corner."[2]

"Well why don't dey tell us what corner, so we can go round there. If we can get some of dis resiprocity by jes going round de corner, I is a man dats going to start turning right now."

"Well dey say dat business is on de upgrade."

"Maby its stalled on de grade. Looks like cording to our business, we is on de grade and our brakes won't even hold and we slipping backwards, what dey say about us of 'em dats on de upgrade but going de wrong way?"

"Well he says he has appointed a Remission to disgust dat."

"Well if de members of de Remission don't ride in our Taxicab what good's dat going to do us?"

"Don't you understand, Amos, this is a time and degeneration of

Weekly Articles

Big Business. De little fellow don't count. We is in a period of Mass destruction and you got to be immerged with somebody."

"Who is we going to get immersed with? Ain't de Republicans for de poor man?"

"No, Amos, dats de Democrats what was going to help de poor."

"Well why don't dey help us den?"

"Well dey will help you, Amos, jes as soon as dey helps their selvs, dey ain't doing much better than we is. Dey got to immerge with somebody else dey will be worse off den they is."

"Well who could de Democrats immerse with?"

"Why nobody less 'en its the Republicans."

387 WILL ROGERS SAYS 'RED' CAGLE HAS DECEIVED US!

Well all I know is just what I read in the papers. The last week or so we did have some outside devilment to take our minds off the usual routine. The most diverting instance was the secret service discovering the fact years after it had happened that our great Football player, Red (Christian) Cagle had grabbed a wife under his arm and streaked through the whole Army regulations for a Justice of the Peace.[1]

This event took place years ago, in fact the year Dewey entered Manila, but the Army has been all this time finding it out.[2] In fact they dident want to find it out till after the football season was over. Because with Red off their football team, they would have looked about like Harvard, or Yale or Princeton, or some of those other second division teams. Notre Dame would have sent in Saint Mary's against 'em.

Seems that Red was down home on a vacation one time, and he run onto a mighty pretty girl. He had his cape thrown back so the red lining showed, and to this Southern Bell it looked like General Lee. Red figured out there wasent much else to do on a vacation, so he thought he better marry her.

He dident want to go away and leave her at the perils of those other old Boys down in the cane breaks. He dident know that when you went to West Point you wasent supposed to be accompanied by a marriage certificate.

But the Army don't want you to have any entangling alliances. They figure it gets your mind off football if you have a wife to worry about. They don't care how much you worry about single Girls. You can keep your mind on some little Dame down the Hudson that makes the "Hops" every time the gates are left open, but they don't want you to have your mind as far away as Louisiana.

Well this marriage seemed to just practically ruin him. Up to then he had been a Substitute on the Plebes team, and had never been between the goal post in his life. But after he come back from that vacation why he went plum loco. There just wasent any controlling him. He would no more than get his fists on a Football than he would light out, and run plum off with it.

Every time they would hand him the ball he would start for Louisiana to show it to his Wife. The Army hadent seen such foolishness as this. It was against all Army regulations. They do everything by orders. You breathe by manual, you sleep by tactics, and eat by regulations. Well they knew there was something the matter with this fellow because he was so different from other inmates. Instead of making just a gain, he would make a touchdown.

Then they commenced advertising him. They said here is a Guy that will get us some money at the gate. He was Red headed; that made him pick up where Red Grange left off.[3] So the first thing we knew he was better known than the whole General staff. The Army had a War College, but nobody knew where it was.

But every ten year old child could tell you where Red Gagle was playing every Saturday. Why when the army played Notre Dame in New York as many people come to see Red as did to see Notre Dame play football.

The Army had a drawing card. Nobody knew who the Secretary of War was, but Immigrants could tell you what Red did against Harvard. You could have left it to a vote of the entire U. S., who they wanted to see carry the ball, Cagle or Coolidge, and Red would have won. The Navy quit playing the Army until Red was outlawed by the statue of limitations. They said "We will play the Army but we won't play Cagle." It looked like for awhile it would be Civil war between the two branches of our service.

They was going to quit playing football and go to fighting. It looked bad. Congressmen and Senators were losing their tickets they were cadging for the game. Even the President says, "Boys will you please play." But the Navy says, "No, not while that fellow is going against all the formula's of Military and Naval tactics." You see they knew there was something the matter with him but they dident know what it was. They dident know that it was matrimony that was spurring him on to these great deeds. And the thousands and thousands of people that were paying and fighting to get to see him, neither did they know that they were being deceived.

They were paying their good hard earned money to see fine young unattached manhood battle it out on the field of educational finance with no undue advantages taken by any one. They looked on it as a fair fight, with no one having an advantage. Little did they know that this Hero that they were cheering at that very moment dident have his mind on the Army and its great and glorious tradition, but that he was sneakingly thinking of this little schoolmam away down south under the shade of the old Turpentine trees.

They dident know that he was deceiving not only the great Government but the poor Taxpayers who had used their influence with Washington to get tickets to get into the game. Had they known that this boy had a wife of many years standing they would have risen up in rightous wrath and maby tore the grandstand down.

And what of all the thousands of fair young things with rouge, and lip stick, what of them? Hadent they come with palpitating hearts to see this Hero grab a Harvard man and throw him not only for a loss, but out of the park? Here was rank deception being practiced before their young gin-clouded eyes.

Who would pay money to see an old married man do something? It was taking the romance out of the great game. How could you make an Idol out of a Husband? Wasent College based on Football? And wasent football based on finance and romance? What does a hundred thousand people care what happens to a married man? And besides hadent he cheated the government? Hadent he got an education all the time making them think he was a fine worthy upstanding single man, when at heart he knew that he was married and unworthy of Government support?

Did he think the Government was going to go round trying to educate married men? Their marriage was their education. So it just looked like the case of Benedict Arnold. I don't know what they will do with him. I suppose they will lynch him. He has just simply spoiled Football for a lot of us. We will never see a man make a touchdown now, that we won't wonder if his wife is watching.

388   TARIFF ARGUMENTS 'NEVER ACCOMPLISH ANYTHING AT ALL'

All I know is just what I read in the papers. I just been reading the weekly paper "Times." You know that's just about the best thing out on the happenings of the week. They give their own slant on what has happened and they must have a bright up-to-date bunch of young fellows on there that give you real low-down. I was just sitting here tonight reading it.

It tells you what the President has been doing that week, and what the Senate, and the House. Course most of these are short, but that's been in ever since Mr. Hoover was inaugurated and called them in special session.

Mr. Ford issues a statement last week that this new tariff bill if passed will be the worse thing in the world for all of us. You see a lot of manufacturing establishments try to cover up their own business ability by having the Government protect them against somebody that handles their business better than they do.

They can always holler "Cheap labor!" But the cost of transportation to this country more than makes up for that. So every little Industry that can't make a big profit hollers for protection.

We won't see the real effects of this till we have all these other Countries passing restrictive tariffs against us. You can't stop the other fellow from shipping his goods to us without him doing something to get even.

Some of the smartest and most conscientious men in our National life have been divided on the tariff question. It's not all Politics, a lot of it is a matter of real opinion, based on a long study. All Democrats don't agree on it and no two Republicans have exactly the same opinion on it. So let's give the old boys back there the benefit of the breaks. They are just up against something that is above them.

Arguing tariff is sorter like argueing religion. There just ain't any answer. If a business thrives under a protective tarriff, that don't mean that it has been a good thing. It may have thrived because it made the people of America pay more for the object than they should have, so a few have got rich at the cost of the many. There is never any way of estimating the damage done by a tariff, that is how much other countries retaliate in different ways. Mr. Grundy might be making Pennsylvania rich, but at the cost of the friendship of all our foreign friends.[1]

You got to sorter give and take in this old world. We can get mighty rich, but if we haven't got any friends, we will find we are poorer than anybody.

Nations are just like individuals. They get mad and fight just like individuals. Their feelings are hurt even quicker than Individuals. They do everything just like one person. So that's the way it is with wealth and position.

We might be the wealthiest Nation that ever existed, we might dominate the world in lots of things, but as Nations are individuals, why we are just an Individual, and because we are richer than all our

Neighbors or than anybody else, that don't necessarily mean that we are happier or really better off.

We don't all envy our Town or State's most wealthy man. We see lots of reasons why we wouldent trade places with him. We not only look at this wealth but we look at all the other sides to him. We may know how he is all wet in lots of ways. So we may say, "Yes, he has got money, but what else?"

Well, now that is the way we are liable to become. We are known as the wealthiest Nation of all time. Well, in the first place we are not. The difference between our rich and poor grows greater every year. Our distribution of wealth is getting more uneven all the time. We are always reading, "How many men payed over a million dollar income tax." But we never read about "How many there is that are not eating regular." A man can make a million over night and he is on every page in the morning.

But it never tells who give up the million that he got. You can't get money without taking it from somebody. They don't just issue out new money. What you got tonight that you dident have last night must have come from somebody.

We have dozens of Magazines that print success articles, but you go broke and see what you can do to get your life story published. Yet the going broke might have made a real man out of you. You may be just starting in to live. We do love to talk in big figures. We love to read in big figures. The old boy that dident get the breaks and couldent make the grade we don't care much for.

So that's the way we have become to look on nations. We are judging them all by the size of the Navy, or their Territory, but we don't give a hoot about their character, or maby a hundred fine things about them. If they don't amount to something in a big way they are a joke to us, "What do we care what a tariff bill does to them? Are we in the business for them or for ourselves?"

So we are liable to get a bad kick back from a lot of this highhanded stuff we are pulling. We are riding a high horse at this time. So it takes a pretty smart man to tinker with this tariff.

We are liable to go do something here we won't live down very soon. It's all right to help out the folks back home, and bring every voter some kind of relief, but you want to be mighty careful at whose expense you bring it. It does look like we ought to be able to manage our affairs so that we could get along and still sorter be friends with folks, too. But this tariff thing has sure got two sides to it, and they are not political sides either. It's a smart man's business, it's not just for mere Politicians to mess with.

389   CONCERNING COURT, MORROW, AND TEXAS

1930

Well all I know is just what I read in the papers. I just been reading in the news about the presentation of some of our Americans at the Court of St James. I remember Ambassador Dawes telling me about what a time he was having picking out the ones that were to be presented.[1] He wanted to turn it over to the Senate to decide which ones to present. Well they had it and as usual wealth won out.

You have often seen the add "Campbells Soup." Well that add has netted dividends, for offspring Charllote bent the knee to the King and Queen.[2] It just shows you what advertising will do for you. The thermos bottle people have got into the Social heat by producing an client to courtesy to their Majestys. Everybody that has ever taken a bottle on a picnic contributed to her social success. The Radio people entered a Daughter, Elizabeth.[3] While the World has been listening in they have themselves had their ear to the Society ground, and when the time come they tuned in with Lizzie.

But while all these National advertised ingredients were "going Social" don't think the Cigarette was idle. No Sir, Old Gold had a test and sent their fair daughter. Doris Duke "walked a mile" through Buckingham Palace to get a peek at George and Mary.[4] Campbells soup had nothing on Campbells Cigaretts. Old Chesterfield was there in all its debutante finery. The Stotesburys entered a fair maid for the test in the person of Miss Francis Hutchison.[5]

Atlanta come through and it wasent Coca Cola either. It was some of the Hoke Smith troop.[6] So it looks like the whole thing run pretty near to form. I kinder thought Dawes would pick out a bunch of Girls in our land who had accomplished something. You know last year America got a lot of favorable publicity by Helen Wills crashing into what up to then had been "Who's Who in Debutantville."[7] Helen made it on backline drive. She could stand in Buckingham Palace and place one in Windsor Castle. So it was thought well maby they will start to introduce Girls who have swum a Channel, speeled all the words right, stuck to the phone during a fire, or done some noteworthy thing. But, no it was the same old racket. The bank book got you in. Achievement couldent hurdle a flock of Credit slips.

The whole thing is the prize "Hooey" thing of all time. They don't get to say a word. The Queen don't say a word to them. They just come by, do a little bum courtesy and then they are through for the day.

It compares in importance about like voting the Democratic Ticket at a Presidential Election. You vote but it don't mean anything. Dawes added the only Democratic touch to the whole thing by having on breeches of a decent length. The Ambassador from Russia, "Comrade" somebody or other, he wore knee breeches but he had a Sweater on. So that squared him with the Proletariot.

Old New Jersey is all excited over the coming election. Mr. Morrow was practically all set, as he should have been, to go in the United States Senate.[8] He is not only the class of the race but of all their races for some time. It takes a Statician to name any of New Jersey's Senators in the past years. So this little fellow would have given them a dignity and importance that they have been sadly lacking in. Plus an ability that is unusual in anyone running for the Senate. Because he announced himself on the Prohibition question, and give the best straight forward explanation of his stand, why up jumps a Dry. He has the same chance being elected as I have to supplant Charley Chaplin as the World's greatest Comedian.[9] But this old Boy just saw a chance to get back into print, so he announced that he would run, not by popular demand, but by personal inclination. So that splits the thing all up. Now he could be in the Senate ten years and nobody would ever know what State he was from, while Morrow would be a power in there. His ability would stand out like a Traffic light in that body.

Been interested in the scheme of my old friend Jack Garner of Texas.[10] Jack wants to divide up the great State of Texas into five states. Why he.wants to stop at five nobody knows. If he is going to split the old open range up, why why not make job of it.

The papers state that Texas would make 220 States the size of Rhode Island, and 54 the size of Connecticut, and six time bigger than the whole of New England. Jack wants more Senators to offset that mess from the east. Well let's make some Rhode Islands out of it, and that will give us (220 times as big). That's 440 Senators. Now that ought to satisfy anybody, even if you are fond of Senators, 440 ought to get us about what Pennsylvania has been getting with their two.

Our old friend Mussolini broke a silence last week. When all the rest of the World was talking on dissarmament he remarked as per such, "Though words are beautiful things, Ships and Aeroplanes, are much more beautiful." That old Lad spoke a palate full. He knows the Nations that are great are the ones that have something in the way of side arms. He knows that without an Army and Navy they will never be able to find room for his growing population.

That fellow has kept Italy on the up-grade for all these years, and all the time everybody says, "Oh, he can't last." I have said ever since I met him in 26, that he was by far the greatest Guy I had ever met, and there has never been a day since then that I have changed. He has done more for his Country than any man ever did for one in a like time. You don't see 'em shooting at him any more do you. He is a Whiz, that baby is. I have never yet seen him propose a fool thing.

390   MISS SOUTHERN DEMOCRACY ASKS ALIMONY

Every once in awhile something shows up in the way of real humor, and it's generally by somebody that most everybody else never heard of. In the case I am presenting to you it says in there that it was presented by a Mr. A. Berkowitz, but anyhow whoever it is, let's get him some credit, and maby spoil his life by making a writer out of him. A Mr. F. W. Kuhn, of Troy Alabama sent it to me as a clipping from the Birmingham Age-Herald. The case is that "Miss Southern Democracy is sueing Senator Tom Heflin for Divorce."[1] It's a bear and I want you to read it. Course they use Tom as the example but it's really hitting at all the Hoovercrats.

I havent heard much from Tom's race lately, but I bet they have a tough time cleaning him. Those town boys might be against him but when he pulls off his old alpaca, and gets to illustrating the weakness of his opponents with those Negro stories, (which he can tell like nobody else) why he will give 'em a tough battle. But let me repeat you this just as is. The Petition follows:

"Miss Southern Democracy complaintant, vs Thomas J Heflin, alias 'Cotton Tom' Heflin, alias 'Admiral Tom' Heflin, respondent, in the Circuit Court of Jefferson County, Alabama, tenth Judicial Circuit of Alabama, in equity. To the honorable William M Walker Judge of said Court, Humbly complaining your complaint, Miss Southern Democracy shows unto your honor the following facts as a basis of complaint.

"First, that your Complaintant is over the age of 21, and has been a boni fide resident of the Sovereign State of Alabama since the year 1865. Your Complaintant retains her maiden name in this bill, for reasons well known to this court and the world at large.

"Second—That the respondent, Thomas J Heflin, is over the age of 21, and though absent from the State a boni fide resident of the State.

"Three—That your complaintant and respondent were married to each other in the fall of the year 1894, at Lafayette, Alabama, where the respondent was a lowly Cotton grower, and where your complaintant, through her aid and influence, first aided the respondent to the rank of Public officer of this great State. Your complainant will in all fairness aver that until the time of the acts herein complained of the respondent was a model husband. That his courtship at Lafayette was swift and ardent, that down through the years respondent was loyal and true, and appreciative of helping hand of complaintant, which in love bestowed upon him many high offices, finally the Toga of United States Senator, in November of the year 1920.

"Four—Your Complaintant avers that she and the respondent lived together in holy blissful union untill the first Tuesday after the first monday of November of the year 1928, at which time they seperated and have not lived togeather since. Your Complaintant charges that in the spring of that year she first noticed changes in her erstwhile model Spouse. He began to stay out late at nights, with dissreputable Characters known as Republicans, That he would come home in a bad mood and mutter "Raskobite," That he no longer fed and cared for the pet Donkey, that had been their comfort during their married life.[2] But brought into their happy home an ungainly Elephant. Your complaintant further charges that he was cruel to her, and threatened to break her up and destroy her forever, that he shamed her in the presence of her Enemies, by speeches so threatening in tone that your complaintant was made to blush and hang her head in shame. That he failed to support her, and furnish her with those necessities of life, and that on said November day he utterly abandoned her, leaving her broken and destitute, and beset by many foes, and he charges that at the time he abandoned her, she was wrong, unchaste, and defiled.

"Your complainant avers that she was ever faithful and true and brought to respondent blessings never before reaped by any man. That she gave to him the best years of her life, and now she has grown frail and weak and cannot support herself, and that but for friends would have long ago been forced to spend her years in want and poverty. Furthermore complainant avers that respondent is in good health, strong, and well able to work, and Complainant being without relief except in a Court of Equity, and prays that your Honor will cause him to plead answer, to this bill, within the time and manner required, and shall pay to Complainant such a sum as will be nessasary for her support and maintanence, in accordance with her station in life, and suitable permanent alimony for her future support.

"Complainant further prays that upon final hearing of this case, your honor will render a decree forever dissolving the bonds of matrimony existing between these two. And that your complainant again be permitted to plunge her adventurous prow once more into the

1930

bevexed waters of the seas of connubiality and cast her fortunes with any man who gains her affections in the contest, for her favor provided for by the law of her Fathers home."

signed A Bekowitz. Solicitor for the complainant. Footnote, — The respondent is required to answer each and every paragraph of the foregoing bill of complaint. But NOT under oath, answer under oath hereby being expressly waived.

A Bekowitz

391 OLD NOAH RAISED HIS OWN WINE

Well all I know is just what I read in the papers, and in the letters that I get after spouting on the "Raddy-ho," (and say by the way, you know we used to kid Al Smith about the way he pronounced that word,) well we just now come to find out that he was right all the time and the rest of 'em all was wrong. Yes Sir Al was absolutely right. Then these people would write me and say, "Why don't you name some of the words that Mr Hoover miss-pronounces?" and then they would name 'em.

Say, what would I know about them? If that's all the people in this country had to worry about, why we would be sitting pretty fine. If there was nothing wrong with us but our pronunciation we would be well off.

But talking about getting letters from Folks, I have had more letters about my broadcasting a week or so ago on Prohibition than I have on any one of the other subjects, and 98 percent of them agreed not with the subject so much as the fact that what I had to say about it was that "We were tired of listening to both sides of the argument and dident care what happened to it." Well you would be surprised the amount that are really tired of it and wish the whole word and subject would pass out of our every day usage. They have asked me so may of them to try and give them something in print of what I did say, and especially they wanted the real dope on whether the stuff about Noah was on the level or not.

Now it sure was. You know I wrote a little book all on Prohibition away back in about 1819. It was called "Will Rogers on Prohibition" and published by Harper and Bro, along with another one called, "Will Rogers on the Peace Conference" and when I was writing this one on Prohibition I remembered that the Bible had a lot to say about drinking and wine, so I borrowed me a Bible, and I started in to read it just to see what I could get that applied to Wine.

Weekly Articles

Well I really had the surprise of my life. I hadent read over a few pages till I run onto this early story of the wild life of our original Ancestor, Noah. The way the book started off it looked like I would get what I wanted right off the reel and that if I used all that was said in regard to wine that I would have to issue it in two volumes.

You see that's one wonderful thing about the Bible—there was no censorship in those days. Of course now some of our Churches hold Conferences and cut out certain parts that they think don't belong in there. Or change them according to what they think should be said instead of what was said. In other words we are always having somebody improving on the words of the Lord. That's even worse than a Scenario Writer brightening up Shakespeare.

Then here just the other day I went to that wonderful play in New York called "Green Pastures" and, say, by the way don't miss it, it's the greatest thing I ever saw.[1] It's the play as you probably know that really enacts all the scenes of the Bible in the every day homely way that the real old down home Negroes think that it is. There is one Character of the Lord, just an ordinary fellow, walking among them and talking to 'em about like any old Preacher. He offers some of his subjects, "Here Brother Noah, is a good ten cent Cigar." Another time when he is having a tough time with his subject he says, "This job of being the Lord is no cinch."

Going around with him all the time up in Heaven is old Gabriel, and he keeps saying to Gabriel, "Look out Gabriel don't toot that horn yet." Gab is always shining up the old Alto Horn. It's the most simple, and the most impressive, and the most reverent thing you ever saw done on a stage. And it's exactly like those old Camp meetings that I have gone to down home in Oklahoma, and it comes about as near being right as some of these other more so-fisticated religions that we have. These Negroes take what the Lord said literally and not what they thought he ought to have said, so don't miss that show if you have to go clear to New York to see it.

But what I started in to tell you was about old Noah. Well in this show they got him building the Ark right there on the stage. The Lord is telling him what to put in it, and Noah asks about the snakes, and the Lord says, "Sure we got to have snakes." "Well," says Noah, "don't you think Lord that we better take a jug of spirits along with us in case one of the snakes goes haywire and bites somebody during the rain?" So the Lord told Noah to take the Jug, and the Noah says, don't you think Lord I better take two Jugs. "No," says the Lord, "Only one Jug." "But," says Noah, "two Jugs would balance the boat, put one on each side." "No," says the Lord, "Put the one jug in the middle of the Boat." So you see everybody seems to be pretty well wise to old Noah. He wasent hardly what you would call the backbone of the Anti Saloon League.

You see it was in the early Chapters of Genesis that it reads, "And he became a Husbandman and planted a Garden." You see the minute he got married he started right in raising the ingredients that go with married life. So you see you don't want to prevent wine raising. You want to prevent marriage.

Then it says, "he drank of the wine and was drunk." Not just a little tight or about half loaded, but drunk. And I expect in those days and times among those old Timers, when they admitted anyone was Drunk, I expect he filled the bill. Now the Lord dident seem to mind it, in fact it was on account of his drinking that he picked Noah to gather all these Animals into the Ark, he was the only one that had seen all of 'em. So Noah just went out and every time he needed another pair of Animals he would just take another drink, in fact two drinks for he always had to have a he and a she, all but a Democrat and its mate. He run out of wine just as he was looking for the mate to the Democratic He, and that's today why there is so few drinkers in the Democratic party. They are the Party of law and decency, all due to Noah running out of wine.

392 WILL AND SHARKEY TALK IT OVER

Well, all I know is just what I read in the papers, and what I run into as I prowl hither and thither. You know I have often said in answer to inquiries as to how I got away with kidding some of our public men, that it was because I liked all of them personally, and that if there was no malice in your heart there could be none in your "Gags," and I have always said I never met a man I dident like.

Even out in Chicago last week, why there is just an awful lot of fine things about the old town besides bullet holes. It's one of the most progressive Cities in the World. Shooting is only a side line. It's a great place. You only have to meet it to know it good. Well that's the way it is with humans, you read a lot of other people and kinder form a certain opinion. Now there has been a whole lot in the papers here lately about the much discussed Prize fight between Jack Sharkey and this young fellow Schmelling, and the Sport writers have had a Carnival for a year or so writing about the "Gabby Gob," and million and one titles that denoted that he was nothing but a big breeze.[1] Well I was up in Boston a week or so ago and it was just a day or so after that famous fight, and through a mutual friend I happened to meet this fellow Sharkey. Had a long chat with him and he drove me out to his home and met his wife and three great kids. I had always kinder admired him in spite of what was said, for he had always had the reputation of being a very clean living family man and well liked by his neighbors. Now when your Neighbors don't get wise to you you must be pretty straight laced.

Well he told me a lot about the fight, and he told it in a very straight-forward way. He dident have any crying to do, or any Alabi's. He says he knows that he hit the fellow right on the belt, but he don't think it was below it. He says he ducked down very low to avoid a punch from Schmelling and he started this punch from his position and that the other fellow come in at him fast and that it landed lower than he had expected but not a foul. He said he never seemed like he was having an easier fight, that between every round he couldent hardly believe it, that here he was fighting for the very World's Championship and having the easiest time of his career. He said he had trained hard and expected much more opposition out of the fellow, and when this thing come and was standing over in the corner with his hands on the ropes just waiting for them to declare him the winner, why when they held up the other fellow's hand here is his words, "Well my chin dropped and it hit me on the chest, (low down on the chest) and it almost knocked me out. My heart went down and down out of one leg then hopped across into the other and come up a ways and stopped dead.

"Here I was with the Championship in my lap and blowed it again. My first thoughts were, what will my wife think of me? Here I am noted for pulling something right at a time when I had the most at stake and here I was doing it again."

Well it was really pathetic to hear the fellow explain it. He says "I just look like I can't keep from doing something when the very most is at stake. But it all comes in the game, maby I have had a few lucky breaks too only they don't show up so plain. I am proud of one thing, I did keep my head and dident go plum cuckoo like I used to do when things went wrong. I at least won over myself if I dident win over the German."

Not even his worst enemy accused him of any deliberate foul, so it was pretty tough to be sitting there not the Champion of the World after you had had it in your lap and then thrown it away. To show his good faith in the affair he offers to fight any time and for nothing only his training expenses. He said the German was a fine young fellow and dident claim the foul because he knew he wasent. But that naturally he thought he was as the blow right in the pit of the stomach on the belt line would naturally make anyone think they were hit low. He also said he dident blame the Boy from trying to make all he could out of the championship. (Now at that time they hadent awarded him the real Championship.) But Sharkey said that they should, that he won the fight and he should be given all that goes with it.

He has a lovely home out in the fashionable section of Boston. It's built and furnished all in good taste. (That is as far as I am able to judge.) At least it had none of the ingredients of us Movie folks homes out in Beverly.

His wife's Grandfather and Grandmother live with them, and they have three awfully cute kids, a little Girl five, another four, and a little boy two. He told of the terrible hissing he got when he come into the ring with the American Flag around him. Not only he told me but others that knew, that was not Sharkey's idea at all, it was thrown on him as he left the dressing room and he tried to protest, but they told him, "No it's great, wear it." He would try to push it off as he was walking up the isle, and they told him, "You cant shove the flag aside now its got to stay on there. What will people say if they see you throw the flag down in the isle?" He says, "My I was with the Navy, I know what the flag means. I know where it's to be used and where not. But it was just another example of seeming to do the wrong thing at the very right time."

Now he has got to sit around. He can't fight anybody till the Commission tells him. If Schmelling won't fight till next year neither can he. "Here I have to lay idle all this time. I like to fight, it keeps me in better condition. But what can you do? You are in their hands. It's big Business now, and if it's better for them that I lay idle all this time, why that's what I am to do. When I was coming up I could fight every night and no one objected, but now that I am a big shot, they tell me when to fight, what to eat, where to train, how long to train, who to fight. It's politics now and not a Sport."

393   ALL ABOUT CHICAGO

Well all I know is just what I read in the papers, and what I see as I prowl the hinterlands. Now let's get this Chicago thing straightened out. I was out there for a whole week right here lately, and talked with everybody that I thought might know something of the real condition as it is out there. Course it was kinder like Politics, you have to discount about 90 percent of what each side says. But the main thing we did find out, and that was that as far as crime in proportion to its population, why it has less than anybody's town. There has been lots of men killed here, but they have been gangsters, and 90 percent of them have been killed by their own Gang, not by a rival Gang. It's been by their own, for some double crossing and holding out on their bosses.

You see they have very elaborate systems of checking up on you, the same as any big business has of checking up on their clerks or employees, and the minute they discover that you are not handing over all the "loot" or that you might be dealing with some rival enterprise, why they what is called, "Put you on the spot." That means you are sentenced, and if your last insurance is not paid, it would be well to look into it, for you are "not going to be with us long." But if you go along and do your work and turn in all that's coming, why you have nothing to fear, and maby get a raise, the same as in any other business.

You see lots of people think that all this Racketeering and Bootlegging and corruption is just a fly by night affair, run on a slipshod haphazard way. Well you never were more wrong in your life. You know as a matter of fact there is nothing as old as crookedness. It started away back when Eve used some political and Sex influence on poor old Dumb Adam to get him to gnaw on a forbidden Apple. Old Cain slew Abel, or visa versa, I don't know which. But anyhow it was an argument over the spoils.

So you see on account of its age it's not a fly by night Industry. Meanness has always been better organized and conducted than righteousness. So these Lads here are really of an old and ancient (and sometimes) honorable profession. Chicago has no more cussedness than any other City but it's been better advertised. They have never lacked for newspaper space. If out of town papers wouldent supply it why their own would.

Naturally there is different Gangs, as there is different groups in every line. People are going to drink, and somebody has to supply it to them. People are going to gamble, and somebody has to prepare them a place to do it. It was of course in the early days back in 1819 or 20 a small business, but it grew and grew far beyond even the expectations of its most optimistic boosters, till today Bootlegging and Racketeering of various sorts are not a business, it's an Industry.

There is no such thing as a little Bootlegger, no more than there is a little Banker. The day of the little Banker in a small town is past. He is a Member of a chain. He is a subsidiary of some big Concern. Well that's what this is. The little fellow can't live in this business on his own, he has to work for some one else. He can't go out and buy his goods and peddle it to you on his own. No he simply makes delivery,

1930

and it's for the chain. He is simply an order clerk, or delivery man, or one of dozens of other menial work hands in this great and intricate Industry. It's not done by some little fellow with a few hundred dollars capital, it's done by Financiers. It takes more capital to invest to insure the safe delivery of Liquor into Chicago and distribute it around than it does for to do the same thing with your milk, your bread or even your meat. They have to control ships, aeroplanes and trucks by the hundreds. High wages.

Then look at an expenditure that none of the other basic commodities have to meet, and that is Protection. Talk about a Tarriff wall! Why the tarriff is only collected by one party and that's at the port of entry. But with this there is no end of the collectors who are there to levy tributes. What percent of the cost of a bottle, do you think goes to Protection? Why say there is more collecting than there is selling.

So you see all this entails a pretty big Organization. It not only takes millions to operate one of these big going concerns, but it takes a lot of a lot of other things. So you see this stuff all comes under the heading of "Big Business," and the big ones have to look after and protect their customers. You can't kill off your customers, neither can you afford to let them maby go to some other firm. You have to strive to please. So they try their best to run it as you would a legitimate business.

Another thing, it's not so much that Chicago is such a terrible drinking place, but it is the clearing House the same as they are in the Wheat, or Cattle Market. The nice little decent towns that you never read about what's going on there, well they must get their stuff through Chicago. It comes in here from Canada, by every known conveyance. Then it's made here lots of it, and it's cut here. Then it goes out to the various branch places for delivery. Well that's a tremendous business, when you supply America thirst, why you have been to a supplying.

So this gang thing is bigger than most people realize. They are too smart to go and kill each other off. They don't do that. The ones that are killed are the ones that have pulled something on their own bunch, such as not handing over everything, or have done some sort of double crossing. Then they have them bumped off. Naturally the Police know what it is, and they are not going to break their neck in an argument where they know, no innocent are going to suffer, but they don't go out and shoot somebody down just for the sake of getting his money. No they get thirs too easy for that. They don't have to resort to that. They have a big business and they run it in a BIG legitimate way.

Now what's going to be done to stop 'em? Well it's as I have said off hand I can't think of anything unless the "Town's best people" quit drinking. These Boys couldent get far if nobody was buying. The demand must be there to create the market. So that's all we got to do to stop the whole thing. It don't seem much does it? Maby by next week everybody will have turned decent.

394 NEWS FROM MINNESOTA

Well all I know is just what I read in the papers, and what I see as I prowl hither and thither. You know week before last I had a fine week up among our Nordic Brothers in Minneapolis. You know they live and prosper and get along better than any other distinct bunch of folks we have in this Country. They are about the best Farmers we have in this Country, and even they are having a tough time making farms pay, and when they can't do it why it's time for the rest to let 'em foreclose and get a filling station and get out. Dairying is what saves them up there, and hard work has something to do with it. For those old boys really work. They have beautiful Cities, some of the loviliest parks and beautiful lakes, and lots of private homes. The Apartment epidemic hasent hit 'em yet, and what a rush they are getting to those Lakes for the vacation period. Bands of boys and girls from southern States are all coming here to summer Camps.

They say there is ten thousand lakes in the state of Minnesota alone. You know there is three or four different bunches up here. The general impression is that everything is a Swede, but these Norweigans, and Danes are just as proud of their Native land and will tell you they come from a better country than Sweden. But the great part about it is they all get along fine together. Any rivalry is good natured. That Maverick of the Senate, Senator Shipstead, who is supposed for lack of name to be a farmer-Laborite, he is strong up here.[1] I met him in Washington for the first time a few weeks ago and he said he had been reading some of my junk, and that he thought He and I had about the right idea that both sides were wrong about 90 percent of the time, and that's the way he votes, he just guesses at the side that is the furtherest wrong and votes against them, with the side that is maby the less wrong.

Like all Towns they was mighty dissapointed in their Census Reports. Minneapolis was trying to reach the half million, and they only got about 462,000. St. Paul about a third less.

You see what causes all this dissapointment in these Cities is

1930

these Chamber of Commerces. They start yapping about what they have in their Town, and they tell it so long that they get their people to believing it, and then when the Government comes along, and the people have to really be there, and NOT just accounted for by a Luncheon Club Speaker, why the old Census Boys can't dig 'em up as easy as the "Speaker of the Day." But what a difference does it make what your town is? A growing City is just like fifty Guys starting to climb up a ladder. While you are trying your best to get one rung higher, why the babies at the top like New York and Chicago are skipping rungs by the dozens, so that even if you climb your relative position is the same. When Minneapolis gets a million, Chicago will have fifteen, so what's the answer? But it's sure does make a good Chamber of Commerce rally talk.

Well sir I was up there one night and who do you think dropped in on me but, Doctor Mayo, the old Country Doctor of Rochester Minn.[2] Mrs Mayo was with him, and another accomplice from down in Nashville, Tenn, I forget his name, but he is head of the Committee that is raising money for Tennessee to build a combined monument to its 3 Presidents of the United States, Jackson, and Johnson, and I don't know who to the other was. Well they want to build one while this present wave of Prosperity is on. They want to get it built before a Democratic Administration gets in and demoralizes the country. This fellow is from Nashville. He had his Daughter with him. He and Charley Mayo are prowling around trying to drum up some trade for his little medical practice out there. They say he has in addition to dosing out calumel and assaifititi to the ailing Norweigans, he has put in a branch line of "Operation" while you wait. Somebody give him a knife, and he and a Brother of his will have your frame into kindling wood before you know it. He had been over in Italy, and it was reported that he was going to slice into Mussolini and cut out his French Complex. So that give me a chance to get in my Monologue about Mussolini and the Castor Oil.[3] Well as we were sitting in a Drug Store at the time having a drink, my Castor Oil story naturally reminded him of one. (That's the worst part about a story, you can't hardly tell one that it don't remind somebody of another one.) But this one of his was a good one. It's all right for his wife, (and by the way a lovely, sweet-faced grey-haired young looking Woman) she and the other fellow's daughter were there, so don't stop reading this out loud, go ahead.

A Woman come into a Drug Store and asked the clerk if there wasent some way he could fix up Castor Oil so that it would be tasteless and not objectionable to take. He said he could, while she was sitting at the Soda Counter waiting he asked her if she wouldent have a cool refreshing drink of some kind, and he handed her a glass of Sasspharilla. She drank it, and after waiting a few minutes she noticed that he was not doing anything toward giving her the Castor oil she had asked for, so she asked him for it. "Why Lady you have already taken it."

"Already taken it?" she hollered, "Why it wasent for me, it was for my Sister."

He is full of stories, and is a great little fellow. Gosh when you think of what those fellows have done! That's what you call being a real Benafactor to mankind.

You know to me the greatest thing they have done, and that is the system of charging everyone in proportion to what they can pay. Course some let a yell out of them like a hoot Owl, and claim that they paid more than so and so, but it's the greatest system ever invented. All Doctors should make enough out of those who are well able to pay, to be able to do all work for the poor free. That is one thing that a poor person should never be even expected to pay for is medical attention, and not from an organized Charity, but from our best Doctors. But your Doctor bill should be paid like your Income tax, according to what you have. There is nothing that keeps poor people poor as much as paying Doctor bills. It always wipes out their savings, and it's that fear of not being able to pay is what makes it ten times worse on them. It ought to be a law, not only a custom.

395   IT'S HARD TO TELL WHAT TO BELIEVE NOWADAYS

Well, all I know is just what I read in the papers. With Mr Coolidge writing for the papers why we got a lot of new reading to do now. He had one in the other day that kinder jarred all of us, and made us wonder if he wasent having a Ghost Writer do some of his stuff. It advised the working man to spend his money, and buy everything that he could possibly afford, and in that way help out the whole economic thing, so that it would put more money into circulation, and make more jobs for those that had none. Now that is absolutely going against all the laws we have been brought up too. We have always been taught to save and put by every dollar that we could, and not buy anything unless we absolutely needed it, and to spend no money for things that we could do without. Now all at once we are advised by everybody to start spending, so it will help somebody else. Imagine telling the working man to spend, that if he don't put his money into circulation why he won't have a job very long. That is what Mr Coolidge said. Now that sounds so unlike him. Here is a man that the whole basis of his popularity is based on his economy and thrift, and all at once to help out a situation, why he says "Spend." So it's hard to tell what to believe nowadays.

Speaking of Prosperity, which is about all we are doing is speaking of it, why I read with great interest the other day the celebrating of the ninty some birthday of our genial benafactor Mr Rockefeller Sr, and it brought back many happy thoughts of my meeting with him every winter when I would play my little "talk dates" at Daytona Beach Florida.[1] He would always come to the Auditorium and bring all the people from his winter household, servants and all. The three years I did that, he was right there in the audience, and was always well versed on Topics, as on Oil Gravity. He knew as much about the dissarmament Conference as he did what the "Dutch Shell" were doing. I always had a few local jokes about him, and would go down off the "Rostrum" and shake hands with him and he would quietly ask me to come to his home on the following morning and have breakfast with him, at eight oclock. In fact after the first time, I would not only give him the chance to ask me, but would encourage it. I would stand by his seat till he had to do something to get rid of me, so the easiest thing would be to "Come have breakfast with us?"

Then after a fine breakfast, when he would give us all a dime each as he come down in the morning, we would go nearby to the Golf Course, and he would play eight holes. It took a pretty tough day, that kept him away. The reason for the eight holes only was that the eighth hole was over by a back road where he could have his car meet him, and go direct home from that hole. I don't play the game, (not even at three at night for money) but he made lots of the holes in what you call Par. He was always straight down the course, not so terribly far, but ON IT.

The old fellow looks like he is extremely happy and satisfied, and I think feels that he has been of some service to his Country as well as to the passing Motorist. He has not only filled the Country's tanks, but has filled many a diseased man with hope of a cure.

Then it's the lesson he has been to other rich men. We all have a good deal of Sheep in us. If somebody does something, we are awful liable to jump over the same place he did. So it's his lesson to other rich men, that has made them more liberal. Now we have hardly any great rich man that has not some form of Charity that he is extremely interested in. They know that to just be rich in this Country is no longer any novelty. It's not the wealth they had that we remember, it's what they did with it. Just last week the Prince of Wales made almost a prayer over the Radio that England might develop some one in their Country comparable to Rockefeller in philanthropy.[2]

That's about the biggest single praise that has come his way. When the future ruler of a great Kingdom asks for a similar man in their Country, you must have accomplished something. He is a great old fellow and I tell you this Son of his is a wonder.[3] He gives away money with fine judgement.

Well let's get some comedy subject into this serious piece someway, so here goes, THE SENATE MET IN AN EXTRA EXTRA SESSION AGAIN. Now that ought to keep you laughing all summer. They let Congress go home for good behaviour, but they kept the Senate in.

They are there argueing over the London Treaty. Of course that just happens to be thing they thought of at the moment; if it wasent that it would be something else. They are trying to find out what Mr Ramsey McDonald said to Mr Hoover when they were out on the Rapidan River last fall.[4] It's always hurt them that they wasent invited to be present and hear every word said, so now they demand that Mr Hoover give them the Menu of that visit. What in the world does what was said and done eight months ago have to do with a six inch gun or an eight inch gun? We got to shoot 'em with guns and not with old Notes and letters from the Foreign Embassies.

Course Mr Hoover is all set out there in his camp, and while these old Boys are argueing and cussing each other over something that is going to pass, why he is out there in old Virginia dragging in the Trout, and giving these Lads the Ha Ha. He has 'em working after hours with no time and a half for overtime. In other words they are just staying for the argument and not for any results. They know the treaty will be passed, and to do so at the least expense would be the proper thing. But not for a Senator. But Mr Hoover gets the last laugh.

396 YES, IT'S HOT IN CALIFORNIA!

Well all I know is just what I read in the papers, and what I know when I am there to know it. Now don't let them tell you it hasent been hot here in California the past few weeks. Brother it's been roasting, and we havent got the usual Alabi, "It's the humidity." We havent even got any of that. Course it's been cool in the nights. (That is fairly cool.) I am not going to be too big a liar just for the sake of the State. It's just been hot, that's all. Of course the papers out here can always kill off hundreds with the heat some place back east. But I think the Editors here were so overcome they couldent even get up enough energy to kill any off with a headline back there.

You can publish all the statistics and junk you want but I guess the whole country has been hit pretty hard. But I lay it to the Stock Market crash last fall. Soon as the market gets a little better we will have some cold weather. Yes we are liable to have snow just as soon as the Market gets better.

Say you know what we got out here besides the heat. Well it's a Fish they call it Grunion, (Not Grundy) Grunion.[1] At a certain time of the day and year why it washes right up on the bank or beach rather. You can tell where I did all my early swimming. It's just a few inches long and pretty small even in a story. Well people go to the Beaches by the Fordsfull and after a big wave come in why they make a dive and tackle these things with their hands, and the funny part of it is, they know when it's going to happen just like an eclipse. The papers all announce it, "Grunion will appear on such and such a Beach at 9:43 Tuesday night, July 12, 1930. If there is any change in the Grunions' arrival time, like there was in Amos and Andy's, why it will be announced as soon as we hear from them."[2] And by golly sure enough at 9:43 on said night, a wave come in and sure enough riding it in was old man Grundy, (I mean Grunion). Well everybody was a Tackle or a halfback, they made a flying tackle at 'em, and when their heads were pried out of the sand, it was found that each hand held two and three ounces of Grunion. So you see California again will get the reputation of being the biggest liars on earth by saying they can catch fish right out on the dry land, and the Rascals won't be lying. They will be telling the truth for the first time in years.

See by the papers that Mr Hoover's western vacation trip has been cut to two weeks in the Rockies, all on account of Hiram Johnston wanting to argue over the Treaty.[3] He knew it would pass. But that made no difference to him. So he just kept everybody in Washington during this terrible weather. Course Mr Hoover is not so bad off, as he has fixed him up a Camp out in Virginia some place, and I reckon it's pretty cool there.

But the President should be compelled to leave Washington early in the summer, even if he is forced to miss Johnston. Mind you I believe Hy is sincere about this, but he knew it was going to pass, and all he had to do was to register his opposition, and not drag it out into all this mess. He and Senator Dave Reed had a pretty set to last week.[4] Dave told him he could go and see the papers, and learn all that was in them, but that he would not be allowed to show them to anybody else. Well Hy went up in the air, he said he could not conceive on any Senator ever looking at anything and not be able to tell about it. So he certainly bawled Davey out.

To have to read something and then keep it to yourself dident appeal to him in the least. Well we have no monopoly on kicking on the Treaty. England says we got the best of it. That shows they have a sense of humor. And in Japan they are hollering their heads off, they say their Delogation dident bring home enough ships. So if there is that much dissatisfaction, it's like I have always preached, why hold these things? There is always more hatreds formed at any meeting than there is friendships, no matter what they agree too they know they should have done better. The Nations in this world that get along and never have any trouble are the ones that never meet in conference at all.

The minute you confer you find out each other's short comings. But anyhow what difference does it make? The minute a war breaks out Treatys don't mean a thing anyhow. If England went to war tomorrow, do you think this being bound to only a given number of ships would hold good? Say they would break that Treaty the minute they could get some boards and carpenters and start building. Everything is all right when things are going good, but when it's bad, then nothing means anything. You naturally got to look to self preservation.

But who cares about all that? Say did you know they arrested a Girl here in Hollywood the other day? She was driving down our main thoroughfare with nothing on but a heavy tan, not a stich. A Modern Lady Godiva. She dident even have the advantage of long hair. You remember the old original over in Coventry England, (by the way I played there in Vaudeville, many years ago, tain't far from Shakespeare's old stomping ground,) well that Lady had a horse, and she had a mane longer than the horse's. But this one here the other day had traded her "Cayuse" for a Chevrolet Roadster, and her hair was short. Course this is all from heresay. I *would* miss it.

I think she come clear for it's awful hard to tell when a woman is nude nowadays and when she is fully clothed. If the worst come to the worst she could always say it was an evening dress. But we do have great time out here, with Women driving nude and fish attacking people right up on dry land, and the heat 120 in the shade. We have lots of fun here. Come on out we will put you in the Movies.

397   HOW ARE YOUR TEETH AND TOENAILS?

1930

Well all I know is just what I read in the papers, and what I hear over the Radio during the various toothe paste hours. I tell you it's a lucky thing for us that people's teeth are in such bad shape or we never would get any amusement at all. In the old days when we did nothing with our teeth till we died off, why we had no amusement at all, we couldent turn a dial and get our favorites Amos and Andy.[1] Tooth paste has been responsible for more good laughs than Barnum's Circus has, and you can use the wrong kind too.[2] According to the announcers, there is various kinds that cause decay, while their kind brings on added growth, so you got to be mighty careful.

Course the best thing in the world in the old days was to chew on a tough piece of steak, or kinder gnaw on and around a bone. But nowadays on account of having to buy so much toothe paste why it don't leave enough to get the steak to whiten and toughen the teeth. A good old rump steak would give your teeth more exercise and build up a foundation than a steel tooth brush would.

But these lettuce sandwitches just don't offer much resistance to the old Molars and they don't get much exercise on them. Malted milk over a soda fountain just might as well be inhaled as far as the teeth is concerned. This Caviar assisted by Cocktails is another National dish that don't offer much physical resistance to the eye teeth. In fact as far as the old Tusks are concerned there is really no reason for owning them.

An old toothless man or Woman is not inconvenienced in the least with our modern type of food. There is nothing that comes in cans that he can't bulldog with ease and comfort. Our more rough type of food nowadays is a ham sandwitch, and the Boys that slice it fix it so that the teeth have no function to perform in its digestion.

Most of our up to date food is by absorptution. It melts in your mouth, so when the old Tooth brush gets a crack at the teeth it's about the only thing they have encountered since babyhood. You have to brush 'em for they have had nothing rub up against 'em lately.

A wolf has the best looking teeth in the World. They are always white. Even the announcer won't tell you that there is film forms over them. But on the other hand look what the old Coyote misses. He never did hear about Madam Queen. He don't the King fish from a Setter pup. He has nothing to console his lonely hours only chewing on some competitor. He has the whitest teeth, but he is not informed on how many times a day the little Baby Wolves should grab a tube of "Never tarnish" and scrape the wisdom teeth.

Weekly Articles

On account of no particular demand for teeth it will only be a short time till we will be hearing over the Radio ways and means to maintain 'em at all, for we will quit growing 'em. You quit walking and you will soon have no legs. You stop arguments and you will soon have no Senators. You stop anything and nature provides that it will be discontinued, and you stop using the teeth only for artificial purposes and you will soon see there will be none. So then we will have to find something else to occupy our time and adds.

You know the old toe nail has never received its proper amount of public care and instruction. It won't be many years before we will be a tuning in on "Calvin and Herbert, those two boys who will tickle you for the next half hour on personal expereinces while prowling in the undergrowth of National incompetence. They come to you by permission of the Anti Ingrowing Toe Nail Company. Have you watched your pedal extremities lately? The toe is an important ingredient of the system. All National ills can be traced, detourly, to the toe, so watch your toes. The Anti Ingrowing Toe Nail Co. have devised a concoction that head toe nails out in the right direction. Just a little application night and morning. Remember, watch the Kiddies, and don't forget, Calvin and Herbert every evening, brought to you by the Anti Ingrowing Toe Nail Co."

If this Country had static for a solid month, there is no telling what would become of people's teeth. But everything is sorter drifting to the sanitary anyhow. In the old days when we wasent so sanitary, why we were strong enough to withstand all the germs. But nowadays we have to be careful of the Microbes for if they get a hold on us we are gone. We are not physically able to withstand 'em. In the old days as many as wanted to could drink out of one cup, and the last one would just shake his head and swallow down Mike-Robies just as fast as they would acumilate. But now the old individual cup won't go for over one sitting, or it will knock the second individual right into the infested class. The old fashioned Goard that the whole family drank out of from birth till death, would kill off more of the modern population than a war. We just ain't built to stand the assults and batteries of an unwrapped-in-paper containers. New handkerchiefs, everything is bundled up seperately. Nothing comes in the gross anymore.

But while we have lost in strength and endurance we have gained in amusement and instruction. For there is not an hour of any day that some one on the Air don't keep us warned of what lies in wait for us in case we don't use their remedy. There is just more different things that can happen to us than there used to be. An open cuspidor is not only passe, but it's a social horror.

WILL DIPS INTO THE BLUE

Well all I know is just what little I read in the papers. Somebody just sent me a clipping I see here and it says who has been left off and who added to the Social Register. Now that is a laugh ain't it? (I would be dropped if I ever got on for saying "ain't.") If all the undemocratic things you can think of just off hand, that is the prize "Hooey," a book to tell you who is good Parlor Hound and who is a sort of Mongrel around the tea table.

I see just offhand here that Polly Lauder, (a niece of Harry Lauder's) who married Gene Tunney has been dropped from the "Register."[1] If she had married a Society Bootlegger she would have made the grade but when she married Gene, a man who had been a pretty fare type of Gentleman who's only fault in his profession was that he shook hands with you before knocking you Cuckoo, why they right away said that Polly dident grade up to par. She had been negligent in picking a Mayflower weed. Tunney's name never had been in "Baloney sheet." But it had to tell in there who she had "promised to Love honor and break clean in the clinches with," so in that way it had to name Gene. So in a kind of a back alley way his name was in there, not intentionally, but in there. So I guess that's why they had to drop Polly's. They left her in there for one year to see if she wouldent repent and come back to Cocktail cavalcade, but as she dident why they just got themselvs a great big eraser and she dropped in Social oblivion. And I bet that just about broke that girl's heart. For here she had spent a lifetime picking out parents who were eligible, and now she had gone and flopped after working hard to make the grade, and here at the last minute flunk. Now what can she do, where can she go? Decent people won't have anything to do with her. Everybody will look at her and say, "Why that's Polly Lauder! She used to be somebody and was fine and social. But they dropped her right off the Book and here she is practically Destitute of all the other Members of the great Fraternity of those who are somebody by grace of proper propogation, (and ordering enough books)."

You see there is something you might not know. If your name goes in you order so many books. It's not exactly a philanthropic organization, and it's not exactly to keep track of those worth while. It's just sorter like all the rest of us are when we really admit it, it's to get the dough. Now about what Gene did was (as he couldent fight Dempesy any more and that big income wasent coming in) why he decided to cut down on his Charaties and this happened to seem to them to be the least necessary, why they discontinued their subscriptions to this Elite Periodical and they give 'em so many months

Weekly Articles

warning and then when the Tunneys dident come through why they just washed 'em up.²

All of which gets us back to "What is Society and what is a Gentleman?" Well of course it's easy to define a Gentleman, a gentleman is to my way of thinking a man that can play Golf and don't say so. But as there is so few in fact it has been discussed whether there is any at all.

Now as to "What is Society?" Society is any band of folks that kinder throw in with each other, and mess around togeather for each others disscomfort. Any little or big group of folks that sorter flock together are "Society" in some form or other. The ones with the more money have more to eat and drink at their affairs, and their clothes cost more, and so that's called "High Society." Now the morals or personal behaviour of its Members have nothing to do with it. The oftener they can crash the front page the solider they are in their fraternity. And it's sorter heriditary. No matter who you raise up in your family Zoo why they naturally inherit your space in the "Social Register." Your personall accomplishments have nothing to do with it. Mind you the Tunneys are not alone. Caruso's wife was in there, and after she married him, they scratched her out.³ So they evidentally have a pet aversion to "Tenors." Now there I kinder agree with 'em. There should be something done about Tenors, otherwise you encourage 'em.

Rear Admiral Byrd is among the missing.⁴ Guess he has been running around these Poles when he should have been at home taking care of his duties in the drawing room. But can you imagine leaving Byrd out, when his family have more record of breeding and tradition than half the book put togeather?

Then here is a fellow that I bet it just broke him right square up when he opened the book and found he was out on his ear. That's Henry Ford. Transportationally he is a Giant, but socially he is a Gnat. I can just imagine his embarrassment when he found that out. For he has been so ambitious, and has strived all his life to be somebody, and now to find that he dident make it. Little Boys will be pointing him out on the running boards. "Oh look there is Henry Ford, he is not in the Social Register! Don't touch him he will contaminate you."

So for downright amusement in reading matter that Register will compete with the Congressional Register and College Humor.

1930

399 KANSAS, COOLIDGE, AND THERMOMETERS

Well all I know is just what I read in the papers. And outside of the thermometer reports, there just ain't much in the newsprints nowadays. This heat thing accompanied by drouth has had everybody pretty bad scared up. Mr Hoover dident go away on his vacation as expected. He got right after it. Course there is not much a man can do when it's heat that's bothering us. He can advise everybody to sit in the shade, and avoid the sun as much as possible. Then if it's rain they need why advise them to raise crops that don't need much rain.

Kansas had an election a week or so ago, and Mr Hoover seemed mighty pleased when his backer from there was nominated by a big majority. It was thought that Kansas on account of being a sort of an Amateur Farming State might go against the Administration because the heat had spoiled the crops, but they dident, they voted for a good friend of mine, Henry Allen.[1] (Well he is a friend of Hoover's too.) Henry is an old Crony of William Randolph White, only Henry gets elected.[2] Henry had been in Washington as a stop gap Senator and evidently did pretty good. He was about the best dressed Senator there. Course that's not much of an accomplishment, as he could be that and still be taken up for indecency among good Society.

So take it all in all it looks like Mr Hoover is going into the late summer pretty well intrenched. Course the Southern Republicans have broke out against him, which would be expected, for there must be something the matter with a Southerner that would be a Republican. So they are naturally in the observation ward all the time anyway. There is some Guy down there named Mann, and he hasent got quite all the appointments that he expected for his Campaign money and he is out for The President's scalp in 32.[3] But by that time maby Mr Hoover will apoint him on some Commission and he will be all O. K. again. A Politician is just like spoiled Kid. If he feels that his stick of candy is not the longest why he will let out a yap that will drown out the neighborhood.

Mr Coolidge is still going along, knocking out his 150 words a day. I am sorry I ever started that idea of wiring in a little dispatch every day on current events. We will have everybody in the world trying it before long. But he has had some mighty nice reading, and some sound advice. Not that anybody is interested in advice whether it's sound or not. In fact the sounder it is the less it's received. But he has done a good job has Mr Coolidge, and I hope he keeps it up. Course it will be against him if he ever wants to run for anything. But there is no job that pays as good as it does, so why would anyone want to run for anything. No Columnist was ever elected to anything any time any place.

This conducting a columns is considered a kind of a low grade type of human endeavor. It's not classed among what might be called the Arts. It's just a kind of a stop gap to keep the Cayote from the doorstep, and as a dignified proffession it's sorter null and void. It's just sorter in the papers to break your jump on the way over to the advertising pages. But while it does not bring home the Literary praise it does fetch in some buck-wheat cakes accompanied by bacon. It can be sneered at till meal time; then it has its good points.

There has been a good deal of trouble out in the Dakotas about the history that Mr Coolidge was supposed to write on a rock.[4] It was to run 500 words and give the history of America and still not go into details. Well 500 words don't allow you much history. Course we never had much history, but like all Nations we think we have. While we can't trace our Ancestors back any further than you can trust a Congressman, why we naturally think we are saturated with "Tradition" when as a matter of fact it's only payments on objects that we are immersed in.

Well the Sculptor dident like the history that our Ex President had cooked up so he made as we say in the eighth art, (the Movies) why he made some re-takes on the manuscript. It seems that Mr Coolidge had with an eye to future Campaigns given our History from a Republican standpoint. There had been Democrats engaged in our history but only in the capacity of Villans. We had reached our present state of taxation by the far sightedness of the Republican Organizations. Well this Gutsom Borglum, who is a foreigner by birth, but an Atlanta Georgian by argument, he had studied his history of our land from the standpoint of Stone Mountain and Major Cohen, and Congressman Upshaw.[5] He believed that Lee, Davis and Jackson participated in our early escapades, while Mr Coolidge took the view that we had reached our present indebtedness by the sole aid of the Grundy's, the Reeds, the Lodges, and the Vares.[6] He had taken his history of America from the Congressional Record, while Gutsom wanted his from the Atlanta Constitution. Coolidge believed that Jefferson was a fictitious Character, and that the income tax was entirely due to Alexander Hamilton, (the inventor of a time lock safe).

Well poor Dakota dident know what it was all about, all the interest they had in the matter was to furnish the Mountain. They just wanted something that a Tourist could read, or have read to him. In fact the more controversy the more would come to read. What constituted our early history dident mean a thing to my old Friend

Beulow and his co-horts.⁷ The Dakotas just said "we got the rock. Print an Aimee McPherson sermon on it, just so somebody will burn out his break bands to come and see it."⁸ If they leave the Coolidge version on there, they should advertise it, "Come and see the Republican history of America in 500 words."

400   THIS CIVILIZATION OF OURS

Well all I know is just what I read in the Papers. Now I have been perusing the Periodicals with an eagle eye, and to save my soul I can't see a thing that will bear repeating. Premature Golf has got us by the ears, and America has a putter in its hand.¹ It's been a godsend to vacant lots. They look beautiful at nights, but in the day time when the lights are not on, the Gingerbread kinder crops out. But it's been a great thing, the working men who put them in, and at a time when Prosperity was at what you might say was its lowest ebb. In fact it wasent even ebbing.

They say "It started in old Chatanooga a long time ago." Now I know Chatanooga pretty well, it's a great old town. Lookout Mountain is perched at its doorstep. Adolph Ochs the Publisher and Owner of the great New York Times comes from there.² But this Snare Drum Golf that started from there has got the town more publicity than Mr Ochs or the Battles of Chicamagua, or Lookout Mountain, or even the Bend in the river. To look at it you wouldent think that it was the City that was the start of the whole of America "picking it up and putting it down."

But those old Southerners are mighty ingenious. You know it was a Guy in Memphis that started this Piggly Wiggly business. He figured that if somebody give you a basket and told you to go to it, that you would take up more junk than if somebody was digging it out for you. The Woman instinct would naturally make her believe that the fellow looking in the bag at the finish might overlook something.

But anyhow he made a great thing of it, and say, by the way, I want to ask him, that man Saunders, (Owner of his own name) what he ever did with that invention for parking Automobiles.³ He took me while I was in Memphis one time and showed me a working model of it, and I thought at the time that it was the greatest thing I had ever seen. It was a gag like an elevator, with cages on both sides. One coming down and one going up, and it stood about twenty or thirty stories or cars high. You drove into a cage with your car, got out, and shut the gate, and it automatically went on up till an empty space

Weekly Articles

come along, and it stopped there to wait for the next car, and your car went on up. You remembered the number of the elevator it was in, when you come for it you pressed your number and it went over the top and on down the other side, and when it reached the ground it stopped, and you drove it out. The whole thing could go on a lot twenty feet wide, and that deep, and would park all these cars. Well anyhow it was a great idea, looked sorter like a Ferris wheel. I wonder what he ever did with it.

Speaking of Politics, I was up at a Rodeo at Salinas, California the other day, and their great speciality there is riding Bucking Bulls. Well the Governor was there and as he was up for re-election he spoke and casually reminded the people that a vote for him would not be un-appreciated.[4] Well just as he would reach an important part of his address why out would come a bucking bull and maby throw a Cowpuncher higher than a Republican Tarriff bill, and the crowd would roar and applaud. The Governor would start again, "As I was saying, I have down more for Monterey County and ----------Ba, ba. "Ride him Cowboy, hook him Cow!" "Monterey County has been my special pet in handing out appropriations," and "Here comes another one, watch that Baby buck! What a Bull! You are riding him pretty Boy!" "If I am re-elected, I will give..." "Set in the middle of that Animal old hand!"

Well all this went on for quite a spell, and we never could find out what the Governor had done for old Monterey County. From the looks of the Bulls there dident seem much that he could do for old Monterey County. What the County needed politically was noiseless bulls. Well they finally wanted me to go over and deliver a Theme song on the Merits of Herbert and Calvin, or "What the Republican Party has done to us." But not me, I wouldent go over there and compete with those Bovines. "Bull" is all right but not when you are competing with the original. I could have told 'em in a minute what was the matter with Old Monterey County, Cal. or old Rogers County Okla, or Brown County Indiana.

We are just stepping too fast. In the old days we figured the world owed us a living, now we figure he owes us an Automobile, a Player Piano, and Radio, Frigid Air, and Clara Bow.[5] The Automobile is to take you places you would be better off if you dident go to. The player Piano is to discourage you from trying to play your own simple little tunes that your folks spent so much on your learning. The Radio is for Pepsident. The Frigid Air is too give you ice water when you would be better off if you dident load up on it, and Clara Bow will just lead you plum astray. She will give a Country boy the wrong impressions.

But it's all coming under the heading of higher Civilization. Till now it's a case of what is Civilization. Was our old folks dumb and dident know nothing? Say don't you kid yourself, those old Boys in their youth could take a big silver Dollar and go out and corrall more "Hot times" than we ever thought of. There is many a Barrimore hid behind long whiskers.[6] Say they did a lot of prowling in their time. A horse and Buggy could take you so far that it wasent impossible to walk home, but it was inconvenient. Even back in my time, when I was going good, I have come dragging in from a dance horseback, by daylight.

We wasent making payments on as many things, but we was making some mighty nifty "Whoopee." Your Mother gets mighty shocked at you Girls nowadays, but in her day her Mother was just on the verge of sending her to a reformatory, so we just got to live and let live and laugh the thing off. The Republicans got the Country and what can you expect?

401 SEEING OUR FRONT YARD IS GREAT FUN

Well all I know is just what I read in the papers, or what I see while prowling. Well sir a week or so ago had a great trip. We were starting to go to the famous Lake Tahoe in California to film the old Frank Bacon play "Lightnin'" right on the ground that it was laid on.[1] You know it was a hotel on the Nevada and California line, and the Divorcees would stop there and it had a California address but in reality you would be living in Nevada.

Well Fred Stone and his family were out at our little ranch at Santa Monica spending a little vacation with us, so we all decided to go up.[2] We first hit out for Yosemite. I hate to admit it but I had never been there. My family had, but not me, and Fred and his folks hadent been. If you never have been there, don't miss it. It's great sight. I am not going to tell you about it for you can get folders that can make it wilder than I can.

First place they have one of the most unique Hotels you ever saw. In fact lots of dandy places to stop. Everybody was apoligising for the falls, as on account of the Republicans giving us no more rains than they have why there hasent been in years as little water coming over. But there was some, and it would give you an idea of where they were and what could happen to some water if it did happen along that way, what a drop it would get.

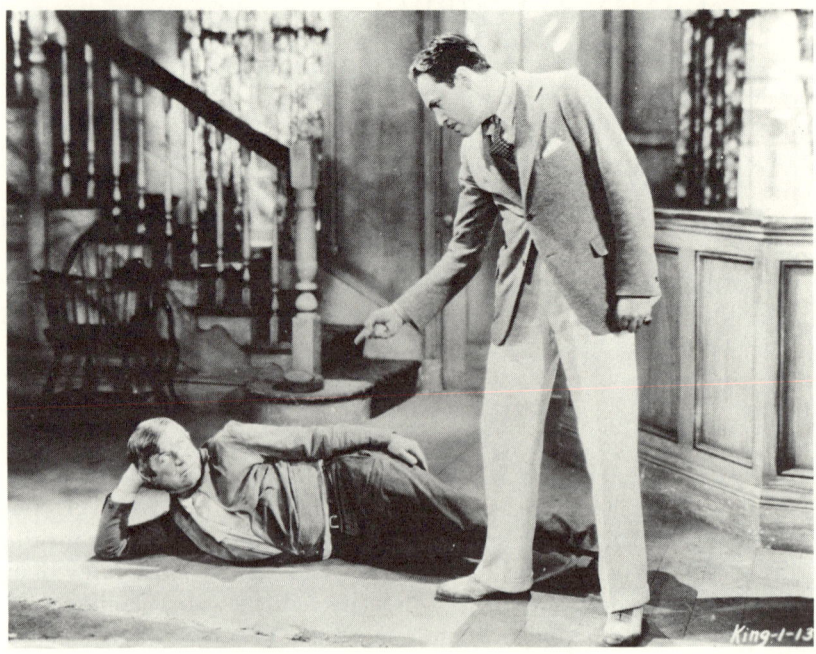

Will Rogers as a resort hotel operator, "Bill Jones," in the motion picture Lightnin' (Fox Film Corporation, 1930).

1930

    We took drives and we took walks, and then we had a Barbecue down on the river bank on the gravel bar. They sure do know how to cook up steaks, and they sent their old Cowboy Banjo player and singer down and he was sure good. He had lots of old ones I hadent heard in years, and he had some I had never heard. Then they had an awful good Cowboy Rope spinner and Fred and I got a kick out of him, for we had both wrestled with one of those things long enough to know how hard it really was.

    There was just 10 or 12 in the party, and then Fred picked up the old rope and he roped like he hadent been off it a day. It will take more than an Aeroplane to knock that Guy out. Then he sang a lot of his old songs from his various hits. I tried a little rope, but I was getting too old and fat. I took up eating again. Down there by the moonlight, and a campfire, and hemmed in by partitions that are three thousand feet straight up, I tell you New York's Yosemite, down in those Canyons can't touch it. You would see little deer playing around. Then we went to see the fire fall, on a high cliff. They build every night a big log fire, and as it burns into small embers, just at nine oclock they push it over in a steady stream that lasts several minutes these burning embers, and here you are almost a mile straight down, and see this fall over this great precepice, and at one of the Camps a women sang that beautiful Indian song, "The waters of Minnetonka."

    Well it was a beautiful sight. Then we went to see 'em feed the bears. There is lots of bears in there, and they take the garbage from the hotels, and have little pits built like tables, and spot lights up in the trees, and it's on the bank of this beautiful little river, and all the crowd are just across on the opposite side. They put all the food in these places, and then they turn the lights on, and all at once right across the river is all these old bears, fussing and eating, and playing. They put food up on an old standing tree trunk, and they climb up there for it, and then the Naturalist of the park gives a very entertaining talk on them. They go to sleep in the fall in caves, and old trunks of trees, and they don't come out or wake up till spring, and their little ones are born during this sleep, and they only weigh about a pound at birth, and they sleep and suck their paw.

    They feed 'em, otherwise they would break in people's tents to get their bacon, or they will go into a car when parked at night if they smell food in there. You are not supposed to feed 'em from your hand but they have a hospital there for the ones that do. Well we started early the next morning, and went out of their in our cars, by the eastern way, the Tiago Route, and it is without a doubt the most beautiful trip I ever saw. It's about 225 miles from there to Lake

Tahoe, by way of Mona Lake and that's the one where there is nothing lives in.

I don't know why, for they dident have any naturalist there to tell us. That's how come me to know so much about the bears. They are getting very fine roads, that is for mountain roads all over these places, and touring through America now is really becoming a real pleasure. We swung over into Nevada from all this Big Trees and Pine timber, down into the desert Country, then by the most beautiful watered valleys, with mighty pretty Cow ranches in 'em, that made my mouth water. Then up over another high mountain pass and there was this wonderful Lake Tahoe, over six thousand feet up in the air, with one hundred miles of shore line, and nobody knows how deep, and beautiful and marvelous places all around it. It's right in the heart of all the old California and Nevada mining places that have made history.

The state line runs through the lake. We drove over to Virginia City, the mining town that built the great San Francisco. $800,000.000, eight hundred million taken from there. Now it's just almost a Ghost town. It's Mark Twain's old town where he worked on the paper.[3] Fred crawled in the window of the old Opera House, and dug around in the dressing rooms and stage. That was the hit of the trip with him. He said he had never played there in the early days but he had played lots of 'em like it, around the middle west. Then to Carson City, Nevada, one of the most picturesque and historic old State Capitols we have, saw where Corbett and Fitsimmons fought the famous "Solar Plexus" fight.[4] Fred got a kick out of that for he used to box with Corbett all during his Championship days, and Corbett always said he would have been a Champion middleweight if he had taken it up as a profession. He was always the best boxer, (and fighter) of any Actor we ever had on the stage. Then to Reno, which is only forty miles from the lake. But Reno I will have to take a whole Chapter to tell you about it, and its "Industry." But if you want to have a good time, I don't care where you live, just load in your kids, and take some congenial friends, and just start out. You would be surprised what there is to see in this great Country within 200 miles of where any of us live. I don't care what State or what town. I tell you Henry Ford has been good to us.

402 AIRPLANES, LADIES, AND POLITICS

Well all I know is just what I read in the papers, or what I "Contact" from hither to thither. I sure did hate missing that big Air

1930

Show in Chicago. I think that is becoming to be the one great show we will have. Just think how it will grow in importance when everybody really goes to traveling by air, and it's coming all the time. They have some big 32 passengers ships out here between Los Angeles and Frisco and they are full all the time.

There is really something to see at one of those shows. You take Automobile shows and all you have to do is to go in the show rooms in every town and you see the same thing you can at a show, and they have them so perfected that about all that ever shows up new at a show is some new fangled Cigar lighter, or odd shape door knobs. But at an air show there is hundreds of entirely different models that you had ever seen before. Then to see fellows like Al Williams, the great Ex Naval Flyer (who they all say is one of the best in the world) and Jimmy Doolittle who can fly and land blind, only by using instruments and all the dozens of others.[1] Now it's a real show.

You know I was reading the other day about the big Military air show they had held in England the other day, and they had a battle between an invading army of them, with the other side protecting the City, and with the speed and the altitude that the Bombing plane can make now, they found that it was almost impossible to keep them away. That is if they dident know they was coming. They say there has to be some way of detecting when they are coming so they can go up and be ready for 'em. As it is now by the time they leave the ground and get to an altitude of 18 and 20 thousand feet why they have already dropped their bombs and gone. They have Bombers now that travel 175 miles an hour.

While we were up at Lake Tahoe in the heart of the Sierra Nevada Mountains we would see the mail plane sometimes going over the mountains. They had to get a high altitude to make it, and there is not much chance of landing if the old Put Put goes bluey, and they do that both ways in the night too. I tell you when you get an air mail letter from away out here, you just ought to stop and think what a chance a half dozen fine young men have taken with their lives to get you that letter there one, two or three days earlier. Gosh that's a risky old game over these mountains at night.

Well let's see what other shows we had lately. Out our way for the last few weeks Aimee and Ma McPherson have just about run the spotlight ragged.[2] We can't find out if Aimee really did swing on Ma or not. Then to make the argument better why the "Face histing" entered into it. Ma said Aimee had her face re-upholstered, Aimee said she dident. Ma said that her (Ma's) nose was broken, Aimee said she broke it putting it in the Church's business, and in the meantime the Congregation never lost its faith. It was with 'em, nose or no nose, face or two faced, it didn't matter. They went down to her beach House in Malibu, (by the way there's where all the Pajama Actorines cavort). Well it seems that Aimee had a beach House, and the Choir would go there and sing to her. Nobody sang to Ma but she never did stop denouncing. So us poor readers have just been about run ragged trying to keep up with so many different developements. It seems that our various assortment of Clergymen, and Clergywomen, won't give one of the ordinary paying congregation a chance to make the front page. Bishop Cannon no more slows up or re-marries or does something, than Aimee and Ma are ready for a go.[3] And speaking of Ma's why I havent communed with you since Ma Furgeson was defeated for the nomination, and of course the election, for it was on the Democratic side, and Texas has about been cured of its last election's short sightedness.[4] Democrats are coming back in the fold so fast and praying for forgiveness that it looks like a bargain sale.

This fellow Sterling that beat Ma is a fine fellow.[5] It took a good man to beat Ma. Got to give her and old Jim credit they come back mighty strong, and the large vote she received certainly showed that old Texas thinks a lot of the old Gal yet. There has been an awful lot of people defeated this year in the primary. Everybody was running that could get some cards printed. It was a great year for the printers.

We got an awful good man beat in Oklahoma for the Senate nomination, Wrightsman.[6] But he was up against another case of too much opposition. It was our old time Senator Gore, the first blind man, (physically) to sit in the Senate.[7] He lost out away back during one of those early Republican landslides. There is going to be a lot of changes in Washington when the boys gather after the next election. Democrats are going to make some big gains for the people are sore at Hoover because they had to go back to work and couldent just make a living by buying a stock and selling it to the other fellow at a raise. Then him not giving 'em rain, has hurt him. Then the people will get all excited around November over wets and drys, and the law will stay like it is, and the thirsts will be quenched as usual, then the "Hooey" will die out till then we will have the same thing over again. Oh, hum!

403   WHERE'S ALL THIS FARM RELIEF?

Well all I know is just what I read in the papers. Here about a week or ten days ago we had quite a mess of news happening. But here lately it's pretty well bogged down. When those Frenchmen was

1930

flying the Ocean, and Lindy was receiving 'em, you know that must have been quite a Novelty.¹ Think of Lindy meeting somebody instead of being met. But he did a mighty gracious thing, as he always does. When those boys landed he was right there, to give them the glad hand of welcome, and it was real too. For he is for anything that is for the good of aviation whether he is the one doing it or not. Yes sir he and Annie was there.²

Well those fellows had a right to make that trip. They were real Aviators in the first place, and they had made every known preperation and taken every precaution. The trouble with most of the other trials that have failed, they were by practically unknown Aviators, and they were just taking a chance, and figuring maby they could make it. You see when those Germans come meandering in here by way of the North Pole and way stations (which by the way was a great trip) why that stirred the French. You let a German do something and even if it's wrong the Frenchmen will want to out do him. Now that they have it done, I look to have to put up immigration laws against visiting foreign Aviators. They will be dropping in here so fast that Grover Whalen will have to be shaking hands with both mits.³

Then Mr Hearst getting thrown out of France was awful big news away back in the same days the Frenchmen were landing.⁴ He went on over to England and they received him with open arms, and even asked him to write something about them. France got sore at something he wrote about 'em, and England with their minds on what could be accomplished by publicity, as they had seen it done by America, they said, "Sure W. R. publish any of our old Treatys you want. We will even write you one to publish, go ahead, write what you want and stay as long as you like." Well anyhow they lost a mighty good spender, when they let him go. Outside of Flo Zeigfeld he does things in a bigger way than any man I ever knew.⁵ Course Zeigfeld, the Marharajah of Johdpurr can't travel and operate like Zeigy.⁶

Well let's see what else there is in the prints. I thought we was going to have some Farm Relief to report to you by this sabbath day. But the commissions are just gathering data. They won't take the farmer's word for it that he is poor. They hire men to find out how poor he is. If they took all the money they spend on finding out how he is, and give it to the Farmer he wouldent need any more relief. But soon as winter comes he will be OK, soon as snow flies he can kill Rabbits, that will be the biggest relief he has had so far.

Well the elections will be breaking out pretty soon, and a flock of Democrats will replace a mess of Republicans in quite a few districts. It won't mean a thing, they will go in like all the rest of 'em, go in on promises and come out on Alabi's. If the Farmer could harvest his promises he would be sitting pretty. The party that's in and not doing so good, when the election comes they throw him out, but all these things happen on what they call the "Off Years," on those years the Republicans see that things go pretty good. So what happens at the coming one won't have a thing to do with the big finals in 32.

I tell you what I bet you. I bet you that Hoover walks in, in 32. It looks kinder goofy for him now. But by then we will have heard him knocked so much that we will begin to feel sorry for him and figure that he hasent had a chance, and by then the Farmers that want relief now will be starved to death, and a new crop will be along that have sold the old farm and put in a "Minature" so he will walk in. There is something about a Republican Administration that it only functions one year in four. But they make sure that year is the presidential election year. So now is the time to take some bets. Paste this up and drop me a line around November 32. Never mind what happens at this one that's coming up in a few weeks, that's only a decoy. That's just to keep the Democrats enthused, and keep them from giving up their character.

By the way all the reports from New Yaork are that Jimmy Walker is folding up and going into the old camphor balls.[7] Well Jimmy has had a good run and it won't worry him much. He has kept 'em fooled for quite awhile, and has made 'em about as good a man as any of the rest of 'em. Jimmy could at least make 'em a good speech. He called in a hundred prominent citizens to disscuss "graft" with him. A man naturally wouldent call in 100 poor men to disscuss graft, they would have no technical knowledge of the subject. These 100 met and adjourned without adopting any resolution to either halt or increase it. It seemed everyone was satisfied as it is.

404 WHAT DO YOU KNOW ABOUT NEVADA?

Well all I know is just what I read in the papers, and what comes along where I happen to be messing around. I don't care where, or how much you have traveled, if you want to hit a unique neck of the woods go up around Lake Tahoe, and over into Nevada, Reno, Carson City, Virginia City, all those Hot Springs up around there, then that Lake Tahoe 6300 hundred hoofs high, 26 miles long and 12 wide, and all the resorts around it, and the California and Nevada line running right through the lake. In fact it makes a bend right in the lake.

1930

It's not only the unique country, it's the people too that you run onto up there. Lots of Frisco people have their summer homes up there. The Fleishackers have a great place, and he goes back to his business and rounds up a new gang of guests and brings 'em up for every week end.[1] He has got that big old Boy that played such great football for Standford, and a fine big Kid he is too, and not spoiled. This Fleishacker is the man that every big business man or financier knows. I have heard more tales of big men being temporarily in need of money and going to the phone and calling up "Herb Fleishacker" and he would fix 'em up. I never heard of a business man that had done as many good deeds for his friends.

Then down the Lake further on Emerald Bay Mrs Knight has I'll bet is the most unique House in America, a Sweedish House.[2] Now we never thought about the Swedes having houses. We just kinder pictured 'em being born, and then leaving the next day for Minnesota, and then live in American made homes. But say on their native heath those Johnsons know how to live. This house of hers is absolutely authentic, and it's the most livable thing I ever saw, all heavy substantial stuff; lots of fireplaces, up off the floor level, and most of them in the corners of the room, and low ceilings, and heavy pannelings, and the outbuildings have sod covered roofs, and it's in a great setting, as she owns Emerald bay, and it's backed up with those giant saw tooth mountains, and a big waterfall coming down at the back of the place. Then another great one is Anita Baldwin's summer place just off the big lake on Fallen Leaf Lake.[3] It's log, the biggest ones you ever saw. The Living room with the highest ceiling, and everything in it is Indian, and I mean authentic Indian, as she has one of the greatest Indian collections in America. A great part of it is now in the Southwestern Museum. There is not one thing you see or touch when you get in that house that's not Indian, or Indian design. Dishes, Knives, Forks, all the cushions of the chairs and settees are cowskin covered, sofa pillows are woven corn husks. She has the oddest mantel in her room. Her Father Lucky Baldwin made his first big money in mining, and you've all seen these piles of rocks of odd colors, and mineral contents that most old homes used to possess, (I know we had some and I been trying for years to find out what become of them). Well she has a concrete mantel, and on the out edges of that mantel is all these wonderfully valuable pieces of mineral, imbedded in the concrete, and of course hers was valuable as it was a fine collection of her Father's that had come from his diggings in the old "Comstock" not many miles from where these are now. I was admiring some of her Indian Baskets, and happened to say that I wanted to get hold of some, and she said, "Over in Carson City there

Weekly Articles

is some very nice ones, they were made by a very famous Washoe Indian Woman now dead, but they are rather dear, they run about ten thousand each." When I regained part consciousness, I thanked her for the information and asked if she thought I could get a slight reduction if I sent over and got say a dozen or so. I wouldent give ten thousand dollars for the basket they had Moses stored away in the bullrushes in.

But we must get away from homes and get to the real interest up around Nevada, and thats the "Divorcees." All of 'em don't live in Reno. They live over on, or near the California line, they have to serve three months. If they leave the State during that time and stay a week, they have to add that on to their sentence at the end. Most of them are young women. There is on an average of about 2,000 here all the time. Two Judges in Reno are trying cases most all the time. Judge Bartlett, one of Nevada's most famous Judges was down to watch us shoot our Picture, and he is a mighty pleasant, shrewd, fine little fellow.[4] He tells me that a great percentage of the women who come, it's planned and premeditaded with the Husband. He has fallen in love with somebody, or she has, or they both have, and they have decided they can't tough it out so they claim desertion, or something, and the alimony is generally arranged beforehand between them, if any.

It's a funny colony, and it ain't funny, it's sad. You talk to these women, and the most of 'em would like to go back and have another try with the husband. But they are game and they won't come till he wires, and he is all hopped up over some other younger Gal, and he don't wire, and they sadly go through with it. Course you don't hear the man's side out here. They don't always tell you about the man they are going to marry the next day after the decree. But it's really pitiful. Course there is the old Stagers here who think no more of changing husbands than they do their brand of Gin. But there is many a heart break here, and lots of children, that's the tough part. Some of them their Mothers told me they hadent told them yet, they thought they were just here for a summer vacation. Divorce ain't so bad I guess when it's only the participants suffer, but it's sure tough on the children. Well anyhow it's a great Industry, and I guess about the only way to stop it is to stop marriage.

405   IN MARK TWAIN'S COUNTRY

Well all I know is just what I read in the scandal sheets, and what I hold a clinic over as I prowl hither and non. Well sir I must tell you more about that mining town of "Bodie," Cal. It was one of the famous mining camps of later days, but had been practically deserted for years, but with the demand for gold here lately and the improved and cheaper method of extracting it, there was a revival of the famous old place. Harry Carr, one of the best newspaper men on this or any other coast, had been up there writing wonderful stories of what it meant to a mining town to be convalescing, and about to reach good health again.[1] He claimed the thing was running almost as wide open as one of our big Cities, that the gambling and drinking was in a small way on a comparison with New York or Los Angeles.

Well in my times, (I am talking like one of the early Pioneers,) I have seen some of the boys foolishly, and at times otherwise, lay a small wager on the outcome of what later would be apparent as a hazardous game. And in passing by I had peeped in under swinging doors and there would be men sipping various nectars. Well Mrs Rogers and I were just out prowling around. We were working on spoiling a fine old classic, and had been taking a great part of the Scenes on the original site where the play was laid, at Lake Tahoe. Mr Henry King our Director had told me that he had seen just about all of my face that he desired for exterior photographic purposes, and that if I wanted I could head for home, and as they had a few more days without me I needed'nt be in any hurry to get to home.[2] Well that was right up my alley. I bet a lot of you like this too. I love to drive around and look over queer places, especially historic old spots. Well that Country up around in the mountains of California, why you could be there from now on, just looking at places that you had read about all your life.

Right under our nose was "Donner Lake" the place where the most famous of all pioneer stories of hardships, why there was where they had spent the winter within fifteen miles of the summit but just to late to get over. That's where perhaps the only case of cannibalism was ever practiced in our country. It was afterwards admitted on the very best of authority that they actually had to resort to the use of human flesh to exist. It was one of the greatest stories of pioneer life. If you havent read the "Life of the Donner Party" you don't know nothing of suffering and hardships. The California Societies are doing a great deal to preserve the spirits and history of these things and they have a fine monument to commerate the spot. Then we went over practically the route that they hoped to make, from Donner Lake to Sutter's Fort, (now Sacremento) and through the old fort as it is preserved today by patriotic citizens, and it should be but it's kinder a travesty on justice that while they kept the Fort, they did nothing for the man, that made the Fort and saved the early settlers.[3] He died destitute in Washington trying to get a little dab of money from our great Government, a mere pittance of what he had spent on preserving the life of some of the early settlers.

There is a story, the life of that fellow Sutter. All the gold was found on his place. He owned all the country. He developed it, he improved conditions there, and yet by the aid of thieves, courts, and injustice, he lost the whole thing. Yet he had done more for his Country, real constructive work, than Washington had, up to the time he was chosen to lead our Army. California should have maintained him in splendor for the balance of his days if he had lived even till Farmers got relief. But you get the life of this fellow Sutter, and it will make any other Autobiography look like the life of an Interior Decorator. But we got to be on our way. Then we went down through all the old early 49 camps, Sutter Creek, Angels Camp, in Caliveras, that's the exact home of Mark Twain's Jumping frog, and really the story that did more to make Twain than any other one thing he ever did. They have Frog Rodeo there every year, Frog Singing, Frog Jumping, and wind up by eating all the frogs that had contested, and everybody wind up with a Frog in their throat. Then Brete Hart was there and all his stories are around in that country.[4] Jackson, one of the early ones, I had made two pictures there previously, and hadent been back for ten years.

They got a great bunch of folks, Italian Americans, fine citizens, and the most hospitable people on you ever saw. Sure glad to see the old place again. Then to Senora, another old timer, but which held on fine, and is today a real little town. Then over Senora pass. Scenery, Oh Boy what views! But it's getting late we must get to Bodie. It's away over near the Nevada line in the sage brush desert. My wife was afraid to go, she had read Carr's articicles and she was looking for whooping, shooting, and gamboleering. Well the poor Devils, the night before, just twenty four hours to correct time announcement, why the Pro-Hi's, had raided the place, broke all the booze in 13 saloons, put 15 men under 1500 hundred dollar bonds, and you should have seen the place this night. Our car was the only thing moving in the town. Indignation meetings consisted of two and three huddled in front of what had been a saloon door. It was still lighted up, but saspharilla was their diet. It was a real surprise raid. The mines hadent opened that day, for they had had no sustenance for 24 hours and couldent work. I talked with them, but it was almost like speaking over the body of a fallen comrade. Their voice was not only reverent but parched. They couldent understand why they out of 120 million people should be discriminated against. Why should they be the only example of Prohibition? They felt that their work demanded as much or more liquid fortitude as is allowed toilers on Wall Street. They estimated in low tones the amount of Bootleggers that these officers must have passed in their trip away out in this desert, from San Francisco where they had come. It will always remain in my memory as the saddest one town I ever saw.

406 WILL TAKES A HISTORY LESSON

Well all I know is just what I read in the papers, and what I get through the mail. Arthur Brisbane and I have been having a good natured kidding through the papers about Russia.[1] Arthur kinder believes that Russia should be recognized, and me I don't know whether they should or not. Lords, that's a Diplomat's business not mine. I am not getting Diplomatic wages. I am only getting acting wages. They are in a position to do quite a little trade with us, so if you want to base everything on a purley dollar and cents basis why we better not only recognize 'em but go out and look for 'em.

But then we know that they spend a great deal of money on propaganda to ferment revolution, and that nothing would be so welcome to them as to read some day where everybody that had a clean shave and more than $2.50 cents had been blown up with a bomb, why then you kinder wonder if it's good to deal with folks that don't wish you any better than that. But that's got nothing to do with it, what I am getting at is the interesting letters this fellow Brisbane writes. I am going to show you one he wrote me that I just got yesterday. I don't think he will mind me publishing this, it's personal, but not too personal for me to collect my weekly fee on, especially when it is better by far than anything I could write.

My Dear Rogers,

Now that I have established your credit as a multimillionaire, and that you have destroyed mine by making me out in the public prints as destitute, which by the way I regret to say is an extremely accurate description, let us talk seriously about Russia. This Country including its brightest intellects, even your own, fail to appreciate the importance of what is going on in Russia.

You know that when Louie the sixteenth came back from shooting at Fontainebleau on a certain 14th of July he wrote in his diary "Rein," meaning in the French language, "Nothing." He hadent shot anything, and he simply wrote down that nothing had happened. But that was the 14th of July on which the

Bastlie was destroyed, and later as a consequence of that "Rein" day, they just casually chopped off his head.

The King of Persia asked, "Where is Greece?" and said to his royal remembrancer, "Remind me sometime to go down and destroy that little Country." His descendants learned about Greece when Alexander came from Macedonia with 30,000 men and sent him flying to his death, went through his line of war Elephants and took his Country.

All of which leads up to the fact that Will Rogers should study and analize, and understand Russia, not dispose of it with a wave of a hand like some foolish Wall Street Broker who buys Karensky Bonds and bellyaches because they are not paid.[2] We dident pay the bonds issued by the South.

I have no doubt that the Russian experiment will fail eventually, being based on pretense of unselfishness and brotherly love, which have no existence among human beings.

But its experiments in Industry, in world competition, and efficincy may cost some of the old Capatalist civilizations dear, if they ignore it. Alexander's Empire fell, dwindling down to the Cleopatra and Mark Anthony foolishness, but not until he had put an end forever to the old Persia. So you ought to warn your readers to not underate Russia. Many years ago when you was a little Boy, (Thanks for that kind compliment Arthur) I told Klaw, Erlanger, Frohman and Brady that someday Movies would sweep the country and be in every town.[3] They thought I was crazy. Well look and see.

Now you take old Cato with his "Carthage must be destroyed" and keep saying every day at the end of your "piece" in diamond type, "Watch and beware of Russia." This is talked into my phonograph in my automobile on my way in from Long Island to New York, hence the length.

Yours sincerely,
A. Brisbane

Now wasent that a fine letter. You know he is a great fellow. I wish you all could know him personally, along with his uncanny grasp of things he has got a lot of humor, there is many a sly laugh imbedded in his sermons on many subjects. Now he is sincere about this Russia thing too. He does know enough about it to know that they are going somewhere, and we better watch out while they are on the way. I think on the other hand that he has kinder been Propagandered on 'em, and he has perhaps got the brighter side, for they were a pretty seedy looking outfit when I visited them in 1926. Course they might have changed a lot. We have. Nobody would ever thought we would be walking on our uppers to have looked at us in 26. Why we had a gold mine and thought it couldent run out. Now he is a smart man, and I am going to take his advice, and really give a little more serious thought and time to see what they really are doing, for Lord knows we all want to see 'em make it go, for if they can make it better for everybody, instead of just for a few why they will have practically revolutionized the World. But all that Cato, and Carthage, and Persia, and Greece, and Macedonia, and Louie the sixteeenth, and "Rein" and all that was lost on me. He was getting a long way from Russia telling about all those old Birds. But the Rascal can quote anything. And I guess he is right, anyhow I havent got time to look it up. Any man as high salaried and busy as he is, that will sit down and take his valuable time to write my Sunday article for me, I am not going to find any faults with it as to facts. I will dissagree with him every day if he will write my articles for me. Anyhow if I ever answer him, I can't talk about those old fellows. I will have to refer him to, Senator Grundy, Al Capone, Tom Heflin, Aimee, and just the ones that I know.[4] But anyhow Arthur, I am much obliged to you, and I will take care of Russia from now on.

407   IT'S ANOTHER OFF YEAR

Well all I know is just what I read in the papers. See where Henry Ford is prowling around over in Europe, and he gets tons and tons of mail and it's addressed to him as "his Highness Henry Ford." They think he is King over here. Well he is not exactly what you might refer too as one of our menial Subjects. Over in a Museum in Berlin they have the first car made in Germany, and perhaps the World, for it was made in 1885, it only had three wheels. It was the "Benz" made by Karl Benz.[1] But up to going to press he has not been able to get it. Germans wouldent take his check I guess. But he did buy two old watches, and a new hat.

Was you ever through that place in Derborn where he has all the old Vehickles stored? If you rode in your young days in old wagon, or sled, or a buggy and have in your old years of reminencing wondered what become of it it's right in Henry Ford's shed. I never saw in all my born days as much plunder as there is in there. Old thrashing Machines, dozens of 'em, old saw mill engines, old fire Engines, Old Handsom Cabs. Everything under the sun that ever dragged one person from one place to another is in there, so I can sure imagine how he must have wanted that old crate.

Can you imagine the excitement he must cause over there? For he is the one man in America that they have an idea what he makes and what he does, and I imagine that his retinue is about one half of what a second rate Movie Star would have traveling over there. I doubt if he has a Secretary with him.

Oh yes, and then we just been reading where the Russians turned down some kind of an order of Tractors. If they did turn down that order of a thousand Tractors as we heard they did, (They were Ford Tractors) why I guess that will cut his trip short, for that would be a pretty hard financial blow and he couldent afford to be prowling around over there then, as it was on the profit and expectation of that order that he made the trip.

Well sir before you know it there will be another election along to pester us. What they have those things for nobody has ever been able to tell. It's just to distribute the jobs around so one man won't have it all the time. Most of the men that are in are trying to stay in and all that are out are trying to get in. This is what they call an off year. What they mean by that is everybody is running but the President.

These off years the Democrats generally make a pretty good showing, and this fall looks like their chance to get a gang of Guys in the Senate and House. Of course they will offset what advantage they have by splitting among themselvs, on the wet and dry plan. They will make that an issue when it's only a habit.

Funny race up in Massachusetts. They dug up a fellow named Coolidge, an Irishman, and a Democrat.[2] He used to be Mayor of Fitchburg, along when Calvin was Mayor of Northampton. They claim the fellow is no kin to Calvin. But I know one time up in Vermont I was playing a town, I think it Rutland or somewhere, and in my audience that night, I had been tipped off was a first Cousin of Cal's and he was a Democrat, and I had a lot of fun kidding with him. Met him afterwards and he was a dandy fellow. I don't know how he got strayed off from the herd while they was all going orthadox. He, (this fellow Coolidge) is running against William Butler, an old friend of Mr Calvin Coolidge's.[3]

Oh yes and this other Coolidge that's running is a wet! Imagine a wet Coolidge! Nature does produce some queer angles. Don't know if Mr Coolidge will take the stump to help out his old friends or not. He is still working on his daily Column and can always say he is too busy. He is mighty schrewd and knows how to keep out of these hometalent fights. New York pretty near everybody is running as a wet. Both Republicans and Democrats know there is more wet votes than there is dry ones so they both jump that way. That shows right there that the whole thing is not on the level, for everyone of these public men come out just according to the way the wind is blowing where they live. Now some of them must have some personal opinion that is not just along with the majority of voters all the time.

New Jersey Morrow took a brave stand when it meant something.[4] He wasent sure he was on the right side or not, but he come out against it. Not that it might have been the right thing to do, but it at least planted him as a man with his own opinion and he was willing to stand by it. But with all the messing and argueing over it at the election it won't mean a thing. Nothing is going to be done about it any more than farm relief, or unemployment relief.

No matter who you elect to go to Washington, that hasent got anything to do with Prohibition, for it has to be repealed by the States, or the men that you don't send away. Not during any of our lifetime will it be repealed for it takes two thirds of the States, not two thirds of the votes. Arizona could offset a State as big and as thickly settled as New York or Massachusetts.

Ohio they got so scared at their convention, they was afraid to do anything, so they just voted as favoring Prosperity and went home. They have a new term now called the "Weaslers." The Weaslers are anyone that is afraid to jump either way. They feel that their state is still doubtful and they claim they havent made up their minds. So from now on you are in for one of the longest and most nonsensical arguments, all over something that they couldent change if they wanted too. Democrats will make quite a few gains and the Wets will perhaps make some, but the whole thing will mean nothing in our lives. All we do is just dig up their salary, and they all get the same price, Republican Democrat, Wet, or Dry. There is no way we can win.

408 WARS AND RUMORS OF WARS

Well all I know is just what I read in the Papers. There is some pretty big stuff in the papers nowadays, but it's kinder under cover. Did you ever kinder stop to figure it out, this old World of ours as a whole is not sitting so pretty just at the present time. Did you know that there is an awful lot of parts of Europe that is just sitting on what the old time Orator used to call a Powder Keg? Well it is.

We can't pick up a paper that from one to a hundred don't prophesy that Prosperity is just around the corner. But let me tell you that war is nearer around the corner than prosperity is. I don't mean so much for us right here. But I mean over in Europe. That Russia is kicking up an awful lot of dust, and Germany is harboring a terrible lot of dissatisfaction, that Hitler has got 'em all stirred up over there.[1] He made a speech last week in which he advocated the breaking of the Versailles Treaty, he said that it was made by a lot of old men, who most of them were about ready to die, and now here was a lot of young men grown up and they had to carry all this burden, for which they were not directly to blame, and that it was only a matter of time till they just wouldent do it. They would say, "Well come on France, what are you going to do about it? We cant be any worse off if you come in and take over our Country than we are now."

Then those little Balkan Nations, they are like a little mess of stray Terriers anyhow, they just as well be fighting as like they are. This has been about the longest they have ever been between wars. I see the other day where Russia was just on the verge of invading Roumania. They have always had it in for them and figured they only had to take a couple of days rations and rounds of ammunition and go over and take that Country anyhow.

Russia and Poland are always on the verge of war. I remember when I was over in both countries in the summer of 26, why they were growling at each other like a couple of Fat Prima Donas on the same Opera bill. Then Italy is ranting around down there trying to pick up some more country and outlet for their population. France is watching them with an Eagle eye all the time, and that's just what Mussolini wants, he had rather worry France than anything. France feels that she would have no trouble whipping them, but if she went down there to do it, Germany would take that opportunity to get at them and she just don't want to have to take the chance. Then the Checko-Slovakians feel kinda hemmed in down their way, and of course the Turks, there is nothing that irks a Turk so much as peace.

Austria, they just been so bad off since the last war that they know there would be no way that war wouldent be welcome to them. Bulgaria has started all the rest of them, her and Serbia, and they don't want to lose their reputations, they want to go down in history as having started all the big ones.

All this whole mess have no more love for each other than a litter of Hyenas, they either lost or gained territory during the last war, and they feel those that did gain that in another war they could grab off even more, and the ones that lost can't see how they could possibly make that mistake again, and that if given a chance to play the same hole over again they could make it par the next time. I try to read all that all those old World Diplomats write over there, and there is not a line of it that is not in regard to another war. They just can't write a prescription without predicting what will happen in the next great war. Their whole minds is on it, and from all that I read of them there is no two that seem to give anywhere near the same possible lineup. It's like the National and American League if when time come to play the Worlds series they would just take all the players from all the Clubs in their League and then choose up and play the other side. No one knows where the thing will start or with who. No one knows how the line-up will be, for they don't know who will be fighting who. Some of them that hate Russia like poisen will want to join her on account of her strength. They will all want to wait and see who looks like the winner. They did that in the last war, quite a few staid out waiting for the best offer. Lots of pretty smart men think that is one of the biggest contributing factors to our present state of economic unrest, is that all big finance is afraid of what will happen in the near future, and they don't know where it will end up. That's why everybody is hanging on to what they got. There is more in the wind than just our little local condition over here. We got as much as we ever had, there is just as much money, as many to eat, and as many to feed, as many to buy. But still our conditions are uncertain. Why? Just because it's things outside our own land that is worrying 'em. They know that signs are not right all over the World. Look at South America. When during our lifetime has there been as many disturbances at one time? No sir the whole thing is world wide, we are effected by it less than anyone.

If we keep our nose clean and don't start yapping about somebody elses honor, or what our moral obligations are, we might escape it. But it's going to take better Statesmanship than we have been favored with heretofore. But the way we are now we are mighty lucky to have nothing but a little business depression that is bothering us. But think what those other poor Devils are up against.

409 TROT OUT THE POLO PONIES

Well all I know is just what I read in the papers. I was just sitting here tonight reading a very beautiful Horse Magazine called, "Polo." It is the issue that tells of the great Internation Match played between England and America, and it gives the very detail of each play, and also tells of the sale of the Horses after the match. You know I was just thinking it might be interesting to some of you to know something especially about the horses, for you don't have to be a polo nut to be interested in good horses.

There was $335,000 worth of horses sold at public auction after

Will Rogers playing his favorite sport, polo.

the games. The British sold 48 head for $183,400. The Americans 36 head $73,200, and the Australians 25 head for $77,600. The British averaged pretty near $4,000 a horse. The Americans only about $2,000 and the Australians $3,000. The reason the Americans dident bring as much was the fact that most of the best horses played by the American team was privately owned and was not put up for sale at all. The ones sold were just the ones that were owned by the Polo Association.

The games are pulled off under the management of the US Polo Association. They guarantee the British team their Transportation and expenses and all which is taken out of the Gate receipts, and this year the Association had themselvs bought up quite a string of Ponies for our team. Heretofore they had depended entirely on the generosity of other players loaning their best horses to the big team. But this year they bought some themselvs, and sold them after the games. The Australians dident of course play in the big matches, but they had brought a great team over here who had created quite a fuss over in England. It was composed entirely of Brothers, four young men from 22 to 28, the Ashton Brothers, and their Father and Mother were with them.[1] They had a very fine string of Ponies, were supposed to be a little smaller than our Boys have been playing. But they were very handy, and a lot of them were so well reigned that you could play them in a snaffle bit Bridle. Of course some individuals sold their Horses. Charley Wrightsman a fine young Sportsman and member of our Clubs out here on the coast was good enough to mount Eric Pedley, the sensation of the games, and a fellow Coast Player.[2] Eric had gone back there to try out a time or two before in International matches, but he never had a proper chance for he wasent properly mounted, but this time Charley sent back twenty head just for Eric to play through the test Matches on.

You know a horse is really from 60 to 70 percent of the game. That's about the ratio the Experts figure it. If you can't beat a man to the ball why there is no use going. It's speed, and more speed that counts with those big League fellows. Us Punks can lope around and have a lot of fun on a pack of old Hounds, but if we was among those fast fellows we would get run over.

Most of the Horses that make those big games are Thoroughbreds, or three quarters so. An awful lot of them are bread and raised on western ranches, and lots of them have run cattle. Polo has not only been a recreation or Hobby of a lot of rich people, but it's been a God-send to the Horse business. It has done more to establish the breeding of good horses than even races have. Now it is a big business, and there is dozens of men just prowling all over the west buying likely "prospects" for Polo. The game is growing so fast and the demand for horses so great that it's a real business now.

The Argentine has really furnished more horses to our International game than we have. They have been breeding good Horses down there for years. I was down there in 1901 and I saw well bread Horses on ranches then, while we was breeding nothing but just old range Ponies. I worked my way on a Stock boat to South Africa from Buenos Aires and we had on board a couple of hundred thoroughbred horses to restock a ranch in Africa after the Boer War.

White Slave an English bred mare played by the English brought $13,000 Bucks, that was the top price, bought by Laddie Sandford.[3] Lady Luck, another English one, owned and played by Lewis Lacey, the great Argentine and English Player brought $10,000, and an Australian mare Isobel, $10,000.[4] Course lots of them brought 1500, and a thousand, but even at that price you are sitting on quite an expensive hunk of horseflesh. And you can't always tell the ones you give the more for may not turn out to be the best. It's sorter what suits certain men. No two humans are the same and no two horses either. Nobody can look at a horse and tell what he is worth. He is worth to you just how good he is to you and how bad you want him and how well he suits you.

Why would any horse be worth the same to any two people? All the Colleges have taken up Polo now, and that's a great boost for it, and this thing of it costing all this money is a lot of Hooey. You can back three or four old fifty dollar crow bates and have as much fun with the game as Jock Whitney, or Laddie Sandford, who each have perhaps from a quarter to a half million just in their Polo Strings alone.[5] That half million to them is just like us buying an extra bowl of Chili. The boy on the sand lot gets just as big a kick out a home run as Babe Ruth, and the Dub Polo Player on a hired horse gets just as much kick out of making a goal as Hitchcock.[6]

It's a great game, and it learns you to ride quicker than anything on earth for when you start hitting at the ball you forget about how you are going to stay on, you just do it unconsciously. Age don't keep you from playing it. Arthur Brisbane's Father in law, Steward Carey, he is in his seventys.[7] Plays twice a week at Meadowbrook. I was 51 Saturday, and played Sunday, (after coming from Sunday School). I dident play good, but I had as much fun missing, as the others did hitting. I am going to play till my whiskers get tangled up in the horse's tail.

410 STRANGE TALE OF A HARVARD CANNIBAL

Well, all I know is just what I read in the papers, or what I find out one way or another. Here a couple of weeks ago I wrote a Sunday Article and it mentioned the Donner Party at Donner's Lake as being our only case of Cannibalism ever practiced in our abundant Country. Well then some man wrote me and told me of a case of a man named Packer in Colorado, and so I wrote a Daily prescription about him, stating the Judge's charge to the Jury, and admonishing him for eating up all the Democrats in the County.[1] If he had just eaten up a Republican why the Judge, (a fine old high type Democrat from Arkansaw) would have perhaps given the man a pension instead of a sentence. Well now we got that much straight.

We first wrote of the Donner Party, by the way if you havent read its history do so, it's the most dramatic piece of life ever lived by a band of our brave Countrymen, and Women. Well then comes this other case of this fiend eating the Democrats, and these two cases must be all there is, or otherwise I would have heard of any others, for people love to write letters and tell you of any other cases, even of cannibalism.

Well now comes a long and very interesting letter from a man named N E Guyot, whose letterhead says Kingman Arizona, and he gives me the exact details of this last case.[2] It seems he was in Colorado at the time. Now a lot of folks thought I was just kidding when I wrote of this Packer, and the story of the Democrats but it was the gospel truth. I certainly wouldent make light of a thing so serious as eating a Democrat. We are reaching a time in our existence when we need every one we can muster. We got to get some prosperity mixed up in our National existence, and as the coming November reaches the election day, we are coming out in numbers that will astonish the Natives. So I certainly was serious and was relating a historical fact. But wait, let Mr Guyot tell you, "It was in the Northwestern part of Colorado, San Juan mountains, ten miles from the Town of Lake City, on a plateau that is called on Government survey, 'Cannibal Plateau.' It was here that Packer through a severe snow storm murdered and devoured his Prospector companions." Now those are some mere facts but here is the things I want you to get. It's the history of this fellow Packer before he started in subsisting on the minority party. Packer was a Harvard Graduate, and graduated in '66. He was a Law Student and started practicing in Boston. What I am getting at is that the only case of a person willfully devouring human flesh was by the Alumni of the great

Harvard, so Harvard has not only produced the least understandable English in our fair land, but produced the only living Cannibal.

Then he was a Lawyer, that of course seems natural, their proffession is an offshoot of the cannibal proffession. They generally skin 'em alive. Packer did have the good taste to destroy 'em and get 'em out of their misery. Most Lawyers delight in seeing their victims suffer. It was the winter of 72 and 73. There was six Companions, and they were all well equipped with provisions. But in the snow they got lost from their Burros. Mr Guyot in his letter says that it was the first time, and perhaps the last that a Lawyer was ever permitted to accompany a band of Prospectors into the mountains. He always waits till they go out and find it, and then he gets his share by showing 'em where to sign their name. But Packer was afraid they would come back and find another Lawyer so he just went along with 'em. But ain't that strange that a Lawyer is never allowed out with Prospectors?

Well it seems there was dissension from the start over allowing him to come to kill and eat him. But that dident go with the Judge and Jury. They knew no man could ever be so hungry that they would eat a Lawyer.

Now I was wrong in one little misstatement about the case, I had heard that he was hung. He was not. Colorado was then a Territory and the game laws did not protect Democrats. Even to this day in some States it would not be considered illegal to eat one. So they give him forty years in Canyon City Jail. That was a little over six years for each one he ate. You would have to eat at least ten or more to get life according to Colorado justice. He dident stay in there that long. Along in 99 when Civilization and the Denver Post hit us, why them and other papers started a campaign to release him. There was a tight election coming on, and them being Republicans, they wanted to let him out hoping he would eat up some more Democrats before November 4th.

Then they brought up that the Judge, Judge Gerry (originally of Arkansaw, and a Democrat by birth and breeding) had been biased in the trial, that no Democratic Judge should sit in a case, where it was Democrats that had been eat.[3] The Editorials of the Denver Papers of that time all brought out this injustice. That it was a blot on the fair name of Colorado that a Harvard man shouldent be able to eat what he liked. Well anyhow the papers got him out, and the fair name of Colorado was saved, and since then they have never convicted, or even tried a man, for murdering, robbing or otherwise maiming a Democrat, Viva Democracy.

After this Packer fellow was released from the Jail, he went to

Cripple Creek and inserted an advertisement in the local papers, asking for men with means to accompany him on a prospecting trip. Not a Soul went. Oh Yes! I forgot to tell you he was the Son of a missionary, and in his youth had spent some time in the South Sea Islands. That's how he acquired this taste. A Missionary, a Lawyer, a Harvard Graduate, I want to tell you Illiteracy is a blessing.

411 WELL, LIFE AIN'T SO TOUGH

Well, all I know is just what I read in the papers, and what I hear over the radio, and, as the papers haven't had anything, and the static has been bad, ignorance is rampant. This week Bernard Shaw talked over the Radio. That was the high point of Radio broadcasting.[1] He made the rest of us that sometimes use that medium, that I think we all ought to retire and just let him say it. You know he is a brilliant old Bird. He never says what you are looking for him to, but he always says what you are glad he did say.

Italy had another big wedding, one of the daughters married Boris of Bulgaria.[2] They went away off down to some little town in Italy to marry, it seems there was a Justice of the Peace down there that she liked. It rained during the wedding, which means that it wont turn out very good. But it wouldent have turned out very good even if it hadent rained, for poor old Boris just got about another war to go.

He ain't so old, only about 32, but there will be a war pretty soon, and of course no European war can be official unless Bulgaria is a participant, and then Boris will get thrown out on his ear. The first thing you know the King of Italy will be the Father of more deposed Queen Daughters-in-law than anybody.

Mussolini seems like he is going along pretty strong. Saw a picture in the Movies the other day where he had an awful mess of young fellows drilling and saluting him. France is still leary of him. She is afraid to go down and pounce on him, for fear Germany will hop on her during their chastisement of Italy. That's why Mussolini traded this Queen to Bulgaria, was in case of any little national uprising in Europe, that Bulgaria would respect their Father-in-law and join Italy. It's the oldest line of Hooey and Diplomacy in the world and Europe is to try to gain Allies by marriage.

They think if they can marry one of their Royal Family into another Royal Family that that binds 'em closer. Nobody couldent have been much closer bound together than Germany and England.

They had been marrying each other like rabbits for generations, yet when the time come they turned against each other like Brothers.

So those poor devils of Royal parentage just go along, go where they are sent. I doubt if the gal had ever seen this Boris Bird, till he come prancing down the center aisle.

But we havent got any time to mess away our time worrying about them. What are we doing right here in the old home precinct? When you read this, our usual November Follies will have passed into the discard. Election day will be a relic, and we will wake up with some more of 'em. There is a good deal of excitement rather synthetic, but anyhow excitement, in some quarters, as to who will go on the Government pension list after this election. In New York State all is hopped over the Governor's race. I don't know just how Roosevelt will fare, but I sure do know he is a fine high class man.[3] I suppose he lost a lot of support by not spanking Tammany and sending 'em to bed, but he is a fine man never-the-less, and I guess this other fellow is too, I don't know him.

It looks like the Democrats will get in a bunch of new ones. They always do mighty well on these off years. We get 'em in on off years and get 'em out on Presidential years. But it give some people something to get worked up over, and get all excited over. It don't mean anything. We been staggering along now about 155 years under every conceivable horse thief that could get into office, and yet here we are, still going strong.

I doubt if Barnum's circus, or Hagenback's Wild Animal Circus has housed as many different kinds of species as has been in our Government employ during its existence.[4] Yet as bad as they are they can't spoil it, and as good as they are they can't help it. We are just a river flowing along. We have a drought year, and we have a flood year. They build dams to stop us, but we just fill up and flow on over 'em, so there is really nothing that can be done about us. We are just flowing to the sea. Corruption can't retard us, and reformers can't assist us, we are just flowing along in spite of everything.

A good man can't do nothing in office because the system is against him, and a bad one can't do anything for the same reason. So as bad as we are better off then any other nation, so what's the use of worry.

412   IT WAS A GREAT ELECTION

Well all I know is just what I read in the papers, and all I have read in the last week is about the Democratic uprising of November

1930

4th. It was my birthday and the Boys of the party really did themselvs proud in my honor. The Republicans were looking for a punch in the jaw, but not for a kick in the pants at the same time. Why there was men beat at this wake that thought they had a deed to their seat. We will kinder start in alphabetically with the disasters and take 'em in that order, starting with Illinois.

An old Democratic friend of mine J. Ham Lewis, who has red whiskers, and a green vest to match, used to be in the Senate away back during the days when we was fixing it so there would never be another war.[1] If my Emily Post Etiquette book serves me right I think he is about the only Democrat in some distance to get a red whisker in that stately hall.[2] And after all these years here he is going back. His facial adornment has shed from a Clara Bow red to a kind of a Henna gray, and the old vest has got many an egg spot concealed behind its pearl buttons.[3] But Ham can curry one and bathe the other and he will make a new entrance into the old "Arena Del Toros."

It wasent only that he got back in there, but it was the spectacular manner that he did it. The Republicans had their strongest Woman up against him, Ruth Hanna McCormick.[4] She had spent a few hundred thousand in the Primaries, but evidently forgot to spend any on the race. That would be like spending all your money in Taxi fare to go the ball game, but none to spend to get in after you got there. But Ruth made a mighty fine race, and maby it's just as well she is not in there. I don't think a woman belongs in there. Not a nice woman anyhow. It's funny how a smart Political Woman like her couldent have guessed right on the Prohibition thing. How anybody could go wrong on what Illinois would do is beyond me. Ham he won't make 'em as good a Woman as Ruth would, but he will make 'em a good man.

Then continuing alphabetically we come to Oklahoma. Another old resident of the Senate got back after all these years. Our Blind man, Senator Gore.[5] He used to be a fixture in there from our Country. Then when he happened to be able to see further than the mob during the war why he lost out; now when the mob has caught up with him, and they can look back instead of having to look forward why they send him back in there. That gives Oklahoma two Democrats, which is of course as it should be, for we are liberty loving people.

You going to hear an awful lot in the next few years about a man from South Dakota named Beulow.[6] He is a Democrat and from South Dakota. Now that's like a Zulu being discovered on the Behring sea. He is a comical old rascal, with a lot of humor and about twice as much common sense as humor so he will be out of place two

Weekly Articles

ways in the senate. Watch him and remember his name, B-E-U-L-O-W and if he is to speak anywhere near you don't miss him.

Course the old timers got back in without even opposition like Pat Harrison, and Joe Robinson of Arkansaw.[7] They will be in the Senate when the Farmers get relief. Joe Robinson is mighty liable to be the Democratic Nominee in '32. It will be between him and Franklyn D. Roosevelt, and they are both mighty fine men.[8] Joe if they want a dry, and Roosevelt if they want a wet. But the wets seemed to kinder swamp everything at this meelee and are gaining strength every day, so in '32 it looks like the wet Candidate will have the edge at the Nomination.

Still the west got a long way to go yet. You see those States that voted wet this time were ones that were known to be wet all the time, when you start voting on it all through the middle west and south you will find a different tale, so both Parties will be up against it as to just what to do in '32. They will want to be wet for the wet voters and dry for the dry voters, and they won't know which one has the most votes, and they will be busier than a Bird Dog trying to figure which way to jump. That gives you a pretty good line on Politics; their personal feelings have nothing to do with it, it's which way will the most votes be. I believe a Candidate would go over Niagra Falls if he was sure the wind was with him.

413 HOW TO GET ON PAGE ONE

Well all I know is just what I read in the papers. And about all you read is Murder. A Robbery, Another Murder, Another Robbery. Then a train hits a loaded Auto. (They never hit 'em till they are Loaded.) That's why more people are not killed by a train is because there is so few really loaded auto's. An Engineer is careful that way, he won't hit a car with only one or two in it, he watches close and always calls his shots and gets a covey of 'em.

Then in between these above mentioned Columns in the Newspapers there will be a fellow in the home town that has just killed his wife and attempted to kill himself. That brings up another odd coincidence. Why is it that an attempted suicide that is going to kill somebody else along with himself, why is it they never miss the other party but they are poor shots on themselves? You would think as close as they are to themselves that they couldent miss. But they most generally do. They seem to be able to hit everybody else they shoot at but themselves.

1930

Out here in Los Angeles the other day we had a fellow who wanted his wife killed and instead of killing her himself, and then missing himself, why he hired another fellow to do it, and what do you think he give him, $1.30. He admitted it, and the husband admitted it. That about holds the record for low wages. That's a mighty poor ad for our Town when they are working for that kind of pay.

Murder by contract has always been a fairly well paid industry outside Chicago and New York. Of course there has been an over supply of men in that business, but in these outlying Villages it has always cost anyone pretty dear to hire someone for that type of work. But this old Boy just did it for $1.30 and all in dimes. AND THEY ARE GIVING HIM A TRIAL. A community that would go to the expense of trying a Bird like that why that's about all we deserve. There is some things that go beyond the law.

Then in between all these items, along about Sunday and Monday the paper has to always leave space for Auto accidents that happen on the way home from Football games. It looks like the poorer the ball team the bigger the accidents. And I don't care how big the score is the casualty list will be bigger. They run about two Co-eds, and one student injured to each point made by the team.

Then you must always leave one Column on the front page for Prominent men to Predict Prosperity in. Maby it was a big Dinner, and Mr. "I'll Fix Everything" is the Guest of honor. Maby he got rich selling "Motto Cards" or Machine Guns. But the Associated Press carries his prediction that "The trend is upward."

Then there is always a Column for Russia for they will have been in some kind of devilment during the previous night. Last week they said that the World was plotting against them. Then named the men that have it in for 'em. Well they will get all their people excited over that, and that will be in the papers for awhile till somebody thinks of something else.

Brazil or the Argentine can't stay on our front pages over a week at a time and then they have to have a pretty fair grade of Revolution to stick that long. We welcomed their incoming President up here this summer and when he got back home they did too. They welcomed him with another President. So now we find that we spent a lot of "Public Reception and dinner dough" on the wrong fellow. It ought to teach us something, never spend a dime on an elected President from any of those Countries till he is inaugurated. There is many a slip between the Poles and the White House in the Tropics.

Hitler over in Germany we have had his column pretty vacant here lately.[1] He has just about run out of Gags. You just can't stay on that old page continually, the strain is too great. You can't think of enough things to do.

Mussolini has come nearer doing it than anyone we ever had during our time. He jumps up and slaps some country down with a statement more often than any other man that ever lived. He gets on there once a week or more, if he is going good. He keeps France so busy denying and denouncing that they don't know what it's all about.

Bernard Shaw can make the front page any time he wants to express an opinion about anything, from Einstein's Theory, to the cultivation of Whiskers or Birth Control among Authors.[2] He is the highest paid Author in the World, yet he has given away more free stuff to the papers than any man that ever lived. For everything he ever said was news, and everything any other Author even said was Publicity.

The poor old Editorial pages are just about passing out. Nothing that is not accompanied by pictures of the actual killing will interest anyone any more. The readers don't want advice any more. That's what's the matter with this country; it's been advised to death. An editorial might explain the right course for everyone to pursue, but who wants to pursue it? An instructive Editorial is kinder like the lines they used to have at the top of the old copy writing book. It was a fine sentence, and it sounded just like what you ought to do, but you just copied it and went on.

A picture of Mary Garden getting off the boat is of more importance than what Opera she is going to appear in.[3] Her and "Old Tack" out in Amarillo can get in an argument and make up and get the town more advertising than the low price of wheat can.[4]

Then you have to leave room in there some place for the "Columnist." Pretty near every paper is afflicted with a mess of us. We are flourishing through a certain reign of insanity that perhaps won't be permanent, and woe be to any of us who take the whole thing serious. I think even Mr. Coolidge knows that as soon as the Country is thoroughly adjusted that we will be in some essential line, with a smaller recompense but an easier conscience. But with all its faults the old Paper is our daily bread. Sometimes it's burned, and sometimes not cooked to suit us but we got to have it everyday and its intelligence is always in keeping with its readers.

414 A WORD ABOUT EVERYTHING

1930

Well lets see what about the last "Fortnight." You know there is another one of those things we got from the English. We used to dident know any more what Fortnight meant than an Einsten speech.[1] But now we can just take a month apart and split it up into a couple or three Fortnights just like we had always been used to it. Then "Week End." That's another one we grabbed off from our British relations. "Week End" we used to think it referred to some dissabled extremity of the human body, and instead of naming the disease they just referred to it as the "Week end," maby misspelling it purposely. But now we can't hardly wait for Friday or Saturday to come so we can boast what we are going to do over the week end.

We not only stole the word from the British but the idea. Americans in the old days stayed over Saturday and Sunday, the same place they stayed on Monday, Tuesday, and Wednesday, they stayed at home. We dident start prowling just because it was the last of the week. You used to love your home. You loved to spend time in it. You knew to travel about meant putting up with inconveniences, meeting a lot of people, sleeping in strange beds and you just dident like to go. But now sentencing a man to stay at home over a few "Week ends" is like sentencing him to Sing Sing. He must go away, "his work has been so confining."

And you know come to think of it we nailed a many a thing from the British. We used to make fun of them because they had Busses on their streets instead of Street cars. Well here we are 25 years later adopting that very custom. A street car is getting to be a thing of the past, and all are looking for the Busses to ride on, and the same Double deck ones that we rave over were over there running when Cromwell and Shakespeare were about. Now we are getting around to their Five and six oclock tea. Course it's not Tea here, but it's the same Alabi that is used. You knew we take credit for being a lot faster than we are. We cop a lot of things and then the first thing you know we are claiming them as our own.

You know no Nation has a monopoly on good things, each one has something that the others could well afford to adopt. But that wasent what I started in to gab about at all, it all come about through writing unconsciously the word "Fortnight." I wanted to run over with you what had transpired in the newsprints.

All I know is just what I read in the papers, and there has been a lot of Prosperity talk passed under the bridge since I last communed with you. Mr Hoover's Commission that he appointed to find out if anyone was drinking, why they first upset the Country with a kind of a temporary announcement that they would recomend that they thought a modification would be about the right thing, then the next week they come out and said No they wouldent recomend a modification, that they would recomend a continuation of present drinking. They have been almost two years sampling stuff to really find out what the people are drinking. Well the people were drinking so many different kinds of things that it took the Commission that long to get around. They are going to turn in a "Joint" report. That comes from their late association. Then each one is going to be allowed to tell his own story in his own way, that will be known as a Minority report. What they said in the main report they can deny in the single report, it's kinder like Double Entry Bookkeeping. The red ink is to deny what the black does. We have kinder forgot who was on this Committee outside of Mr Wickersham, and that's one reason for wanting to turn in seperate single reports, it will kinder get the other members before the public.[2]

Course Mr Hoover can't do only what he is sworn in to do. People look to him to settle the whole thing, why he has been sworn to obey and enforce the laws to the best of his ability and that's what he has done. I bet personally he wished that the whole mess was all so soused that he would never hear of 'em again. You know it ain't right to tangle a President up in a social fight among ourselvs. He shouldent be asked to settle Prohibition any more than he should the short dress problem. That's up to the wearers, and this other is up to the Drinkers. He has got too many important things to do to be messing his time away with that. But we will await their report, for it will be interesting to know just what people are drinking, and if Mr Wickersham settles it, he will perhaps occupy the same position in this Country that Mussolini does in Italy.

415   WHEN THEY HOLLER, GIVE
        'EM A CONFERENCE

Well all I know is just what I read in the papers. Been reading a lot about India lately on account of this Conference they have been holding in London. When India gets a little uneasy and unruly why England gives them a Conference. They invite 'em all to London and the King meets 'em, and they have a few public functions and they all wear their turbans and baggy silk pants, and all are allowed to make speeches, and the papers make over 'em, and they go home.

They come for freedom and go home with press notices. They are

1930

pretty near like American tax payers in that respect, just give 'em a little voice some time, and make 'em think they are getting some place and they go home happy. Well this last one in London was the biggest one in a long time, for the unrest was the biggest. Conferences are always in proportion to public disscord.

The King made a public speech to 'em just like he did for the nations at the Disarmament Conference last January. You know those English are smart. They know how to handle more different kinds of people than anybody. Now we can't do that, that's why we are no good as Colonizers. But Britain can go in anywhere and they got all the pomp and glory that most Natives like. Then they are smart enough to always make them think they are doing part of the management of their country themselves. When as a matter of fact they won't be doing anything, but they can be made to look like it.

Now this Indian Conference, with over 50 Indian Princes, controlling over half of India, well for them to get to London and be made over by Royalty and the British Government why that just sits them off pretty for another few years. Course they are not looking for complete Independence for India, for that would do away with their own feudal power, for each one of those Babies where he comes from is the "Borah" of his hills.[1] Bill on his native heath never had any more power than they do. Some of those birds rule over a municipality as big as one of our big States like New York. All the taxes and toll are paid to them individually, they don't have to be bothered with an election every four years to see who is the head man. He is born the head man and stays "Him" till he passes out.

Some of 'em coming to London brought their wives. They not only kept them veiled, but when they went out through the lobby of the Hotel they had attendants one each side, back and front of them with a screen affair, where they could not be seen. If they went to a Theatre they had the box screened in so they could see out but anyone else couldent look in and see them. I remember seeing one of 'em at a Polo Game where her Husband, the Marajah of some kind of "Singh," was playing and his wife was in a big Rolls Royce all boxed in like a furniture truck, and she had a peep hole she could watch the old Rajah caper around but nobody couldent look in and see her.[2] This was a game over in London, but I can imagine what London is when there is about fifty Retinues of these there at once. Each one would try and naturally outdo the other, so they all brought a band of Coolies with 'em. They can wear more gold braid than a Movie King of a mythical Kingdom. Why I'll bet their pajamas they sleep in looks like a Bull Fighter's braided rompers.

India is full of casts. They got more Castes than we have Commissions. They got one caste that is called the "Untouchables." They are not even allowed to let their shadow fall across one of the upper classes. We can't imagine it over here for we just have two or three different ones, the Republicans and the Democrats. The Democrats have always occupied our lowest position. They could let their shadow fall anywhere, but in an elected official position. They were kinder like the "Untouchables." They just had to live from pillar to post and eke out any existance they could find. But it looks like here lately the lower caste with us is coming to the front, and in London there was two Untouchables at the Conference with the others. So along about 1932 it looks like Serf days will be over and the lower classes will go to the top.

This fellow Gahndi wasent there.[3] I think they got him in jail again. When there ain't any more news from India why the English are jailing Ghandi. He is an odd kind of a duck. We havent got anyone over here to in any way compare with him. He is looked on as a kind of a Prophet. I guess Coolidge would come nearer fitting him in that respect than anyone else. Then he is a Preacher too, kinder like Bishop Cannon when he was feeling good and at himself, sorter combined Politics and preaching.[4] But Ghandi always preached "No violence." He always said agree to everything England wants, but don't do it, sort of a synthetic resistance.

In build and physique from the looks of his pictures, we havent got anybody like him unless it is Will Hays.[5] Bill is set up a good deal like Ghandi from the architectural standpoint. He has got a following a good deal like William Jennings Bryan used to have.[6] They sure believe in him. We havent got anyone that has a following comparable to him here now. If either one of our "Classes" had one like him, they would run 'em for President. Well anyhow they dident take him to the Conference, he would have stole all the thunder from the gold Turbaned Rajahs.

Now Britain ain't going to give them any more "Home rule" than we are going to give the Farmers relief. They will just have a big time and all go home, and use the old Alabi like we do with the Phillipines, "You are not ready for your Independence yet."

When we got ours, if history ain't an awful liar, we sure wasent in much shape to handle it. "You are hungry but you are not able to eat."

416 CONCERNING MUCH HOOEY

Well all I know is just what I read in the papers. Well I just picked up an old paper that had President Hoover's speech that he delivered at the opening of Congress. You know it's in the President's contract that one of his duties is to deliver a Message to the Hired hands when they meet in session. It's supposed to give them the "condition of the Country." You see Congressmen and Senators are not supposed to know anything about the "Country" and they generally don't, so the President issues his message. He starts out, "Substantial progress has been made during the year in national peace and security. Education and scientific discovery have made advances. Our Country is more alive to its problems of spiritual and moral welfare." Now there is a mighty good opening paragraph, especially when you would think it would be kinder hard to see where we had got ahead much in the last year. But he found some mighty worthy things about us. I like that line "Substantial Progress has been made."

You see it leaves a good deal to argue over as to just what constitutes "Substantial." When a fellow is going to hire you and he ain't going to give you much he always says, "I will give you a substantial stipend." It's a kind of a way of making it look like you are getting something and yet, you figure it out and you are not. But it was a mighty good word to use under the circumstances. It come in kinder like the old other White House word "Choose," there was just no telling exactly what it meant. So this "Substantial" covers up quite a good deal of ground.

He says we have made some "Substantial" progress in Peace and security. Well if you got the Peace you have naturally got the security. He means that we got more peace than we did have, we will say a year ago. We wasent fighting anybody a year ago, and we are not fighting anybody now but ourselves, we are all laying it on each other. But it's a kind of a "Substantial" blame. Of course we are nearer war than we were a year ago, for each day you live you are nearer it, for it's in the future and you draw nearer it every day.

Now that brings us to Security. Now we havent done much along the security line, outside the dissarmament Conference in London, which wasent hardly able to be called "Substatial." But Mr Hoover has done all in his power to try and further peace and at the same time leave us a Musket loaded in the corner at the same time. Well that's as it should be. It's all right to go to these Conferences. But it's always well to come home and reload your gun after each one is over.

But we must get on down the message. Here we been all this time on the first paragraph. He says that education has made some strides.

Weekly Articles

Well that's pretty hard to say. I wouldent (and neither did he) call it "Substantial" strides. It's awful hard to tell what education is. Lots of our people have learned a lot of things since last year. Now whether they was the things they ought to know will take a lifetime to find out. So I guess education has advanced. But I expect knowledge has gone back during the past year, at least we act like it.

He says that "During the last 12 months we have suffered with other Nations from economic depression." Yes and we have suffered a lot alone too. In fact I would go even further than the President and say that we had suffered "Substantially," or even "gross substantially." You see that's how a lot of people try to make us feel good is to tell us how bad somebody else is off. I don't know what kind of a streak or complex it is in anybody that gives 'em a kind of a delight to know that somebody else has lost a leg along with you, and if they happen by chance to have lost two and you only one, why then your day is just complete. I don't believe that I could get much nourishment to be starving in a room, and have the keeper come and say, "The other fellow has been starving two days longer than you have." I still believe that I would be just as hungry as I was before. But there is some people that could just get fat on just nothing but such news.

Now he kinder tries to explain the cause of World depression, that's where they all fall down. They offer every manner of different excuses. Why don't some of 'em just say, "Boys I don't know where this thing come from any more than I know where a Radio announcer springs from. If I did I would do something about it." But No they go on explaining their Theories, and by the time they get through they have forgot how to settle it.

In the first place there is no reason to know where all this come from. If a snake bites you you ain't gong to stop and study out where he come from and why he was there at that time, you want to start figuring on what to do with yourself right then. He however went on to show that we did have a lot of assets left, and was in pretty good shape.

They show that there is just as much of everything as there ever was, and all that. But they don't tell that what's the matter with us is the unequal division of it. Our rich is getting richer, and our poor is getting poorer all the time. That's the thing that these great minds ought to work on. Not be figuring out what the cause of this depression was, but let us fix our taxes, or our government work, and our whole system so we can kinder keep it split up a little better. What we got now is "Substantial" unemployment, and that's the thing that needs fixing. Never mind World Court, and Dissarmament, and all that Hooey.

417   LISTEN TO THE GRANDSON TALK!

1930

When your Grandchildren are sitting around some Penal Institution at recreation time, they will talk of the time away back when their parents and grandparents used to tell about a certain man that flourished from around 1920 to 1940 and from then on. Children will be as they are today, they will have to be taught who was President around all that era. But the same as we today remember Jessie James, and Paul Revere and a few of those without any particular aid from history, why we will remember this man. These confined Grandchildren of ours will say, "Yes we have great Coaches today, we have great Teams. But dad says every play they know was originally done away back in his childhood by Knute Rockne who founded Notre Dame.[1] This Notre Dame was just another Stubblefield College. They cut down the tall grass, dammed up the creek, and made another one of those Indiana Institutions of learning that flourished on practically every quarter section throughout the State. Well it was going along, it had a few old Uniforms, and some secondhand Footballs. But they had never played any further away from home than you could make in a day Coach. On Sunday the results of their games would be listed along with Harvard, Yale, Princeton, Penn, and Columbia, and all of that ilk. They had never made the headlines along with Alabama, Georgia, Northwestern, Army, Navy, and all the other Big-Shots. Well from what Grandad says, this Rockne blew in there, and went to school. He was a Swede, or a Norweigen, or a Dane, or some of those Ski Jumping Nations up in there. He dident know a Football from a footpad. But these Pumpkin seed Boys was kicking one around there and playing what they humorously referred to as Football. They let him play with 'em just for comedy purposes, and for a Swede, or a Norweigen, or a Dane, he turned out to be might good. Along about then they started throwing forward passes, so to have some more fun they got to throwing 'em to this Swede, or Norweigen, or Dane. Well instead of this Swede, or Norweigan or Dane dodging 'em, why he got to catching 'em, and Ski'ening over the line with 'em. Well then he graduated, for they won't let you stay in one of these Schools but four years, no matter how little you know. They got a rule they make you graduate whether you want to or not. Then when they graduated him, then come the problem, what was he going to do? He hadent finished from Harvard so he couldent sell Bonds. He was just a Swede, or Norweigan, or Dane football player and there wasent a whole lot of market for a Football Player. That was back in the days when Football was a recreation and not a Racket. So he says to himself why can't I coach? I have missed enough signals during my years on the team to entitle me to instruct others.

Weekly Articles

"So he found some boys that dident know much more about the game then he did, so he started coaching 'em, the first thing you know he was helping to coach Notre Dame. Well he dident think he was much of a Coach till he got to seeing some of the others. The head Coach got a job at what he thought was a real high Goal University, and Knute took over the team. Well from that day football left the red and started to making gains into the Credit, the black side of the Ledger. When the graduating class would receive their invocation, he would ask to say a few words to 'em, boys what is your aim through life? Why sir to make a living. No it's not, it's to send a football player to Notre Dame, that's your life work. Send me a Football Player.

"BUT when the football player got there he knew what to do with him. He told 'em that football was a game of the head, and not of the feet and hands. Well it just wasent no time till Notre Dame had got out of the weeds, and raised their Scholastic standing a half dozen touchdowns, and you started reading about it. It wasent just a Buckwheat College, it was right up in the money. It was filling more Stadiums than any of 'em. He then originated the unique idea of playing a real team every Saturday, instead of about three a season. Then come his climax, as my old Gradparents have told me. He was a great Kidder. He was to play a game on the coast against their best, and their Sporting Writers had boosted their team up till it looked like practical death for Knute to even go on the field with 'em. Well he started in before they left Chicago, saying that his team dident have a chance, that they would be beat, as they had lost their only Star. Well on the Coast they fell for it, and when he got to Tuscon, Arizona to practice, why he was supposed to have lost another Star, a Mr. Mullins.[2] The Sporting Writers come down to see who he was practicing in Mullins place and they noticed a No 31. They looked it up and it was a Mr Hanley.[3] But when the game started a gent named Occonner was the starter.[4] Nobody had ever heard of him, but nobody will ever forget him. Then the news leaked out that during this Arizona practice he had been wearing Hanley's sweater. But no sporting writer had ever thought of that. Well he kidded 'em right up to game time, and even got the odds against his team. Well Gradpap says that when they kicked off Notre Dame got ahold of the ball and never give it back to the other side all day. But the thing that Gradpap laughed about was the way this fellow Rockne just kidded the pants off the whole Pacific coast from the time he left South Bend till he got back. Barnum Gradpap says in his balmiest days never made such a Sucker out of folks with his side show as this Knute fellow did singlehanded, outside of what his team did to the others.[5] He even told 'em that next year they would beat him that bad. Well everybody was surprised to know that they would play 'em again next year. Nobody ever heard of the Kaiser wanting a return date.[6]

"But I have just heard Gradpa sit by the hour and tell some of the Komical things this Rockne did in his day. Yes sir, Gradpap says he is the one that made Notre Dame more famous than Oxford and Cambridge. This Swede, or Norweigan, or Dane, or Lithuanian, or whatever he is."

418 EUROPE TOO DEEP FOR WILL

Well all I know is just what I read in the papers. Spain blowing up the way it did broke in for a lot of news. I was over there messing around in Spain about four years ago. Had a long chat with that Primo Rivera, who was then dictating for the Country.[1]

He "Dictated" me a long special message as to what he was trying to do with the country, and I used it in the *Saturday Evening Post* just as he gave it to me. He is the fellow that while the Ambassador and I and our Commercial Attache was in his office talking to him why he reached down in his office drawer and dragged out some of the best wine that was supposed to be Oh, Lord knows how old, he said it was. It was one of the best official touches of hospitality I run onto while over there. He looked like he was doing a pretty good job with the Country. But No, they must get rid of him, and they have never looked like anything since.

Now this King I also met and he seemed mighty able, and a good fellow.[2] But Boy when they turn against you, all you have ever done don't mean a thing. You can say what you please about "dictators" but when he is a good man it's the best form of Government there is. It's just like a business that's run by one good man, the whole trouble with it is, you never know what will happen when the "Dictator" is dead or thrown out. Any one of our big men could take this country and run it fine, if he just dident have to mess with any Political machine, or a lot of red tape.

Now you take Mussolini. Lots of 'em knock him, and say that's a terrible form of Government. But you wait till he passes out and see what happens to that Country. Still he told me on that same trip that he was getting his system so well organized that it would carry on after his death. But I doubt that, for now he absolutely is doing what he thinks is best for his Country, and he has never even by his severest Critics been accused of doing anything for gain for himself. In fact he is a poor man. You know those fellows they got an awful lot

Weekly Articles

of pride, and they want to go down as a big man, and he is really a big help to that Country. Course every Country thinks they need a different kind of Government. We think we must have Democracy and we get it too, right in the neck sometimes. But as bad as we are we seem to get by better than anybody else, outside of Switzerland.

There must be a smart little Country, they fight all around 'em, and all they do is just turn their necks to see which side they are fighting on. They sell to all sides, house and feed all sides, and still wind up without getting into it.

Since I got started in on all this foreign mess, which I don't know any more about than you do, you know come to think of it nobody knows anything about any Country not even his own. The smartest Statesmen are the worst fooled when anything comes up right quick. I think a Country is harder to understand than a woman. There really ain't anywhere where you can put your hand on a Country. Its heart is not at its Capitol as some think.

It's not in its biggest Cities. It's not in the Country. All at once some little something happens, and you hear what the Country has done, and nobody knows where it was done from or really who instigated. It's a great kick to sit and hear somebody say, "Well I lived in France for years, I know what France will do. I know the heart of the real France." Well the poor fellow is not purposely lying. He really thinks he does. Or somebody will sit and tell you what the Englishman will do under certain conditions. Nobody knows what anybody will do.

Every day brings new conditions, new ideas, new alighnements. Politicians don't make up people's minds like they used to. Pretty near every old Bird you meet is thinking for himself. This Radio, and more Newspapers, and Movie Weeklies, and all that have made one fellow think he is just as smart as the other one. He don't want anybody coming along telling him what he ought to think.

Now they say France is just getting along better than anybody. Still after the war everybody that thought they knew France predicted that there was no way for them to come out of it. When we was all a-buying stock, and waiting till the next day to sell it at a Profit, not even asking what it paid if anything, why France was working. We was speculating off each other. We dident see how in the World anything could ever be lower in price than it was then. We was the smart Guys. "What a Sucker people are to work when they can get this easy dough." That was our slogan.

Now we are bundling the Gold back to France and they are where we would have been if we hadent gone "Cuckoo."

England is having their troubles for they always had a bunch

1930

that would never work, they was just bred not to work. Their Labor Government is having tough sledding, almost as bad as our efficiency Government is. It sure is a bad time for a man to get ambitious and want to get into Politics. There has never been a time when Public office was at such a low ebb, and maby not on account of the man in there as it is just general conditions. Sometimes its just a case of a good man in at a bad time. It's like sending the first string in after the game is too far gone to do any good. There is nothing you can do but just try and keep the score down, that's the way with a good man being elected to office nowadays. It's just a case of try and relieve what little misery he can.

We got to get some other kind of distribution of money. The rich never had as much, and the poor as little. But we better not do anything about it till we see how the Russians turn out. They been pretty quiet the last couple of weeks. They are studying up some devilment to pull on the World. A Russian just loves misery, and he wants to get as many in on it as he can. He wants to share it among friends as well as foes.

Well the football season is over now, so maby we can start some foolishment of some kind. Hoover and the Senate have made up, so we will just sit around and wait for some other Calamity to happen.

WEEKLY ARTICLES — 1931

419   AMERICANS GOT THEIR MODERN TASTES ON CREDIT

Well, here it is 1931, and what are we going to do about it. Don't look like we are going to be able to prevent it. That's one thing the Lord sure did regulate. He fixed so one year would just follow another one whether you had a calendar or not. He left us in doubt about everything else. We don't know when it's going to rain, snow, sunshine or anything. We don't know when we are to get sick, rich or die. We don't know who is going to follow us on when we are gone. We don't know what will happen to Prohibition, we don't know when or where the next war will break out.

We sure are dumb. But he did let us know what day followed what day, and made it so it would happen, no matter what happened. There has been 1930 of these same New Years roll around just since we been reckoning time, and I reckon a couple of million before that, kinder in porportion to whether you believe in Noah and his Ark, or the old monkey swinging by the tail theory. But never mind how we all got here. What we got to do these hard times is to worry about how we are going to stick here as long as we can without getting hungry.

We got to make some resolutions as well as interest and tax payments in this joyful season. It's the starting of a new year of trials and tribulations, and if everybody that does anything is caught it will be mostly trials. We have just about broke the record when it comes to having done devilment during this last year. There has been more people and more commandments broke in 1930 than in any year since away back when old Sodom and Gomorrah was the local New York and Chicago of its day.

We havent had such a bad year in comparison to years we used to have, but we have had a disappointing year, for it's been a bad year in comparison to the last eight or ten years. We have been just going like a house afire, and we couldent see any reason why we shouldent keep right on burning. We didnt see how we could ever run out of fuel. Our tastes were acquired on credit, and we wanted to keep on enjoying 'em on credit. But a guy knocks on the back door during the year 1930 and says, "Here, pay for the old radio or we will haul down your aerial." "Get out of that bath tub we got to take it back." "Get out of that hoot nanny, you been driving it without payments long enough."

Well, that was a sort of a jar. The man talked so nice when he sold it to us, we had no idea he would ever want it back. Why we had kinder got used to all this and took it as a matter of fact. If you never had a fifty cents cigar why a nickel one is mighty satisfying, but let you get to puffing on a real one for awhile and the old nickel one is going to be mighty nauseating.

Well everybody had just made things, and sold things, and it just looked like one of these endless chains where everybody gets a pair of $4 shoes for $1.25. They do but a fellow finally comes and gets the other $2.75. Well, that's what has happened to us this last year. It wasent what we needed then that was hurting us, it was what we was paying for that we had already used up. The country was just buying gasoline for a leaky tank. Everything was going into a gopher hole and you couldent see where you was going to get any of it back.

You see in the old days there was mighty few things bought on credit. Your taste had to be in harmony with your income, for it had never been any other way. I think buying autos on credit has driven more folks to seek the revolver as a regular means of livelyhood than any other contributing cause. All you need to make a deferred payment on anything now is an old rusty gun. I don't reckon there has ever been a time in American homes when there was as much junk in 'em as there is today. Even our own old shack has got more junk in it that has never been used, or looked at than a storage place. Most everybody has got more than they used to have, but they havent got as much as they thought they ought to have. So it's all a disappointment more than a catastrophe. If we could just call back the last two or three years and do our buying a little more carefully why we would be O.K.

But things turn pretty quick, and with the government helping out like it is finally going to, why we are liable to get out of this bog hole before we know it. And it will be a good thing for everybody in the long run. We was just getting the idea that nothing could go down in price, we thought the only way it could go was up. Just buy it and hold it a day or so that's all we thought there was to finance. Well, from now on you are going to find some mighty careful folks. A Salesman knocking on our door now with some new fangled pet knife is going to have to be mighty good to even get in the door much less make a sale. The Lord just kinder looked us over and says, "Wait, you folks going too fast, slow up and look yourself over, a year of silent meditation will do you good. Then when you start again you will know you got to get it by working and not by speculation." So the old year just gone is liable to prove in the long run a mighty beneficial year after all. It may bring us back to our senses.

420   IT HAPPENS EVERY 100 YEARS

Well all I know is just what I read in the papers. I was just reading a thing here where just exactly 100 years ago there was a long Editorial in the papers asking the people not to get panicky, that they had had a bad year, but that "Fundamentally the Country was sound," and that they looked for things to pick up, that there had been an overproduction of Overshoes, Red Underwear, knitted things about the length of a well rope, that you wrapped and rewrapped around your neck and also tied 'em over your ears.

Then there was too many lanterns on the market, for the amount of night work that was being done. There was also a glut of the Market on Mustache Cups. The men wasent buying them like the Producers had thought, they was just letting the old upper lip foliage drain right through the Coffee. It told of the evils of Mass production, that you shouldent produce faster than the buying power. If I remember I think the Republicans were in then too. And oh, yes, they was going to try and get the farmer some relief, going to give him some ammunition so he could shoot him some meat to eat. Oh yes, they was going to work on the roads, too. The President had just appointed some Commissions, one to look into and see what the Boys was drinking. Now all this was just exactly 100 years ago, so you see every 100 years we have what is humorously referred too as "Depression." It's always temporary. That it happens every 100 years proves that it will pass away. But it is funny how there is really nothing new under the sun. I sho was glad to get hold of this old article for it proves that we have had these things before and lived 'em down and we can this one. But regardless of bad times we got the Xmas holidays over in fine shape, and the New Years. Biggest excitement over the holidays was "The Young Pioneers" of New York. They put on a Burlesque of Xmas, and the birth of our Savior, and the Xmas Spirit, that must have been mighty gratifying to their Parents.

A Xmas in Russia would just suit them fine. But you just try to pay the fares of any of them and offer to send 'em, and you would

1931

have to call out the Marines. The old Communist preaches his doctrines, but he wants to do it where he is enjoying the blessings of Capitalistic surroundings. He preaches against the Pie, but he sure eats it.

Congress adjourned for only a week, so they been back at it again for about ten days. Back at what? Why back at what they was back at before. What was they back at before? I don't know but they still back at it whatever it was. Some talk of a Special Session after this one is over on March 4th. But its not what you would call by "Popular Demand."

Wickersham Committee havent turned in their report yet, so we don't know if the Country is drinking or not, or if so, what?[1] But as soon as they report why we will get that problem straightened out right away.

Mr. Hoover weathered quite a storm with his hired hands, but seemed to have come out on top and is in better shape than he has been in a good while. The boys have called him about everything they could think of, and as everybody laughed it off, why they have about decided to let him alone for a while. McKellar of Tennessee just discovered Xmas week that Hoover had been in England for some time, that's about a record for being behind times.[2]

Got a nice letter the other day from Barney Baruch.[3] I had about a year and a half ago, just before the crash, sorter half way decided to get a little dab of some kind of stock. Everybody all around me was just rolling so in profits, that it made my little joke telling stipend seem mighty little. I had never, or havent yet, got a dollar that I dident tell a joke for, either on stage or paper, so I knowing Barney mighty well, and having a mighty high regard for him personally and as being the last work in business, so in my little talk with him I asked him to invest in his own way a little dab that I thought I could spare.

Well I had to naturally tell him something of my affairs, so I told him what I owed, mostly on unimproved Real Estate. Well he liked to have thrown me out of his Wall Street Office. "You owe that much, and you want to take some of your money and buy stocks? Say you go home and pay your debts. Lord knows how long it will take you to do 'em. But pay what you can of 'em. You won't like this advice, no man does. He don't want to pay his debts as long as he thinks he can make an easy dollar in something else. I wouldent invest a dollar for you anyhow, things are too high, they don't look good. Now go start paying on your debts."

That's the nearest I ever came to owning stock. (I mean outside of a few horses, and cattle.) Less than a month from the day I was in his office the Bust come. So every few months he writes me and asks me how I am making out on the debts, and how much I got 'em whittled down.

You know he is kinder the Angel for the Democratic Party, that is if you could call anyone connected with the Democrats an Angel. And he is forever trying to pay 'em out of debt, so I am writing him and tellin him, that I am just as good a business man as he is. That he can't keep the Democrats out of debt any more than I can keep myself. So whenever you hear of the Democrats being out of debt I will be too.

421 LET'S GIVE EVERY MAN A JOB!

Well all I know is just what I read in the press. Course those five hundred that come in out of the woods down in Arkansaw and demanded food for their families, that was a real sensation.[1] It caused more than any one item that had appeared in a long time. Now those folks down there sho was hungry or they wouldent have come in and asked for food for if there ever was proud people it's them. They don't believe in accepting Charity.

Well the Government woke up and voted $15,000,000 for food right away. At first the Government said they would try and provide money to get the Farmers some seed for their next crops, but that they wouldent give them money for food as that would be too much like the "Dole," that's the thing they do in England when you can't get work they give you a certain weekly allowance, and it's called the "Dole." Course everybody over there says it hasent worked out, and that it was a mistake to start it.

But I guess the ones that have been receiving it and buying their bread, don't think that it is such a terrible blunder, so that's the way it is. It sorter depends on which side of the fence you are on.

If you live under a Government and it don't provide some means of you getting work when you really want it and will do it, why then there is something wrong. You can't just let the people starve, so if you don't give 'em work, and you don't give 'em food, or money to buy it, why what are they to do? What is the matter with our Country anyhow?

With all our brains in high positions, and all our boasted organizations, thousands of our folks are starving, or on the verge of it. Millions of bushels of wheat are in Granaries at the lowest price in twenty years. Why can't there be some means of at least giving everybody all the bread they wanted anyhow?

Here they are starving in Arkansaw and in our adjoining State of Oklahomea they are feeding their wheat to the stock to try and get rid of it.

Oil, there was never such an overproduction of oil in the World, and yet Gasoline was never much higher. But there you have a business that's in the hands of a few men, and they see that the price is kept up. It's not regulated by supply and demand it's regulated by manipulation. If the Farmer had a Rockefeller among them, you wouldent see them pulling off a hundred different ways, and no two agreeing on what to do.[2]

Now this Farm board I been reading all I can about 'em, on both sides, and Lord knows there is sure two sides. If ever a Gang of fellows that are, (we all know trying to do some good) ever kicked up a dust it's them. Now take Mr. Coolidge for instance he had always kinder kept his typewriter out of Government affairs.

He had always stuck pretty well to writing on the merits of the ten Commandments, and the Merits of "Hard work, perseverance, and taking care of your Oppurtunities."

But even he said that the Government going in and buying wheat to try and stabalize the market was bad dope. Well, that is about the first flat footed statement that he has come out on since he advised everybody to advertise. But on the other hand Mr. Hoover put some mighty fine men on that Farm Board, and it don't seem hardly that they could all be so terribly wrong. But it's like argueing the tarriff, no two can agree on just where it should start or stop.

But the main thing is we just ain't doing something right, we are on the wrong track somewhere, we shouldent be giving people money, and them not do anything for it, no matter what you had to hand out for necessities, the receiver should give some kind of work in return. Cause he has to eat just the same when he is laying off as when he is working.

So every City or every State should give work of some kind, at a liveable wage so that no one would be in actual want. Of course it would cost the taxpayers more money, but if you are making it, and all your fellow men are not why you shouldent mind paying a good slice of it for the less fortunate. Course the big man's argument, and all the heavy Taxpayers' alabi is that when you take too big a slice from a man as taxes it takes that much more out of his investments and might cut down on money being put into enterprises. But it dident work that way after the war, and during it why income taxes run as high as seventy percent on every dollar earned, and yet there was more money being made and put into things than there is now.

If your Income Taxes go to help out the less fortunate, there could be no legitimate kick against it in the world. This is becoming the richest, and the poorest Country in the world. Why? Why, on account of an unequal distribution of the money.

How can you equalize it? By putting a higher surtax on large incomes, and that money goes to provide some public work, at a livable wage. I don't mean a wage that is maintained in other lines. I mean a wage is provided for the unemployed. That is if you could in no way find a job, you could go to some State or National, or City or Country Public work, that would give you say four hours a day work, instead of the usual eight.

You wouldent be accepting Charity. But you would be doing honest work for it, until you could get employment in some line that was not public work, and at a regular wage. It wouldent cheapen labor. It would only cheapen Public works, the thing that belongs to all the people, and the thing they would like to have cheapened. But it would be an Insurance against not having anything to do.

There is nothing that makes a man feel better than to know that no matter how bad things break he has something to fall back on, that he can make a living out of. It would be a glorified Community Chest idea, only instead of it being doled out to you as Charity you would work for it. There would never be any real Unemployed. The so-called unemployed would be working for the State or Government a guaranteed number of hours each week, at a living wage.

Now that we got that settled all we have to do is get by Congress and see if the Republicans will vote a higher Income tax on the rich babies. It might not be a great plan, but it will DAM sure beat the one we got now.

422 AND SO TO BED

I used to write a good deal about what I read in the papers. But you know I been reading a lot of these other Writers of Sundays, and they write mostly about themselvs, and they seem to be doing mighty well too.

It seems that away back in Caesar's or Heflin's or somebody's early days there was some old Writer called Pepy, and all he did was just write what he did.[1] Well he dident do much, (but write) for there wasent much to do in those days. Oh yes, drink. Well he had some kind of peculiar ways of saying things and his spelling was bad, (I can't personally stand anybody with bad spelling, I am off anybody that can't spell.)

But this old fellow could make nothing sound good the way he laid it on the line. He had two expressions, and if he just hadent happened to use them, why none of our modern Writers could have copied him, for that's all they can copy him in, they just use these two lines over again and again and think they are doing a Pepys. One was "Laye late," and the other was "Woke betimes." Well I am going to do some of that "Lay lating" and "Woke betimes."

I will start on my trip east from California a couple of weeks ago. The night before I started I "Lay late." No I dident, it was two nights before I started that I lay late. The morning that I started I dident lay so late. In fact I dident lay hardly at all. I had to catch an Aeroplane that was leaving away over in Burbank, Cal. (that's not Burbank's home, it's Jim Jefferies') and I was away out at my little ranch at Santa Monica.[2] It was leaving around Five oclock and you can't do much "laying late" and make that kind of a getaway.

My Oldest Son Bill was to drive me, and that meant I had to get up just one hour earlier than usual in order to start trying to get him up. Well anyhow I "Woke betimes." I woke betimes because I had two alarm clocks set for the job, and they both went off thirty minutes early.

Well 3:30 A M is pretty tough time to start a diary. Should be working on a Dairy, and juicing a Jersey Heifer at that hour. Well it was dark, and we drove in toward Hollywood, and got pretty near through it before we saw a single car. Hollywood is so wild that there wasent even a Street lamp burning at that hour. We got to the field, bought my Ticket for Ft Worth Texas, had some Baggage Excess, (I told my wife I dident need all three of those shirts). Stood around about half asleep, and then had a cup of Coffee. I don't do much eating when I am on Plane, or getting on one. I am mighty easy to get sick. It's a big three, Wasp Motored Fokker Plane. It's still dark when I tell the Kid goodbye, and to take good care of my Ponies, and to stay off 'em, and only play his own.

Burbank and Glendale look mighty sparkling like from the early dawn, then out over Los Angeles. It's spread out, well you have to look at it by lights to see how far it is spread out. Then we hit for out over Pomona, and on over through the mountain pass at Banning and the fashionable Palm Springs. Then nothing to see till we hit Phoenix, or near Phoenix where the Irrigation lads start in. Those thousands of flat squares are beautiful from the air.

At Phoenix was met by a band of Citizens that wanted me to stay over or come back to a big affair where they were going to have 17 rail road Presidents at the Fruit Shippers Convention, and they was going to have a Golf Game, between the seventeen and seventeen Vice-Presidents were to Caddy for them. That would be nothing new, they have been carrying the Bag for 'em all the time. But it give Vice-Presidents a chance to do something. Then the rest of the Audience was composed of other Vice-Presidents. But they did plan on having a great time and I hear they had it. They give me a big box of the finest dates I ever ate. (Smuggled over from California I bet.) Then on down over Tombstone, Arizona, and the next gas stop was Tuscon. Another Deligation had some kind of a "Racket" they wanted me to stop over and enter into. No it was Douglas where this bunch was. It was on the Mexican line. I wouldent have minded stopping there. Then on the El Paso, had Lunch, changed Pilots, got there about 1:30 P M about three days ride on the train, then started across Texas.

Now you have started something. Oh Yes I am leaving out some of these "Woke Betimes." At each stop I "Woke Betimes" for I slept all the rest of the way. Well I "Lay late" at Big Springs and like to not "Woke Betimes" to see another Deligation, that wanted to draw my attention to a 15 story brick hotel that I would pass over as we passed over the town on leaving. Associated Press man there, and he got everything wrong but the name of the Town and misspelled it.

Then to Abiline, (Sweet Abiline, My Abiline, in all my dreams). I havent sung that old song since 1920. There I woke betimes and Amon G. Carter had a special Plane to meet me to take me to Ft Worth.[3] For he dident want me to have to see Dallas. Had a nice night there, woke betimes, met a lot of nice folks that was going to handle my little Charity tour through the State, then flew up to Tulsa, where met equally as nice bunch for Okla. Then drove my Auto 45 miles to Chelsea, and spent the night at my only Sister's home, saw a new Niece baby, nice Baby to, had fine visit, lots of my family.[4]

Will Rogers and Amon G. Carter, publisher of the Fort Worth *(Texas)* Star-Telegram.

Weekly Articles

Lay late. No not there, awoke betimes, then caught the plane for St Louis, was going to Chicago, but just as both planes was pulling out grabbed the one for Columbus, Ohio, and New York. Comedians never know what they are doing. Wouldent take the money for my fare on the plane so everybody had to wait till they went and got the ticket fixed up. They will trust the Pilots with your life but not with $19 which was the fare to Columbus. Got to Indianapolis, was met by some Newspaper friends and Co-workers of the Indianapolis News. Talked about Kin Hubbard, the late Humorist, "Abe Martin."[5] They told me my junk had took his old place on the back page, (which it had occupied for 25 years). Imagine me trying to replace him. That would be like Clara Bow replacing Mrs Chapman Catt.[6] So long, I am going to Lay late.

423   SOME POLITICAL CRADLES HAVE SHOATS IN THEM

Well all I know is just what I read in the papers, and what I see. Well here the last few weeks I have seen more than I have read. They say that travel is an education to you. Yes and it's a bother too. But I must go back a couple of weeks in order to get at some of the old stuff I saw.

First place I saw some mighty poor farms flying over Missouri, eastern Oklahoma, and Indiana, on my way to Washington. Just little renter shacks, and it was snowing and lots of 'em dident look like they had any wood, much less food. You see it's the country folks that are suffering more than the city ones, in this hard year.

Well I got into Washington and went of course immediately up to "Opera Comique" both ends of it, the Senate and the House. First in to see Nick Longworth in the Speaker's office.[1] That's my official headquarters while at the Capitol building. I leave my overcoat there, (that's trusting) and I work out of there. Phoned Jack Garner, the Democratic Leader, and told him the Democratic Party were ready to caucus, and he come right over.[2] He told me the next time I come that I could still use that same office, and phone out to Nick to come over and see me there. It's going to be mighty close as to who will be Speaker of the next house.

Next over to see Tilson Republican Leader but a nice fellow in spite.[3] Then I hiked for the Senate for there is where the fireworks were operating, as they was argueing over whether the Government was to feed its folks or its folks were to feed its folks. Joe Robinson of

1931

Arkansaw was fighting for his Amendment to provide 25 million for food, and he was backed by all the Democrats, and all the "Wild jackasses."⁴ That's what Mr. Moses called the Insurgent Republicans one time just before election last year.⁵ It got a laugh and cost his side two million votes, so that really could be called the two million dollar laugh.

Gillette of Mass. was talking against the Government going into the food business just for our own home talent, he thought we should send something out to the other Countries, but that we could find some way of tiding our personal hunger over till something turned up, or the Market picked up, or something.⁶ Right in the middle of his "America second," why Senator Caraway, who really reminds one of Felix the Cat, in the Movies, who you know is so wise and walks around with his hands behind him studying.⁷

Well Caraway, was prowling up and down, and one of the Boys in the Press stand says, "Caraway is thinking up one now to hit him with," and sure enough he kept sidling over toward the Republican side. You know they have a line drawn there so you can tell the Republicans from the Democrats. They have to have nowadays; there is no other way telling. Well Caraway said, (You know this Caraway is a smart one, and very sarcastic, he bowls 'em over with a well-placed Bon Mot, and it not only floors 'em but the hurt remains), well he said, to Gillette who is from Mass.,

"What about that time when Salem Mass. was destroyed by flames, or was it Witches, and the Government appropriated money to help the distressed, you Senator Gillette was in the House of Representatives, did you say then that it was a Dole, did you say it was 'bad Precedent' to set, answer me?"

Well, poor Gillette was in the hole, that gag about the Witches of Salem had got him groggy, and he was sorry that Salem had ever had a fire. Well he said that he dident vote for the relief, or against it either, he just answered "Present," then Felix pounced on him again, (he was just playing with him from paw to paw,) "You just voted Present did you, well that's courageous Statesmanship. Your State was stricken, they needed help, but their Congressman voted neither to help, or not to help, he just announced that he was there."

Tom Heflin in the last days of his stay in there made one of his while I was in the gallery.⁸ They were going to go down to Alabama and investigate Tom's election as he says there was frauds in the counting of the votes, he feels that he was elected but counted out. They can do that. Well his opponent had sent word that he welcomed the investigation. But Tom said that was just a gallant gesture, that he dident welcome the investigation and he told this story to illustrate it.

"Down in my old fine State of Alabama at Hot Springs was Rastus Lincoln, a Nigger. His white Neighbor had lost a Shote, little spotted one weighing about ninty pounds. Well the Neighbor got the Sheriff and went looking for the hog, and they went to Rastus house. He was sitting on front of the fire place rocking a cradle and singing a baby song, with the covers in the cradle all tucked in both head and foot till you couldent see a thing of the Baby. 'Rastus you seen Jones hot?' 'Oh no sir I ain't seen him, you can serch the place, I ain't see the Shote tall.'

"They searched, but found nothing, then they asked, 'What's in the cradle?' 'Thats my baby Gentlemens, that's my little baby.' 'Let us see the Baby?' 'Oh no, the Baby is sick and the Doctor said if I raised the kivvers on the Baby and the air hit him he would die. You can't see the Baby.' But they went toward the cradle and started to lift the quilt, and Rastus said, as he moved toward the door, 'I can't stand and see him die, I just got to go.' And he did right out the door and across the cotton patch.

"They lifted the Kivvers and there lay the 90 pound hog, and that's what will happen when you Investigating Commite get to my old State of Alabama. You won't find my people are crooked. My people in Alabama are the finest people God ever let live. I love my People in Alabama. I am not saying a word against the great folks of Alabama. I dont want any blot to be on them. It's the crooked Politicians that done it. It's not the fine people of Alabama. They are the finest folks on this green earth. They elected me. They done it fairly. But the crooks counted me out, and that's why I want this election investigated. You come to Alabama and lift the Kivvers and you will find the Hog."

424 WILL AND AL TALK THINGS OVER

Well all I know is just what I read in the papers, and what I happen to see prowling hither and thither. I was in New York a couple of weeks ago and I decided that before I left there I would like to see Al Smith. I hadent seen him in a long time and had always been an admirer of him. I just wanted to see him and see how he was, and how he was feeling. So I phoned him, and he said "Come right on down." He is right across the street from that wonderful Empire Building, in a corner suit overlooking it.[1]

This building belongs to Jesse Jones a mighty well known Democrat. He is the fellow that bought the Democratic Convention for

Houston, Tex.[2] He owns these buildings all over the Country and rents 'em mostly to Republicans.

Well Al never looked better in his life, and I have known and been seeing him around New York for many years. He started in of course by showing me the 90 story building, out of the window that gave us the best view of it. It did look wonderful. It's got some sort of outside structual steel work that looks like Illinum, and in the sun it just glistens. Then he started in showing me old pictures on the wall of his office that showed early scenes in New York. He showed some of the old houses on the lower east side where he lived, one under the very shade of Brooklyn Bridge. Then the old home on Oliver Street. He is without a doubt the most sentimental prominent man I ever met. He glories in the past. He had one that showed the old Theatrical team of Harrigan and Hart, who made their great fame in the "Mulligan Guards."[3] It was in a large frame with dozens of the old time favorites, including the old Theatres that they played in. He would hum to you the tunes of those old favorites.

It was hard to tell which he looked on with more pride, the highest building in the World that he was actually in charge of its construction, or his harking back to the days when he was the principal performer in all Amateur Theatricals, and they do say he himself was a splendid actor. He could have done anything that fellow. He sure beams personality. He is human if there ever was one.

I don't care whether you agree with him politically or not, the person don't live that could meet him and be with him awhile that wouldent go away not liking him. He does a hundred little things and mannerisms that make you feel that he is one of you. There is no put on, or front with Al, he is just Al, unlike anybody else in the World.

I had just come from the White House a day or so before and was telling him about how Mr Hoover was worked up over this relief business. Well Sir I bet Mr Hoover has not even among his own party a single man that has a much sympathy and good feeling for him than Al Smith. There was no put on about it, he really meant it when he would talk of the many things that had seemed to go wrong through no fault of the President's, yet he had to bear the brunt of them.

Here was a man that had been in office long enough to know what you can be blamed for. No Sir Hoover's best booster is Al Smith, and he had just been working with Ex President Coolidge on a Committe to give away an Estate that had been left to Charity, and he had the highest praise for Coolidge too, and he says, as I have always maintained, that Mr Coolidge has a great sense of humor, and he would tell some of it that happened during their deliberations.

We went over to the Democratic Club for lunch, and he got to

Weekly Articles

telling about the animal pets that the children had at the mansion in Albany. He built almost a Zoo there to house them. How a big pet Bear that they had raised from a cub, had got loose and got over into a girls' Orphanage, and they was all scared to death for fear he would hurt somebody and instead these Kids has him pulling and wooling him around and they couldent hardly get him away from them. They was feeding him bread and jam. He would tell of his dogs his Kids had. One a great Newfoundland, that in the summer when it was so hot they would fix him in the basement, and then out and keep the hose on him. He could tell you every characteristic of every dog, the more trivial a subject the more interesting he could make it. No hard feeling, no rancor toward anybody. An Unique man, with a unique record, polled more votes than all the other Presidents that were elected, with the exception of Mr Hoover. I doubt if he wants to run again.

Even if he don't he will retire into private life one of the most, yes the MOST, popular men of our time. He is the most human of our present day figures. He is not from the soil, but from the cobblestones, and he knows after all they all are human and just alike.

425 ON THE WING FOR CHARITY

Well all I know is what I read in the papers, and Brother listen I havent read a paper in two weeks. We been going too fast to read. Talk about an aerial circus, a One Night Stand troop, a Karnival! But we are a combination of all these and then some more.

I started my little tour to raise some extra money for the needy and unemployed in Texas. Started in Austin the Capitol. I had been in the Movies for a couple of years, and all the jokes I knew I had used 'em in my pictures. So when I started out on this I was mighty short handed on laughs. My Wife said to me, "You can't go out and do an evening's show. You havent any material."

I told her well Honey, it's for Charity and maby I can get by. She said, "It's a good thing it is for Charity, or you would be in danger of your life."

Then I got to thinking that I dident have much material, so I decided as I was starting in Texas that I better drop by Austin where the State Legislature was in session and get some material. Well that's why I chose it, and it was a God send to me. It turned out great, not that the Texas Legislature is especially humorous. It's not, it's just the average, in fact I think they got a pretty good body there, as Legislatures go. They just hadent done anything, which made them on a par with all others.

They also had a new Govenor who looks like he is starting out on a good administration.[1] He is a very wealthy man, and knows enough Politics not to think he can put in a lot of reform measures. He knows you can't do that. There is where Mr Hoover fell down. He thought all you had to do if you was the Head man was to suggest something and it would be done. Well those Boys don't work that way. They are as jealous of their position as a Governor or a President so they want to be conferred with on anything, so if you start rushing anything by them they just chop your head off.

But this Govenor knows that, and he will do a little trading with 'em. That was Coolidge's long suit. He had that New England swap idea. Course then another thing Congress could never dissagree with Coolidge purposely for they never knew what he wanted. So in that way he got 'em with him accidentally part of the time. But we had a mighty pleasant visit at Austin.

Met all the Ex Governors. Dan Moody who had just gone out.[2] Always liked Dan. He is a fine young fellow. Then in come my old Friend Jim Furgeson.[3] Him and Ma come pretty near getting in again last time. Their slogan was "Two Govenors for the price of one."

Out of there after the Matinee and down to the old historic San Antonio, where we sure had a fine great big House, some nine thousand dollars. The old Cattlemen's organization gave me a reception before our show, and that really kinder got me, for there is one class of men that won't be replaced. Every other line of business is being carried on from Father to Son, and on by newcomers in the same business, but the Old Trail Drivers, and the old time Cattlemen, there can never be any to take on their work. They are the last of one of America's most unique and extraordinary men. Some of the greatest Characters in our whole history were old Cattlemen. Humor they were chucked full of it, and San Antonio is one of their last stands.

Several old time Texas Rangers were there. There is a bunch that have made history. The old Trail Drivers are trying to get enough money to build a monument to the old time Trail driver, and from its model it's very beautiful and I hope the State gives them part of the money to do it, for the Cowman certainly made that State.

That town is a great Aviation center, the Army has two or three of their greatest training places there.

Next morning out of there we had a show scheduled over 250 miles from there, and the fog and rain hit us. Had to drive it. Not So Hot.

Angelo, another real old Cowtown that night, and a big packed house. The next morning still cloudy and rainy. Bobby Cantwell, Oklahoma's crack Pilot still marooned in San Antonio, and Frank Hawkes on his way back from New York (where he had to go but was to return that day).[4] We got out at seven A M, drove 110 miles, put on a milkman's matinee at Ten at Abiline, in Simmons University Auditorium, played to over five thousand dollars.

Then another 110 mile jump, (these are by Auto, no Plane, it's still cloudy and raining) to Breckinridge, Texas. Great Gang again, and Frank Hawkes had jumped on back from New York and there we started in on what was to be the most towns anybody outside of an ambitious Congressman ever made on one trip. We started in on our first jump out of there not so forty, we got stuck in the mud on the take off, and it took half of the Breckinridge till pretty near dark to get us out.

We are in Dave Ingalls' plane, Assistant Secretary of the Navy in charge of Aviations plane.[5] Its had those "Spats" over the wheels to help cut down the wind resistance. Well they are great till they get full of mud. If I had had a can opener I would have sent Dave a present. We made Dallas in the dark, then up early the next morning and flew to Port Arthur, where we showed at twelve, then over to Beaumont for the afternoon, and how those two towns did support the cause! They know all over that country what the need is. You see they take half the money raised for the town and half goes to the Country, and every cent of it is theirs, and I wouldent allow a thing to be charged to the receipts. The town had to give the hall, the Papers the Adds, and everything that come in was theirs.

By this time Frank Hawkes was developing into a fine Monologist, Jimmy Rodgers the Yodler was singing for us and Chester Byers the Champion Roper was roping, and then in Dallas was joined by the Famous Revellers Quartette, who General Motors, and Palmolive loaned me, and the Tenor was released for the trip by Salada Tea people.[6] That all was mighty fine of these big firms for they had to engage someone else, and they allowed these boys' salaries to go on so I was able to get this wonderful aggregation simply for their expenses. Of course these could not be asked to get up in the dead of night and fly to a town like I was to give a show, but they made all the night shows. Two of them dident fly. Both Tenors, so they couldent have made these jumps for the day shows.

It was nice of the National Broadcasting Co to arrange this, for it was an awful jolt to lose these boys from their programmes, but what a hit they were, and what a fine bunch of Boys!

The Texas Co had loaned me Frank Hawkes, and I couldent

1931

even pay for the gas the ship used even if we made a forced landing, there would be one of their wagons with gas waiting for us. No wonder that Hawkes can fly. He has been in every field in every town all over this Country.

I am going to keep this trip up till I find a field that he is not familiar with. It may take a year. He is a great little fellow. I always thought he was a big man, but he is little. Oh I can't get started to tell all this in this time. I got to write you next week about the old Home State of Oklahoma, and then the wife's state of Arkansaw. I am writing this in the Navy "Hell Diver" at five thousand feet, and just landing at Stillwater, Okla. for a ten o'clock morning show. The best A and M College in America. Oh boy he is banking, and diving for the crowd! Good bye!

426   NOTES AND COMMENT
            AT 160 MILES AN HOUR

All I know is just what I see from the air with this Captain Hawkes going 160 miles an hour.[1] I am dinging on this little Corona away up in the air. We are in a Navy Curtis "Hell Diver" plane loaned to us by the Assistant Secretary of the Navy in charge of air.[2] We thought we did some shows in Texas, But Boy when we got into the old home State of Oklahoma, then they showed us how to lay out some shows. I am trying to keep this little diary. You just about have time to write a few words in here and then we have to land and do a show.

This Monday, we are coming into Oklahoma from Texas. It's the only day we havent got a bunch of day shows; we only have the opening show at Oklahoma City tonight. We land about ten o'clock, Captain Hawkes goes to the Hotel, and I get the man to drive me by the Capitol building. You see I wanted to see the other Oklahoma show, the Legislature. I don't constitute Oklahoma's sole Comedy element. Then too I had never met our new Governor, "Alfalfa" Bill Murray.[3] My Dad had known him.[4] They had served on the Constitutional Convention of Oklahoma about 1906.

Papa always said the crowning achievement of that Convention was that they made Hotel Bed Sheets 9 feet long. He used to often say that he dident know why they did it, "as so few of the Deligates had ever had much contact with sheets." Well he is quite a fellow this Murray. He might be called a little Radical by some. But I think he has got some mighty good ideas. That's why I doubt if any of them

Weekly Articles

will pass. You got to get something pretty "Nutty" to get by nowadays. We had a good visit. I had lunch with him in his office. He is supposed to bring his lunch in a paper bag. So I dident take him up at once as I never saw the paper bag that could hold all I could eat. But he said he would sent out, and he did. He don't eat much besides Onions. Well I love onions, but I like meat too. In fact I believe I like meat better than Onions, so he sent out and got me something to eat. Then they made me go and talk to a joint session of the Legislature. I will have to tell you about that some time. Big House in Oklahoma City that night, got over ten thousand dollars.

Tuesday morning. Here we are in the air again, and early, as we have to be at Norman, Oklahoma, the Home of Oklahoma's crack University. It's just a little ways from Oklahoma City. They got a pretty good flying field there. Got a lot of laughs out of the Students and Teachers, for the Govenor was just trying to put through a Bill to tax Teachers salaries, and I claimed I was there lobbying for it. Murray also has it in for the amount of traveling expenses spent by College Athletes. He is trying to put through a Bill to compel every team to play all its games at home. It's kinder hazy in my mind yet. But I think he is going to do it just like chess, over the phone. One team grabs the ball and phones when they kicked off and the other phones back where they caught it and how many yards they made on that play.

This show was at ten oclock in the morning. Captain Hawkes would do an act too, and the "Revellers" Quartette who only did the night shows they come down there that morning and sang for the University.[5]

Then to Chickasha, Okla. There an old Boy runs the biggest Bank that used to go to school with me in Kemper Military Academy about '98. There is a Girls' School there, and we were in their Auditorium. Those Girls sho would giggle when anything did strike 'em funny. They are a great audience. We flew out of there for Ardmore for our night show. Went out to a mighty fine barbecue at Ben Johnston's house, where we joined all the rest of our troop, The Revellers, and Jimmy Rodgers who was with us then, (the Yodler De Lux) and Chester Byers, the Roper.[6]

Up early this morning and we are flying to Duncan. Oh Boy we are met here by a band of Cowboys mounted, and we get on horses. Hawkes is on one, he is the only riding Aviator. Wow what a street full of people. All these places the Theatres are full. Here we are back to the field and off for Lawton, that's right by Ft. Sill, the old Military Fort, and quite a historic old place. After the show there today we went out to the Fort and visited the place where they had

1931

old Geronimo, the Apache Chief incarcerated.[7] We saw the cell, I afterwards knew him at the World Fair in St Louis. As old as he was he used to go out with us at the Wild West Show and Roping Contest on Sundays and rope a steer. I guess he was about the best old Fighter that ever roamed that southern Country. It's a pretty place, Ft. Sill is, and so is Lawton.

Now we are off and flying again over the old Ft. and off for Durant for the night. It's a great life this. Talk about playing one night stands. Some days we play a half dozen. This Hawkes is a sweet flyer, and this Plane is a darb. We knock off 150 miles an hour right along. This is Thursday morning and we are to be at the Oklahoma A. and M. at Stillwater at ten A.M. I had never been there and always wanted to go, as I had a Nephew graduate from there and he has turned out mighty good, and it's a great school.[8] They win more prizes for fat Cattle than any other Agricultural School in the U.S. There is an animal Man there named Blizzard, and he is a Bear.[9] He showed us all their fine cattle.

Enid. Here she is for the afternoon show. Frank is bringing her in, he is high and dropping and side slipping her in fast. You can't write when this thing is doing this. Big hall and a big house full. Now we are off for Ponca City, that's a great little City. That's the place they have a Statue of the "Pioneer Woman." I was there and made a speech at the unveiling of it. That fellow Marlin has done a lot for that town.[10]

Off again this morning early for Shawnee. Big crowd at the field. Here is a niece here to meet me.[11] I drive with her and her husband and Boy to the Theatre.

Ada next. Sounds like a Girl. But it's a town, and a nice one. Now we are off for McAlister. That's the town where I took my Masonic 33 degrees 22 years ago and havent been there since. Gee they got a great Masonic Temple there. I played in the big auditorium, and it's one of the most beautiful places you ever saw.

Now we are off for Muscogee, four shows today. Getting back in my own old Territory now where I know a lot of folks. I used to go to school here at a Girls' school. Thats a fact. Myself and the President's son were the only Boys there. We even roomed in a great big dormitory room with Girls. We were ten years old. I better quit before I get too far into this.

427 WE CAN MAKE SPEECHES IN OUR SLEEP

Well all I know is just what I read in the papers, and all the reading I been able to do is in the air, "lepping" from town to town. But we finally got back home to California. We sure run into some tough weather on the way out. This Hawkes sure did defy the elements.[1] We was a flying through the fog and rain coming from our last stand at Texarkana, Tex. all one morning. We finally worked our way out to the edge of New Mexico and then we got out of the rain and hit a real blizzard, a snow storm. Well sir that Bird started circling and messing around in the air and I had no idea what he was doing, or trying to do. I thought he is only trying to find the ground. But do you know he came down, and made a quick side slip landing. I just thought it was a forced landing on the Prairie, but then I saw it was a little marked off emergency field, he had found it by instruments, not by sight. It was the last one on the way across the mountains till we reached Albequraue, over a hundred miles away.

Now get this. Here was an emergency landing in a storm where you couldent see ten yards, and we hadent got out of the Plane and quit stamping around trying to keep warm, till a Committee of the town was there to ask us to come that night to a Banquet. We had had three solid weeks of Committees, and was flying away to escape 'em, and here was one away out on the Prairies in a snow storm. That's working pretty fast. I want to see some Chamber of Commerce beat that. The School Teachers of Guadaloupe County were having a Banquet over at the Harvey House that night, so Frank Hawkes and I went over and did our usual little act.

We had got so by this time we could do it in our sleep. You could wake either of us up at any hour of the night and we would raise up, Frank would say, "I have been called a Speed Demon, I am not a Speed Demon, I think that Aviation has something to sell that no other line of transportation has, and that is speed. I mean speed within the confines of safety, the whole heavens above is open, and all we have to do is to use it. You can't get any worse hurt flying at two or three hundred miles an hour than you can flying at ninety, so what we have to do is develop planes that will fly at what we now call a tremendous rate of speed. I see the day coming in the not far distant when you will leave New York at noon, fly across the country at the rate of a thousand miles an hour, and reach Los Angeles, at NOON. That sounds crazy but it's not. The sun travels at the rate of one thousand miles an hour. Well if the Plane travels that fast you are keeping up with the sun, so you leave at noon, and as there is three

1931

hours difference in time, it takes you three hours to make it, so you can get there when the sun does, so you leave at noon and arrive at noon. Of course when we fly two thousand miles an hour, you will leave New York at noon, and will fly out and arrive back at noon, in other words you havent been gone at all, and that reminds me of the time I took up a Negro Boy. Will always wants me to tell some jokes too, he has advised me not to get too technical. So I will tell you about the Negro Boy."

So we had this stuff down so pat that we could do it anywhere, or anytime. Frank has a Dandy appearance on the stage, and they like to hear him tell of his trips. Well in case I am called at any hour of the night, I simply roll over on my pillow and start in as follows, "Well folks sure glad to be here with you, glad you are starving, otherwise I would never have met you. You have got nothing on the rest of the Country. We are all starving. We havent had a regular meal since the Democrats were in, and if we wait for 'em to get in again we may never get another one. The Republicans promised us prosperity and we like a half wit believed 'em. But the joke is on them. They ain't eating so regular themselves. Starving ain't so bad, it's getting used to it that is tough. The first three years of a Republican Administration is the hardest. By the end of that time you are used to living on predictions. It seems good to get back in the Old South again, for this is about the only old South we got. Prohibition split us in two politically, and the drouth cut the two halves up into quarters, and the quarters are divided over the tarriff, so that only leaves one eighth of the Party intact, and the Wickersham Report killed off those that could read, and the Hoover Democrats have committed suicide.[2] So the o. d. South is solid in favor of anything that ain't in effect now. This hunger is not local, it's universal.

"Senators are drinking corn when two years ago they would have turned up their nose at less than Bourbon. Lobbyists are working on Commission and starving to death. Wall Street brokers have let the night chouffers go, Rockefeller Sr. is only playing seven holes.[3] The Rapidan dryed up, and the President is using the seine in the potomac. Coolidge hasent had a new ribbon on his typewriter since Northampton raised its tax rate. Borah hasent issued an ultimatum since Idaho silver mines closed for lack of Gold.[4] I am telling you times are tough. When Charley Schwab can't think of an Alabi it's H---."[5]

NOTES

325 Original Manuscript (OM); published: *Tulsa Daily World (TDW)*, March 17, 1929. The texts of the Weekly Articles (WA) published herein come from Rogers' original manuscripts when such documents are available. In all other cases, the texts of the articles are taken from the *Tulsa Daily World*, from some other reliable newspaper, or from the copy issued by the McNaught Syndicate (McN). The dates given indicate earliest publication. The headings accompanying each article are from the original manuscript or from the newspaper cited.

[1]Herbert Clark Hoover, Republican president of the United States from 1929 to 1933.

[2]John Calvin Coolidge, Republican president of the United States from 1923 to 1929. At the end of his term, Coolidge returned to his adopted hometown of Northampton, Massachusetts, where he lived in retirement until his death in 1933.

[3]José Gonzalo Escobar, former general in the Mexican army and commander-in-chief of rebel forces in Mexico from 1928 to 1929.

[4]Plutarco Elías Calles, Mexican military and political leader; president of Mexico from 1924 to 1928. Several Mexican military officers, unhappy with the imposition of the official presidential candidate, rebelled in early 1929 against the government and the strongarm rule of Calles. Calles took charge of federal military operations and by mid-April had quelled most revolutionary activity.

[5]Francisco R. Serrano, Mexican military leader and politician. An instigator of a short-lived rebellion in 1927, Serrano was captured and executed on October 3, 1927.

Arnulfo R. Gomez, Mexican general and leader of the 1927 rebellion.

[6]Juan Andreu Almazán, Mexican medical student who abandoned his studies in 1910 to join the Revolution; federal general who opposed the Escobar rebellion; unsuccessful presidential candidate in 1940.

[7]Gilberto R. Limón, Mexican revolutionist who led a brief, ill-fated rebellion against the government in 1929.

[8]Dwight Whitney Morrow, United States ambassador to Mexico from 1927 to 1930; lawyer, banker, and Republican politician.

326 OM; published: *TDW*, March 24, 1929

[1]For this and all further references to Herbert Hoover see Weekly Article (WA) 325:Note (N) 1.

[2]Theodore Roosevelt, Republican president of the United States from 1901 to 1909; Spanish-American War hero, Progressive party candidate for president in 1912, and world renowned sportsman.

[3]For this and all further references to Calvin Coolidge see WA 325:N 2.

[4]Porfirio Díaz, Mexican military leader, politician, and dictator; president of Mexico from 1876 to 1880 and 1884 until his ouster in 1911.

[5]Francisco Indalecio Madero, Mexican revolutionary and politician; forced Díaz's resignation in 1911 and served as president of Mexico until his ouster in 1913.

[6]Victoriano Huerta, Mexican general and politician. Huerta supported the Madero revolution in 1911 but then deposed Madero and had him killed. Huerta served as provisional president from 1913 until his removal from office by force in 1914.

Francisco "Pancho" Villa, Mexican bandit and revolutionary leader; opponent of the government after Madero's death. In 1916, hoping to draw the United States into war against Mexico, he raided Columbus, New Mexico, killing sixteen persons and burning much of the town. He was assassinated in 1923.

Holbrook Blinn, noted American dramatic actor and theatrical director. Blinn, who made his stage debut in 1878 at the age of six, achieved personal success as a loosely-disguised Pancho Villa in *The Bad Man*. He died in June of 1928.

[7]José María Pino Suárez, Mexican lawyer, poet, and revolutionary; vice president during Madero's ill-fated administration.

[8]Venustiano Carranza, Mexican revolutionary and liberal political leader; president and virtual dictator from 1917 until his assassination in 1920.

[9]Alvaro Obregón, Mexican military officer, revolutionary, and politician; president of Mexico from 1920 to 1924. Obregón was elected again to the presidency in 1928 but was assassinated before taking office.

¹⁰Emiliano Zapata, Mexican revolutionist and champion of agrarianism. Active from 1911 to 1916, Zapata was independent of all other rebellion movements; he ultimately was defeated by Obregón.
¹¹Adolfo de la Huerta, provisional president of Mexico from May to November of 1920; minister of finance from 1921 to 1923.
¹²For Plutarco E. Calles see WA 325:N 4.
¹³Emilio Portes Gil, provisional president of Mexico from 1928 to 1929.
¹⁴For José G. Escobar see WA 325:N 3.

327   OM; published: *TDW*, March 31, 1929

¹Albert Einstein, noted German physicist who received a Nobel prize in 1921 for his work in theoretical physics, notably on the photoelectric effect.
²Mabel Walker Willebrandt, assistant attorney general of the United States from 1921 to 1929, in charge of cases arising from federal taxes and prohibition; played a prominent role in the enforcement of federal prohibition laws during the 1920s.

328   McN; published: *TDW*, April 7, 1929

¹Cornelius "Neil" Vanderbilt IV, American journalist, author, lecturer, cinematographer; member of one of America's wealthiest families. Vanderbilt embarrassed his family with the publication in 1929 of *Reno*, a sensational novel about the Nevada divorce capital.
²A Canadian-registered vessel, *I'm Alone*, was sunk in the Gulf of Mexico by a United States Coast Guard patrol vessel on March 22. The "rumrunner" carried a cargo of more than 2,400 cases of liquor.
³Fiorello Henry La Guardia, Republican United States representative from New York from 1917 to 1919 and 1923 to 1933; mayor of New York City from 1934 to 1945.
⁴Wesley Livsey Jones, Republican United States senator from Washington from 1909 until his death in 1932. The Jones "Five and Ten" Act of 1929 raised the maximum federal penalties for liquor offenses to five years imprisonment and a $10,000 fine.
⁵Newton Booth Tarkington, Pulitzer prizewinning American novelist who wrote such well-known works as *Penrod*, *The Magnificent Ambersons*, and *Alice Adams*.

329   *Los Angeles Examiner (LAE)*, April 14, 1929

¹George Palmer Putnam, American publisher, editor, author, motion picture executive, and explorer; treasurer of the publishing firm of G. P. Putnam's Sons from 1919 to 1930.
²George Hubert Wilkins, Australian aviator and polar explorer who directed several Arctic and Antarctic expeditions and who authored numerous books about his exploits.
³Frank Waterman Stearns, wealthy Boston merchant and ardent supporter of Calvin Coolidge. After he became president, Coolidge provided a permanent suite in the White House for Stearns and his wife.
⁴Vilhjalmur Stefansson, Canadian-born explorer, ethnologist, and author.
⁵Martin Elmer Johnson, American photographer, explorer, and naturalist. With his wife, the former Osa Helen Leighty, Johnson made an extensive expedition to Africa in 1923-1927, returning to the United States with an invaluable photographic record of the then largely unknown continent.
⁶Amelia Mary Earhart, American flier who in 1928 became the first woman to cross the Atlantic in an airplane. She married George Palmer Putnam in 1931.
⁷Belle Wright Willard Roosevelt, wife of Kermit Roosevelt.
⁸Kermit Roosevelt, American soldier, businessman, explorer, writer, and hunter; son of President Theodore Roosevelt (see WA 326:N 2).
   Theodore Roosevelt, Jr., American soldier, writer, politician, and explorer; eldest son and namesake of the twenty-sixth president.
⁹Betty Blake Rogers, wife of Will Rogers. The couple was married at the Blake family home in Rogers, Arkansas, on November 25, 1908.
¹⁰Jesse L. Lasky, Sr., American motion picture producer; co-founder of Famous Players-Lasky Corporation and executive of Paramount Pictures Corporation from 1916 until the depression of the 1930s.

¹¹Robert Edwin Peary, American arctic explorer and naval officer who led the first successful expedition to the North Pole in 1909.

Frederick Albert Cook, American physician and arctic explorer. On his return from an arctic expedition in 1909, Cook claimed that he had reached the North Pole in April of 1908. The claim was denounced and rejected by scientists.

330   OM; published: *TDW*, April 21, 1929

¹Mary Louise Cecilia "Texas" Guinan, Texas-born stage and night club entertainer renowned for her conflicts with prohibition agents and her brash greeting to each customer: "Hello, sucker!"

²Myron Timothy Herrick, United States ambassador to France from 1912 to 1914 and 1921 to 1929; Republican politician from Ohio.

³James Thomas "Tom" Heflin, Democratic United States senator from Alabama from 1920 to 1931. Virulently anti-papist and anti-liquor, Heflin blamed Catholics for his son's highly-publicized bout with alcohol.

⁴Charles Curtis, Republican vice president of the United States from 1929 to 1933. Curtis was the central figure in a social precedence controversy involving his half-sister and official hostess, Dolly Curtis Gann, and the matrons of Washington society.

⁵Emily Price Post, American writer and columnist, famous for her advice on manners and social etiquette; author of the bestseller *Etiquette* (1922).

⁶Henry Lewis Stimson, United States secretary of state from 1929 to 1933. Stimson earlier had served as secretary of war in the cabinet of William Howard Taft, as special presidential representative to Nicaragua, and as governor general of the Philippine Islands.

⁷William Howard Taft, Republican president of the United States from 1909 to 1913; chief justice of the United States Supreme Court from 1921 until his death in 1930.

⁸Marion Talley, American operatic soprano who created a minor sensation in 1926 by being selected at the age of nineteen for a role with the Metropolitan Opera of New York City. She "retired" in early 1929, purchasing a Kansas farm with her earnings as a singer.

331   OM; published: *TDW*, April 28, 1929

¹William Dawes, American revolutionary patriot who rode with Paul Revere on April 18, 1775, from Lexington toward Concord, warning residents of the approach of British troops.

²Charles Gates Dawes, United States ambassador to Great Britain from 1929 to 1932; Chicago financier, Republican politician, and former vice president of the United States. "Hell 'n Maria" was one of his favorite expressions.

³Louis Leon Ludlow, Democratic United States representative from Indiana from 1929 to 1949. As a correspondent for Indiana and Ohio newspapers, Ludlow was a member of the congressional press galleries for twenty-eight years prior to his election to Congress.

⁴Hamilton Fish, Jr., Republican United States representative from New York from 1920 to 1945.

⁵John Charles Linthicum, Democratic United States representative from Maryland from 1911 until his death in 1932.

332   OM; published: *TDW*, May 5, 1929

¹Heflin (see WA 330:N 3) unsuccessfully sought Senate condemnation of a person who tossed a bottle at him following a Ku Klux Klan rally in Massachusetts in March of 1929.

²Frederick Huntington Gillett, Republican United States senator from Massachusetts from 1925 to 1931; one-time congressman and Speaker of the House.

³Joseph Ridgway Grundy, American textile industrialist and banker; president of the Pennsylvania Manufacturers' Association from 1909 to 1930. A leading protectionist, Grundy was elected as a Republican to the United States Senate in late 1929; he served for less than one year.

⁴George Herman "Babe" Ruth, popular professional baseball player who

achieved fame as a home run slugger with the New York Yankees from 1920 to 1935; inducted into the Baseball Hall of Fame in 1936.

Charles Francis Adams, American lawyer and financier; United States secretary of the navy from 1929 to 1933.

[5]John Nicholas Ringling, wealthy American showman who with his several brothers entered the circus business in 1884, eventually assembling one of the world's largest circuses.

[6]The *Mayflower* was the presidential yacht that Hoover decommissioned early in his administration as a move to cut expenses.

333   OM; published: *TDW*, May 12, 1929

[1]Alfred Emanuel "Al" Smith, Democratic political leader; governor of New York from 1919 to 1920 and 1923 to 1928; unsuccessful candidate for the presidency in 1928.

[2]Henry VIII, king of England from 1509 until his death in 1547; known for his break with the Catholic Church and his many wives.

[3]For Tom Heflin see WA 330:N 3.

[4]Thomas Wolsey, English prelate and statesman who served as Henry VIII's lord chancellor and adviser.

[5]*Cradle of the Deep*, the romanticized tale of a young girl's life on a South Sea schooner. Originally purported to be the autobiography of Joan Lowell (Mrs. Thompson Buchanan), the 1929 bestseller proved a hoax.

[6]For Texas Guinan see WA 330:N 1.

[7]*The Front Page*, a newspaper melodrama produced for Broadway in 1928 by Ben Hecht and Charles MacArthur and twice adapted for motion pictures.

334   OM; published: *TDW*, May 19, 1929

[1]John Wanamaker, Philadelphia department store magnate and philanthropist; United States postmaster general from 1889 to 1893.

[2]William Penn Adair, Georgia-born Cherokee tribal leader.

[3]Boies Penrose, longtime Republican "boss" of Pennsylvania; United States senator from 1897 until his death in 1921.

[4]Andrew William Mellon, United States secretary of the treasury from 1921 to 1932; financier and industrialist from Pittsburgh, Pennsylvania.

James Couzens, Republican United States senator from Michigan from 1922 until his death in 1936; industrialist and former mayor of Detroit.

[5]Arthur Brisbane, American newspaper writer and editor whose column, "Today," appeared in more than 200 daily and 1,200 weekly newspapers. Brisbane, a leading booster of the United States, often wrote on the theme "Don't sell America short."

[6]William Randolph Hearst, powerful American publishing tycoon and Democratic politician; proprietor of a large chain of newspapers and magazines.

[7]Horace Greeley, nineteenth century American journalist and political leader; founder in 1841 of the *New York Tribune*.

Frank Andrew Munsey, American publisher; owner of the *New York Evening Sun* and *Evening Telegram* newspapers and *Munsey's* and *Argosy* magazines.

[8]George Horace Lorimer, American editor and publisher; editor in chief of the *Saturday Evening Post* from 1899 until his death in 1937.

[9]Philip Danforth Armour, American industrialist; founder and head of the meatpacking firm Armour & Company.

[10]William Hale "Big Bill" Thompson, Republican mayor of Chicago from 1915 to 1923 and 1927 to 1931. A devoted Anglophobe, Thompson was a founder of the "America First" movement.

[11]Samuel Insull II, Chicago public utilities magnate with vast holdings throughout the Midwest. Overexpansion caused the collapse of his empire in the 1930s.

[12]William Wrigley, Jr., Chicago industrialist who in 1891 founded William Wrigley, Jr., & Company, manufacturer of chewing gum.

Samuel George Blythe, American editor and political writer; longtime contributor to the *Saturday Evening Post*.

[13]Alice Roosevelt Longworth, daughter of President Theodore Roosevelt, wife of Speaker of the House Nicholas Longworth, and prominent Washington hostess.

¹⁴Smedley Darlington Butler, United States Marine Corps officer. A former head of the Philadelphia Department of Safety, Major General Butler commanded the Marine Corps detachment in Nicaragua in the 1920s.

335   OM; published: *TDW,* May 26, 1929

¹Robert P. "Bob" Hewitt, licensed transport pilot from Philadelphia.
²For Pancho Villa see WA 326:N 5.
  Augusto César Sandino, Nicaraguan revolutionary who supported a liberal insurrection in Nicaragua in 1926 and waged guerrilla warfare from 1927 to 1932 against United States Marines who intervened in the conflict.
³Arnold Rothstein, prominent New York City gambler and racketeer who was murdered in a Manhattan hotel room in November of 1928. The case was never solved.
⁴For the *Mayflower* see WA 332:N 6.
⁵Edward Beale "Ned" and Evalyn Walsh McLean, Washington society figures. Ned McLean was the publisher of the *Washington Post.*
⁶John Roll "Jock" McLean, eldest son of Ned and Evalyn McLean.
⁷Evalyn Washington "Emily" McLean, only daughter of the McLeans.
⁸For Alice Roosevelt Longworth see WA 334:N 13.
⁹Nicholas Longworth, Republican United States representative from Ohio from 1903 to 1913 and 1915 until his death in 1931; Speaker of the House from 1925 until his death.
¹⁰Under the debenture plan for farm relief, exporters of agricultural products would receive debenture certificates that would equal one-half the tariff duty assessed upon a comparable import.
¹¹Mack Sennett, Canadian-born American motion picture producer and director, known as the "king of comedy"; creator in 1913 of the famous Keystone Kops.
¹²Smith Wildman Brookhart, Republican United States senator from Iowa from 1922 to 1926 and 1927 to 1933; member of the maverick progressive faction of the Republican party.
  Simeon Davison Fess, Republican United States senator from Ohio from 1923 to 1935. Fess and Brookhart were feuding over Brookhart's alleged lack of support for the Hoover administration.
¹³Alice Longworth and Dolly Curtis Gann (see WA 330:N 4) were embroiled in a bitter battle over the social precedence issue.
¹⁴Reed Smoot, Republican United States senator from Utah from 1903 to 1933; Mormon church official and Utah sugar beet producer; proponent of high tariffs, especially on foreign sugar.
¹⁵For Mabel W. Willebrandt see WA 327:N 2; for Texas Guinan see WA 330:N 1.
  James Cannon, Jr., bishop in the Methodist Episcopal Church, South, from 1918 until his death in 1944; an ardent and active prohibitionist.
¹⁶For Tom Heflin see WA 330:N 3.

336   OM; published: *TDW,* June 2, 1929

¹For *Cradle of the Deep* see WA 333:N 5.
²For Henry VIII see WA 333:N 2.
³Florenz "Flo" Ziegfeld, Jr., American theatrical producer, best known for the *Ziegfeld Follies.* First produced in 1907, these elaborately-staged musical revues featured a bevy of beautiful chorus girls and many of the leading stage performers of the day. Rogers appeared with the *Follies* from 1916 to 1925.
⁴Sam Hardy, American actor featured on stage in the early 1920s and in scores of motion pictures in the 1920s and early 1930s.
⁵Marion Davies, blonde American comedienne who enjoyed a long starring career from 1917 to 1937 in vaudeville and motion pictures.
⁶For Tom Heflin see WA 330:N 3; for Reed Smoot see WA 335:N 14.
⁷Francis Hackett, Irish-born American novelist and biographer whose works include *Henry the Eighth* (1929).
⁸Edward VII, king of Great Britain and Ireland from 1901 until his death in 1910.
  George V, king of Great Britain and Northern Ireland from 1910 until his death in 1936.

Edward Albert, prince of Wales from 1911 until his succession to the British throne in 1936; extremely popular as a bachelor prince.

⁹Alphonse "Scarface Al" Capone, notorious Chicago gangster leader who became a symbol of lawlessness in the 1920s.

¹⁰Arthur, prince of Wales and eldest brother of Henry VIII; died in 1502.

¹¹Isabella I, queen of Castile from 1474 until her death in 1504; chief benefactor of Christopher Columbus and his expeditions to the New World. By her marriage to Ferdinand of Aragon in 1469, the modern nation of Spain was founded.

¹²For Mabel W. Willebrandt see WA 327:N 2.

¹³Ferdinand II, king of Aragon from 1479 until his death in 1516; joint sovereign of Castile with his wife, Isabella I.

¹⁴Dawes (see WA 331:N 2) headed a special commission in Santo Domingo in 1929 to audit the finances of the Dominican government.

¹⁵Catherine of Aragon, daughter of Ferdinand and Isabella of Spain; first queen of Henry VIII; abandoned by Henry in 1531 after she failed to produce a male heir.

¹⁶For Thomas Wolsey see WA 333:N 4.

¹⁷Anne Boleyn, mistress of Henry VIII. She secretly married King Henry in 1533, prompting the nullification of his marriage to Catherine of Aragon.

337   OM; published: *TDW,* June 9, 1929

¹For Henry VIII see WA 333:N 2.

John Barrymore, distinguished American stage and screen actor; member of one of the foremost American families of actors.

John Gilbert, American motion picture actor who first achieved success as a romantic leading man in 1924 in *His Hour.* Gilbert's career was cut short by the advent of "talkies" in the late 1920s.

Benito Mussolini, dictator of Italy from 1922 to 1943; founder and leader of the Fascist movement.

For Tom Heflin see WA 330:N 3.

John Roach Straton, Baptist ministerial leader from New York City who gained national prominence as a fundamentalist, prohibitionist, and anti-papist.

²For Catherine of Aragon see WA 336:N 15.

³For Anne Boleyn see WA 336:N 17.

⁴Greta Garbo, Swedish motion picture actress. Garbo, noted for her haunting beauty and sultry sexuality, arrived in Hollywood in 1926, where she soon became one of the highest paid performers in films. She retired in 1942.

Peggy Hopkins Joyce, American vaudeville, stage, and screen actress whose six marriages and countless engagements brought her much publicity.

⁵Mary Boleyn, older sister of Anne Boleyn and mistress of Henry VIII.

⁶William Carey, husband of Mary Boleyn and attendant to Henry VIII.

⁷Henry Percy, suitor of Anne Boleyn and son of the earl of Northumberland.

⁸For Thomas Wolsey see WA 333:N 4.

William Edgar Borah, Republican United States senator from Idaho from 1907 until his death in 1940; powerful chairman of the Senate Foreign Relations Committee.

⁹Clement VII, pope of the Roman Catholic Church from 1523 until his death in 1534. Clement refused to sanction the divorce of Henry VIII from Catherine of Aragon.

¹⁰Martin Luther, German religious reformer; professor at the University of Wittenburg from 1511 to 1546; father of the Reformation in Germany.

¹¹Mary I (Mary Tudor), daughter of Henry VIII and Catherine of Aragon; queen of England and Ireland from 1553 until her death in 1558.

¹²Elizabeth I, only child of Henry VIII and Anne Boleyn; queen of England and Ireland from 1558 until her death in 1603.

¹³Jane Seymour, third wife of Henry VIII.

¹⁴Anne of Cleves, German-born fourth wife of Henry VIII.

¹⁵Hans Holbein the Younger, German portrait and historical painter; court artist to Henry VIII.

¹⁶Thomas Cromwell, earl of Essex, English statesman who held many posts under Henry VIII, including lord privy seal and lord great chamberlain. He was beheaded in 1540.

¹⁷Catherine Howard, fifth wife of Henry VIII; beheaded in 1542 for adultery.

¹⁸Thomas Culpepper, cousin of Catherine Howard with whom he had an adulterous relationship.
¹⁹Katherine Parr, sixth and last wife of Henry VIII.
²⁰For Francis Hackett see WA 336:N 7.

338   *TDW,* June 16, 1929

¹Charles Augustus Lindbergh, American aviator who made the first solo, nonstop transatlantic flight in 1927. In June of 1929, Lindbergh married Anne Spencer Morrow, daughter of Ambassador Dwight W. Morrow (see WA 325:N 8).
²James Joseph "Gene" Tunney, American boxer who reigned as world heavyweight champion from 1926 until his retirement in 1928.
   George Bernard Shaw, leading British playwright, novelist, and literary critic. Among his works are *The Devil's Disciple* and *Pygmalion.*
³Charles Spencer "Charlie" Chaplin, legendary English-born comedian who starred in several classic American and British films. He was widely known for his portrayal of the "Little Tramp."
⁴For Mabel W. Willebrandt see WA 327:N 2.
⁵For the debenture plan see WA 335:N 10.
⁶For the Gann-Longworth controversy see WA 330:N 4 and WA 335:N 13.
⁷Lou Henry Hoover, wife of President Herbert Hoover.
⁸For Babe Ruth see WA 332:N 4.

339   OM; published: *TDW,* June 23, 1929

¹For the Prince of Wales see WA 336:N 8.
²For Henry VIII see WA 333:N 2.
³For George V see WA 336:N 8.
   Mary, queen consort of Great Britain and Northern Ireland; wife of George V.
⁴For this and all further references to Benito Mussolini see WA 337:N 1.
⁵Miguel Primo de Rivera y Orbaneja, Spanish military and political leader; dictator of Spain from 1923 to 1930.
⁶Ingrid, princess of Sweden who was rumored to be engaged to the Prince of Wales.
⁷For Isabella I see WA 336:N 11.
   Charles VIII, king of France from 1483 until his death in 1498.

340   OM; published: *TDW,* June 30, 1929

¹Jessie De Priest, wife of Representative Oscar Stanton De Priest of Illinois, the first black to serve in Congress since the 1880s.
²Warren Gamaliel Harding, Republican president of the United States from 1921 until his death in 1923.
   Thomas Woodrow Wilson, Democratic president of the United States from 1913 to 1921.
³For Charles A. Lindbergh see WA 338:N 1.
⁴For Charles G. Dawes see WA 331:N 2.
⁵For the Prince of Wales see WA 336:N 8.
⁶Owen D. Young, Chicago attorney and corporation executive; chairman of an international conference in 1929 that formulated the Young Plan for payment of German reparations.
⁷John Pierpont Morgan, Jr., chairman of the board of J. P. Morgan & Co., one of the most influential banking firms in the world and the major lending house to the Allied nations during World War I.

341   OM; published: *TDW,* July 7, 1929

¹For William Howard Taft see WA 330:N 7.

342   OM; published: *TDW,* July 14, 1929

¹Lindbergh (see WA 338:N 1) helped to found Transcontinental Air Transport, a unique, short-lived "wedding" of air-rail transportation.

343 OM; published: *TDW*, July 21, 1929

[1] Amon Giles Carter, publisher of the *Fort Worth* (Texas) *Star-Telegram* and influential civic leader of Fort Worth and booster of Texas.
[2] Harry Hazel Culver, Southern California real estate developer and bank executive; founder and builder of Culver City, California.
[3] Paul Whittier, aviator son of Max Whittier, California oilman and one of the original developers of Beverly Hills.
[4] Slade Hulbert, unidentified.
[5] Loren Mendell and Roland B. "Pete" Reinhart, two West Coast fliers, set a world record for endurance flying in July of 1929. The mark was broken less than one month later.
[6] William Gibbs McAdoo, Jr., naval veteran of World War I, graduate of Princeton University, and California businessman and sportsman; son of William Gibbs McAdoo, Sr., United States secretary of the treasury from 1913 to 1918 and prominent candidate for the Democratic nomination for the presidency in 1920 and 1924.
    A. E. McManus, Jr., British-American flier; former aviator with the Royal Air Force.

344 OM; published: *LAE*, July 28, 1929

[1] George Woodward Wickersham, former attorney general of the United States who headed a famous presidential commission in 1929 that surveyed the enforcement of the Eighteenth Amendment.
[2] James Ramsay MacDonald, British Labor party leader who served as prime minister of Great Britain in 1924 and from 1929 to 1931 and 1931 to 1935.
[3] Nancy Langhorne Astor, American-born wife of Lord Waldorf Astor and, as a British subject, the first woman elected to the House of Commons, serving from 1919 to 1945.
[4] Aristide Briand, prime minister of France from 1909 to 1911, 1915 to 1917, 1921 to 1922, 1925 to 1926, and in 1929.
    Raymond Poincaré, prime minister of France from 1912 to 1913, 1922 to 1924, and 1926 to 1929. He also served as minister of finance and held other high governmental posts.
[5] For Owen D. Young see WA 340:N 6.
[6] Aimee Semple McPherson, American evangelist who preached a Pentecostal, fundamentalist, faith-healing doctrine. McPherson, who enjoyed a great following in the 1920s and 1930s, was the founder of the International Church of the Foursquare Gospel based in Los Angeles.
[7] Robert Marion La Follette, Jr., Republican United States senator from Wisconsin from 1925 to 1947.
[8] Robert Marion La Follette, Sr., leading progressive Republican politician who served as congressman and senator from Wisconsin and as governor of the state. He died in 1925.

345 OM; published: *TDW*, August 4, 1929

[1] Man O' War, American-bred race horse which won twenty of twenty-one races from 1919 to 1920 and set five American track records during a brief racing career.
[2] George Middleton, American dramatist who wrote numerous successful plays produced since 1902, including *The Cavalier* and *The Sinner*.
    For Robert M. La Follette, Jr., see WA 344:N 7.
[3] Glenn Frank, American educator and editor; president of the University of Wisconsin from 1925 to 1937.

346 *TDW*, August 11, 1929

[1] Max Siegfried Schmeling, German boxer who held the world heavyweight championship from 1930 to 1932. The most successful professional boxer in German history.
[2] Chiang Kai-shek, Chinese general and political leader; president of the Chinese Nationalist government from 1928 to 1931, 1948 to 1949, and 1950 until his death in 1975.
[3] For this and all further references to Al Smith see WA 333:N 1.

⁴Edward Grey, British statesman who served as secretary of state for foreign affairs from 1905 to 1916 and who was a prominent figure in the diplomatic confrontation before World War I. His memoirs and papers were published in 1925 and 1926.

347   McN; published: *TDW*, August 18, 1929

¹Edward Vernon "Eddie" Rickenbacker, American aviator and airline executive who as a flight commander during World War I personally disabled twenty-six enemy aircraft.

²For Reed Smoot see WA 335:N 14.

³William James and Charles Horace Mayo, American surgeons who co-founded the world famous Mayo Clinic at Rochester, Minnesota, in 1889. The brothers remained active at the clinic and an affiliated research foundation until their deaths in 1939.

⁴Francis Heenen "Peaches" Browning, fifteen-year-old New York City schoolgirl who married Edward West Browning, a wealthy fifty-year-old real estate operator, in the spring of 1926. The couple lived together for ten months and then, after a widely-publicized trial, separated.

⁵Edward Clarence Moore, well-known surgical specialist and physician in the Los Angeles area and, later, a clinical professor of surgery at the University of Southern California. Moore performed gall bladder surgery on Rogers in the summer of 1927.

Percival Gordon White, Los Angeles physician and specialist in internal medicine; partner of Dr. Edward Moore.

348   OM; published: *TDW*, August 25, 1929

¹David Aiken Reed, Republican United States senator from Pennsylvania from 1922 to 1935.

²For Reed Smoot see WA 335:N 14.

³For Charles A. Lindbergh see WA 338:N 1.

⁴Mark Sullivan, American newspaper columnist and radio commentator who began his career as a muckraker but who later became a spokesman for conservative Republicans.

⁵Jackie Coogan, American motion picture child star who was immortalized as "The Kid" in a Charlie Chaplin film of the same name in 1921; later appeared on radio and television.

⁶For Joseph R. Grundy see WA 332:N 2.

349   OM; published: *TDW*, September 1, 1929

¹Grace Anna Goodhue Coolidge, popular former first lady; wife of President Calvin Coolidge.

²Rex Ellingwood Beach, American novelist and miscellaneous writer, noted for his rough-hewn portrayals of frontier life in Alaska.

³Lois Kimsey Marshall, wife of Thomas Riley Marshall, Democratic governor of Indiana from 1909 to 1913 and vice president of the United States from 1913 to 1921.

⁴For Nicholas Longworth see WA 335:N 9.

⁵Arthur Capper, Republican United States senator from Kansas from 1919 to 1949; editor and owner of the *Topeka* (Kansas) *Daily Capital, Kansas Farmer, Capper's Farmer*, and other publications.

350   OM; published: *TDW*, September 8, 1929

¹Elizabeth Page Poindexter, outspoken wife of Miles Poindexter, former United States senator from Washington and ambassador to Peru.

²Philip Snowden, English statesman and Labor party leader; chancellor of the exchequer in 1924 and from 1929 to 1931; married to the former Ethel Annakin.

³For Nancy Astor see WA 344:N 3.

⁴For Tom Heflin see WA 330:N 3.

⁵Dawes (see WA 331:N 2) was the principle author of the Dawes Plan of 1924 for the payment of German reparations.

⁶For William E. Borah see WA 337:N 8.

Byron Patton "Pat" Harrison, Democratic United States senator from Mississippi from 1919 until his death in 1941.
[7] For Joseph R. Grundy see WA 332:N 3.
[8] Kemal Pasha, Turkish general and political leader; president of Turkey from 1923 until his death in 1938. Kemal Pasha, who inaugurated sweeping social and political reforms in Turkey, later took the name, Ataturk.

351 OM; published: *TDW*, September 15, 1929

[1] Elihu Root, American attorney and statesman; United States secretary of war, secretary of state, and senator; after 1915, represented the United States on various diplomatic missions.
  Charles Evans Hughes, American attorney, Republican politician, and jurist; former governor of New York, United States Supreme Court justice, and secretary of state; chief justice of the Supreme Court from 1930 to 1941.
[2] For William E. Borah see WA 337:N 8; for Reed Smoot see WA 335:N 14; for Joseph R. Grundy see WA 332:N 3.
[3] For Aimee Semple McPherson see WA 344:N 6.
[4] For Mabel W. Willebrandt see WA 327:N 2.
  James John "Jimmy" Walker, dapper and flamboyant Democratic mayor of New York City from 1925 to 1932.
[5] John Davison Rockefeller, Sr., American oil magnate who organized Standard Oil Company in 1870 and who dominated the industry until his retirement in 1891.
  Henry Ford, American automobile pioneer; founder of Ford Motor Company.
  Joe Toplitsky, Los Angeles realtor and insurance executive.
[6] Oscar Stanton De Priest, Republican United States representative from Illinois from 1929 to 1935; first black to serve in Congress since the 1880s (see also WA 340:N 1).
[7] For Tom Heflin see WA 330:N 3; for Peggy Hopkins Joyce see WA 337:N 4.
[8] Robert Tyre "Bobby" Jones, American amateur golfer who was one of the all-time great players of the sport; winner of four United States Open championships, three British Open crowns, and five United States amateur titles.
  Martha Jane "Calamity Jane" Burke, American horsewoman, sharpshooter, and frontier character of the Old West.
[9] Gus Orville Nations, Saint Louis attorney and former director of prohibition agents in Missouri. In a syndicated newspaper series, Mabel Willebrandt accused Gus Nations and his brother, Reginald Heber Nations, of allowing the Griesedieck Brewery Company of Saint Louis to brew and sell illicit beer.

352 *TDW*, September 22, 1929

[1] Brigham Young, American religious leader who headed the Mormon Church from 1847 until his death in 1877. He directed the mass migration of Mormons to the Great Salt Lake Valley in Utah and served as the first governor of the territory.
  Joseph Smith, founder of the Mormon Church in 1830 and leader during the movement's early years in the United States.
  Joseph Ray, nineteenth century American educator and physician; wrote a popular series of algebraic and mathematical schoolbooks.
[2] Charles B. "Charlie" Irwin, Wyoming rancher, wild west showman, railroad lobbyist, and race horse owner; a commanding figure and personality, he weighed 500 pounds at the time of his death in 1934.
[3] For Reed Smoot see WA 335:N 14.
  John Benjamin Kendrick, Democratic United States senator from Wyoming from 1917 until his death in 1933.

353 OM; published: *TDW*, September 29, 1929

[1] Drumgoole was the correct spelling.
[2] For John D. Rockefeller, Sr., see WA 351:N 5.
[3] For Joseph Ray see WA 352:N 1.
  William Holmes McGuffey, nineteenth century American educator, best remembered for his series of *Eclectic Readers* for schoolroom instruction.
[4] Glenn Scobey "Pop" Warner, famous American football figure who coached at

Carlisle Institute from 1899 to 1903 and 1907 to 1914 and at Stanford University from 1924 to 1932.

354   OM; published: *TDW*, October 6, 1929

[1] *They Had to See Paris*, Rogers' first "talkie," had its world premiere in Los Angeles on September 18, 1929.
[2] An airliner crashed in western New Mexico during a storm on September 8, 1929, killing all eight persons aboard.
[3] Sallie Clementine Rogers McSpadden, a sister of Will Rogers; wife of John Thomas "Tom" McSpadden, rancher of Chelsea, Oklahoma.
[4] Robert Westmoreland "Bobby" Cantwell, early Oklahoma aviator who flew as an executive pilot for oilmen and as a private transport flier.

355   *TDW*, October 13, 1929

[1] Abie's Irish Rose, one of the longest running plays in the history of Broadway theatrical productions. Anne Nichols wrote the comedy, which opened on May 23, 1922, and played before approximately two million theater-goers during its lengthy run.
[2] Anne Pennington, American dancer who often performed in the *Ziegfeld Follies* and who won fame as the dancer with the "dimpled knees."
[3] Ben Ames Williams, American novelist and short story writer whose works include *All the Brothers Were Valiant* and *Audacity*.
[4] Ringgold Wilmer "Ring" Lardner, American humorist, novelist, playwright, and short story writer, famous for his baseball and other sports tales; author of *Big Town, What of It?*, and *Round Up*.
[5] Andrew "Andy" Tombes, American vaudevillian and motion picture character actor, active in the entertainment business until his retirement in 1955.

356   OM; published: *TDW*, October 20, 1929

[1] J. Ramsay MacDonald (see WA 344:N 2), accompanied by his elder daughter, Ishbel, made an official visit to the United States in October of 1929.
[2] For Joseph R. Grundy see WA 332:N 3.

357   OM; published: *TDW*, October 27, 1929

[1] For J. Ramsay MacDonald see WA 344:N 2 and WA 356:N 1.
[2] William B. Shearer, American shipping lobbyist, naval expert, and proponent of United States preparedness. Shearer, who attended an international disarmament conference in 1927 as an observer for the American ship-building industry, was accused of working to break up the conference. The Senate Naval Affairs Committee conducted an investigation and early in 1930 cleared Shearer of all allegations.
   For Aimee Semple McPherson see WA 344:N 6.
[3] Connie Mack (Cornelius McGillicuddy), American professional baseball player and manager; manager of the Philadelphia Athletics from 1901 to 1950.
[4] Lewis Robert "Hack" Wilson, American professional baseball player who starred in the outfield for the Chicago Cubs from 1926 to 1931; renowned as a home run hitter.
[5] Thomas Alva Edison, American inventor and scientist, famous for such innovations and improvements as the incandescent electric lamp, the phonograph, and the microphone. Edison, who celebrated his eighty-second birthday in 1929, was the honored guest at a Golden Jubilee of Light celebration hosted by Henry Ford at Dearborn, Michigan, on October 21.
[6] For this and all further references to Henry Ford see WA 351:N 5.
[7] John Burroughs, American naturalist and essayist who died in 1921. Among his nature works are *Wake-Robin, Bird and Bough*, and *Field and Study*.
[8] Harvey Samuel Firestone, American industrialist who organized and built Firestone Tire and Rubber Company.

358   OM; published: *TDW*, November 3, 1929

[1] Edsel Bryant Ford, president of Ford Motor Company from 1919 to 1943; only son of Henry Ford.

For Thomas A. Edison see WA 357:N 5.
²Charles Michael Schwab, American industrialist who founded Bethlehem Steel Corporation in 1904.
³John Davison Rockefeller, Jr., son and namesake of the Standard Oil Company magnate (see WA 351:N 5); manager of the family philanthropies.
Otto Hermann Kahn, German-born American financier who was a partner in the powerful banking firm of Kuhn, Loeb & Company of New York City from 1897 until his death in 1934.
⁴Benjamin Barr Lindsey, American jurist and social reformer; proponent of the juvenile court system and "companionate marriage."
Walter Percy Chrysler, American automobile manufacturer. A former president of Buick Motor Company, he later founded and headed Chrysler Corporation.
Albert Russel Erskine, American industrialist who headed Studebaker Corporation, manufacturer of automobiles, from 1915 until his death in 1933.
Albert Fisher, American industrialist who was a major manufacturer of car bodies and trucks.
Walter Owen Briggs, American manufacturer of automobile bodies; president of Briggs Manufacturing Company from 1909 to 1937.
⁵Julius Rosenwald, American merchant and philanthropist; president of Sears, Roebuck & Company from 1910 to 1925.

359   OM; published: *TDW*, November 10, 1929

¹Roger Ward Babson, American businessman, statistician, and business prognosticator.
²Eddie Cantor, American vaudeville, burlesque, theatrical, motion picture, and radio comedian.
For John D. Rockefeller, Sr., see WA 351:N 5.
³For J. P. Morgan, Jr., see WA 340:N 7.

360   OM; published: *TDW*, November 17, 1929

¹For Jimmy Walker see WA 351:N 4.
²For James Cannon, Jr., see WA 335:N 15.
³For Charles G. Dawes see WA 331:N 2.
Carol D. Blymyer Dawes, wife of Charles G. Dawes.
Hiram Warren Johnson, maverick Republican politician; United States senator from California from 1917 until his death in 1945.
⁴For Smith W. Brookhart see WA 335:N 12.
⁵For Otto H. Kahn see WA 358:N 3.
⁶Hiram Bingham, Republican United States senator from Connecticut from 1924 to 1933. Bingham was censured by the Senate in November of 1929 for having placed a lobbyist of the Connecticut Manufacturers' Association on the Senate payroll as his tariff adviser.
⁷For Joseph R. Grundy see WA 332:N 3.

361   OM; published: *TDW*, November 24, 1929

¹For Joseph R. Grundy see WA 332:N 3.
²For Ishbel A. MacDonald see WA 356:N 1.

362   OM; published: *TDW*, December 1, 1929

363   OM; published: *TDW*, December 8, 1929

¹Wilhelm II, emperor of Germany from 1888 until his abdication in 1918; led Germany into World War I.
²Edward Fitz Randolph "Eddie" Vail, California cattleman and philanthropist; close friend of Rogers.

364   OM; published: *TDW*, December 15, 1929

¹For Texas Guinan see WA 330:N 1.

²Abbott Lawrence Lowell, American educator, political scientist, and author; president of Harvard University from 1909 to 1933.
Charles William Eliot, American educator, scientist, mathematician, and author; president of Harvard University from 1869 to 1909.
Clarence Cook Little, American biologist, cancer specialist, and educator; president of the University of Michigan from 1925 to 1929.
For Glenn Frank see WA 345:N 4.
Knute Kenneth Rockne, Norwegian-born football coach at Notre Dame University from 1918 until his death in 1931. In thirteen seasons as head coach, Rockne directed the Fighting Irish to 105 wins, 12 losses, and 3 ties.
Nicholas Murray Butler, American educator, philosopher, and Republican politician; president of Columbia University from 1902 to 1945; co-winner of the Nobel peace prize in 1931.
³Christian Keener "Red" Cagle, football star at the United States Military Academy in the late 1920s. Cagle was forced to resign from the academy in 1930 after it was disclosed that he had married in 1928 despite academy rules prohibiting the marriage of cadets.
⁴John Joseph Pershing, popular American military officer, known as "Black Jack," who commanded the Allied Expeditionary Force in Europe during World War I and who served as Army Chief of Staff from 1921 to 1924.
⁵Albert James "Albie" Booth, Jr., star football player at Yale University from 1929 to 1931. Booth led the Bulldogs to fifteen wins, five losses, and five ties with excellent running, passing, punting, and dropkicking.

365   OM; published: *TDW,* December 22, 1929

¹For Owen D. Young see WA 340:N 6; for John D. Rockefeller, Jr., see WA 358:N 3.
²For Andrew W. Mellon see WA 334:N 4.
³William Scott Vare, Republican political leader in Pennsylvania and United States congressman. Vare was elected to the Senate in 1926, but because of charges of excessive campaign expenditures he was never permitted to qualify, eventually being unseated in December of 1929.
⁴Grundy (see WA 332:N 3) served in the Senate from 1929 to 1930.

366   OM; published: *TDW,* December 29, 1929

¹For Bobby Jones see WA 351:N 8.
Oscar Baun "Pop" Keeler, American sports reporter, widely known as the "dean of the nation's golf writers"; friend and biographer of Bobby Jones.
²William Fox, Hungarian-born American motion picture producer who was one of the early power-wielders in the industry.

367   OM; published: *TDW,* January 5, 1930

368   OM; published: *TDW,* January 12, 1930

¹For Charles G. Dawes see WA 331:N 2; for Dwight W. Morrow see WA 325:N 8.
Joseph Taylor "Joe" Robinson, Democratic United States senator from Arkansas from 1913 until his death in 1937; minority leader of the Senate from 1923 to 1933.
For David A. Reed see WA 348:N 1.
Hilary Pollard Jones, American naval officer who attained the rank of vice admiral before retiring in 1927. Jones and the other individuals that Rogers mentioned represented the United States at the London Disarmament Conference of 1930.
²For Charles Evans Hughes see WA 351:N 1.
³Hugh Simon Gibson, American career diplomat who served as United States ambassador to Belgium from 1927 to 1933; formerly held similar posts in Poland and Switzerland; chairman of the American delegation to the preliminary commission for the disarmament conference at Geneva, Switzerland, from 1926 to 1927.
Andrew Theodore Long, American naval officer; member of the general board of the Navy from 1923 to 1930; naval adviser to Gibson at Geneva.

369 McN; published: *TDW*, January 19, 1930

[1]Humbert, crown prince of Italy, married Princess Marie Jose of Belgium on January 8, 1930. The princess' mother, Queen Elizabeth of Belgium, was a former duchess of Bavaria.
[2]Victor Emmanuel III, king of Italy from 1900 to 1946. He was married in 1896 to Princess Elena, daughter of the future king of Montenegro.
[3]Alfonso XIII, king of Spain from 1886 to 1931. His reign was marked by the dictatorship of Primo de Rivera (see WA 339:N 5).
[4]For George V see WA 336:N 8.

370 OM; published: *TDW*, January 26, 1930

[1]Thomas Edwin "Tom" Mix, famous American cowboy motion picture star; one of the greatest box office attractions in the history of the screen.
[2]For John N. Ringling see WA 332:N 5.
[3]Zachary Taylor "Zack" Miller, owner of the 101 Ranch near Ponca City, Oklahoma, and organizer of the 101 Ranch Wild West Show, which frequently made world-wide tours from 1906 to 1931.
[4]Attilio Henry Giannini, American physician and banker; brother of Amadeo Peter Giannini, founder of the Bank of Italy, predecessor of the huge Bank of America. Attilio, who supervised the family's banking interests in New York City, was a leading pioneer in the financing of motion picture productions. His wife was the former Leontine Denker of Los Angeles.
[5]John Pierpont Morgan, Sr., founder of the influential banking firm of J. P. Morgan & Company.
For John D. Rockefeller, Sr., see WA 351:N 5.
[6]Earle Charles Anthony, California automobile distributor, service station developer, and radio station owner.
[7]Winfield R. "Winnie" Sheehan, American motion picture director and producer; vice president of Fox Film Corporation from 1921 to 1935.

371 OM; published: *TDW*, February 2, 1930

[1]Margherita Grassini Sarfatti, Italian writer and book reviewer; author of *The Life of Benito Mussolini*, an international bestselling biography in 1925.
[2]For Joseph R. Grundy see WA 332:N 3.
[3]Paul Whiteman, American bandleader who became famous in the 1920s for pioneering "sweet style" as opposed to the traditional "classical" jazz.

372 *TDW*, February 9, 1930

373 *TDW*, February 16, 1930

[1]Waldorf Astor, English statesman and newspaper publisher; husband of Lady Astor (see WA 344:N 3).
[2]Thomas Cromwell, English statesman during the reign of Henry VIII; noted for his harshness as a church agent in the dissolution of small monasteries.

374 McN; published: *TDW*, February 23, 1930

[1]For George V see WA 336:N 8.
[2]Horatio Nelson, British naval hero noted for his service in the Napoleonic wars. He won many key engagements, including the Battle of Trafalgar in 1805, wherein he lost his life just as the British victory was assured.
[3]For Charles G. Dawes see WA 331:N 2.
[4]Elizabeth Cutter Morrow, American educator, social worker, and poet; wife of Ambassador Dwight W. Morrow.
Ewilda Miller Robinson, wife of Senator Joe Robinson of Arkansas.
Adele Wilcox Reed, wife of Senator David A. Reed of Pennsylvania.
For Carol D. B. Dawes see WA 360:N 3.
Ynés Reyntiens Gibson, Belgium-born wife of Ambassador Hugh S. Gibson.
Frances Lovering Adams, wife of Secretary of the Navy Charles Francis Adams.

Mabel Wellington White Stimson, wife of Secretary of State Henry L. Stimson.
⁵For J. Ramsay MacDonald see WA 344:N 2.
⁶For the Prince of Wales see WA 336:N 8.
⁷For Anne Morrow and Charles A. Lindbergh see WA 338:N 1.

375   McN; published: *TDW*, March 2, 1930

¹For Charles G. Dawes see WA 331:N 2.
²For the Prince of Wales see WA 336:N 8.
³For Queen Mary see WA 339:N 3.

376   *TDW*, March 9, 1930

¹For Grace A. Coolidge see WA 349:N 1.
²For Joe Robinson see WA 368:N 1.
³For Carol D. B. Dawes see WA 360:N 3.
⁴For Charles G. Dawes see WA 331:N 2.
⁵For Frank W. Stearns see WA 329:N 3.
⁶Mary Pickford, American silent film actress who won wide acclaim and legendary renown as "America's sweetheart."
⁷For Charles A. Lindbergh see WA 338:N 1.
⁸For William E. Borah see WA 337:N 8.

377   *TDW*, March 16, 1930

¹Coolidge was asked to dedicate a dam named in his honor on the Gila River, 130 miles southeast of Phoenix, Arizona.

378   *TDW*, March 23, 1930

¹For Julius Rosenwald see WA 358:N 5.
²For Edsel B. Ford see WA 358:N 1.

379   *TDW*, March 30, 1930

¹For J. Ramsay MacDonald see WA 344:N 2.
²For Scarface Al Capone see WA 335:N 9.
³Jess C. Andrews, Indiana livestock operator; head of the International Livestock Exposition in Chicago.
   Carl G. Fisher, Indiana businessman and realtor who conceived and built the Indianapolis Speedway in 1909 and who developed Miami Beach and other resort cities in Florida.

380   McN; published: *TDW*, April 6, 1930

¹For Theodore Roosevelt see WA 326:N 2.
²For Joseph R. Grundy see WA 332:N 3.
³For Reed Smoot see WA 336:N 14.
⁴For Brigham Young see WA 352:N 1.
⁵Edwin Sidney Broussard, Democratic United States senator from Louisiana from 1921 to 1933.
⁶Royal Samuel Copeland, physician and former New York City health commissioner; Democratic United States senator from New York from 1923 until his death in 1938.
   For Andrew W. Mellon see WA 334:N 4.
⁷Key Pittman, Democratic United States senator from Nevada from 1913 until his death in 1940.
⁸Sam Gilbert Bratton, Democratic United States senator from New Mexico from 1925 to 1933.
⁹Kendrick (see WA 352:N 3) operated a large cattle and sheep ranch near Sheridan, Wyoming.
¹⁰Park Trammell, Democratic United States senator from Florida from 1917 until his death in 1936.

Duncan Upshaw Fletcher, Democratic United States senator from Florida from 1909 until his death in 1936.

381   *TDW,* April 13, 1930

382   McN; published: *TDW,* April 20, 1930

   ¹For Anne Pennington see WA 355:N 2.
   ²For Flo Ziegfeld see WA 336:N 3.

383   OM; published: *TDW,* April 27, 1930

   ¹William Howard Taft (see WA 330:N 7) died on March 8, 1930.
   ²For Joseph R. Grundy see WA 332:N 3.

384   *TDW,* May 4, 1930

   ¹Bryant Baker, English-born sculptor who arrived in the Unied States in 1916 and became noted for his many busts and heroic statues of famous Americans.
   ²Ernest Whitworth Marland, Oklahoma oilman and Democratic politician; served as United States congressman and governor of Oklahoma in the 1930s.
   ³Zachary "Zack" Mulhall, pioneer Oklahoma rancher and early-day wild west showman.
   ⁴Gordon William "Pawnee Bill" Lillie, Oklahoma rancher, wild west showman, oilman, and banker.
   ⁵James "Jimmy" Rider, rancher-farmer from Talala, Oklahoma.
   ⁶For Zack T. Miller see WA 370:N 3.
   ⁷William Vann Rogers, eldest son of Will and Betty Rogers; known as Will Rogers, Jr.
   ⁸For Sallie Rogers McSpadden see WA 354:N 3.
   ⁹Patrick Jay "Pat" Hurley, United States secretary of war from 1929 to 1933; Tulsa lawyer and businessman.
   ¹⁰William Judson Holloway, Democratic governor of Oklahoma from 1929 to 1931. Holloway, who was elected lieutenant governor in 1926, became governor on the impeachment and removal from office of Henry S. Johnston.
   ¹¹Robert Quillen, American editorial writer and columnist for many newspapers and magazines in the United States and Canada; resident of Fountain Inn, South Carolina.

385   *TDW,* May 11, 1930

   ¹For Mary Pickford see WA 376:N 6.
   Douglas Fairbanks, Sr., swashbuckling American actor and hero of many silent screen spectaculars; husband of Mary Pickford.
   ²For John D. Rockefeller, Sr., see WA 351:N 5.
   ³For Andrew W. Mellon see WA 334:N 4.
   ⁴For Aimee Semple McPherson see WA 344:N 6.

386   *TDW,* May 18, 1930

   ¹"Amos 'n Andy," long-running radio serial first broadcast in 1928. It featured two white comedians, Freeman Fisher Gosden and Charles J. Correll, in every male role. The escapades of two black taxi drivers and their friends in Harlem attracted an enormous and faithful listening audience.
   ²For Andrew W. Mellon see WA 344:N 4; for John D. Rockefeller, Sr., see WA 351:N 5; for Scarface Al Capone see WA 336:N 9.

387   *TDW,* May 25, 1930

   ¹For Red Cagle see WA 364:N 3.
   ²George Dewey, American admiral whose naval forces defeated a Spanish fleet at the Battle of Manila in 1898.

³Harold Edward "Red" Grange, star football halfback and All-American at the University of Illinois from 1922 to 1925. Grange left college in 1925 to play professional football with the Chicago Bears.

388   *TDW,* June 1, 1930

¹For Joseph R. Grundy see WA 332:N 3.

389   OM; published: *TDW,* June 8, 1930

¹For Charles G. Dawes see WA 331:N 2.
²Charlotte Kelsey Dorrance, daughter of John Thomas Dorrance, president of the Campbell Soup Company and orginator of canned soup.
³Elizabeth Brinton Kent, daughter of Arthur Atwater Kent, Philadelphia innovator and manufacturer of radios.
⁴Doris Duke, American tobacco heiress and socialite; daughter of James Buchanan Duke, one of the founders of the American Tobacco Company.
For George V see WA 336:N 8; for Queen Mary see WA 339:N 3.
⁵Frances Hutchinson, granddaughter of Edward Townsend Stotesbury, Philadelphia financier and railroad magnate.
⁶Hoke Smith, former governor of Georgia and United States senator. His second wife, Mazie Crawford Hoke, was presented at Buckingham Palace on May 15, 1930.
⁷Helen Wills, famous California tennis player who won her first of seven United States Open titles in 1923 at the age of seventeen. She also won twelve Wimbledon championships.
⁸Dwight W. Morrow (see WA 325:N 8) was elected as a Republican to the United States Senate in 1930 to fill a vacancy. He served from December of 1930 until his death the following October.
⁹For Charlie Chaplin see WA 338:N 3.
¹⁰John Nance "Jack" Garner, Democratic United States representative from Texas from 1903 to 1933; Speaker of the House from 1931 to 1933; vice president of the United States from 1933 to 1941.

390   OM; published: *TDW,* June 15, 1930

¹For Tom Heflin see WA 330:N 3.
²John Jakob Raskob, American industrialist who resigned his executive position with General Motors Corporation in 1928 to serve as Democratic national chairman for Al Smith's presidential campaign. Heflin opposed Smith and Raskob in 1928.

391   OM; published: *TDW,* June 22, 1930

¹*The Green Pastures,* a Pulitzer prize winning play by Marcus Cook Connelly, was first produced in 1930. It is based on Roark Bradford's *Ol' Man Adam an' His Chillun* (1928).

392   OM; published: *TDW,* June 29, 1930

¹Jack Sharkey, American prizefighter who held the world heavyweight title from 1932 to 1933.
Schmeling (see WA 346:N 1) won the heavyweight championship on a foul by Sharkey in the fourth round of a scheduled fifteen-round bout in New York City on June 12, 1930.

393   OM; published: *TDW,* July 6, 1930

394   OM; published: *TDW,* July 13, 1930

¹Henrik Shipstead, United States senator from Minnesota from 1923 to 1947. Originally elected to the Senate as a Farmer-Laborite, Shipstead later switched to the Republican party.
²For Charles H. Mayo see WA 347:N 3. He was married to the former Edith Graham.

³For the story of Mussolini and the castor oil see Rogers' *Letters of a Self-Made Diplomat to His President.*

395   OM; published: *TDW*, July 20, 1930

¹For John D. Rockefeller, Sr., see WA 351:N 5.
²For the Prince of Wales see WA 336:N 8.
³For John D. Rockefeller, Jr., see WA 358:N 3.
⁴For J. Ramsay MacDonald see WA 344:N 2.

396   OM; published: *TDW*, July 27, 1930

¹For Joseph R. Grundy see WA 332:N 3.
²For "Amos 'n Andy" see WA 386:N 1.
³For Hiram W. Johnson see WA 360:N 3.
⁴For David A. Reed see WA 348:N 1.

397   OM; published: *TDW*, August 3, 1930

¹For "Amos 'n Andy" see WA 386:N 1.
²Phineas Taylor Barnum, American showman who was a cofounder in 1881 of the famous Barnum and Bailey Circus.

398   OM; published: *TDW*, August 10, 1930

¹May Josephine "Polly" Lauder, debutante heiress of Greenwich, Connecticut, who married boxer Gene Tunney (see WA 338:N 2) in Rome, Italy, on October 3, 1928.
   Harry Lauder, popular Scottish singer and songwriter who was knighted in 1919 for entertaining troops during World War I.
²William Harrison "Jack" Dempsey, American boxer who held the world heavyweight title from 1919 until he lost the crown to Tunney in 1926.
³Enrico Caruso, Italian operatic star who was the leading tenor of the Metropolitan Opera in New York City from 1903 to 1920. After his death in 1921, his many recordings perpetuated his fame. His wife was the former Dorothy Park Benjamin, daughter of a prominent New York City patent attorney.
⁴Richard Evelyn Byrd, American naval officer and explorer, renowned for his expeditions to the North and South Poles in the 1920s and 1930s.

399   OM; published: *TDW*, August 17, 1930

¹Henry Justin Allen, Republican United States senator from Kansas from 1920 to 1930. A newspaper publisher and former governor, Allen was appointed to the Senate in 1929 to fill a vacancy. He handily won the Republican senatorial primary in 1930 but lost the general election.
²William Allen White, owner and editor of the *Emporia* (Kansas) *Gazette* from 1895 until his death in 1943; Republican politician; recipient of a Pulitzer prize in 1923. Rogers often interchanged the middle names of White and fellow publisher William Randolph Hearst (see WA 334:N 6).
³Horace A. Mann, Republican politician and one of the managers of Hoover's campaign in the South in 1928; founder of an anti-administration organization of southern Republicans.
⁴Coolidge was asked in January of 1930 to write a 500-word history of the United States to be inscribed on Mount Rushmore. He wrote a text, but the sculptor of the project disliked it and asked him to contribute another version. Coolidge's death in 1933 left the work unfinished.
⁵Gutzon Borglum, American sculptor who supervised the work at the Mount Rushmore National Memorial in South Dakota and designed and did much of the labor on the Confederate memorial at Stone Mountain, Georgia.
   Octavus Roy Cohen, American fiction writer, noted as the author of a series of Negro stories set in his native South.
   William David Upshaw, Democratic United States representative from Georgia from 1919 to 1927; leading prohibitionist and religious fundamentalist.

⁶For Joseph R. Grundy see WA 332:N 3; for David A. Reed see WA 348:N 1.
Henry Cabot Lodge, leading Republican figure; United States senator from Massachusetts from 1893 until his death in 1924.
For William S. Vare see WA 365:N 3.
⁷William John Bulow, Democratic governor of South Dakota from 1927 to 1931.
⁸For Aimee Semple McPherson see WA 344:N 6.

400   OM; published: *TDW*, August 24, 1930

¹A miniature golf craze swept the country in the early 1930s.
²Adolph Simon Ochs, publisher of the *New York Times* from 1896 until his death in 1935; publisher of the *Chattanooga Times* from 1878 until his death.
³Clarence Saunders, Memphis grocer who revolutionized the industry with the Piggly Wiggly supermarkets. After losing control of the stores in 1924, Saunders established another grocery chain known as "Clarence Saunders, Sole Owner of My Name."
⁴Clement Calhoun Young, Republican governor of California from 1927 to 1931.
⁵Clara Bow, vivacious American motion picture actress who symbolized the flapper age and the "the roaring 20s" as the "It" girl of the decade. Bow personified playful feminine allure.
⁶The Barrymores—John (see WA 337:N 1), Lionel, and Ethel—comprised one of the most famous and successful family of actors in the United States.

401   OM; published: *TDW*, August 31, 1930

¹Frank Bacon, American actor and playwright; co-author of *Lightnin'*, which had a long, uninterrupted theatrical run in New York City from 1918 to 1921.
²Fred Andrew Stone, well known American stage and screen actor. In 1903 he created the Scarecrow role in the theatrical production of the *Wizard of Oz*. Stone was one of Rogers' dearest friends.
³Mark Twain, pen name of Samuel Langhorne Clemens, American author and humorist. Twain resided in Carson City in 1861 and in Virginia City in 1862, during which time he prospected for gold and silver and wrote for a local newspaper.
⁴James John "Gentleman Jim" Corbett, American boxer who held the world heavyweight title from 1892 to 1897. One of the first of the modern-day scientific boxers, Corbett retired from the ring in 1903. He later appeared on the stage, in motion pictures, and on radio.
Robert Prometheus "Bob" Fitzsimmons, English-born prizefighter who won the world heavyweight championship from Corbett in a famous bout at Carson City, Nevada, on March 17, 1897. He lost the title two years later.

402   OM; published: *TDW*, September 7, 1930

¹Alford Joseph "Al" Williams, Jr., research pilot with the United States Navy from 1917 to 1930; holder of several air records and aviation awards.
James Harold "Jimmy" Doolittle, American flier noted for his speed marks set in the 1920s and 1930s, his interest in commercial aviation, and his later heroism during World War II.
²Minnie Pearce "Ma" Kennedy, evangelist and mother of Aimee Semple McPherson (see WA 344:N 6); credited with much influence in the development of her daughter's early career. On August 18, 1930, Kennedy appeared at a Los Angeles health center with a broken nose. The press reported that McPherson had inflicted the injury during a fight with her mother a few days earlier.
³For James Cannon, Jr., see WA 335:N 15.
⁴Miriam Amanda Wallace "Ma" Ferguson, Democratic governor of Texas from 1925 to 1927 and 1933 to 1935.
⁵Ross S. Sterling, Texas oilman and newspaper publisher who was elected governor of Texas in 1930. A Democrat, Sterling served as governor from 1931 to 1933.
⁶Charles John Wrightsman, Tulsa lawyer, oilman, and Democratic politician.
⁷Thomas Pryor Gore, Democratic United States senator from Oklahoma from 1907 to 1921 and 1931 to 1937.

403   OM; published: *TDW*, September 14, 1930

[1] Two Frenchmen, Dieudonne Coste and J. Maurice Bellonte, completed the first nonstop flight from Paris to New York City on September 3, 1930. For Charles A. Lindbergh see WA 338:N 1.
[2] For Anne Morrow Lindbergh see WA 338:N 1.
[3] Grover Aloysius Whalen, New York City merchant and civic leader; police commissioner from 1928 to 1930; long-time official "greeter" for the city.
[4] For William Randolph Hearst see WA 334:N 6.
[5] For Flo Ziegfeld see WA 336:N 3.
[6] Ibrahim Ibni Almarhum Abu Bakar, sultan of Jahore from 1895 until his death in 1959. Sir Ibrahim, who ruled his rubber-rich southern Malaya state with the aid of British advisers, was one of the wealthiest men in the Far East.
[7] For Jimmy Walker see WA 351:N 4.

404   OM; published: *TDW*, September 21, 1930

[1] Herbert Fleishhacker, California lumberman, utilities magnate, banker, and philanthropist. His eldest son, Herbert Fleishhacker, Jr., played football at Stanford University from 1927 to 1929.
[2] Ella J. Waters Knight, wife of William Henry Knight, a San Francisco cartographer, astronomer, and publisher who played a leading role in the naming of Lake Tahoe.
[3] Anita M. Baldwin, heiress to the estate of Elias Johnson "Lucky" Baldwin, early-day San Francisco mining stock and land speculator.
[4] George Arthur Bartlett, Democratic United States representative from Nevada from 1907 to 1911; district court judge at Reno, Nevada, from 1918 to 1931.

405   OM; published: *TDW*, September 28, 1930

[1] Harry Carr, widely read reporter and columnist for the *Los Angeles Times* from 1897 until his death in 1936.
[2] Henry King, American motion picture director, noted especially for his sentimental, nostalgic American period films; active as a director from 1915 to 1961.
[3] John Augustus Sutter, nineteenth century California trader who founded a colony on the site of modern-day Sacramento. Gold was discovered on his property in 1848, and in the subsequent "rush" he lost his land to squatters.
[4] Francis Brett "Bret" Harte, American writer of humorous short stories. In 1868 Harte cofounded the *Overland Monthly,* a literary magazine which he published in his adopted California and in which appeared the first of his renowned stories of local color, "The Luck of Roaring Camp."

406   OM; published: *TDW*, October 5, 1930

[1] For Arthur Brisbane see WA 334:N 5.
[2] Alexander Feodorovich Kerensky, Russian revolutionary leader who served briefly in 1917 as prime minister in the first revolutionary government; overthrown in November of 1917 by the Bolsheviks.
[3] Marc Klaw, American theatrical producer, active from 1881 until his death in 1936.
    Abraham Lincoln Erlanger, American vaudeville and theatrical producer; former partner of Klaw.
    Daniel and Charles Frohman, American theatrical producers and managers. Charles, the younger of the two brothers, became known as "the Napoleon of the Drama." He lost his life when the *Lusitania* sank in 1915.
    William Aloysius Brady, American theatrical and motion picture producer and talent manager; sports promoter.
[4] For Joseph R. Grundy see WA 332:N 3; for Scarface Al Capone see WA 336:N 9; for Tom Heflin see WA 330:N 3; for Aimee Semple McPherson see WA 344:N 6.

407   OM; published: *TDW*, October 12, 1930

[1] Karl Benz, German engineer and pioneer in the construction of motor-driven vehicles; founder of the automotive firm of Benz & Company.

²Marcus Allen Coolidge, Massachusetts manufacturer and Democratic politician; United States senator from 1931 to 1937. He was not related to President Calvin Coolidge.
³William Morgan Butler, Massachusetts lawyer, textiles manufacturer, Republican politician, and former United States senator.
⁴For Dwight W. Morrow see WA 325:N 8 and WA 389:N 8.

408   OM; published: *TDW*, October 19, 1930

¹Adolf Hitler, chancellor and Fuehrer of Germany from 1933 until his death in 1945. By 1930 Hitler's National Socialist (Nazi) party had grown sufficiently to raise a serious challenge to the established German government.

409   OM; published: *TDW*, October 26, 1930

¹The Ashton brothers—James Hay, Robert R., Geoffrey, and Phillip—comprised one of the most famous polo teams in Australian sports history. Their father, James Ashton, a Sydney businessman, and their mother, Helen Willis Ashton, accompanied the brothers on their tour of the United States in 1930.
²Charles Bierer "Charley" Wrightsman, California sportsman and oil producer; son of Charles J. Wrightsman (see WA 402:N 6).
   Eric L. Pedley, champion California polo player and one of the top American polo players in the history of the sport. Pedley and Wrightsman often competed with Rogers at sports clubs in the Los Angeles area.
³Stephen "Laddie" Sandford, New York City sportsman who owned one of the most important racing and polo stables in the country; sponsor of the famous Hurricane polo team.
⁴Lewis L. Lacey, Anglo-Argentine polo player who represented both England and Argentina in international competition. The Argentine team that he took to London in 1922 went unbeaten and later won the United States championship.
⁵John Hay "Jock" Whitney, American banking and mining heir and sportsman; owner of Greentree, a leading stable of racing and polo horses.
⁶For Babe Ruth see WA 332:N 4.
   Thomas "Tommy" Hitchcock, Jr., American polo player; foremost polo player of all time. He first gained international stardom in 1921 and remained outstanding for almost two decades thereafter. He was killed in World War II.
⁷For Arthur Brisbane see WA 334:N 5.
   Seward Carey, businessman from Buffalo, New York, and a member of the famous Meadowbrook Polo Club on Long Island.

410   OM; published: *TDW*, November 2, 1930

¹Alfred E. Packer, legendary "man-eater"; only man convicted of cannibalism in the United States (1883).
²N. E. Guyot, pioneer western prospector.
³Melville B. Gerry, early-day judge in territorial Colorado.

411   *TDW*, November 9, 1930

¹For George Bernard Shaw see WA 338:N 2.
²Boris III, king of Bulgaria from 1918 until his death in 1943. King Boris married Princess Giovanna, daughter of King Emmanuel III of Italy, on October 25, 1930.
³Franklin Delano Roosevelt, Democratic governor of New York from 1929 to 1933; president of the United States from 1933 until his death in 1945.
⁴For P. T. Barnum see WA 397:N 2.
   Karl Hagenbeck, German animal trainer and circus director, renowned for exhibitions of "wild" animals. After the death of Hagenbeck in 1913, his son, Karl Lorenz Hagenbeck, carried on the family profession until his death in 1948.

412   OM; published: *TDW*, November 16, 1930

¹James Hamilton "Ham" Lewis, Democratic United States senator from Illinois from 1913 to 1919 and 1931 until his death in 1939; noted for his tonsorial splendor.

²For Emily Post see WA 330:N 5.
³For Clara Bow see WA 400:N 5.
⁴Ruth Hanna McCormick, Republican United States representative from Illinois from 1929 to 1931. McCormick, who failed in 1930 in a bid for a Senate seat, was the daughter of Ohio industrialist and politician Marcus Alonzo "Mark" Hanna and the widow of publisher and congressman Joseph Medill McCormick.
⁵For Thomas P. Gore see WA 402:N 7.
⁶Bulow (see WA 399:N 7) was elected to the United States Senate in 1930. He served from 1931 to 1943.
⁷For Pat Harrison see WA 350:N 6; for Joe Robinson see WA 368:N 1.
⁸For Franklin D. Roosevelt see WA 411:N 3.

413   *TDW*, November 23, 1930

¹For this and all further references to Adolf Hitler see WA 408:N 1.
²For George Bernard Shaw see WA 338:N 2; for Albert Einstein see WA 327:N 1.
³Mary Garden, Scottish-born operatic soprano who made her American debut in *Thais* in 1907. She appeared with the Chicago Civic Opera Company from 1910 until her retirement.
⁴Gene Alexander Howe, editor of the *Amarillo* (Texas) *News-Globe* from 1924 to 1935; writer of a popular column under the pseudonym of "Old Tack."

414   OM; published: *TDW*, November 30, 1930

¹For Albert Einstein see WA 327:N 1.
²For George W. Wickersham see WA 344:N 1.

415   OM; published: *TDW*, December 7, 1930

¹For William E. Borah see WA 337:N 8.
²Genga Singh, Indian maharaja, soldier, and sportsman; maharaja of the Bikaner state from 1887 until his death in 1943.
³Mohandas Karamchand Gandhi, Indian political and spiritual leader known as the Mahatma, or Great Soul; principal leader of the Indian struggle for independence from Great Britain, a goal finally attained in 1947.
⁴For James Cannon, Jr., see WA 335:N 15.
⁵William Harrison "Will" Hays, president of the Motion Picture Producers and Distributors of America from 1922 to 1945; known as the "czar" of the motion picture industry.
⁶William Jennings Bryan, prominent Democratic politician, known as the "Great Commoner"; thrice unsuccessful Democratic candidate for the presidency; United States secretary of state from 1913 to 1915. Bryan died in 1925.

416   OM; published: *TDW*, December 14, 1930

417   OM; published: *TDW*, December 21, 1930

¹For Knute K. Rockne see WA 364:N 2.
²Lawrence "Moon" Mullins, star fullback for the Notre Dame University football team from 1928 to 1930.
³Daniel "Dan" Hanley, third-string fullback for Notre Dame University in 1930.
⁴Paul "Bucky" O'Connor, halfback for the Fighting Irish from 1928 to 1930. In a game against the University of Southern California on December 6, 1930, Rockne inserted speedy O'Connor at fullback to replace the injured Moon Mullins and the inexperienced Hanley. In order to mislead USC, however, Rockne directed Hanley and O'Connor to exchange jerseys.
⁵For P. T. Barnum see WA 397:N 2.
⁶For Kaiser Wilhelm I see WA 363:N 1.

418   *TDW*, December 28, 1930

¹For Primo de Rivera see WA 339:N 5.
²For King Alfonso XIII see WA 369:N 3.

419   *TDW,* January 4, 1931

420   *TDW,* January 11, 1931

¹For George W. Wickersham see WA 344:N 1.
²Kenneth Douglas McKellar, Democratic United States senator from 1917 to 1953.
³Bernard Mannes Baruch, American businessman, statesman, and Democratic political adviser and financial contributor; confidant of several presidents.

421   *TDW,* January 18, 1931

¹Five hundred farmers marched through the business district of England, Arkansas, on January 3, 1931, demanding food for their drought-stricken families. Two days later, the Senate voted to add $15 million to a $45 million drought relief bill passed earlier by the House. The House, however, later refused to approve the added expenditure.
²For John D. Rockefeller, Sr., see WA 351:N 5.

422   McN; published: *TDW,* January 25, 1931

¹For Tom Heflin see WA 330:N 3.
Samuel Pepys, official in the English naval department and noted diarist. His diary, penned between 1660 and 1669, was written in a unique system of shorthand, complicated with foreign words and invented ciphers.
²Luther Burbank, American horticulturist who first took up market gardening in 1868 and who developed the Burbank potato and new and improved varieties of other cultivated plants.
James J. "Jim" Jeffries, American prizefighter who held the world heavyweight title from 1899 until his retirement in 1905. One of the strongest men ever to enter the ring, Jeffries later became a successful businessman, operating a commercial farm at Burbank, California.
³For Amon G. Carter, see WA 343:N 1.
⁴For Sallie Rogers McSpadden see WA 354:N 3.
Lucia Eaton, grandniece of Will Rogers and granddaughter of his sister, Sallie.
⁵Frank McKinney "Kin" Hubbard, American caricaturist and humorist on the staff of the *Indianapolis* (Indiana) *News* almost continuously from 1891 until his death on December 26, 1930. Hubbard created the colorful cartoon character "Abe Martin."
⁶For Clara Bow see WA 400:N 5.
Carrie Lane Chapman Catt, American suffrage leader and lecturer who was prominent in the campaign resulting in the adoption of the Nineteenth Amendment to the United States Constitution.

423   McN; published: *TDW,* February 1, 1931

¹For Nicholas Longworth see WA 335:N 9.
²For Jack Garner see WA 389:N 10.
³John Quillen Tilson, Republican United States representative from 1909 to 1913 and 1915 to 1932; majority leader in Congress from 1925 to 1931.
⁴For Joe Robinson see WA 368:N 1.
⁵George Higgins Moses, Republican United States senator from New Hampshire form 1918 to 1933; president pro tempore of the Senate from 1925 to 1933.
⁶For Frederick H. Gillett see WA 332:N 2.
⁷Thaddeus Horatio Caraway, Democratic United States senator from Arkansas from 1921 until his death in 1931.
⁸For Tom Heflin see WA 330:N 3.

424   McN; published: *TDW,* February 8, 1931

¹Smith served as president of the corporate enterprise that built the Empire State Building, which when it was completed in 1931 became the tallest building in the world.
²Jesse Holman Jones, Houston lumberman, oilman, land developer, newspaper publisher, civic leader, and Democratic party booster; chairman of the Reconstruction Finance Corporation from 1933 to 1939.

³Edward Green "Ned" Harrigan, American theatrical writer, producer, and actor.

Anthony "Tony" Hart, American theatrical entertainer of the nineteenth century, renowned as a member of the famous performing team of Harrigan and Hart. The duo debuted *The Mulligan Guards* in 1873.

425   McN; published: *TDW*, February 15, 1931

¹For Ross S. Sterling see WA 402:N 5.
²Daniel James "Dan" Moody, Jr., Democratic governor of Texas from 1927 to 1931.
³James Edward "Jim" Ferguson, Democratic governor of Texas from 1915 to 1917 who was impeached for several reasons, including misappropriation of state funds. He attempted to run for governor again in 1924, but a court ruled that he could not be a candidate, whereupon his wife, Miriam "Ma" Ferguson (see WA 402:N 4), entered the race and won.
⁴For Bobby Cantwell see WA 354:N 4.
Francis Monroe "Frank" Hawks, American aviator who established numerous transcontinental and point-to-point speed records in the 1920s and 1930s.
⁵David Sinton Ingalls, United States assistant secretary of the navy for aeronautics from 1929 to 1932; Republican politician from Ohio.
⁶James Charles "Jimmie" Rodgers, popular American recording artist of the 1920s and 1930s who became known as the "Father of Country Music." Many of the 111 songs which Rodgers recorded featured yodeling.
Chester Byers, world champion roper and rodeo performer from Oklahoma. Rogers gave Byers some of his first lessons in roping.
The Revelers Quartet, one of the first "precision" singing groups on radio, featured James Melton and Lewis L. James as tenors, Elliott Shaw as baritone, and Wilfred Glenn as bass.

426   McN; published: *TDW*, February 22, 1931

¹For Frank Hawks see WA 425:N 4.
²For David S. Ingalls see WA 425:N 5.
³William Henry "Alfalfa Bill" Murray, Democratic governor of Oklahoma from 1931 to 1935.
⁴Clement Vann "Clem" Rogers, Indian Territory rancher, banker, and Cherokee tribal leader; father of Will Rogers. Murray and Clem Rogers served as delegates to the Oklahoma constitutional convention of 1907.
⁵For the Revelers Quartet see WA 425:N 6.
⁶Rogers probably referred to Roy M. Johnson, pioneer oil producer in southern Oklahoma and former newspaper publisher at Ardmore. Johnson was one of the primary benefactors at Rogers' benefit performance in Ardmore.
For Jimmy Rodgers and Chester Byers see WA 425:N 6.
⁷Geronimo, Apache war leader who directed his fellow tribesmen in an extended campaign against white settlers and soldiers in the Southwest in the 1880s. He finally capitulated and settled with other members of his tribe as farmers and stock raisers at Fort Sill, Oklahoma, where he died in 1909.
⁸Maurice Rogers McSpadden, nephew of Will Rogers and son of Rogers' sister, Sallie Rogers McSpadden; graduate of Oklahoma Agricultural and Mechanical College (later renamed Oklahoma State University).
⁹Warren Lale Blizzard, American educator and agricultural specialist; head of the department of animal husbandry at Oklahoma Agricultural and Mechanical College from 1920 to 1939; later, dean of agriculture.
¹⁰For E. W. Marland see WA 384:N 2.
¹¹Lasca Gazelle Lane Luckett, niece of Will Rogers and daughter of one of his sisters, Maud Rogers Lane.

427   *TDW*, March 1, 1931

¹For Frank Hawks see WA 425:N 4.
²For George W. Wickersham see WA 344:N 1.
³For John D. Rockefeller, Sr., see WA 351:N 5.
⁴For William E. Borah see WA 337:N 8.
⁵For Charles M. Schwab see WA 358:N 2.

INDEX

"Abe Martin" (cartoon): 230
Abie's Irish Rose (play): 73
Abilene, Texas: 228, 236
Actors and actresses: 73, 75, 81, 83, 233
Ada, Okla.: 239
Adair, William Penn: 24
Adams, Charles Francis: 19
Adams, Frances L.: 119
Adams, John: 19
Adams, John Quincy: 19
Advertising: 80, 153
Afghanistan: 26
Africa: 11, 120, 200
Agriculture: 91; *see also* Farmers
Alabama: 21, 155-57; election in, 231-32
Alabama, University of: 215
Albany, N. Y.: 234
Albuquerque, N. M.: 72, 240
Alexander, _____: 103
Alexander the Great: 192
Alfonso XIII, king of Spain: 106, 217
Allen, Henry J.: 175
Amarillo, Texas: 72, 208
American Civil War: 85
American Magazine: 41, 111
American Mercury (magazine): 24
American Revolution: 16, 65, 121
"Amos 'n Andy" (radio show): 146-48, 169, 171
Andreu Almazan, Juan: 3
Andrews, Jess C.: 130
Anne of Cleves: 32
Anthony, Earle C.: 107
Anti-Saloon League: 118, 159
Apache Indians: 125
Apartments: 164
Appian Way: 112
Aquitania, S. S.: 113
Ardmore, Okla.: 238
Argentina: 69, 200, 207
Arizona: 71, 125, 126, 144, 195, 201, 216
Arkansas: 69, 87, 120, 201, 202, 206, 224, 225, 231, 237
Armenia: 131
Armour, Philip D.: 24
Arnold, Benedict: 150
Art: 126, 176
Arthur, prince of Wales: 28, 29
Arctic, aero-exploration of: 13
Ashton, Geoffrey: 199
Ashton, James H.: 199
Ashton, Phillip: 199
Ashton, Robert R.: 199
Astor, Nancy L.: 49, 61; home of, 115-18

Astor, Waldorf: home of, 115-18
Atheists: 95
Athletes, in colleges: 238
Atlanta, Ga.: 176
Atlanta Constitution: 176
Aurora, Ill.: 9
Austin, Texas: 234, 235
Australia: 91, 119, 199, 200
Austria: 196
Automobiles: 177, 178, 193; Ford models, 17, 53, 145, 169; dealers in used, 66; compared to aviation, 72; manufacturers of, 81; Studebaker models, 94; Buick models, 101, 127; Cord models, 101; Cadillac models, 127; accidents involving, 134, 206, 207; Chevrolet models, 170; exhibits of, 183; credit purchases of, 221
Aviation: 54, 71, 72, 86, 101, 120, 185, 227-28, 230, 235, 240-41; in U.S., 44; endurance flights, 45-47; accidents, 71; and war, 103-104; exhibit in Chicago, 183; exhibit in England, 183

Babson, Roger W.: 82-83
Bacon, Frank: 179
Baker, Bryant: 140
Baldwin, Anita M.: 187-88
Baldwin, Elias J. (Lucky): 187
Balkans: 196
Banks and bankers: 91, 107, 162
Banning, Calif.: 228
Barnum, P. T.: 171, 216; circus of, 204
Barrymore, John: 30, 179
Bartlett, George A.: 188
Baruch, Bernard M.: 223-24
Baseball: 8, 25, 75, 197; World Series of 1929, 78-79
Beach, Rex E.: 59
Bears, at Yosemite National Park: 181
Beaumont, Texas: 236
Belgium: 19, 38
Benedictines: 15
Benz, Karl: 193
Berkowitz, A.: 155, 157
Berlin, Germany: 193
Beverly Hills, Calif.: 46, 102, 130, 140, 161
Bible: 92, 157-59
"Big business": 124, 127-29, 147-48, 162, 163
Big Spring, Texas: 228
Bingham, Hiram: 86
Birmingham (Ala.) *Age-Herald:* 155
Birth control: 7, 18, 208

266

Black Hills, S. D.: 47
Blinn, Holbrook: 5
Blizzard, Warren L.: 239
Blythe, Samuel G.: 24
Bodie, Calif.: 189
Boer War: 200
Boleyn, Anne: 30-33
Boleyn, Mary: 30-31
Booth, Albert J., Jr.: 95
Bootlegging and bootleggers: 79, 84, 104, 127, 133, 134, 162-63, 173, 191
Borah, William E.: 31, 62, 63, 124, 241
Borglum, Gutzon: 176
Boris III, king of Belgium: 203, 204
Boston, Mass.: 4, 11, 17, 19, 20, 21, 104, 123, 159, 161, 201
Boston Tea Party: 8
Boulder Dam: 58, 65
Bow, Clara: 178, 205, 230
Boxing: 41, 159-61, 182
Brady, William A.: 192
Bratton, Sam G.: 132-33
Brazil: 126, 207
Breckenridge, Texas: 236
Bremen, S. S.: 108
Briand, Aristide: 49
Briggs, Walter O.: 81
Brisbane, Arthur: 24, 191-93, 200
Brockton, Mass.: 18
Brookhart, Smith W.: 27, 86
Brooklyn Bridge: 233
Broussard, Edwin S.: 132
Brown County, Ind.: 178
Browning, Francis H. (Peaches): 55
Brutus: 111, 112
Bryan, William Jennings: 212
Buckingham Palace: 106, 118, 153
Buenos Aires, Argentina: 200
Bulgaria: 196, 203
Bullfighting: 1-2, 97, 211
Bulow, William J.: 177, 205-206
"Bumming": 72
Burbank, Calif.: 227, 228
Burbank, Luther: 227
Burke, Martha J. (Calamity Jane): 64
Burr, Aaron: 24
Burroughs, John: 80
Business: 77, 151; mergers in, 127-28; *see also* "Big business"
Businessmen: 96, 97, 135
Butler, Nicholas Murray: 94
Butler, Smedley D.: 25
Butler, William M.: 194
Byers, Chester: 236, 238
Byrd, Richard E.: 174

Cagle, Christian K. (Red): 95, 148-50
Calamity Jane: *see* Burke, Martha J.
Calipatria, Calif.: 92-93
Calaveras County, Calif.: 190
California: 34, 45, 49, 71, 72, 85, 91-93, 96, 97, 106, 107, 133, 178, 179, 182, 186, 188, 189, 190, 227, 228, 240; historians of, 92; climate in, 168-69; newspapers in, 168-69
Calles, Plutarco E.: 1, 3, 6
Cambridge University: 217
Canada: 117, 163
Cannibals and cannibalism: 11, 189, 201-202
Cannon, James, Jr.: 27, 85, 184, 212
Cantor, Eddie: 83-85
Cantwell, Robert W. (Bobby): 72, 236
Capital: 65
Capitalism: 223
Capone, Alphonse (Scarface Al): 28, 129-30, 147, 193
Capper, Arthur: 60
Caraway, Thaddeus H.: 231
Carey, Seward: 200
Carey, William: 30-31
Carr, Harry: 189, 190
Carranza, Venustiano: 5
Carson City, Nev.: 182, 186, 187
Carter, Amon G.: 45, 228
Carthage, ancient: 192, 193
Caruso, Dorothy P. B.: 174
Caruso, Enrico: 174
Castor oil: 165-66
Catherine of Aragon: 29-30, 31-32
Catt, Carrie Chapman: 230
Cattle: 66, 72
Cattlemen: 235
Caviar: 171
Censorship: 158
Census: 133; of 1930, 164
Central America: 54
Chain stores: 127-29
Chambers of commerce: 92, 93, 126, 165, 240
Chaplin, Charles S. (Charlie): 34, 154
Chapultepec Castle: 5
Charity: 81, 166, 167, 173, 224, 226, 228, 233, 234
Charles VIII, king of France: 38
Chattanooga, Tenn.: 177
Chelsea, Okla.: 67, 71, 142, 228
Cherokee Indians: 57, 67, 142-43
Cherokee Nation: 68
Cherokee Strip: 142-43
Chewing gum: 84, 136
Chiang Kai-shek: 53
Chicago, Ill.: 13, 17, 24, 26, 53, 64, 101, 128, 159, 165, 183, 207, 216, 220, 230; crime in, 129, 161-64
Chicago Cubs (baseball): 78, 79
Chickasha, Okla.: 238
Children, maturity of: 100
Chile, embassy of: 15
China: 25, 48-49, 52-54, 125-26; American relations with, 52; Japanese relations with, 52; British relations with, 53
Chocolate: 93
Christians, early: 111
Christmas: 100-102, 222-23

267

Chrysler, Walter P.: 81
Church of England: 31
Cimarron, N. M.: 72
Circus business: 107
Cities: 165, 218
Civil engineers: 69
Civilization: 101, 126, 129, 179
Claremore, Okla.: 23, 34, 57, 113, 142
Clemens, Samuel L.: 182, 190
Clement VII, pope: 31
Cleopatra: 93, 192
Clergymen: 92, 128, 133-34, 158, 212
Cleveland, Ohio: 45
Coffeyville, Kans.: 11
Cohen, Octavus Roy: 176
Colleges and universities: 150; education at, 69; presidents of, 69; athletes at, 238
Colorado: 201, 202
Columbia University: 215
Columbus, Christopher: 29, 57, 126
Columbus, Ohio: 230
Comedians: 72, 84-85, 154, 230
Communists: 223
Concord, Mass.: 16, 17
Conferences, international: 134, 170, 210-12, 213
Confidence: restoring of, 89-91, 95-96; in public officials, 130
Confucius: 52
Congressional Record: 22, 176
Connecticut: 154
Contests: 71
Coogan, Jackie: 57
Cook, Frederick A.: 13
Coolidge, Calvin: 1, 4, 6, 11, 14, 16, 20, 23, 26, 38, 40, 41, 42, 51, 57, 59, 60, 63, 67, 80, 93, 94, 96, 106, 122, 124-25, 129, 131, 137-40, 144, 145, 149, 166-67, 172, 175-76, 177, 178, 194, 208, 212, 225, 233, 235, 241
Coolidge, Grace A. G.: 58-60, 122, 123-24
Coolidge, Marcus A.: 194
Copeland, Royal S.: 132
Corbett, James J. (Gentleman Jim): 182
Corruption: 204
Cosmetics: 76
Cosmopolitan (magazine): 41
Cotton: 93
Court of Saint James: 24, 29, 120, 153-54
Couzens, James: 24
Coventry, England: 170
Cradle of the Deep (book): 21-22, 27
Credit, buying and selling on: 112-13, 220-21
Crime: 129-30, 206-207, 208; in Chicago, 161-64
Cromwell, Thomas: 32, 33, 115-16, 209
Cuba, sugar from: 55
Culpepper, Thomas: 33
Cults: 91
Culture: 126

Culver, Harry H.: 45
Culver City, Calif.: 45, 46
Curtis, Charles: 15

Dallas, Texas: 45, 228, 236
Dams: 124-25, 126, 129
Dancing: 100
Davies, Marion: 28
Davis, Jefferson: 176
Dawes, Carol D. B.: 85, 119, 123
Dawes, Charles G.: 17, 29, 40, 62, 85, 102, 118-19, 120, 121-22, 123, 153, 154
Dawes, William: 17
Dayton, Ohio: 25
Daytona Beach, Fla.: 167
Dead Sea: 92
Dearborn, Mich.: 80
Debts: 112, 223-24
Debutantes: 120-22; at Court of St. James, 153-54
Democracy: 121, 137, 218; in the South, 155-57
Democratic National Convention: of 1932, 13; of 1928, 69, 232-33
Democratic party and Democrats: 3, 11, 15, 25, 28, 31, 40, 49, 53, 56, 60, 61, 65-66, 68, 85, 86, 88, 89, 100, 111, 125, 127, 132, 138, 140, 148, 151, 153-54, 159, 165, 176, 184, 185, 186, 194, 195, 201, 202, 204, 205, 206, 212, 224, 230, 231, 232, 241
Dempsey, William H. (Jack): 173
Denmark: 38
Denver, Colo.: 202
Department of the Treasury, U. S.: 24, 58, 61, 66
De Priest, Jesse: 38
De Priest, Oscar S.: 64
Detroit, Mich.: 19, 49, 81
Dewey, George: 148
Diaz, Porfirio: 4, 5
Dictators: 106, 217
Diets: 55, 109
Diplomacy and diplomats: 61, 62, 121-22, 191, 196-97, 203
Disarmament: 4, 76, 78, 125-26, 154, 214; international conferences on, 19-20, 102-104, 108, 113-15, 118-20, 123, 126, 130, 134-35, 143-45, 167, 168, 169-70, 211, 213
Divorce: 75, 86, 121, 132, 155, 179; involving Henry VIII, 29-33, at Reno, Nev., 188
Dogs: 50
"Dole": 224, 225-26, 230-31
Doolittle, James H. (Jimmy): 183
Donner Party: 189, 201
Dorrance, Charlotte K.: 153
Douglas, Ariz.: 228
Drought: 175
Drumgoole School: 67-69

Duke, Doris: 153
Duluth, Minn.: 13
Duncan, Okla.: 238
Durant, Okla.: 239

Earhart, Amelia M.: 11
Earthquakes: 71
Eclipse, of the sun: 144
Economic depression: 197, 214, 220-26, 230, 241
Edison, Thomas A.: 79-82; son of, 82
Education: 39, 103, 150, 213-14
Edward Albert, prince of Wales: 28, 36, 61, 120, 121, 167; marriage of, 40
Edward VII, king of England: 28
Eighteenth Amendment: 6, 8, 64; *see also* Prohibition *and related topics*
Einstein, Albert: theory of, 6, 208; speech by, 209
Elections: 85, 186, 194, 201, 204-206; in Kentucky, 85; in New York City, 85; in Virginia, 85; of 1932, 130; presidential, 153-54, 175, 206; in New Jersey, 154; in Kansas, 175; in New York state, 204; in Illinois, 205; in Oklahoma, 205; in South Dakota, 206; in Alabama, 231-32
Electricity: 80
Eliot, Charles W.: 94
Elizabeth I, queen of England: 32
Elks clubs: 63
Elmer the Great (play): 75
El Paso, Texas: 3, 124, 228
Emerald Bay: 187
Empire State Building: 232, 233
England: 28, 29, 32, 52, 55, 64, 65, 76, 87, 104, 106, 114, 115, 117-22, 126, 130, 167, 170, 185, 197, 199, 203-204, 210-12, 218-19, 223; naval superiority of, 8-9, 61, 114, 118; reigning family of, 37; government of, 40, 61, 76, 219; prime minister of, 49; Chinese relations with, 53; aviation exhibit in, 183; customs in, 209
English Channel, swimming the: 121, 153
English language: 119
Enid, Okla.: 239
Equador: 9
Ericson, Leif: 126
Erlanger, Abraham L.: 192
Erskine, Albert R.: 81
Escobar, Jose G.: 1, 2, 3, 6
Etiquette: 205
Europe: 32, 40, 65, 96, 108, 136, 193, 195, 203
Evolution, theory of: 220
Executions, of Mexican rebels: 2, 4

Fairbanks, Douglas, Sr.: 144
Fallen Leaf Lake: 187

Farmer-Labor party: 164
Farmers: 77, 88, 131, 224, 225; governmental relief for, 4, 7, 16, 18, 21, 27, 35, 42, 47-48, 51, 62, 85, 88, 185, 186, 190, 195, 206, 212, 222; in Minnesota, 164; tenant, 230
Fashions: 170; changes in, 135-37
Fast Company (film): 75
Federal Farm Board: 225
Federal Reserve System: 14, 16, 24, 65, 77
"Felix, the Cat" (cartoon): 231
Ferdinand, king of Aragon: 29
Ferguson, James E. (Jim): 235
Ferguson, Miriam A. (Ma): 184, 235
Fess, Simeon D.: 27
Financiers: 82, 84, 163
Firestone, Harvey S.: 80
Fish, Hamilton, Jr.: 18
Fisher, Albert: 81
Fisher, Carl G.: 130
Fishing: 85
Fitchburg, Mass.: 194
Fitzsimmons, Robert P. (Bob): 182
Fleishhacker, Herbert: 187
Fleishhacker, Herbert, Jr.: 187
Fletcher, Duncan U.: 133
Florida: 6, 96, 107, 133
Flys: 65
Football: 51, 67-69, 94-95, 99, 101, 148-50, 207, 215-17, 219
Football stadiums: 68
Ford, Edsel B.: 80, 128; children of, 82
Ford, Henry: 64, 79, 80-82, 96, 103, 112, 127, 145, 147, 151, 174, 182, 193-94; reconstructs village, 81-82
"Fortnight," definition of: 209
Fort Reno: 72
Fort Sill: 238-39
Fort Worth, Texas: 45, 227, 228
Fox, William: 99
France: 9, 14, 24, 29, 31, 34, 38, 39, 40, 49, 64, 90, 114, 115, 124, 126, 134, 143, 165, 184, 185, 191, 196, 203, 208, 218
Frank, Glenn: 51, 94
Franklin, Benjamin: 23, 24; as ambassador, 24
Freedom: 210
French language: 119
Frohman, Charles: 192
Frohman, Daniel: 192
The Front Page (play): 22

Gambling: 88, 89-90
Gandhi, Mohandas K.: 212
Gann, Dolly C.: 27, 35
Garbo, Greta: 30
Garden, Mary: 208
Garner, John N. (Jack): 154, 230
Gasoline, price of: 225
Geneva, Switzerland: disarmament conference at, 19-20, 103, 108, 123

Geography: 69
George V, king of England: 28, 36, 106, 118, 119-20, 134, 153, 211
Georgia, University of: 215
Germany: 9, 32, 36, 38, 49, 52, 61, 185, 193, 196, 203-204, 207
Geronimo: 239
Gerry, Melville B.: 202
Gettysburg, Battle of: 73
Giannini, Attilio H.: 107
Giannini, Leontine D.: 107
Gibson, Hugh S.: 103
Gibson, Ynes R.: 119
Gilbert, John: 30
Gillett, Frederick H.: 18, 231
Glendale, Calif.: 228
Godiva, Lady: 170
Golf: 97-99, 167, 174, 228; players of, 98-99
Gomez, Arnulfo: 2
Gore, Thomas P.: 184, 205
Graft: 18, 66, 79, 112, 186
Grand Canyon: 44, 145
Grange, Harold E.(Red): 149
Grant, Ulysses S.: 45
Greece: 192, 193
Greeley, Horace: 24
The Green Pastures (play): 158
Greenville, S. C.: 143
Grey, Edward: 54
Grocery stores: 66
Grundy, Joseph R.: 18, 58, 62, 63, 77-78, 86-87, 88, 89, 97, 111, 132, 133, 138, 151, 169, 176, 193
Grunion fish: 169
Guadalupe County, N. M.: 240
Guinan, Mary L. C. (Texas): 14, 22, 27, 94
Guns: 129-30
Guyot, N. E.: 201, 202

Hackett, Francis: 28
Hackett, Thomas: 33
Hagenbeck, Karl: circus of, 204
Hamilton, Alexander: 24, 176
Hanley, Daniel (Dan): 216
Happiness: 145, 152
Hardin-Simmons University: 236
Harding, Warren G.: 38, 80
Hardy, Sam: 28
Harrigan, Edward G. (Ned): 233
Harrison, B. Patman (Pat): 62, 206
Hart, Anthony (Tony): 233
Harte, Francis B. (Bret): 190
Harvard University: 39, 148, 149, 150, 201, 202, 203, 215
Hawks, Francis M. (Frank): 236-37, 238, 239, 240-41
Hays, William H. (Will): 212
Hearst, William Randolph: 24, 185
Heflin, J. Thomas (Tom): 14, 18, 19, 21, 27, 28, 30, 62, 64, 155-57, 193, 227, 231-32

Helen of Troy: 121
Henry VIII, king of England: 21, 28-29, 30-33, 36, 38, 115
Herrick, Myron T.: 14
Hewitt, Robert P. (Bob): 25
Highway commissions, state: 112
History: 103, 104, 112, 114, 125, 126; of U. S., 176-77
Hitchcock, Thomas, Jr.: 200
Holbein, Hans (the Younger): 32
Holland: 126
Holloway, William J.: 142
Hollywood, Calif.: 28, 45, 72-74, 109, 170, 227
Hong Kong: 69
Honolulu, Hawaii: 22, 144
Hoover, Herbert C.: 1, 3, 20, 26, 27, 32, 35, 47-48, 51, 55, 56-57, 61, 62, 65, 66-67, 76, 77, 78, 79, 80, 81, 85-86, 88, 89, 91, 93-94, 95-96, 104, 106, 108-109, 123, 124, 125, 131-32, 135, 142, 144, 145, 147, 151, 157, 168, 169, 172, 175, 178, 184, 186, 209, 210, 219, 222, 223, 225, 233, 234, 235, 241; cabinet of, 79; speech by, 213
Hoover, Lou H. (Mrs. Herbert C.): 35, 39, 81
Hoovercrats: 155
Hopi Indians, Snake Dance of: 144-45
Horse racing: 50, 68
Horses: 197, 199, 200
Hotdogs: 66
Hot Springs, Ala.: 232
House of Commons, British: 117, 130
Houston, Texas: 25, 69, 233
Howard, Catherine: 33
Howe, Gene A. (Old Tack): 208
Hubbard, Frank M. (Kin): 230
Huerta, Adolfo de la: 5, 6
Huerta, Victoriano: 5
Hughes, Charles Evans: 63, 103
Hulbert, Slade: 46
Humanists: 143
Human race: 50-51
Hunger: 65, 212, 214, 224-25, 231, 241
Hurley, Patrick J. (Pat): 142
Hutchinson, Frances: 153

I'm Alone, sinking of: 9
Idaho: 87, 241
Idealism: 77
Idealists: 114
Ille de France, S. S.: 113
Illinois, election in: 205
Illiteracy: 203
Imperial Valley, Calif.: 91-93
Income, distribution of: 152, 214, 219, 226
Independence, Kans.: 11
India: 210-12
Indiana: 18, 178, 215, 230

Indianapolis, Ind.: 230
Indianapolis News: 230
Indians, American: 17, 34, 67, 69, 125, 126, 129, 142, 181, 187-88
Indian Territory: 11, 67
Ingalls, David S.: airplane of, 236, 237
Ingrid, princess of Sweden: 38
Insull, Samuel II: 24
Insurance and insurance companies: 14
Inventions: 80
Iowa: 27, 144
Irishmen: 95, 194
Irwin, Charles B. (Charlie): 66
Isabella I, queen of Castile: 28-29, 38
Italian-Americans: 190
Italy: 37, 114-15, 126, 134, 143, 154-55, 165, 196, 203, 210, 217; royal wedding in, 105-106

Jackson, Andrew: 165
Jackson, Thomas J. (Stonewall): 176
Jacksonville, Fla.: 35, 133
"Jamaica ginger": 128, 131, 139
James, Jesse W.: 215
Japan: 32, 48-49, 113, 114, 125-26, 143, 170; relations with China, 52; relations with Russia, 52
Japanese language: 119
Jefferson, Thomas: 57, 62, 65-66, 132, 176
Jefferson County, Ala.: 155
Jeffries, James J. (Jim): 227
Jersey City, N. J.: 22
Jerusalem: 145
Jews: 100
Johnson, Andrew: 165
Johnson, Hiram W.: 85-86, 169-70
Johnson, Martin E.: 11
Johnson, Roy M.: 238
Jones, Hilary P.: 102, 103
Jones, Jesse H.: 232-33
Jones, Robert T. (Bobby): 64, 99
Jones, Wesley L.: 10
Joyce, Peggy Hopkins: 30, 64
Juarez, Mexico: 3
Jubilo (film): 75
Julius Caesar: 111, 115, 227

Kahn, Otto H.: 81, 86
Kansas: 11, 71; election in, 175
Kansas City, Mo.: 69; Republican convention in, 51
Keeler, O. B. (Pop): 99
Kemper Military Academy: 23, 238
Kendrick, John B.: 66, 133
Kennedy, Minnie P. (Ma): 183-84
Kent, Elizabeth B.: 153
Kentucky, election in: 85
Kerensky, Alexander F.: 192
Kiawanis clubs: 63

King, Henry: 189
Kingman, Ariz.: 201
Klaw, Marc: 192
Knees: 136-37
Knight, Ella J.: 187
Knowledge: 145, 214
Kuhn, F. W.: 155
Ku Klux Klan: 63, 95

Labor: 76
Lacey, Lewis L.: 200
Lafayette, Ala.: 155-56
La Follette, Robert M., Jr.: 49, 51
La Guardia, Fiorello H.: 10
Lake City, Colo.: 201
Lake Tahoe: 179, 182, 183, 186, 189
Land, scarcity of: 134
Lardner, Ringgold W. (Ring): 75
Lasky, Jesse L., Sr.: 13
Lauder, Harry: 173
Lauder, May J. (Polly): 173-74
Lawton, Okla.: 238, 239
Lawyers: 63, 201, 202, 203
League of Nations: 4, 19; American relations with, 64
Lee, Robert E.: 148, 176
Legs, of women: 135-37
Leviathan, S. S.: 103
Lewis, J. Hamilton (Ham): 205
Lexington, Mass.: 17
Liberty: 205
Liberty Bell: 23
Liberty Hall, reproduction of: 82
Lightnin' (play): 179
Lightning: 71
Lillie, Gordon W. (Pawnee Bill): 142
Limon, Gilberto R.: 3
Lincoln, Abraham: 4, 24, 82, 112
Lincoln Highway: 112
Lindbergh, Anne Morrow S.: 45, 120, 185; marriage of, 33-34
Lindbergh, Charles A.: 39, 43-45, 56, 57, 120, 124, 185; marriage of, 33-34
Lindsey, Benjamin B.: 81
Linthicum, John C.: 18
Liquor: 15, 18, 86, 163
Literary Digest (magazine): 130
Literature: 126
Little, Clarence C.: 94
Liverpool, England: 53
Lobbying and lobbyists: 58, 59, 79, 80, 86-87, 88-89, 241
Lodge, Henry Cabot: 176
London, England: 115, 116, 117, 121, 122, 210-12; disarmament conference at, 102-104, 108, 113-15, 118-20, 123, 126, 130, 134-35, 143-45, 167, 168, 169-70, 213; fog in, 118, 119
Long, Andrew T.: 103
Long Island, N. Y.: 140, 192
Longworth, Alice Roosevelt: 24, 26-27, 35

Longworth, Nicholas: 27, 59, 230
Lookout Mountain, Tenn.: 177
Lord's Supper: 75
Lorimer, George H.: 24
Los Angeles, Calif.: 23, 45, 46, 53, 54, 57, 71, 72, 131, 145, 183, 189, 228, 240
Louisiana: 132, 149
Louis XVI, king of France: 191, 193
Lowell, Abbott L.: 94
Luckett, Lasca G. L.: 239
Ludlow, Louis L.: 18
Ludlow, Vt.: 41
Luncheon clubs: 93, 165
Luther, Martin: 32

McAdoo, William G., Jr.: 47
McAlester, Okla.: 239
McCormick, Ruth Hanna: 205
MacDonald, Ishbel: 76, 89
MacDonald, J. Ramsay: 49, 76, 78, 79, 119, 129, 130, 168
Macedonia: 192, 193
McGuffy, William H.: books by, 69
Mack, Connie: 78, 79
McKellar, Kenneth D.: 223
McLean, Edward B.: 26
McLean, Evalyn W. (Emily): 26
McLean, John R. (Jock): 26
McManus, A. E., Jr.: 47
McPherson, Aimee Semple: 49, 64, 78, 145, 177, 183-84, 193
McSpadden, Maurice R.: 239
McSpadden, Sallie C. Rogers: 71, 142, 228
Madero, Francisco I.: 5
Madison, Dolly: 24
Madison Square Garden: 142
Magazines: 137
Malibu, Calif.: 184
Manchuria: 53
Manila, Philippines: 148
Mann, Horace A.: 175
Man O' War (race horse): 51
Manufacturers Association of Pennsylvania: 77
Manufacturing and manufacturers: 77, 88, 132
Mark Antony: 111-12, 192
Marland, E. W.: 140, 239
Marriage: 39, 75, 137, 148-50, 159; among actors, 188
Marshall, Lois K. (Mrs. Thomas R.): 59
Marshall, Thomas R.: 59-60
Mary I (Mary Tudor): 32
Mary, queen consort of England: 36, 153
Maryland: 18, 47, 57
Massachusetts: 1, 18, 138, 139, 194, 195, 231
Mass production: 18, 222

Mayflower (colonial ship): 126, 173
Mayflower (presidential yacht): 20, 26
Mayo, Charles H.: 55, 165-66
Mayo, Edith G.: 165
Mayo, William J.: 55
Mediterranean Sea: 34
Mellon, Andrew W.: 24, 97, 132, 145, 147
Memphis, Tenn.: 177
Mendell, Loren: 46
Metropolitan Opera, New York City: 81
Mexico: 1-4, 13, 92; American relations with, 1; military school in, 2; military in, 3
Mexico City, Mexico: 1, 3, 54
Miami Beach, Fla.: 130
Michigan: 81
Middleton, George: 51
Midwest (as a region): 206
Military, in Mexico: 2, 3
Miller, Zachary T. (Zack): 107, 142
Millionaires: 17
Milo Park, N. J.: 82
Miniature golf: 177, 186
Minneapolis, Minn.: 164, 165
Minnesota: 18, 51, 164-66, 187
Missionaries: 203; in China, 53
Mississippi: 63
Missouri: 230
Mix, Thomas E. (Tom): 107
Mona Lake (Calif.): 182
Money: 18
Monopolies, in business: 127-29
Montana: 87
Monte Carlo, Monaco: 89
Montenegro: 64, 105
Monterey County, Calif.: 178
Montgomery Ward Company: 127-28
Moody, Daniel J. (Dan), Jr.: 235
Moore, Edward C.: 55
Morgan, J. P.: 40
Morgan, J. P., Jr.: 83, 107
Mormons: 132
Morrow, Dwight W.: 3, 102, 154, 195
Morrow, Elizabeth C.: 119, 120
Mortgages: 93
Moses: 188
Moses, George H.: 231
Moslems: 145
Motion pictures: 36, 55, 75, 107, 109, 123, 128, 170, 176, 218, 231, 234; Rogers in, 69, 72-73, 75; innovations in, 73
Mount Rushmore: 176-77
Mulhall, Zachary (Zack): 142
The Mulligan Guards (stage show): 233
Mullins, Laurence (Moon): 216
Munsey, Frank A.: 24
Murder: 40, 86
Murray, William H. (Alfalfa Bill): 237-38
Muskogee, Okla.: 239
Mussolini, Benito: 30, 37, 78, 105-106,

115, 154-55, 165, 196, 203, 208, 210, 217; biography of, 109

Nashville, Tenn.: 165
National Anthem: 18, 27
Nations: 217-19; comparison between, 152
Nations, Gus O.: 64
Navajo Indians, blankets made by: 133
Negroes: 155, 158; in Washington society, 38-39; at West Point, 64
Nelson, Horatio: 118
Nero: 111
Netherlands: 38
Nevada: 66, 132, 179, 182, 186, 188, 190
New Amsterdam Theatre: 83
New England: 16, 17, 154, 235
New Jersey: 195; election in, 154
New Mexico: 71, 132, 240
Newport, R. I.: 17
Newspapermen: 18, 43-44, 56-57, 119, 134, 189
Newspapers: 87, 113, 146, 162, 166, 206-208, 218; in Mexico, 1; contests sponsored by, 71; in California, 85, 168-69; columnists for, 176, 208; editorials in, 208
New Year's: 100, 102, 103, 220, 222
New York (state): 18, 48, 132, 194, 195, 211; election in, 204
New York City, N. Y.: 3, 6, 9, 26, 29, 43, 50, 71, 73, 83, 94, 104, 106, 107, 108, 142, 149, 158, 165, 181, 186, 189, 192, 207, 220, 222, 230, 232, 233, 236, 240, 241; election in, 85
New York Times: 177
Niagara Falls: 206
Nicaragua: 15, 16, 25, 26, 115
Nineteenth Amendment: 6, 8
Noah: 157, 158-59, 220
Norman, Okla.: 238
Northampton, Mass.: 123, 139, 194, 241
Northern Lights: 21
North Pole, exploration of: 11, 13
Northwestern University: 215
Norway: 38
Notre Dame, University of: 94-95, 148, 149, 215-17
Nudity: 170

O'Connor, Paul (Bucky): 216
Obregon, Alvaro: 5, 6
Ochs, Adolph S.: 177
Ohio: 27, 195
Oil: 65; overproduction of, 225
Oilmen: 140
Oklahoma: 56, 68, 71, 72, 96, 108, 127, 142, 158, 178, 184, 225, 228, 230, 236, 237-39; history of, 17; farm land in, 88; election in, 205; state legislature of, 237-38
Oklahoma, University of: 238
Oklahoma City, Okla.: 128, 237, 238
Oklahoma Constitutional Convention (1906): 237
Oklahoma State University: 237, 239
"Old Tack": *see* Howe, Gene A.
Old Trail Drivers Association: 235
Omaha, Nebr.: 64
101 Ranch Wild West Show: 101, 142
Onions: 238
Oolagah, Okla.: 142
"Open Door": 52
Opera: 16, 196, 208
Opium: 53
Orators: 69
Osage Indians: 142, 143
Otoe Indians: 142
Overproduction: 222
Oxford University: 217

Packer, Alfred E.: 201-203
Palm Springs, Calif.: 228
Panama Canal: 9
Parents: 9
Paris, France: 24
Parks: 66
Parliament, British: 118
Parr, Katherine: 33
Pasadena, Calif.: 94
Pasha, Kemal: 63
Patriots and patriotism: 16-17
Pawnee Bill: *see* Lillie, Gordon W.
Peace: 115, 213
Peary, Robert E.: 13
Pedley, Eric L.: 199
Penn, William: 23, 24
Pennington, Anne: 73, 75, 136
Pennsylvania: 19, 62, 77, 81, 87, 97, 120, 129, 132, 151, 154
Pennsylvania, University of: 205
Penrose, Boies: 24
Pepys, Samuel: 227
Percy, Henry: 31
Perpetual motion: 131
Pershing, John J.: 95
Persia: 192, 193
Peru: 61, 122
Philadelphia, Penn.: 19, 23, 25, 78, 79, 82, 97, 129, 145
Philadelphia Athletics (baseball): 79
Philadelphia Sequi-Centennial Celebration (1926): 78
Philanthropy and philanthropists: 81, 167-68
Philippines: delegation from, 15; sugar from, 55; independence for, 212
Phoenix, Ariz.: 228
Physicians: 165, 166
Pickford, Mary: 123-24, 144
Piggly Wiggly supermarkets: 177
Pilgrim's Progress (book): 21

Pima Indians: 125
Piño Suarez, Jose M.: 5
The Pioneer Woman (monument): 140, 142-43, 239
Pittman, Key: 132
Pittsburgh, Penn.: 19
Plymouth, Vt.: 41
Poincare, Raymond: 49
Poindexter, Elizabeth P.: 61
Poker, 88
Poland: 196
Policemen: 89
Politicians: 7, 76, 94, 96, 124, 127, 129, 131, 152, 175, 204, 218, 232
Politics: 8, 51, 58, 61, 62, 77, 124, 131, 151, 161, 178, 206, 212, 217, 219, 235; in New York, 6, 7; women in, 6-8, 205
Polo: 3, 72, 197-200, 211
Pomona, Calif.: 228
Ponca City, Okla.: 140, 239
Ponca Indians: 142
Port Arthur, Texas: 236
Portes Gil, Emilio: 6
Portugal: 37
Post, Emily P.: 15, 205
Post offices: 127-28
Poverty: 65, 148, 166, 214, 224
Prayer: 119, 144-45
Preliminary Disarmament Conference (1926-27): 103, 108, 123
Primo de Rivera y Orbaneja, Miguel: 37, 217
Prince of Wales: *see* Edward Albert
Princeton University: 148, 215
Profanity: 21, 22, 66
Prohibition: 64, 67, 103, 104-105, 113, 122, 133-34, 154, 157-59, 162-64, 184, 190, 194-95, 205, 206, 209-10, 220, 222, 223, 241; enforcement of, 8-9, 10, 14; opponents of, 67; *see also* related topics
Propaganda: 104
Prosperity: 73, 83, 96, 97, 132, 137, 165, 167, 241; predictions of, 207, 209
Protestants: 95
Psychology: 124
Publicity: 129
Public works: 225-26
Pullman railroad cars: 63
Putnam, George P.: 11
Puzzles: 71

Quillen, Robert: 143

Raccoon coats: 94
Racketeering and racketeers: 83, 162
Radcliffe College: 35
Radio: 78, 142, 157, 178, 203, 218; announcers on, 81
Railroads: 81; legislation concerning, 86; owners of, 91
Ranching: 72
Raskob, John J.: 156
Raton, N. M.: 72
Ray, Joseph: mathematics book of, 68
Real estate: 223
Realtors: 92
Reed, Adele W.: 119
Reed, David A.: 56, 102, 169-70, 176
Reform, in government: 235
Reinhart, Roland B. (Pete): 46
Religion: 63, 91, 151, 183; war in Turkey over, 62
Reno, Nev.: 8, 182, 186, 188
Republican National Convention, of 1928: 69
Republican party and Republicans: 15, 31, 49, 51, 58, 60, 64, 65, 66, 77, 81, 85, 88, 111, 120, 133, 138, 140, 148, 151, 156, 175, 176, 177, 178, 179, 180, 184, 186, 194, 195, 201, 202, 205, 212, 222, 226, 230, 231, 233, 241; insurgents among, 231
Revelers Quartet: 236, 238
Revere, Paul: 16, 17, 215
Revolutions: 207; in Mexico, 2, 3-6; U. S. reaction to, 20; in Portugal, 37-38
Rhode Island: 32, 126, 154
Rickenbacker, Edward V.: 54
Rider, James (Jimmy): 142
Ringling, John N.: 19, 107
Robinson, Ewilda M.: 119
Robinson, Joseph T. (Joe): 102, 123, 206, 230-31
Rochester, Minn.: 165
Rockefeller, John D.: 64, 68, 83, 107, 145, 147, 167-68, 225, 241
Rockefeller, John D., Jr.: 81, 96, 168
Rockne, Knute K.: 94-95, 215-17
Rodeo: 178
Rodgers, James C. (Jimmie): 236, 238
Rogers, Betty Blake (wife): 13, 51, 69, 71, 72, 75, 83, 84, 90, 106, 108, 137, 189, 234, 237
Rogers, Clement Vann (father): 237
Rogers, William Penn Adair (Will): attends bullfight, 1; in Mexico, 1; as polo player, 3, 197-200; with polar explorers, 11-14; as traveler, 13, 179, 181-82, 189; on Boston stage, 19; as reader of books, 21-22, 28; Cherokee ancestry of, 24, 67, 143; with *Ziegfeld Follies*, 28, 75, 89, 136; *Ether and Me,* 33; "Illiterate Digest" of, 33; as Shriner, 34; in vaudeville, 36, 170; in motion pictures, 55, 69, 72-73, 75, 102, 107-108, 111, 140, 179, 190, 234; as writer, 58; early education of, 67-69, 239; as football player, 68; horses of, 68; children of, 69, 71, 75; family of, 69, 71-72, 228; in Oklahoma, 69; as air traveler, 71, 72, 80, 106-107, 124, 140, 227-28, 236-41; as investor, 83-85, 223-24;

274

childhood of, 100-101; in England, 106, 115-22, 134, 170; as train passenger, 107; as ship passenger, 113; at disarmament conference, 118-20, 123, 134; on radio, 127, 157; at dedication of *Pioneer Woman*, 140, 142-43; as comedian, 145; *Cowboy Philosopher on the Peace Conference*, 157; *Cowboy Philosopher on Prohibition*, 157; "lectures" of, 167; as speechmaker, 178; Santa Monica ranch of, 179; at Yosemite National Park, 179-80; and roping, 181; in Russia, 192; in Argentina, 200; birthday of, 205; in Spain, 217; drought relief tour of, 228, 234-41; at St. Louis World's Fair, 239; as Mason, 239
Rogers, William Vann (son): 142, 227, 228
Rogers County, Okla.: 93, 178
Roman Catholics: 15, 30, 31, 32, 95
Rome, ancient: 109, 111-13
Rome, Italy: 21, 29, 31, 32
Romeo and Juliet: 75
Roosevelt, Belle W. W. (Mrs. Kermit): 11, 13
Roosevelt, Franklin D.: 204, 206
Roosevelt, Kermit: 13
Roosevelt, Theodore: 4, 131
Roosevelt, Theodore, Jr.: 13
Root, Elihu: 63, 64
Rose Bowl: 94
Rosenwald, Julius: 81, 128
Rosh Hashanah: 100
Rotary clubs: 126
Rothstein, Arnold: 26
Royalty: 121, 211; marriages involving, 36-38, 105-106, 203-204
Rumania: 196
Rumrunning: 9
Russia: 36, 37, 48, 52, 53, 69, 154, 191, 192, 193, 194, 195, 196, 197, 207, 219, 222; relations with China, 52, 53; relations with Japan, 52
Ruth, George H. (Babe): 19, 36, 200
Rutland, Vt.: 194

Sacramento, Calif.: 189
Saint Louis, Mo.: 34, 230; world's fair at, 239
Saint Mary's College (Indiana): 148
Saint Paul, Minn.: 164
Salem, Mass.: 231
Salinas, Calif.: 178
Salton Sea: 92
San Angelo, Texas: 236
San Antonio, Texas: 235
Sandford, Stephen (Laddie): 200
Sandino, Augusto C.: 26
San Francisco, Calif.: 22, 107, 182, 183, 187, 191

Sanitation: 172
Santa Claus: 100-101, 102
Santa Monica, Calif.: 227; Rogers' ranch at, 179
Santo Domingo: 29
Sarfatti, Margherita G.: 109
Saturday Evening Post (magazine): 23, 24, 75, 217
Saunders, Clarence: 177
Savings: 166-67
Saxophones: 101
Scandals: 85, 86
Schmeling, Max S.: 52, 159-61
Schwab, Charles M.: 81, 241
Science: 213
Scientists: 144
Sears, Roebuck and Company: 128
Seattle, Wash.: 13, 35
Sennett, Mack: 27
Serrano, Francisco R.: 2
Seymour, Jane: 32
Shakespeare, William: 22, 28, 158, 170, 209
Shanghai, China: 53
Sharkey, Jack: 159-61; family of, 160, 161
Shaw, George Bernard: 34, 203, 208
Shawnee, Okla.: 239
Shearer, William B.: 78, 79
Sheehan, Winfield R. (Winnie): 107
Sheridan, Wyo.: 132
She Stoops to Conquer (film): 75
Shipstead, Henrik: 164
Shriners: 34
Siberia: 13
Sicily: 111
Sierra Nevada: 183
Singh, Genga: 211
Sing Sing Prison: 209
Skiing, snow: 215
Smith, Alfred E. (Al): 20, 53, 157, 232, 233-34; family of, 234
Smith, Hoke: 153
Smith, Joseph: 66
Smoot, Reed: 27, 28, 55, 56, 58, 63, 65, 66, 132
Snowden, Philip: 61
Social Register: 173-74
Society: 173-74
Soda pop: 66
Sodom and Gomorrah: 220
Sonora, Calif.: 190
Sonora, Mexico: 5
South (as a region): 53, 175, 206, 241
South Africa: 200
South America: 197
South Bend, Ind.: 94, 95, 216
South Dakota: 176; election in, 205-206
Southern Cross (airplane): 21
South Pole, exploration of: 11
South Seas: 11, 203
Spain: 1, 28, 29, 31, 37, 106, 126, 217; navy of, 126
Speakeasies: 118

Spelling: 227
Spitzbergen, Norway: 13
Staked Plains: 72
Standard Oil Corporation: 127, 128-29
Stanford University: 187
Statesmen: 218
Statue of Liberty: 21
Stearns, Frank W.: 11, 123
Stefansson, Vilhjalmur: 11, 13
Sterling, Ross S.: 184, 235
Stillwater, Okla.: 237, 239
Stimson, Henry L.: 15
Stimson, Mabel W. W.: 119
Stock market: 16, 82-85, 113, 184; buying on margin, 87, 94; collapse of, 87-88, 89-91, 94, 169, 223-24
Stocks and bonds: 127; buying and selling of, 82-85, 135, 215, 218, 223
Stone, Fred A.: 179, 180, 182
Stone Mountain, Ga.: 176
Stotesbury, Edward T.: 153
Straton, John Roach: 30
Straw polls: 130, 133-34
Street cars: 209
Submarines: 91, 113, 114; polar exploration by, 11, 13
Sugar: 66; tariff on, 65, 132
Suicides: 206
Sullivan, Mark: 57
Supply and demand: 225
Sutter, John A.: 189-90
Sweden: 38, 164
Switzerland: 49, 103, 218
Sydney, Australia: 22

Taft, William Howard: 15, 42, 137
Talley, Marion: 16
Tammany Hall: 6, 7, 11, 131, 204
Tariffs: 18, 24, 27, 28, 35, 40, 57, 58, 62, 64, 66, 76-78, 79, 81, 86-87, 88, 105, 122, 124, 131-33, 151, 152, 163, 178, 225; on sugar, 65, 132
Tarkington, Booth: 10
Taxation: 15, 17, 24, 51, 76, 89, 145, 176, 211, 214, 220, 241; reduction in, 97; corporate, 124; on income, 152, 176, 226
Tax "dodgers": 66
Taxpayers: 150, 211, 225-26
Teeth: 171-72
Ten Commandments: 225
Tennessee: 165, 223
Tennis: 26
Tenors: 174
Texarkana, Texas: 240
Texas: 71, 72, 124, 154, 184, 228, 234-37; state legislature of, 234-35
Texas Rangers: 235
Thanksgiving: 89, 102
Thompson, William H. (Big Bill): 24
Tilson, John Q.: 230
Time (magazine): 150-51

Tobacco, use of: 76
Toes: 172
Tombes, Andrew (Andy): 75
Tombstone, Ariz.: 228
Toothpaste: 68, 171
Toplitsky, Joe: 64
Tourists: 13, 66, 121, 144, 177; in Philadelphia, 23
Trammell, Park: 133
Trans-Siberian Railway: 53
Travel: 230
Treaties: 168, 169-70
Treaty of Versailles (1919): 196
Troy, Ala.: 155
Tucson, Ariz.: 216, 228
Tulsa, Okla.: 23, 34, 72, 228
Tunney, James J. (Gene): 34, 173-74
Turkey: 26, 196
Twain, Mark: *see* Clemens, Samuel L.

Unemployment: 214, 226, 234
United States: 197; Mexican relations with, 1; British relations with, 8-9; Indian hospital in, 34; aviation in, 45; French relations with, 49; Chinese relations with, 52; national debt of, 58; foreign relations of, 63; and League of Nations, 64; public lands of, 65-67; government of, 76, 79, 218, 224, 231; "condition" of, 93, 109, 220-26; flag of, 161; security of, 213; history of, 176-77
United States Army: 148-50, 235; horses of, 72; polo team of, 72
United States Capitol: 85, 230
United States Coast Guard: 9, 104
United States Congress and congressmen: 7, 8, 16, 18, 21, 28, 35, 38, 39, 40, 41-42, 47, 56, 57, 77, 79, 88, 93, 94, 95, 104, 105, 108-109, 113, 122, 124, 131, 133, 138, 149, 174, 176, 213, 223, 231, 235, 236; drinking among, 9-10; *see also* United States Senate *and* United States House of Representatives
United States Constitution: 23, 109
United States House of Representatives and representatives: 18, 77, 131-32, 151, 194, 230, 231; *see also* United States Congress
United States Marine Corps: 20, 25, 26, 52, 223
United States Military Academy (West Point): 64, 95, 148-50, 215
United States Naval Academy (Annapolis): 149, 215
United States Navy: 19, 20, 76, 161
United States presidents and presidency: 3, 4, 60, 67, 68, 124, 126, 131, 137, 139, 194, 210; employment of retired, 41-42
United States Secret Service: 148

276

United States Senate and senators: 1, 8, 17, 18, 19, 24, 26, 27, 41, 50, 51, 55, 57, 58, 59, 60, 63, 65, 66, 77-78, 79, 85, 86-87, 89, 94, 96, 97, 105, 109, 111-12, 120, 122, 130, 131, 132, 137-40, 143-44, 149, 151, 153, 154, 156, 168, 172, 175, 184, 194, 205, 206, 213, 219, 230, 241; investigations by, 78, 79, 86-7, 88-89; insurgency among, 138; *see also* United States Congress
United States vice presidents and vice presidency: 140
Upshaw, William D.: 176
Utah: 58, 66, 132

Vail, Edward F. R. (Eddie): 92
Vanderbilt, Cornelius IV: 8
Vare, William S.: 97, 176
Vatican: 15, 62
Vaudeville: 26, 97; Rogers in, 170
Venice, Italy: 112
Vermont: 41
Victor Emmanuel III, king of Italy: 105-106, 203
Villa, Francisco (Pancho): raid on Columbus, N. M., 5, 26
Virginia: 16, 33, 47, 55, 56, 57, 85, 116, 168, 169; election in, 85
Virginia City, Nev.: 182, 186

Walker, James J. (Jimmy): 64, 85, 186
Walker, William M.: 155
Wall Street: 13, 64, 75, 83, 84, 89-91, 96, 127, 135, 191, 192, 223, 241; *see also* Stock market *and other related topics*
Wanamaker, John: 23
War: 13, 18, 19-20, 26, 76, 78, 103, 104, 114, 115, 126, 134, 170, 195-97, 203, 205, 213; between China and Russia, 48, 52, 53-54
War debts and reparations: 49, 62
Warner, Glenn S. (Pop): 69
Washington, D. C.: 15, 18, 25, 26, 27, 31, 35, 40, 47, 55, 59, 77, 78, 79, 80, 85, 88, 89, 109, 119, 142, 150, 164, 169, 175, 184, 190, 230
Washington, George: 4, 16, 23, 24, 45, 57, 62, 65, 125
Washington Conference (1922-1924): 103, 108, 114
Wealth: 65, 80, 87, 129, 151-52, 153, 167, 214, 219, 226
Weddings, royal: 105-106
"Weekend," definition of: 209

Western Union: 17
Westminster Abbey: 116
West Virginia: 57
Whalen, Grover A.: 185
Whiskers: 208
White, Percival G.: 55
White, William Allen: 175
White House: 20, 27, 38, 39, 41, 57, 60, 85, 123, 207, 213, 233
Whiteman, Paul: 111
Whitney, John H. (Jock): 200
Whittier, Paul: 46
Wichita, Kans.: 71, 142
Wickersham, George W.: 48, 210
Wickersham Commission: 209-10, 223; report of, 104-105, 241
Wilhelm II, kaiser of Germany: 92, 217
Wilkins, George H.: 11, 13
Willard Hotel: 26
Willebrandt, Mabel W.: 7, 27, 28-29, 35, 64
Williams, Alford J. (Al), Jr.: 183
Williams, Ben Ames: 75
Wills, Helen: 153
Wilson, Lewis R. (Hack): 78-79
Wilson, Woodrow: 38, 60
Windsor Castle: 153
Wisconsin: 51
Wives, of professional golfers: 99
Wolsey, Thomas: 21, 29, 30, 31
Wolves: 171
Women: 38, 59, 60, 76, 120, 136-37, 170, 177; in politics, 6-8, 205; in aviation, 11; and dieting, 56; and cosmetics, 76
World Court: 4, 63, 214
World War I: 37, 106, 116-17, 196, 205, 218, 226
Wrightsman, Charles B. (Charley): 199
Wrightsman, Charles J.: 184
Wrigley, William, Jr.: 24
Writers: 75, 155, 208, 227
Wyoming: 66

Yale University: 148, 215
Yom Kippur: 100
Yosemite National Park: 179
Young, Brigham: 66, 132
Young, Clement C.: 178
Young, Owen D.: 40, 49, 96
Young Pioneers: 222
Young Voters League: 122

Zapata, Emiliano: 5
Ziegfeld, Florenz (Flo), Jr.: 136, 185
Ziegfeld Follies: 28, 136; Rogers in, 75